STATISTICS
FOR THE
SOCIAL SCIENCES

STATISTICS
FOR THE
SOCIAL SCIENCES

Victoria L. Mantzopoulos

University of Detroit Mercy

Prentice Hall
Englewood Cliffs, New Jersey 07632

Library of Congress Cataloging-in-Publication Data
Mantzopoulos, Victoria L.
    Statistics / Victoria L. Mantzopoulos.—1st ed.
      p.   cm.
    Includes index.
    ISBN 0-13-101320-3
    1. Statistics.   2. Social sciences—Statistical methods.
I. Title.
HA29.A726 1995
519.5—dc20   94-18819
                                      CIP

Editorial/production supervision: Joan E. Foley
Editorial director: Charlyce Jones Owen
Editor-in-chief: Nancy Roberts
Acquisitions editor: Mike Bickerstaff
Editorial assistant: Nicole Signoretti
Supplements editor: Jennie Katsaros
Marketing manager: Kris Kleinsmith
Copy editor: Linda L. Thompson
Design director: Anne Bonanno Nieglos
Designer: Judith A. Matz-Coniglio
Cover designer: Marjory Dressler
Cover art: Marjory Dressler
Illustrator: Gary Moore
Buyer: Bob Anderson

 © 1995 by Prentice-Hall, Inc.
A Simon & Schuster Company
Englewood Cliffs, New Jersey 07632

Printed in the United States of America
10 9 8 7 6 5 4 3 2 1

ISBN 0-13-101320-3

Prentice-Hall International (UK) Limited, *London*
Prentice-Hall of Australia Pty. Limited, *Sydney*
Prentice-Hall Canada Inc., *Toronto*
Prentice-Hall Hispanoamericana, S.A., *Mexico*
Prentice-Hall of India Private Limited, *New Delhi*
Prentice-Hall of Japan, Inc., *Tokyo*
Simon & Schuster Asia Pte. Ltd., *Singapore*
Editora Prentice-Hall do Brasil, Ltda., *Rio de Janeiro*

**To my husband,
Konstantinos Iouanis Mantzopoulos**

Contents

PART II *PROBABILITY STATISTICS*

5 *Probability: Sample Spaces* 72

6 *Calculating Probabilities* 87

7 *Probability Distributions of Discrete Variables* 117

8 *Normal Probability Distributions*   *140*

9 *Sampling Distributions*   *168*

PART III   *INFERENTIAL STATISTICS*

---

10 *Inferential Statistics*   *185*

15 Case Study   *346*

Part IV   *APPENDICES*

A Tables

B Dictionary and Formulas   *368*

Preface

Statistics for the Social Sciences is intended for a college or university beginning or introductory statistics class in the social and health sciences. A basic premise of the text is that students need to focus only on those statistical techniques applicable to their field of study. More importantly, they should use a text presenting fully illustrated examples of information and techniques that they will confront in their future careers. The author understands the anxiety related to statistics. A major source of the anxiety is related to the mathematics. Many students in these fields tend not to be as mathematically advanced as some of their counterparts. Most statistics books ignore their abilities, expecting advanced math skills. This book attempts to alleviate some of the anxiety by developing a step-by-step illustration of the use of all formulas.

The goal of *Statistics for the Social Sciences* is to have an introductory statistics textbook for the social and health sciences that can be completed in one semester. The development of concepts is limited to those necessary to understand and apply a technique. Descriptive probabilities and inferential statistics are covered. The unique feature of the text is the writing and presentation style. It is designed to help students to understand not only what they are doing, but why they are doing it.

The approach of this book is to divide each chapter into sections describing a specific procedure. All concepts and techniques are supported by an example immediately following their presentation. The examples are clearly stated and follow the same format throughout the book. Each example is described as an experiment and is followed by the answer and solution. The solution is a step-by-step discussion, starting with a clear description of the experiment, what techniques are to be employed, why those techniques are employed, and how they are employed. Each section also includes a Learning Aid. The Learning Aid is used as a quick reference to the formula and application, including a fully illustrated application of the major techniques of that section. The chapter ends with a Chapter in Review, presenting a full set of problems using the most important techniques of the chapter. The Chapter in Review allows the students to further sharpen their skills. All supporting statistical and mathematical tables are included in the appendices. Also included is a glossary of basic terms and concepts. Formulas are integrated into the glossary, with additional terms applicable to understanding statistics.

The author has taught statistics for more than 10 years. As a student of statistics, one of her professors said that all statistics is third-grade math made difficult with funny symbols and language. A second professor always said that statistics becomes intuitive. It does. The book evolved from a series of handouts that were supplements to a required text. As students continuously demanded more handouts, they developed into this text.

Supplements

FOR INSTRUCTORS

Instructor's Manual

The *Instructor's Manual* features topic outlines, chapter summaries and objectives, and lecture and discussion suggestions.

Test Item File

The *Test Item File* consists of approximately 40 multiple-choice, 25 fill-in, and 10–12 problem/essay questions for each chapter.

FOR STUDENTS

Study Guide

The *Study Guide* focuses on mastering concepts and includes instructions and examples for working problems using computer software. Each chapter includes learning objectives, a chapter outline, the chapter's formulas (with all symbols defined), and summaries of steps for conducting each procedure, plus a set of self-tests—multiple choice, fill-in, and problem/essay questions. Each chapter concludes with a section on the use of SPSS/PC+ Studentware, MYSTAT (the student version of SYSTAT), and SPSS for Windows.

Acknowledgments

Deep appreciation is extended to David Jackson and Father Frank McGough for their ideas and input. Both have offered their valuable time, assistance, guidance, support, and encouragement. I would like to thank Dawn Bickerstaff, who gave her assistance in the initial stage of developing a method and design of the text. My gratitude is expressed to all the students in my statistics courses, who have assisted in the development of the text as they read and learned from sample chapters and handouts. I would also like to extend my special thanks to Dr. Charles D. Elder, Chair, Department of Political Science, Wayne State University, for his guidance and encouragement, which reach beyond the scope of the text. In addition, the following reviewers provided assistance: Jon S. Ebeling, California State University—Chico; Samuel B. Hoff, Delaware State University; Edward J. Miller, University of Wisconsin—Steven's Point; and Stephen Percy, University of Wisconsin—Milwaukee.

STATISTICS
FOR THE
SOCIAL SCIENCES

What Is Statistics?

1

People often ask why a social or behavioral scientist needs to learn mathematics. What do numbers have to do with studying politics, sociology, or behavior? People tend to associate statistics with mathematics and engineering. However, statistics is not simply mathematics; it is a science in and of itself that goes beyond the mathematics and numbers it employs.

Statistics is the process of making generalizations on the basis of information. As a science, statistics is concerned with three areas: the collection and classification of data; describing and presenting data; and interpreting and drawing conclusions from the data. Almost all fields of study employ the techniques of statistics. The first area is the collection of data. It is briefly discussed in this text, but it is typically addressed more fully in a class on research design or research methods. The second area, describing and presenting data, is the focus of the first unit of this text. Describing and presenting data is referred to as descriptive statistics; it centers around the graphic displays and measurements such as means and standard deviations. The third area, interpreting and drawing conclusions, is divided into two units, probability and inferential statistics.

SECTION 1

Uses and Abuses

It is important to remember that statistics is logic, with mathematics as the tool and application as the goal. Everyone uses statistics every day. Even babies unknowingly apply the techniques of statistics. If an infant desires food, a diaper change, or satisfaction of another need, the infant can associate a cry with the resulting attention. Although the infant is not consciously testing a causal relationship, a recognizable pattern develops.

Playing a game of chance employs the science of statistics, and usually the odds are against the player, as in gambling and lotteries. Making a decision whether to pursue a particular policy, buying an item, employing a method, or admitting students to a college or university are applications of statistics.

People often say that numbers lie, that statisticians can manipulate numbers to prove any point. Some statisticians might attempt to make numbers lie, but these people are the exception, and they can almost always be identified by even a novice observer.

More typically, the numbers do not lie, but the interpretation may be misleading or incorrect. This is often the case in the media. Information is usually presented with an oral explanation. The oral explanation is often slightly different than the visual information. Or the information and the explanation may coincide, but the listeners hear or think they see something else. That is, the consumer misunderstands and misapplies the information.

Most abuses center around the misapplication or incorrect presentation of correct data. A good example of misapplication is the distinction between the two statements that in the United States, most poor people are white and most African Americans are poor. Both statements are correct, although most people think they are conflicting. Carefully analyzing them, the first statement states that of all the poor people in the country, most are white. This should be the case, because white Americans are more numerous than African Americans. The second statement describes a different population. It looks at African Americans only and then distinguishes between nonpoor African Americans and poor African Americans.

Misrepresentation of data tends to center around distorting graphs and tables in such a way that the information is correct, but the visual interpretation is incorrect. Interrupting the axes in bar charts or line graphs distorts the visual by allowing the eye to compare the height of one bar to that of another when the full heights of the bars are not presented. Notice the bar charts in Figure 1.1.

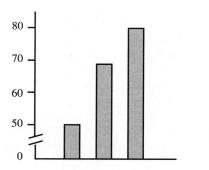 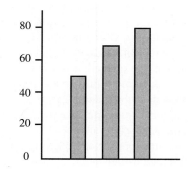

FIGURE 1.1   Bar Charts Representing the Same Information

Both charts present the same information. The first chart interrupts the vertical axis by jumping from 0 to 50; then it shows 50 to 60, 60 to 70, and 70 to 80. The inconsistent increments allow the visual understanding of the bars to be distorted. The second bar looks twice as high as the first bar, and the third bar looks three times as large as the first bar. The second graph does not distort the proportions of the bars, because the increments on the vertical axis are consistent. The heights of the bars in the second graph reflect smaller differences than those that appear to be shown by the first graph.

The third area of statistical abuse involves flaws in the research design. If the design is full of errors, so too will be the data and, therefore, the results. The major areas of concern are sample size, unbiased sampling, and unbiased questions. These concerns are addressed later in this chapter.

Statistics in the Social and Behavioral Sciences

Most fields of the social and behavioral sciences apply the techniques of statistics. Political science, public administration, sociology, social work, psychology, history, economics, humanities, nursing, health sciences, education, and other related areas are only a few of the disciplines that are becoming more and more dependent on statistical analyses.

Political science and public administration are fields that have become very involved in statistically analyzing data for decision-making purposes. Decisions about the feasibility or the effectiveness of a policy confront political scientists and public administrators almost daily. Decision making and public policy-making require an understanding of the problems and issues as well as their causes and effects. But perhaps the most visible statistical question in politics is the recurring question of who will win an election. Public opinion polls and election exit polls have become very popular at the national, state, and local levels of government. Predicting election results requires political scientists to employ more probability analyses than do other social scientists.

Sociologists also frequently use statistics. Their focus may range from determining the impact of policy to describing complex issues such as crime, poverty, and social behavior. The importance of sociological research is reflected in its adaptation to research in other fields, especially the other social sciences.

Social workers are also concerned with the impact of policy but are more concerned with how the consequences of policy decisions affect people's lives. Social workers are concerned with various policy areas, which range from child welfare to reestablishing people who have been separated from the community. A growing body of data is being produced and analyzed in the social work discipline.

The field of psychology also involves statistics. Psychologists use statistics to explain why people act and think the way they do. An example of a research area in psychology is the relationship between genetics and environmental interaction. Psychologists often conduct ongoing studies that observe behavior. The field produces an enormous amount of data, which are often borrowed for analysis in numerous related fields.

History is a field that is now utilizing statistics more frequently. Although the field has been dominated by normative reasoning, empirically analyzing and explaining past events is becoming common and acceptable.

Economics is a field that regularly employs statistical techniques. As a highly quantitative field, economics attempts to explain complicated issues, from the distribution of wealth to problems of capital, wages, and prices.

Humanities is a field that is not often associated with statistics. However, even the more traditional areas of the humanities, such as languages, literature, and philosophy, are using statistics to explain linguistic and literary structures.

Nursing and other areas of health sciences employ statistical techniques in making decisions about health programs, medication, and behavior.

Educators are concerned with the principles and problems related to learning and teaching. Education is a field that is also very involved in statistically analyzing policy. Educators also test various teaching approaches and decide the impact on the learning process. Most fields of study increasingly use statistics. Each discipline is becoming more familiar with the others, and all disciplines increasingly share information.

Basic Terms and Concepts

There are several terms and concepts that must be clearly understood before studying the techniques in statistics. The most important term is *population*. The population is the universal set that is to be analyzed. Even if a sample is drawn from a population, it is the population about which generalizations are drawn.

The population must be well defined by the researcher, so that the inferences drawn are clearly understood. For example, if the researcher wants to describe student ages, the population must be clearly defined as all students in the class, in the school, in the state, in the country, or in the world. The researcher must be as specific as possible.

> **Population** A universal set of all individuals, objects, or measurements whose properties are being analyzed.

It is often difficult to observe or test every element in a population. Sampling techniques allow a researcher to study a population by focusing on a smaller set of elements.

> **Sample** A subset of the population.

The objective of sampling is to collect a sample that is representative of the population. Typically, a sample should mirror the population. There are numerous reasons why it may not, however. One reason is that it is not intended to. However, when attempting to produce a sample that mirrors the population, two major problem areas are sampling error and systematic error. *Sampling error* is the error due to chance. It is the chance that the elements chosen for the sample are not representative of the population. Small samples tend to have a higher probability of containing sampling errors than do larger samples. For example, if one student is sampled to describe the average age of all students, the sample will probably not be representative of the population. However, if several students are sampled, the estimate will more likely be representative. Increasing sample size tends to decrease sampling error.

However, bigger is not always better. If the same kind of element is sampled every time and that element is only one type of many, a systematic error exists. This error will not be corrected by sampling more of the same elements. A *systematic error* is an error in the process of selecting elements in the sample, and it is not corrected by increasing sample size. An example of a systematic error is when people are selected for a public opinion poll by a researcher who stands on a street corner. Only people working or living in that area are likely to pass that particular corner. Another example is testing the average age of students at a college by observing only students enrolled in evening courses. These students tend to be older than students enrolled in day courses. A random selection of elements from the whole population tends to be the best method of preventing a systematic error. Randomization allows every element the same chance of being selected for a sample.

EXAMPLE 1.1

Experiment   A local television station conducts an election poll of 2000 people randomly selected from a telephone list of people who attended a morning talk show over the last 2 years. Identify the sampling error.

Answer   Systematic error

Solution   There are two types of errors: sampling errors and systematic errors. A sampling error tends to occur when the sample size is too small to allow for a reliable inference to the population. A sample of 2000 people is a good sample size and should not pose a substantial sampling error. A systematic error is an error associated with the selection process. Randomization usually controls systematic error. However, though randomization is noted, the list from which the names are drawn is suspect. The list is generated by people who attend a local talk show. The people choosing to attend a talk show probably do not completely coincide with people who vote.

Samples and populations are tested and observed to collect information about certain characteristics of the elements. The characteristics or properties are referred to as *variables*. Variables such as age, education, and marital status are characteristics about objects or individuals that can be described by different values. A value is a classification of a variable. It either can be numerical or can be a nominal attribute that can be assigned numerical values. Age and education are variables whose values are numerical. Marital status is a variable whose attributes, such as single, married, or divorced, must be assigned numerical values for statistical calculations.

Variable A characteristic of objects, events, or individuals that has or can be assigned a numerical value.

As with the population, the variables that are tested must be clearly defined by the researcher in such a way that another researcher can fully comprehend and replicate the measurement if necessary. A variable must be operationally defined, with clear specifications for measuring the characteristics and the values that may be assigned to the responses. The operational definition must be concerned that the measurement does, in fact, measure the variable. That is, it must be determined if the measurement is a valid indicator of the variable.

Value One of the categories or responses of a variable.

The value of a variable associated with one element or individual of the population or sample is often referred to as datum. For example, if Ms Duncan is a student in class and the variable *age* is observed, the value 25 years old is a single piece of data. Ms Duncan's marital status, single, is another value that is a single piece of data.

Variables are classified as discrete or continuous. *Discrete variables* are those that can take on only a finite number of possible values. Because the number of possible values is limited, discrete variables are often said to be counts, as opposed to measurements. Counts need not be full counts, or whole numbers, but instead are said to have a clear beginning and a clear end. *Continuous variables* measure and can take on an infinite number of possible values. A measurement is limited by the measuring device. For example, a scale for weight is limited to the units the scale measures. One scale may report weight in full pounds, another in half pounds, and another in tenths of a pound. The measuring device, the scale, can take on infinite values, because a scale is developed to measure hundredths or thousandths of pounds. The distinction of discrete and continuous variables is important in statistics, because many techniques are better suited for one or the other.

EXAMPLE 1.2

Experiment Identify the following variables as discrete or continuous.

    a. Number of siblings
    b. Distance from home to school
    c. Temperature of the room
    d. Number of red cars in the parking lot

Answer

    a. Discrete
    b. Continuous
    c. Continuous
    d. Discrete

Solution

    a. The number of siblings is discrete, because the number is a count. A finite number of siblings can be identified.

    b. The distance from home to school is continuous, because distance is a measurement. Although a clear beginning and end of the measurement exist (home and school), any measurement reported is an estimate based on the limitations of the measuring device. One device may report miles, another may report kilometers, and yet another may report feet or yards. Each of these units will be estimates where the distance is typically rounded to the nearest mile, kilometer, foot, or yard.

    c. The temperature of the room is also continuous. Temperature is measured and not counted. There are infinite number of ways a thermometer may estimate temperature such as in units of whole degrees or fractions of degrees. Measuring temperature is limited only by the measuring device.

    d. The number of red cars in the parking lot is a count and, is, therefore, discrete. The experiment asks for a count of cars and not a measurement.

A set of values of a variable for each of the elements of a sample or population is also referred to by the noun data. For example, the set of ages for all students in the class is a set of data.

> **Datum** (singular) The value of a variable associated with one element of the population or sample.

> **Data** (plural) The set of values of a variable for each of the elements of the population or sample.

An experiment is a planned activity that generates a set of data. Social and behavioral sciences tend to focus on quasi-experimental designs, which are not usually conducted in a laboratory, as is the case with the so-called physical sciences. A popular technique of quasi-experimental designs is to survey respondents. A survey is an instrument that allows researchers to observe respondents outside of a controlled, laboratory setting.

> **Experiment** A planned activity that generates a set of data.

A parameter is a numerical characteristic of an entire population. Parameters describe populations and are usually represented by Greek letters such as μ or σ. The letter μ (pronounced ''mew''), for example, is the symbol that denotes the mean of a population; σ (pronounced ''sigma'') denotes the standard deviation of a population. The general rule is that the calculation for a numerical characteristic such as a mean or standard deviation is the same for a population or a sample, but the symbol representing the measurement differs.

A statistic is a numerical characteristic of a sample. Statistics describe samples and are usually represented by English letters such as $\bar{x}$ (pronounced ''x-bar'') or s. The symbol $\bar{x}$, for example, denotes the mean of a sample, and s denotes the standard deviation of a sample. Therefore, a mean may be represented by μ or $\bar{x}$, depending on whether it describes a population or a sample. Populations are represented by Greek letters, and samples are represented by English letters.

> **Parameter** A numerical characteristic of an entire population. Parameters are usually represented by Greek letters, such as μ or σ.

> **Statistic** A numerical characteristic of a sample. Statistics are usually represented by English letters, such as $\bar{x}$ or s.

An example of a parameter in the case study on fertility is the mean number of children ever born to all women who have ever been married. The case study can only estimate this mean, since not all women in the world can be observed. A statistic is limited to the actual survey and is defined as the mean number of children ever born to all women in the survey.

Data were defined earlier as discrete or continuous. There is another useful way of classifying data according to their level of measurement. There are four levels of measurement: nominal, ordinal, interval, and ratio. A nominal-level measurement is data whose responses describe qualities or attributes that do not imply magnitude or value. Although values must be assigned for statistical purposes, the values do not specify magnitude. Examples of nominal-level data are religion, color of hair, marital status, or color of cars in a parking lot.

> **Nominal-level measurement** (also known as attribute or categorical measurement) Data whose values describe attributes that do not imply magnitude or order.

Ordinal-level measurements order data from lowest to highest or highest to lowest. Ordinal-level measurements rank data but do not otherwise note magnitudes. The difference between values is not clear beyond their placements in the ranked order. For example, if the class is ranked from shortest to tallest, it is not clear whether the shortest person is 1 inch (in.) or 2 in. shorter than the second or whether the difference between the heights of the first and second shortest is the same difference as between the second and the third. Military rankings are ordinal-level measurements, as are most job rankings, both in public and private institutions.

> **Ordinal-level measurement** Data whose values are ranked or ordered from lowest to highest or highest to lowest.

Interval-level measurements are data that can be ordered and have measurable differences. For example, 1 in. is smaller than 2 in., and the difference between 1 and 2 in. is measurable and identical to the measurable difference between 2 and 3 in. Temperature is also a common interval-level measurement.

> **Interval-level measurement** Data whose values are ordered and have measurable differences.

The fourth level of measurement is ratio. Ratio-level data are similar to interval-level measurements in that they have values that are ordered and have measurable difference. However, unlike interval-level measurements, ratio-level measurements have an absolute-zero starting point. That is, a value of zero for a ratio-level measurement implies an absence of the variable. Zero means zero: The measurement does not exist. Interval-level measurements may contain a zero, but the zero is sometimes arbitrarily set. Temperature is interval because it contains a zero that does not imply an absence of temperature. The fact that there are two popular measurements of temperature, Fahrenheit and Celcius, implies that a temperature of zero is not a natural starting place. Age, height, weight, and money are considered examples of ratio-level measurements. Age, for example, is ratio; zero years old reflects the absence of age.

> **Ratio-level measurements** Data whose values can be ordered, have measurable differences, and have a zero starting point, which implies an absence of variable.

Descriptive Graphics for One Variable

2

The purpose of graphically presenting data is to reduce or summarize the data so that it is quickly comprehensible with the same or better understanding as if there were a full review of the data. For example, if every American is surveyed for marital status, more than 250 million answers would be obtained. A survey of the 250 million answers would probably not result in a full understanding of the distribution of marital status. However, a count of the number of responses in each category presented in an organized table would allow for rapid understanding of marital status in the United States.

The most common graphs and tables are frequency distributions, bar graphs, histograms, pie charts, and line graphs. Computer software programs provide a variety of graphs, for which the user simply inserts the data and labels.

Whether composed by hand or computer, several precautions must be taken to ensure that a graph presents the data appropriately. Be certain that the visual does not distort the meaning of the data. Distortion is very common with bar charts and histograms in which the length of a bar is used to present a number of values. For example, the bar charts in Figure 2.1 represent the same information. Do the visuals provide the same understanding?

The left chart is a more accurate presentation of the data. The visual shows that there are slightly more (about 5 per 100) Democrats than Independents and slightly more (about 10 per 100) Independents than Republicans. The right chart is distorted. Compare the height of the bar for Democrats to the height of the bar for Republicans. Although the numbers represented are the same, the visual suggests that there are twice as many Democrats as Republicans. The symbol // on the vertical axis represents an interruption in the values. Notice that the chart begins at 0 but then increases to 25, with increments of 5 thereafter. *Increments should always be*

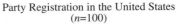

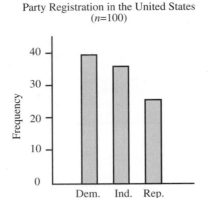

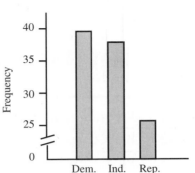

FIGURE 2.1   Bar Charts Representing the Same Information

consistent. There are rare occasions when adjusting the increments would not lead to distortion.

Several general rules exists. Try to make the graph readable and easy to comprehend. Do not make it too complicated or too cluttered. Remember that simplicity is the objective. Round numbers, where appropriate, to reduce the number of digits. If numbers are in thousands, millions, or billions, consider dropping the zeros from the values and note the necessary multiplier in the variable label or title to the graph. Move unnecessary symbols out of the table and into value labels or titles. Symbols such as $ and % can be integrated in the column heads or title of the table so that they are not repeated with every value. Number and label all tables and graphs and all columns, axes, and legends. Note the source of data.

SECTION 1

Frequency Distributions

Frequency distributions provide a simple count of data in terms of the number or percentage of each value of a variable. Noting marital status of Americans as a count of the various responses is an example of a frequency distribution.

Frequency distributions are characterized as ungrouped and grouped. An ungrouped frequency distribution is a simple count of each value for the data. Values grouped or categorized form grouped frequency distributions. For example, if the ages of students in class are presented in a tabulation as 20, 21, 22, and so on, the distribution is ungrouped. But if the ages are categorized in ranges of 20–24, 25–29, 30–34, and so on, the distribution is grouped.

The creation of an ungrouped frequency distribution begins by listing all the values of the variable. The number of occurrences for each value is counted and inserted in a column corresponding to the value. A total should be reported at the bottom of the table to verify that all the data are accounted for. For example, for the set of data 1, 1, 2, 2, 3, 3, 3, 3, 4, 4, 5, 5, 5, 5, and 5, a frequency distribution is begun by establishing a column for the values 1, 2, 3, 4, and 5. A column is also established for a count of each value. The value 1 occurs twice, the value 2 occurs twice, the value 3 occurs four times, the value 4 occurs twice, and the value 5 occurs five times.

Value	Frequency
1	2
2	2
3	4
4	2
5	5
Total	15

EXAMPLE 2.1

Experiment   The following data are ages of students in Dr. Mantz's philosophy course. Create a frequency distribution.

17 17 18 18 18 19 19 19 19 19 19 20 20 20 20
21 21 21 21 21 21 21 21 21 22 24 24 24 25 25

Answer

Ages of Students in Dr. Mantz's Class

Age	Frequency
17	2
18	3
19	6
20	4
21	9
22	1
23	0
24	3
25	2
Total	30

Solution   Begin by labeling the table. The title should be precise but as succinct as possible. Clearly label the columns. The first is the variable age, and the second is the frequency, or number, of each age. Separate the column headings from the data with lines. Write each age in the column for age. (Do not forget the value 23. Although it did not appear in the data, omitting it in the table would interrupt the increments reported.) Count the number of occurrences for each age and insert the count in the column labeled frequency. Total the frequencies to verify all data are accounted for. Close the table with a line.

An ungrouped frequency distribution has the advantage of showing every piece of data. However, if there are dozens of values, an ungrouped frequency distribution can be cumbersome. A researcher strives to use as much data as possible but must also confront the manageability of the data. A grouped frequency distribution allows a large number of values to be presented in a condensed format. Table 2.1 shows a grouped frequency distribution that gives the ages of 7720 women over the age of 30.

TABLE 2.1   Current Age Distribution of Women

Age	Frequency
30–34	1185
35–39	1007
40–44	980
45–49	841
50–54	897
55–59	691
60–64	643
65–69	662
70–74	489
75 and older	325
Total	7720

The values in the distribution range from 30 to perhaps 100. To list 70 or more values would result in a very lengthy table. Collapsing the values into groups produces a manageable table without sacrificing too much of the data. It is, however, unclear where the frequencies occur in each group. For example, in the category 30–34, it is now unclear if the women are all 30, 31, or some combination of ages.

Each category in a grouped distribution is referred to as a *class*. Values in each class must be mutually exclusive; that is, a value can occur in only one class. It is incorrect to make one category 30–35 and then make a second 35–40. A response of 35 could be listed in two classes. Each class should have the same width (increment). The class width is the difference between the lower class limit and the next lower class limit. For the class 30–34, the class width is 5, which is determined by subtracting 30 (the lower limit of this class) from 35 (the lower limit of the next class). If one class width is 5 years (y), all class widths should be 5 y. Class widths should be small enough not to lose too much information. Four to 12 classes provide a good balance between not sacrificing information yet allowing for manageability. The first and last classes may be open-ended, such as in Table 2.1, where the last class is ''75 and older.'' However, open-ended classes pose problems for further calculations and should be avoided if possible.

Grouped frequency distribution A frequency distribution

where

> Values are collapsed into groups or classes.
>
> Values in each class must be mutually exclusive.
>
> A **lower class limit** is the lowest value in a specific class and an **upper class limit** is the highest value in a specific class.
>
> A **class width** is the difference between the lower class limit and the next lower class limit.

EXAMPLE 2.2

Experiment   Identify the class width for the following grouped frequency distribution. Identify the lower class limit for the second class.

Class	Frequency
0–9	11
10–19	10
20–29	9
30–39	10
Total	40

Answer   Class width = 10; lower class limit for second class = 10.

Solution   The class width for each class is the same and is determined by finding the difference between the lower class limit of one class and the lower class limit of the next class. Using the first class 0–9, the lower class limit is 0. The lower class limit of the second class is 10. The difference is 10 − 0 = 10.

There are several ways to present data in a frequency distribution. Thus far, the full count or tally has been presented. Another method of presenting the data is with a relative frequency. A relative frequency is the proportion of each value or class to the total. It can be stated as a percentage or a decimal number. When all values are accounted for, the total of the relative frequencies must equal 1.00, or 100%. To determine a relative frequency, divide the number of occurrences (frequency) for each value by the total number of responses. The symbol f represents the frequency and the symbol Σf represents the summation of f. The calculation must be performed for each value or group.

Relative frequency   The proportion of the frequency of a value to the total number of occurrences.

$$\frac{f}{\Sigma f}$$

A cumulative frequency can also be used to present data in a frequency distribution. A cumulative frequency is a running count of the frequency for a value and all preceding values. The first value in a cumulative frequency is equal to the value in the frequency column, since no values precede it. The last value should equal the total number of occurrences. A cumulative relative frequency is a running count of the relative frequencies of a value and all preceding relative frequencies.

Cumulative frequency distribution   A count of the frequencies or relative frequencies of a value to all preceding counts.

EXAMPLE 2.3

Experiment   Calculate the relative frequency, cumulative frequency, and cumulative relative frequency for the following data.

Class	Frequency
0–9	11
10–19	10
20–29	9
30–39	10
Total	40

Answer

Class	Frequency	Relative Frequency	Cumulative Frequency	Cumulative Relative Frequency
0–9	11	.275	11	.275
10–19	10	.250	21	.525
20–29	9	.225	30	.750
30–39	10	.250	40	1.000
Total	40	1.000	40	

Solution   Begin by determining the relative frequency. Divide the frequency by the total number of occurrences. For the first class, 0–9, divide 11 by 40. For the second class divide 10 by 40. Repeat this procedure for the other two classes. The cumulative frequency is a running count of the occurrences. The first class has a cumulative frequency of 11. The second class has its frequency of 10 plus 11 from the first class (10 + 11 = 21). The third class is 11 + 10 + 9. The fourth class is the sum of all frequencies. The cumulative relative frequency repeats the cumulative method, but with the relative proportions added instead of the frequencies. The first cumulative relative frequency is the relative frequency, because no class precedes it. The second cumulative relative frequency is .275 from the first class plus .250 for the second class. The third class is then .275 + .250 + .225. The fourth class is the sum of all previous relative frequencies. The full calculations are illustrated in the following table.

Class	Frequency	Relative Frequency	Cumulative Frequency	Cumulative Relative Frequency
0–9	11	$11/40 =$ .275	11	.275
10–19	10	$10/40 =$ .250	10 + 11 = 21	.250 + .275 = .525
20–29	9	$9/40 =$ .225	10 + 11 + 9 = 30	.250 + .275 + .225 = .750
30–39	10	$10/40 =$ .250	10 + 11 + 9 + 10 = 40	.250 + .275 + .225 + .250 = 1.000
Total	40	1.000	40	

A LEARNING AID

Frequency Distributions

Calculate the relative frequency, cumulative frequency, and cumulative relative frequency for the following data for the ages of patients in a pediatrician's office on a particular day.

Class	Frequency
0–3	10
4–8	6
9–12	3
12–15	1
Total	20

Step 1   Establish a column for the relative frequency. The relative frequency is determined by dividing the frequency of each value by the sum of the frequencies (total number of observations). Divide each value by 20. The relative frequencies must have a sum of 1.0

Class	Frequency	Relative Frequency
0–3	10	$^{10}/_{20} =$ .50
4–8	6	$^{6}/_{20} =$ .30
9–12	3	$^{3}/_{20} =$ .15
12–15	1	$^{1}/_{20} =$ .05
Total	20	1.00

Step 2   Establish a column for the cumulative frequency. The cumulative frequency is a running count of the frequency column. Add the frequency of a value to the frequencies of all preceding values. The first cumulative frequency is the same as the frequency. The last must equal the total, 20.

Class	Frequency	Relative Frequency	Cumulative Frequency
0–3	10	.50	10
4–8	6	.30	10 + 6 = 16
9–12	3	.15	10 + 6 + 3 = 19
12–15	1	.05	10 + 6 + 3 + 1 = 20
Total	20	1.00	

Step 3   Establish a column for the cumulative relative frequency. The cumulative relative frequency is a running count of the relative frequencies. The first value must equal the relative frequency of the first class and the last value must equal 1.00.

Class	Frequency	Relative Frequency	Cumulative Frequency	Relative Cumulative Frequency
0–3	10	.50	10	.50
4–8	6	.30	16	.50 + .30 = .80
9–12	3	.15	19	.50 .30 + .15 = .95
12–15	1	.05	20	.50 .30 .15 + .05 = 1.00
Total	20	1.00		

Step 4   Present the distribution without the calculations.

Class	Frequency	Relative Frequency	Cumulative Frequency	Relative Cumulative Frequency
0–3	10	.50	10	.50
4–8	6	.30	16	.80
9–12	3	.15	19	.95
12–15	1	.05	20	1.00
Total	20	1.00		

SECTION 2

Frequency distributions are easier to visualize if they are presented graphically. A bar chart or a histogram graphically displays information contained in frequency distributions.

Bar Charts and Histograms

A bar chart, also known as a bar graph, displays discrete and continuous data of any level of measurement, although it is most commonly used for displaying nominal-level data. It is appropriate for grouped and ungrouped data. A bar chart may represent frequencies or relative proportions.

A histogram is a special type of bar chart. A histogram better represents continuous data at the interval and ordinal levels. A histogram may represent frequencies or relative proportions.

A bar chart can be distinguished from a histogram by noting whether the bars are separate or adjacent. Because bar charts represent nominal-level data or discrete data, the bars are not adjacent. Each bar is independent of the others. A histogram represents continuous data; hence the bars are adjacent so values are not interrupted.

The creation of the two graphs is similar. A horizontal axis represents the numerical or alphabetic values of the variable. Alphabetic values refer to nominal-level data, such as marital status, with values including single, married, and divorced. A vertical axis represents the frequencies or proportions. Values are placed on the axes. Values representing the frequencies or proportions should be in equal intervals. Intervals of 5, 10, 50, 100, and so on, are used. The values on the vertical axis do not necessarily correspond to the reported frequencies. For example, if frequencies are 40, 41, and 42, the axis might contain the value 40, where bars for 41 and 42 would be drawn slightly above the mark of 40. The heights of the bars correspond to the frequencies or proportions. The widths of the bars in a histogram represent the class widths. Label the axes and avoid placing values at the top of the bars. Also avoid interrupting the data either on the vertical or horizontal axes. Adjust the scales as necessary to avoid interrupting the axes. This adjustment is very important for bar charts and histograms, because interrupting the axes results in a distorted visual.

The frequency distribution in Table 2.2 can be graphed as a bar chart. The variable in the distribution is marital status, a nominal-level measurement best represented by a bar chart and not a histogram.

Begin by drawing the horizontal axis representing the values of the variable. The values of the variable marital status are single, married, divorced, and widowed. Draw the vertical axis representing the frequencies. The values on the vertical axis must represent the frequencies in such a way that the frequencies are neither too

TABLE 2.2   Marital Status of Students at the University

Marital Status	Frequency	Relative Frequency
Single	78	.503
Married	51	.329
Divorced	22	.142
Widowed	4	.026
Total	155	1.000

extended nor too clustered. Intervals must be consistent. A review of the values shows that the frequencies range from 4 for widowed to 78 for single. Intervals of ten would best represent all the frequencies. Begin the vertical axis at 0 and increase in increments of 10 to at least 80. Draw independent bars for each marital status. The height of the bar represents the frequency. The result is shown in Figure 2.2.

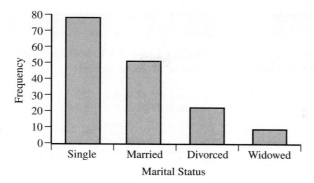

FIGURE 2.2   Bar Chart Representing Marital Status of Students

The following grouped distribution can be transformed into a histogram. The variable is the age of patients visiting a doctor's office on a specific day. Age is a continuous ratio-level measurement that is best represented by a histogram.

Ages of Patients	Frequency	Relative Frequency
10–19	10	.172
20–29	9	.155
30–39	10	.172
40–49	11	.190
50–59	8	.138
60–69	10	.172
Total	58	1.000

Begin by drawing the horizontal axis representing the values of the variable. Ages are grouped into 10-y classes. The lower limit of each class is the lower limit of the bar, and the upper class limit is the upper boundary of the bar. Draw the vertical axis representing the frequencies. The values on the vertical axis must represent the frequencies in such a way that the frequencies are neither too extended nor too clustered. Intervals must be consistent. A review of the values shows that the frequencies range from 8 for the age class 50–59 to 11 for the class 40–49. Intervals of 2 would best represent all the frequencies. Begin the vertical axis at 0 and increase in increments of 2 to at least 12. Draw adjacent bars for each age class. The height of the bar represents the frequency. The result is shown in Figure 2.3.

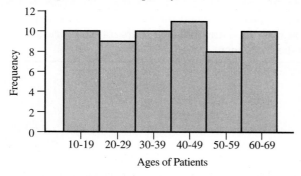

FIGURE 2.3   Histogram for Ages of Patients

EXAMPLE 2.4

Experiment   Draw a histogram for the price of a loaf of rye bread based on the following distribution from a survey of 50 local stores.

Price of a Loaf of Rye Bread (in Dollars)

Price	Frequency
1.25	5
1.26	7
1.27	9
1.28	8
1.29	10
1.30	11
Total	50

Answer

Histogram for Prices of Rye Bread

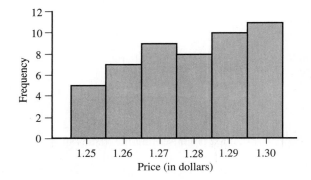

Solution   Begin by identifying price as a ratio-level measurement best represented by a histogram. Draw the horizontal axis representing the price of the bread. Note each price along the axis. Draw the vertical axis representing the frequencies. The values on the vertical axis need to represent the frequencies in such a way that the frequencies are neither too extended nor too clustered. Intervals must be consistent. A review of the values shows that the frequencies range from 5 for the price $1.25 to 11 for the price $1.30. Intervals of 2 best represent all the frequencies. Begin the vertical axis at 0 and increase in increments of 2 to at least 12. Draw adjacent bars for each price. The height of the bar represents the frequency.

A LEARNING AID

Bar Charts and Histograms

Draw a histogram for the following distribution on infant mortality rates of 50 developed nations (rounded to whole numbers).

Infant Mortality Rates of Developed Nations

Rate (per 1,000 Births)	Frequency
8	3
9	6
10	10
11	8
12	10
13	7
14	6
Total	50

Step 1   Identify the conditions for a histogram. A histogram is a type of a bar chart typically representing continuous-interval or ratio-level measurements. Infant mortality rate is a continuous ratio-level measurement (values are rounded).

Step 2   Draw the horizontal axis. The horizontal axis represents the values of the variable infant mortality. The values for infant mortality range from 8 to 14. Label the axis.

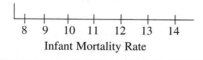

Step 3   Draw the vertical axis. The vertical axis represents the frequencies. The values on the vertical axis need to represent the frequencies in such a way that the frequencies are neither too extended nor too clustered. Intervals must be consistent. A review of the values shows that the frequencies range from 3 to 10. Intervals of 2 would best represent all the frequencies. Begin the vertical axis at 0 and increase in increments of 2 to at least 12.

Step 4   Complete the histogram. Draw adjacent bars for each value of infant mortality. The height of the bar represents the frequency.

Histogram for Infant Mortality Rates of Developed Nations

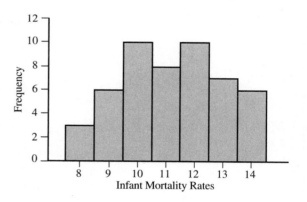

Pie Charts and Line Graphs

Frequency distributions can easily be redone as pie charts and line graphs. Pie charts and line graphs are very popular displays of data because they are easily created and understood.

A pie chart, also known as a circle graph, is a circular diagram that is analogous to a pie, where each value of a variable is equivalent to a different-sized piece of the pie. Pie charts are typically used for nominal-level discrete variables and represent relative proportions. The values in the relative frequency column of a frequency distribution are easily represented in a pie chart.

Line graphs have become very popular in recent years. There are two types of line graphs: One represents frequencies and is known as a frequency polygon; the other represents cumulative frequencies or cumulative relative frequencies and is known as an ogive (pronounced ''o-jive'').

As with other displays, pie charts and line graphs should be kept as simple as possible. Keep unnecessary information out of the display. Move values and percentages to the titles or labels. Many computer software packages create pie charts and line graphs. Many of the packages put percentages or frequencies inside the graphs. Avoid the notations unless the information is necessary for understanding the display. Remember that the purpose of a display is to present a visual aid to understanding. The actual values are not usually necessary.

A pie chart is created by dividing a circle into slices corresponding to the relative proportions of each value or category of the variable. For example, if 50% of a class are females and 50% are males, a pie chart is divided into two equal parts.

The following distribution can be shown using a pie chart.

Marital Status of Students at the University

Marital Status	Frequency	Relative Frequency
Single	78	.503
Married	51	.329
Divorced	22	.142
Widowed	4	.026
Total	155	1.000

Begin by drawing a circle. The circle will be divided into four categories, representing the four values single, married, divorced, and widowed. Focus on the relative frequency column of the distribution. Relative frequencies are written as percents by moving the decimal to the right two places. The relative frequency of single students is .503, which is 50.3%. Draw a line across the circle representing slightly more than 50%. For married students, draw a line representing another 32.9%. For divorced students, draw a line representing another 14.2%. Finally, the remaining portion of the pie should be equivalent to 2.6% for widowed students. See Figure 2.4.

A frequency polygon is a display that is similar to a histogram. A frequency polygon line begins and ends at zero. Dots placed at the tops of the bars of a histogram replace the bars and are connected, forming a line moving up and down across the values of the variable. As with a histogram, the horizontal axis represents the values of the variable. The vertical line represents frequencies.

The histogram in Figure 2.5 can be redone as a frequency polygon. Place the dots in the center of the bar representing the middle of each class. Extend the line at the beginning and end of zero. See Figure 2.6.

An ogive is a second type of line graph; it represents cumulative frequencies or cumulative relative frequencies. For an ogive describing cumulative frequencies, the line must begin at zero and end at the total number of observations for the table. An ogive displaying cumulative relative frequencies must begin at zero and end at

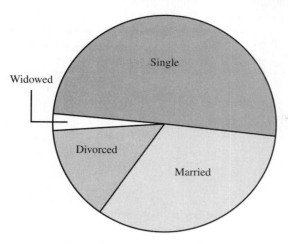

FIGURE 2.4   Pie Chart Representing Marital
Status of Students

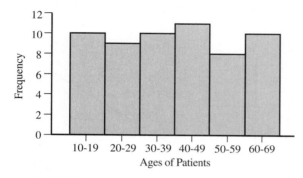

FIGURE 2.5   Histogram for Ages of Patients

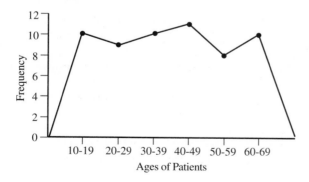

FIGURE 2.6   Frequency Polygon for Ages of Patients

1.00 (or 100% if percents are described). The lines on ogives increase as they travel across the graph. Lines may remain parallel for one or two values, but they must reach the total frequency of 1.00 for the last value. The following frequency distribution is for the price of a loaf of rye bread.

Price of a Loaf of Rye Bread (in Dollars)

Price	Frequency	Relative Frequency	Cumulative Frequency	Cumulative Relative Frequency
1.25	5	.10	5	.10
1.26	7	.14	12	.24
1.27	9	.18	21	.42
1.28	8	.16	29	.58
1.29	10	.20	39	.78
1.30	11	.22	50	1.00
Total	50	1.00		

The creation of an ogive begins with identifying the axes. The horizontal axis represents the values of the variable. For the price of bread, the values are 1.25, 1.26, and so forth. The vertical axis represents either the cumulative frequency or cumulative relative frequency. The values on the vertical axis must begin at 0 and increase in equal increments to the total frequency or 1.00. The ogive in Figure 2.7 represents the cumulative frequency, which begins at 0 and ends at 50.

FIGURE 2.7   Ogive for the Price of Rye Bread

EXAMPLE 2.5

Experiment   Draw a cumulative relative frequency ogive for the price of rye bread from a survey of 50 local stores.

Price of a Loaf of Rye Bread (in Dollars)

Price	Frequency	Relative Frequency	Cumulative Relative Frequency
1.25	5	.10	.10
1.26	7	.14	.24
1.27	9	.18	.42
1.28	8	.16	.58
1.29	10	.20	.78
1.30	11	.22	1.00
Total	50	1.00	

Answer

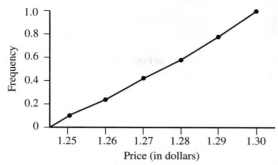

Solution   Begin by drawing the axes. The horizontal axis represents the prices of the bread. The vertical axis represnts the cumulative relative frequency. The vertical axis must begin at 0 and increase in increments representing cumulative frequencies until 1.00 (100%) is reached. Place a dot at each point of the interception of the value and its cumulative relative frequency. The last dot must be at 1.00. Connect the dots to form a line. The line in an ogive always increases or remains stable, but it must reach the total frequency of 1.00.

A LEARNING AID

Frequency Polygons

Draw a frequency polygon for the following distribution of infant mortality rates of 50 developed nations (rounded to the nearest whole number).

Infant Mortality Rates of Developed Nations

Rate (per 1,000 Births)	Frequency	Cumulative Frequency
8	3	3
9	6	9
10	10	19
11	8	27
12	10	37
13	7	44
14	6	50
Total	50	

Step 1   Identify the conditions for a frequency polygon. A frequency polygon is a type of line graph representing frequencies and is similar to a histogram.

Step 2   Draw the horizontal axis. The horizontal axis represents the values of the variable infant mortality. The values for infant mortality range from 8 to 14. Label the axis.

```
   8   9   10   11   12   13   14
        Infant Mortality Rate
```

Step 3   Draw the vertical axis. The vertical axis represents the frequencies. The values on the vertical axis must represent the frequencies in such a way that the frequencies are neither too extended nor too clustered. Intervals must be consistent. A review of the values shows that the frequencies range from 3 to 10. Intervals of 2 would best represent all the frequencies. Begin the vertical axis at 0 and increase in increments of 2 to at least 12.

Step 4   Complete the frequency polygon. Place dots to represent the frequency of each value. The dots replace the bars of a histogram. Connect the dots by starting at zero and ending at zero.

Frequency Polygon for Infant Mortality Rates of Developed Nations

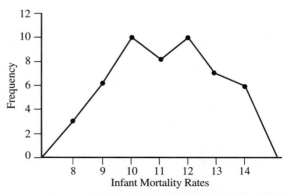

CHAPTER 2 IN REVIEW

2.1 Construct a frequency distribution for the ages of 30 students in Professor Constantine's class.

```
21  31  21  34  19  20  28  30  27  25  25  25
   25  30  27  21  34  19  19  20  21  21  30
          25  25  32  32  31  30  27
```

2.2 A random sample of orders of food items from a menu provides the following information.

Gardenburger	52
Chili	14
Soup	56
Turkey sandwich	23
Club sandwich	17
Tuna salad	18
Chicken salad	15
Chef's salad	40

Construct a frequency distribution, including the relative frequency, cumulative frequency, and cumulative relative frequency.

2.3 A sample of the musical preferences of 70 people produces the following results.

Pop	18
Classical	12
Country	17
Rock	10
Oldies	13

Construct a frequency distribution, including the relative frequency, cumulative frequency, and cumulative relative frequency.

2.4 Construct a pie chart representing the music preferences given in Problem 2.3.

2.5 Construct a bar chart representing the selection of food items given in Problem 2.2.

2.6 A random survey of employees at the Sav-a-Lot store yields the following wages (dollars per hour)

```
7.85  5.25  8.35  6.15  6.25  6.50  4.75  5.10  5.50
   7.25  8.25  6.40  7.00  5.75  5.95  7.50  8.50
              6.10  7.20  7.45
```

   a. Construct a grouped frequency distribution with class widths of $1.

   b. Draw a frequency polygon.

2.7 Draw a pie chart for the following data on education.

Education	Frequency
Elementary	325
Secondary	2,190
Bachelors	950
Masters	400
Doctorate	135

2.8 Draw a bar chart for the following data on the employment status of women.

Employment Status	Frequency
Full time	1871
Part time	1006
Unemployed	19
Not economically active	1104

2.9 Create a grouped frequency distribution with class widths of 5 for the number of children in the third grade in Monroe County.

```
31,  28,  25,  24,  35,  31,  32,  22,  20,  28,  28,
   29,  30,  22,  30,  28,  24,  31,  35,  22,  20,  28,
              28,  24,  30
```

2.10 Draw an ogive for the following frequency distribution describing the number of patients admitted in the county hospital over the past 30 days (d).

Class	f
0–4	3
5–9	5
10–14	10
15–19	13
20–24	9
25–29	9
30–34	7
35–39	6
	62

2.11 With class widths of 1 minute (min), draw a histogram for the numbers of minutes that it took a local ambulance company to reach 16 accidents

```
1.6  5.4  2.8  7.7  3.5  4.5  3.1  2.4
   3.0  7.7  2.5  3.9  7.0  5.4  1.9  4.2
```

2.12 The following grouped frequency distribution represents the ages of women marrying in St. Clair County. Complete the distribution with the relative frequency and the relative cumulative frequency.

Class	Frequency
11–15	8
16–20	10
21–25	16
26–30	7
31–35	4

2.13 Draw a frequency polygon for the following cholesterol levels of patients visiting Dr. Adam's office.

Cholesterol Level	f
190–194	1
195–199	4
200–204	3
205–209	6
210–214	9
215–219	6
220–224	2
	31

20.0	18.3	23.7	19.1	19.1	18.8
17.7	20.8	17.2	20.8	19.4	20.8
21.3	18.0	20.8	22.3	20.8	24.4

Create a frequency distribution representing the count, the relative frequency, and the cumulative relative frequency. Group the data in thousands starting at 17.0 to 17.9.

2.14   A sample of 18 starting salaries for liberal arts college graduates yielded the following results (data in thousands, rounded to nearest hundred):

2.15   The following data represent the number of suicides per 10,000 inhabitants in rural areas in Japan. Construct a grouped bar chart on the number of suicides.

22	10	12	2	10	9	16	11	8	14	11	8	13
10	12	0	10	12	8	11	5	7	10	7	9	9
					6	8						

3

Descriptive Statistics for One Variable

Data can be presented in graphs and charts as a method of reducing what may be a long and cumbersome list of observations. Often, however, even graphs and charts are too cumbersome. Reducing the data to one or two numbers to represent the beginning, center, end, or dispersion of the data is another means of description. These numbers are referred to as measures of central tendency, measures of dispersion, and measures of location.

SECTION 1

Measures of Central Tendency

Measures of central tendency locate the center of a set of data. A measure of central tendency is a single number that describes the general order or magnitude of a set of data. Each measurement describes the center in a different way. A mean, for example, describes the average response. The median describes the midpoint of the data. Yet another measurement, the mode, describes the most common response. Each measurement, although correct, may result in a different description of the data. Since each measurement may describe the center of the data in a different fashion, some measurements are more suited for certain types of data.

The most common measure of central tendency is the mean, more commonly referred to as the *average*. The mean is a measurement that describes the center of a set of data when the data are summed and divided by the number of observations. Recall the usual approach described for calculating an average: Add all the numbers and divide by how many there are.

> **Mean** A measure of central tendency that describes the average response by summing the data and dividing by the total number of elements or observations.
>
> If the mean represents a sample, the symbol is $\bar{x}$.
> If the mean represents a population, the symbol is μ.

Different symbols represent the mean of a sample and the mean of a population. Recall that statistics represent information about samples and are usually represented by English symbols. Parameters represent information about populations and are usually represented by Greek symbols. Though the symbols differ, the calculation is the same.

Formula for Calculating a Mean

$$\bar{x} = \frac{\Sigma x}{n} \qquad \mu = \frac{\Sigma x}{N}$$

where

$\bar{x}$ represents the sample mean.
μ represents the population mean.
Σ (sigma) represents the summation of the values.
x represents each value in the data.
n represents the number of elements or observations in the sample.
N represents the total number of elements in the population.

The calculation of the mean requires adding the values of x and dividing by the number of observations. For example, the mean for the values 3, 4, 5, 6, and 7 is the sum of the values $(3 + 4 + 5 + 6 + 7 = 25)$ divided by the number of values (there are 5 values). The mean is $25 \div 5 = 5$.

EXAMPLE 3.1

Experiment Calculate the mean score on an exam using the following data: 83, 93, 70, 65, 90, 100, 55, 52, 81, 73.

Answer $\bar{x} = 76.2$

Solution The mean is calculated by summing all the values of x and dividing by the total number of values.

$$\bar{x} = \frac{\Sigma x}{n} = \frac{83 + 93 + 70 + 65 + 90 + 100 + 55 + 52 + 81 + 73}{10}$$

$$= \frac{762}{10} = 76.2$$

EXAMPLE 3.2

Experiment Calculate the mean number of children born to 20 women aged 35 to 55 y.

2 0 3 2 1 1 2 3 0 2 4 1 1 3 1 0 2 5 6 3

Answer 2.1

Solution The mean is calculated by summing all the values of x and dividing by the total number of values. The values have a sum of 42. Divide 42 by 20 (the number of women surveyed).

$$\bar{x} = \frac{\Sigma x}{n} = \frac{42}{20} = 2.1$$

The mean can also be calculated when the data are arranged in a frequency distribution. A frequency distribution condenses the data so that a count of each value is reported. The values of x are either given separately or collapsed into groups or classes. Even if the data are not grouped, the values of x cannot simply be added to determine the mean. The number of occurrences of each value is given as a frequency. For example, if the value 2 occurs three times, merely adding the 2 to other values would fail to recognize that it actually occurred three times. Therefore, 2 must be added three times $(2 + 2 + 2)$. When working with a frequency distribution, instead of adding each value the number of times it occurs, it is easier to multiply the value by its number of occurrences. That is, if 2 occurs 10 times, instead of adding 2 ten times, multiply 2 by 10, for a total of 20. The formula for the mean can be adjusted to note the multiplication of the values by their number of occurrences. The symbol f represents the frequency, or number of occurrences.

Mean Formula for a Frequency Distribution

$$\bar{x} = \frac{\Sigma xf}{\Sigma f}$$

where

Σxf represents each value of x multiplied by f.
Σf represents the total number of occurrences, which is the sum of the frequencies.

The adjusted mean formula is applied to all frequency distributions. Do not attempt to apply the original mean formula to a frequency distribution, because it will not count all the occurrences and will result in a wrong answer. *Re-*

member, a frequency distribution mean formula includes f. The denominator in the formula is also adjusted. Although most texts use n in the denominator, this text replaces n with Σf as a reminder to sum the occurrences and not the number of different values. Both symbols, n and Σf, represent the total number of occurrences.

EXAMPLE 3.3

Experiment   Calculate the mean for the number of absences of students in a statistics class.

x	f
0	8
1	7
2	5
3	5
4	5
Total	30

Answer $\bar{x} = 1.73$

Solution   This is a frequency distribution that arranges the data around the number of occurrences for each value of x. For example, eight students missed 0 classes. Instead of listing 0, 0, 0, 0, 0, 0, 0, and 0, the frequency distribution reports the 0 and gives 8 occurrences. The calculation of the mean must consider 0 eight times, 1 seven times, 2 five times, 3 five times, and 4 five times. Multiplying each value of x by its frequency and then adding will result in the same answer as if the values were listed separately. Use a table to ensure the calculations are aligned appropriately. Also, be sure to total the number of occurrences (for the denominator) as 30 and not mistakenly assume n is 5 because there are five different values, 0, 1, 2, 3, and 4.

x	f	xf		
0	8	$0 \times 8 = 0$		
1	7	$1 \times 7 = 7$		
2	5	$2 \times 5 = 10$	$\bar{x} = \dfrac{\Sigma xf}{\Sigma f} = \dfrac{52}{30} = 1.73$	
3	5	$3 \times 5 = 15$		
4	5	$4 \times 5 = 20$		
Total	30	52		

The mean for grouped frequency distributions is found using the same method as used for ungrouped frequency distributions. However, the calculation of a mean from a grouped frequency distribution is only an approximation, since grouping of data involves the loss of precise information on individual observations. That is, if the absences of the students in the previous example were grouped as 0 and 1 with 15 combined observations, it would be impossible to know if all 15 students in the group missed no classes or 1 class. An assumption must be made as to a value of x that will best represent each class. The most accepted value is referred to as the *class mark*, or the *class midpoint*. The class mark is the value in the middle of the class. For example, if a class is 10–12, the class mark, or midpoint, is 11. The value 11 is the best estimate of where the observations of that class fall. When the midpoint is not obvious, the class mark is determined by adding the lower and upper limit of the class and dividing by 2. In other words, the class mark is the mean of the values in each class. Every class has a unique class mark.

The class mark is necessary for the calculation of the mean of a grouped frequency distribution. The mean formula requires multiplying x by the number of its occurrences. But a grouped frequency, by definition, does not have an x. Each class represents several values of x. The class mark is the estimate of x and is used in the calculation of the mean.

EXAMPLE 3.4

Experiment   Calculate the mean birth rate of 20 countries whose rates are given in the following grouped frequency distribution.

x	f
10–19	4
20–29	8
30–39	3
40–49	3
50–59	2
Total	20

Answer $\bar{x} = 30.0$

Solution   Identify the distribution as a grouped frequency distribution. The values have been collapsed into classes, with the observations reported. A grouped frequency distribution does not contain a value of x for each class. An assumption must be made for each class as to where the frequency occurs. Do the four countries in the first class report a birth rate of 10, 19, or another value in the class? Since the information is not available, the assumption is that the countries report a value exactly in the middle of the class. The value in the middle is referred to as the class mark and must be determined for each class. The value in the middle of 10 and 19 is 14.5 [(10 + 19)/2 = 14.5]. The class mark for the second class is (20 + 29)/2, or 24.5. The class mark for the third class is (30 + 39)/2, or 34.5. The class mark for the fourth class is (40 + 49)/2, or 44.5. Finally, the class mark for the fifth class is (50 + 59)/2, or 54.5. Place these values in a table. Note the class marks as the values of x.

Class	f	x	xf
10–19	4	14.5	58.0
20–29	8	24.5	196.0
30–39	3	34.5	103.5
40–49	3	44.5	133.5
50–59	2	54.5	109.0
Total	20		600.0

Calculate the mean using the preceding information. Remember that the numerator is the sum of the *xf* column (600). Also remember that the denominator is the sum of the *f* column (20), representing the 20 birth rates reported.

$$\bar{x} = \frac{\Sigma xf}{\Sigma f} = \frac{600.0}{20} = 30$$

There are advantages and disadvantages to working with the mean as a measure of central tendency. One advantage is that the mean is familiar to most people. Most people know how to calculate the mean, even if they do not know it as the mean. Another advantage is that the mean is calculated with all the available data. A researcher usually attempts to use as much of the data as possible, not discarding information. Another advantage is that the mean is suitable for ratio and interval data and therefore lends itself to further statistical manipulation; that is, the mean is often used for hypothesis testing, estimation, and other more advanced statistical procedures.

However, the mean has a few disadvantages. The mean may be a value that cannot or does not exist in the data. For example, the mean number of children may be determined as 2.5. But can a family have two and one-half children? Also, extreme values affect the calculation of the mean. The set of numbers 3, 4, 5, 6, and 7 has a mean of 5, but so, too, does the set of data 1, 2, 3, 4, and 15. The mean 5 is more appropriate for the first set of data than for the second. The second set includes the extreme value 15, which pulls the mean toward it. Another disadvantage is that the mean is not appropriately suited for nominal- and ordinal-level data. These data do not reflect true values of *x*, and the calculation of the mean can be misleading.

Another measure of central tendency is the median. The median identifies the middle value; exactly half of the data are above the median, and half are below. Visualize listing the data on a piece of paper, spaced equally with the lowest value at the upper edge and the highest value at the bottom edge. If the paper is folded in half, the value at the crease will be the median. Half of the values will be on the upper half of the paper, and half will be on the bottom half.

Median $\tilde{x}$ The middle value of a set of data, where the data are arranged with half of the values above, and half below the median.

The notation for the median is $\tilde{x}$. The symbol above the *x* is a tilde. There are several steps in calculating the median. The first step is to arrange, or rank, the data from the lowest value to the highest value. The second step is to calculate the position where the median value occurs. The position is determined by the expression $(n + 1)/2$; that is, add 1 to the number of values and then divide by 2. The symbol for the position is i. Position i is not the median; it is the location of the median in the data.

$$i = \frac{n + 1}{2}$$

The third step is to find the position determined in Step 2. If i is calculated as 3, count down (or across, depending how the data are presented) to the third value in the ranked data. If i is 4.5, count down to the position between the fourth and fifth values. The fourth step is to identify the median as the value in position i. When position i is a whole number, such as 3, give the value found in the position as the median. If position i is a fraction, such as 4.5, give the median as the value halfway between the existing values. The value between two positions is the mean of the values. For example, the numbers 1, 2, 4, and 5 are ranked from lowest to highest. Position i is $(4 + 1)/2$, or 2.5. There is not a value in position 2.5. The median is determined by finding the value halfway between 2 and 4, which is $(2 + 4)/2$, or 3. The median is 3.

Steps in Calculating the Median

1. Rank the data from lowest to highest.
2. Calculate position $i = (n + 1)/2$.
3. Count across the data to position i.
4. Identify the median.

EXAMPLE 3.5

Experiment   Find the median for the following set of data: 5, 2, 3, 6, 4, 3, 2, 5, 2, 7

Answer $\tilde{x} = 3.5$

Solution   There are four steps in determining the median. Step 1 is to rank the data from lowest to highest: 2, 2, 2, 3, 3, 4, 5, 5, 6, 7. Step 2 is to calculate position i. The number of cases, n, is 10.

$$i = \frac{n + 1}{2} = \frac{10 + 1}{2} = \frac{11}{2} = 5.5$$

Count across the values to position 5.5. Since i is the position, the median is the value between the fifth and sixth values. The fifth value is 3 and the sixth value is 4. The value in the middle position is $(3 + 4)/2$, or 3.5. The median is 3.5.

EXAMPLE 3.6

Experiment   Find the median for the number of children born to 20 women ages 35–55.

2   0   3   2   1   1   2   3   0   2   4   1   1   3   1   0   2   5   6   3

Answer $\tilde{x} = 2$

Solution   There are four steps in determining the median. Step 1 is to rank the data from lowest to highest:

0   0   0   1   1   1   1   1   2   2   2   2   2   3   3   3   3   4   5   6

Step 2 is to calculate position i. The number of cases, n, is 20.

$$i = \frac{n + 1}{2} = \frac{20 + 1}{2} = \frac{21}{2} = 10.5$$

Count across the values to position 10.5. Since i is the position, the median is the value between the tenth and eleventh values. The tenth value is 2 and the eleventh value is also 2. The value in between these two values is also 2: $(2 + 2)/2 = 2$. The median is 2.

The median is a measure of central tendency that is most suited for ordinal-level data. An advantage of the median over the mean is that the median is not influenced by extreme values. The median is commonly used to describe data such as income levels, housing costs, and other measurements of money that tend to contain extreme values.

Disadvantages with the median are many. It does not lend itself to further statistical techniques. It does not make use of the actual values in the data, but only of the number of values that exist. It does not necessarily involve an actual value in the data.

The third common measure of central tendency is the mode. The mode describes the center of the data as the most commonly occurring observed value. The mode is the value with the highest frequency, or the value that occurs more than any other.

Mode The most commonly occurring observed value.

There is no formula or calculation involved in determining the mode. It is determined by observing the data and noting the value with the greatest frequency. For example, the mode of the data 2, 3, 4, 4, 5, and 6 is 4, because it occurs twice, whereas other values occur only once. If the data are presented in a frequency distribution, the mode is the value with the greatest frequency. If the frequency distribution is reporting grouped data, then the mode is estimated as the class mark, or midpoint, of the class with the greatest frequency.

EXAMPLE 3.7

Experiment   Determine the mode for the following set of data:

x	f
6	2
7	3
8	4
9	3
10	2
Total	14

Answer   Mode = 8

Solution   The mode is the value that occurs with the greatest frequency. The value 8 occurs more often than the other values, with a frequency of 4.

EXAMPLE 3.8

Experiment   Determine the mode for the following data:

x	f
1–4	12
4–9	33
10–14	24
15–19	30
20–14	21
Total	120

Answer   Mode = 6.5

Solution   The data set is a grouped frequency distribution. The mode in a grouped frequency distribution is contained in the class with the greatest number of occurrences. The class 4–9 has the greatest frequency, 33. The class mark is the estimate of the mode. The class mark for the class 4–9 is determined by finding the value in the middle of the class. The class mark—and, therefore, the mode—is (4 + 9)/2, or 6.5.

The mode has a few advantages over the other measures of central tendency, including ease of identification. It does not require any calculation other than a class mark if it is determined for a grouped frequency distribution. Though the mode is applicable to all levels of data, it is best suited for nominal data.

The disadvantages of the mode are that it may not exist at all, or many may exist. That is, there are times when each value of x occurs with the same frequency. Sometimes two or more values may occur with equal frequency. If there are two values that have the greatest frequency, the data are referred to as bimodal. A three-way tie is called trimodal.

A LEARNING AID

Measures of Central Tendency

In a recent measles epidemic, one hospital in the city reported 20 cases, one hospital reported 18 cases, one hospital reported 6 cases, four hospitals reported 4 cases, and three hospitals reported 2 cases. Find the mean, mode, and median number of cases for the 10 hospitals.

Step 1   Arrange the data for each hospital in increasing order (from lowest to highest). Although arranging the data is not necessary for the mean, it is required in the median and assists in identifying the mode. Begin with the three hospitals reporting 2 cases. Write 2, 2, and 2. Next list the four hospitals reporting 4 cases as 4, 4, 4, and 4. Repeat this process for each hospital.

$$2, 2, 2, 4, 4, 4, 4, 6, 18, 20$$

Step 2   Calculate the mean. The mean is the sum of the values of x divided by the number of values.

$$\bar{x} = \frac{\Sigma x}{n} = \frac{2 + 2 + 2 + 4 + 4 + 4 + 4 + 6 + 18 + 20}{10}$$
$$= \frac{66}{10} = 6.6$$

Step 3   Calculate the median. The median requires identifying the position i as the location where the median is found. The data are already ranked. Calculate $i = (n + 1)/2$.

$$i = \frac{n + 1}{2} = \frac{10 + 1}{2} = \frac{11}{2} = 5.5$$

Count across the data to the position 5.5, which is between the fifth and sixth values. Because i falls between two values, the median is the value halfway between the values. The fifth value is 4; the sixth value is also 4. The value between 4 and 4 is 4, so the median is 4.

$$\tilde{x} = 4$$

Step 4   Identify the mode. The mode is the most common occurrence. There are four hospitals reporting 4 cases. Because 4 occurs more than any other value, the mode is 4.

Measures of Dispersion

In the ideal research environment, the choice of the measure of central tendency would not be difficult. If everyone were alike, the mean, median, and mode of any measurements would be the same. However, variety does exist. Most researchers focus on the average as the measure of central tendency. Calculating an average implies that all observations are not identical and that variation exists. The variation is the degree to which observations vary from the average. The amount of variation can be calculated with a measure of dispersion.

Measures of dispersion often supplement the mean. For example, the set of data 5, 5, 5, 5, and 5 has a mean of 5, as does the set 1, 2, 3, 4, and 15. The nature of the sets is different, with the first having no variation and the second having variation. To understand the degree of the variability of the data, the mean can be supplemented with a measure of dispersion. The larger the measure of dispersion, the more variability that exists. If no variation exists, the measure of dispersion is 0.

Just as with averages, there are many measures of dispersion, each having its advantages and disadvantages. Variability can be measured by finding the difference between the highest and lowest values, known as the range. Another measure is the mean of the deviations from the mean. The most widely used measures of dispersion are the variance and the standard deviation. The variance and standard deviation measure the squared deviations of the values from the mean.

The range is a simple way to calculate the dispersion of values. The range is calculated by subtracting the lowest value from the highest value. Be sure to scan the data carefully for the highest and lowest values, especially if the data are not ranked.

> **Range** A measure of dispersion that identifies the difference between the lowest and highest value.
>
> $$\text{Range} = H - L$$
>
> where
>
> H represents the highest value.
> L represents the lowest value.

EXAMPLE 3.9

Experiment   Calculate the range for the following set of data: 3, 4, 6, 7, 7, 8, 10.

Answer   Range = 7

Solution   The range measures the difference between the highest and lowest values. Be sure to scan the data carefully to identify the highest and lowest values. The highest value is 10 and the lowest value is 3. The range is the highest (10) minus the lowest (3).

$$\text{Range} = H - L = 10 - 3 = 7$$

The variance is a widely used measure of dispersion. It is also referred to as the average squared deviation and measures the average squared deviation of the values from the mean. After the mean is identified, the distance of each value from the mean is measured, squared, summed, and divided by the number of values minus 1. For example, if the mean is 5 and a value is 4, the distance from 5 to 4 is measured and squared. If another value is 7, the distance from 5 to 7 is measured and squared. This is repeated for each value and the squared distances are summed and divided to give an average of the squared deviations. Variances are never negative. The size of the variance reflects the amount of dispersion, with a larger variance implying more variability than a small variance.

> **Variance**   The average squared deviation of values from their mean.
>
> If the variance represents a sample, it is denoted by s^2.
> If the variance represents a population, it is denoted by σ^2.

The symbol representing a variance differs if it describes a sample or population. The symbol for a sample variance is s^2, and the symbol for a population variance is σ^2 (pronounced ''sigma squared''). It is important to become familiar with the notations, because both will be used in later formulas. There are also two different formulas for calculating the variance. Although both are applied to samples, each formula has an advantage, depending on the presentation of the data.

Formulas for Calculating the Sample Variance s^2

$$s^2 = \frac{\Sigma(x - \bar{x})^2}{n - 1}$$

or

$$s^2 = \frac{\Sigma x^2 - (\Sigma x)^2/n}{n - 1}$$

where

x represents each value of the data.

$\bar{x}$ represents the mean.

n represents the total number of observations.

The numerator of both formulas is referred to as the *sum of the squares*. The concept of the sum of the squares is important in the next chapter. Essentially, to find the sum of the squares, the distances of the values of x from the mean are determined, squared, and summed. The variance is then determined by dividing by $n - 1$. The first formula, with the numerator $\Sigma(x - \bar{x})^2$, is more suited to whole-number data. Subtracting and squaring fractions is cumbersome and can be more easily achieved with the second formula. Also, the first formula requires use of the mean. If the mean is not available or is too time consuming to calculate, the second formula can be used. Both formulas result in the same answer for all data. Most researchers tend to favor the second formula.

Calculate the population variance with the sum of the square numerator from either of the previous formulas, and divide by the total number of elements in the population. The calculations for the population mean, variance, and standard deviations contain N in the denominator, noting the total population size, instead of $n - 1$. Remember to use the appropriate Greek letter in describing population parameters.

EXAMPLE 3.10

Experiment   Calculate the variance using both formulas for the following ages of children visiting a pediatrician's office: 3, 4, 4, 5, 6, 7, 7, 8.

Answer $s^2 = 3.14$ and $s^2 = 3.14$

Solution   Both formulas result in the same answer. The first formula requires the mean. Begin by calculating the mean:

$$\bar{x} = \frac{\Sigma x}{n} = \frac{44}{8} = 5.5$$

Using the first formula, subtract the mean 5.5 from each value of x. Square each difference. Sum the squared differences and divide by $n - 1$. A table helps organize the calculations. The values in parentheses in the table for 3 serve as a guide to the calculations of the other values.

x	$(x - \bar{x})$	$(x - \bar{x})^2$
3	$(3 - 5.5) -2.5$	$[(-2.5)^2]$ 6.25
4	-1.5	2.25
4	-1.5	2.25
5	-0.5	0.25
6	0.5	0.25
7	1.5	2.25
7	1.5	2.25
8	2.5	6.25
Total		22.00

$$s^2 = \frac{\Sigma(x - \bar{x})^2}{n - 1} = \frac{22}{8 - 1} = \frac{22}{7} = 3.14$$

Calculating the variance with the second formula will yield the same result. The columns differ from those just presented. Also, the mean is not needed in the calculation. Use a table to help organize the calculations.

x	x^2
3	(3^2) 9
4	16
4	16
5	25
6	36
7	49
7	49
8	64
$\Sigma x = 44$	$\Sigma x^2 = 264$

$$s^2 = \frac{\Sigma x^2 - (\Sigma x)^2/n}{n - 1} = \frac{264 - 44^2/8}{8 - 1}$$

$$= \frac{264 - 1936/8}{7} = \frac{264 - 242}{7} = \frac{22}{7} = 3.14$$

The variance is a measure of the squared deviations. It is difficult for most people to understand information reported in square units. For example, if a variance measures dispersion in years, its value is given in years squared. The variance can be extended one step further by returning the result to the same unit of measurement as the original data. Extending the variance calculation in this way results in the standard deviation. The standard deviation is the square root of the variance, which is given in the original unit of measurement. If years are involved, then the variance is in years squared, and the standard deviation is in years.

Standard deviation The square root of the average squared deviation from the mean. The standard deviation is the square root of the variance.

If the standard deviation represents a sample, then the symbol is s.
If it represents a population, the symbol is σ.

Notice that the symbols for the variance and standard deviation are similar. The variance involves squared values, and therefore it includes an exponent (^{2}). The standard deviation does not include the exponent. Remember to use the appropriate English or Greek symbol, depending on whether a sample or a population is described. As with variances, the larger the standard deviation, the more dispersion exists in the data. Standard deviations are never negative. If all the data are exactly equal to the mean, the standard deviation is 0.

There are two ways of approaching the calculation of the standard deviation. Either the variance is calculated and then the square root is taken, or the variance formula is noted as the standard deviation with the square root symbol over the complete formula.

Formula for Calculating the Standard Deviation

$$s = \sqrt{s^2} \quad \text{and} \quad \sigma = \sqrt{\sigma^2}$$

$$s = \sqrt{\frac{\Sigma(x - \bar{x})^2}{n - 1}}$$

$$s = \sqrt{\frac{\Sigma x^2 - (\Sigma x)^2/n}{n - 1}}$$

EXAMPLE 3.11

Experiment   Calculate the standard deviation using both formulas for the following ages of children visiting a pediatrician's office: 3, 4, 4, 5, 6, 7, 7, 8.

Answer $s = 1.77$ and $s = 1.77$

Solution   Both standard deviation formulas will result in the same answer, and both are the square roots of the variances. The first formula requires the mean. Begin by calculating the mean.

$$\bar{x} = \frac{\Sigma x}{n} = \frac{44}{8} = 5.5$$

Using the first formula, subtract the mean, 5.5, from each value of x. Square each difference. Sum the squared differences, divide by $n - 1$, and calculate the square root for the final answer. A table helps organize the calculations. The values in parentheses in the table for 3 serve as a guide to the calculations for the other values.

x	$(x - \bar{x})$	$(x - \bar{x})^2$
3	$(3 - 5.5) - 2.5$	$[(-2.5)^2]$ 6.25
4	-1.5	2.25
4	-1.5	2.25
5	-0.5	0.25
6	0.5	0.25
7	1.5	2.25
7	1.5	2.25
8	2.5	6.25
Total		22.00

$$s = \sqrt{\frac{(x - \bar{x})^2}{n - 1}} = \sqrt{\frac{22}{8 - 1}} = \sqrt{\frac{22}{7}} = \sqrt{3.14} = 1.77$$

Calculating the standard deviation with the second formula will yield the same result. The columns differ from those just presented. Also, the mean is not needed in the calculation. Use a table to organize the calculations.

x	x^2
3	(3^2) 9
4	16
4	16
5	25
6	36
7	49
7	49
8	64
$\Sigma x = 44$	$\Sigma x^2 = 264$

$$s = \sqrt{\frac{\Sigma x^2 - (\Sigma x)^2/n}{n - 1}} = \sqrt{\frac{264 - 44^2/8}{8 - 1}} = \sqrt{\frac{264 - 1936/8}{7}}$$

$$= \sqrt{\frac{264 - 242}{7}} = \sqrt{\frac{22}{7}} = \sqrt{3.14} = 1.77$$

If the variance has already been calculated, then the calculation does not need to be repeated to find the standard deviation. Simply take the square root of the variance.

An adjustment of the variance and standard deviation formulas is necessary for frequency distributions. Recall that the mean formula is adjusted by multiplying each value of x by its frequency. The same adjustment must be made when calfjculating the variance and standard deviation of a frequency distribution. If the frequency distribution is grouped, a class mark must be identified first and applied in the formula as x. All *formulas for frequency distributions must include the product of x and f.* Remember, Σf is equivalent to n, the number of observations.

Variance Formula for a Frequency Distribution

$$s^2 = \frac{\Sigma x^2 f - (\Sigma xf)^2/\Sigma f}{\Sigma f - 1} \qquad s = \sqrt{s^2}$$
$$\sigma = \sqrt{\sigma^2}$$

EXAMPLE 3.12

Experiment Calculate the variance and standard deviation of the following grouped frequency distribution.

Class	f
10–19	4
20–29	8
30–39	3
40–49	3
50–59	2
Total	20

Answer $s^2 = 162.895$ and $s = 12.76$

Solution Identify the distribution as a grouped frequency distribution. Find the class mark for each class, which will then be used as the estimation of the x value. The class mark for each class is found by adding the lower and upper limits and dividing by 2. The class mark for the first class is $(10 + 19)/2$, or 14.5. For the second class, the class mark is $(20 + 29)/2$, or 24.5. Calculate each class mark. Place the class marks in a separate column to assist in the calculations. The calculations will require an x column, x^2 column, x^2f column, and xf column. The summations of the f, x^2f, and xf columns are necessary for the final calculations.

		Class Mark			
Class	f	x	x^2	x^2f	xf
10–19	4	14.5	210.25	841.00	58.0
20–29	8	24.5	600.25	4,802.00	196.0
30–39	3	34.5	1,190.25	3,570.75	103.5
40–49	3	44.5	1,980.25	5,940.75	133.5
50–59	2	54.5	2,970.25	5,940.50	109.0
	$\Sigma f = 20$			$\Sigma x^2 f = 21{,}095.00$	$\Sigma xf = 600.0$

$$s^2 = \frac{\Sigma x^2 f - (\Sigma xf)^2/\Sigma f}{\Sigma f - 1} = \frac{21{,}095 - 600^2/20}{20 - 1}$$

$$= \frac{21{,}095 - 18{,}000}{19}$$

$$= \frac{3095}{19}$$

$$= 162.895$$

$$s = \sqrt{s^2} = \sqrt{162.895} = 12.76$$

A LEARNING AID

Measures of Dispersion

In a 30-mile-per-hour (mi/h) speed zone, 10 randomly selected cars are checked for speed. Find the range, variance, and standard deviation of the motorists' speeds. The speeds are: 22, 32, 38, 27, 39, 23, 29, 30, 31, 29.

Step 1 Calculate the range. The range is the difference between the highest and lowest values. Be sure to scan the data carefully when identifying the highest and lowest values. The highest value is 39 and the lowest value is 22. The range is

$$\text{Range} = H - L = 39 - 22 = 17$$

Step 2 Calculate the variance. The variance is the average squared deviation from the mean. There are two formulas for the variance. One formula requires the calculation of the mean; the other does not. Since the mean is not reported, it may be more convenient to calculate the variance with the formula that does not include the mean. Organize the data in a table. An x column and an x^2 column are necessary.

x	x^2
22	484
32	1024
38	1444
27	729
39	1521
23	529
29	841
30	900
31	961
29	841
$\Sigma x = 300$	$\Sigma x^2 = 9274$

$$s^2 = \frac{\Sigma x^2 - (\Sigma x)^2/n}{n - 1} = \frac{9274 - 300^2/10}{10 - 1}$$

$$= \frac{9274 - 9000}{9} = \frac{274}{9} = 30.44$$

Step 3 Calculate the standard deviation. The standard deviation returns the data to the original unit of measurement. That is, the variance 30.44 is in miles per hour squared. The standard deviation is in miles per hour. The standard deviation is the square root of the variance.

$$s = \sqrt{s^2} = \sqrt{30.44} = 5.52$$

Measures of Position

Means and standard deviations are important values that describe data from one population. However, it is often necessary to describe or compare data across two populations. Measures of position are useful for comparing data within one population or between different populations.

The standard score, or z score, is a measure of position that allows data from the same or different populations to be compared. The principle of the standard score is to standardize data to one scale. Standardized data can be compared to other standardized data in regard to their relative positions. The standard score is a popular measure of position and lends itself to further statistical techniques. (A full discussion of the standard score is presented in Chapter 8.)

Standard score, or z score A measure of position based on the number of standard deviations that a given value of x is from the mean.

The standard score is a standardized standard deviation. It measures the number of standard deviations a given value is from the mean. When values are compared from different populations, a z score is calculated for each value based on its mean and standard deviation. All means on the standardized scale are adjusted to 0, and all standard deviations are adjusted to increments of 1 above and below the mean.

Calculation for the Standard Score, or z Score

Sample   Population

$$z = \frac{x - \bar{x}}{s} \quad \text{or} \quad z = \frac{x - \mu}{\sigma}$$

EXAMPLE 3.13

Experiment   Yolanda received a score of 78 on her statistics exam with Professor Miller, where the mean score was 73 and the standard deviation was 3. Michelle received a score of 83 on her statistics exam with Professor Charles, where the mean score was 81 and the standard deviation was 5. Did Yolanda or Michelle do better relative to her class?

Answer   Yolanda did better, relative to her class, than did Michelle.

Solution   Determining if a student did better relative to another student requires comparing the positions of the students on a standardized scale. Each student's score must be standardized with the z score formula and then compared. Begin by calculating Yolanda's score using the information from her class. Second, calculate Michelle's score.

Yolanda: $z = \dfrac{x - \mu}{\sigma} = \dfrac{78 - 73}{3} = \dfrac{5}{3} = 1.67$

Michelle: $z = \dfrac{x - \mu}{\sigma} = \dfrac{83 - 81}{5} = \dfrac{2}{5} = 0.40$

Compare the standardized scores. Although Michelle's original score is higher than Yolanda's, Yolanda's standard score is higher. That is, Yolanda did better relative to her class than Michelle did in her class.

Other common measures of position include quartiles and percentiles. Quartiles and percentiles partition data into several equal parts. Quartiles divide data into four equal quarters. Percentiles divide data into 100 equal parts. Although not addressed here, other divisions exist, such as deciles, which divide data into 10 equal parts. The principle in partitioning data is to determine what proportion of values are lower and higher than a particular score. For this reason, percentiles and quartiles are important tools in education. Entrance exams for universities are based on percentiles, whereas admission is often based on quartiles.

> **Quartile** A measure of position that divides data into four equal parts. The first quarter is denoted by Q_1, the second, by Q_2, and the third, by Q_3.

> **Percentile** A measure of position that divides data into 100 equal parts. Each percentile is denoted by P with a subscript indicating the value of the percentile.

The steps involved in determining quartiles include ranking the data, calculating the position i, adjusting i, counting the data to the adjusted i position, and identifying the quartile or percentile. The data should be ranked from lowest to highest. In the formula, k equals the quartile number or percentile number.

> **Calculating the Position of Quartiles and Percentiles**
>
> $$i = \frac{n(k)}{100}$$
>
> where
>
> i is the position of the quartile or percentile.
> k is the quartile or percentile in question.
> n is the number of cases or scores.
> k for percentiles is equal to the percentile in question.
> k for quartiles is $Q_1 = 25$, $Q_2 = 50$, or $Q_3 = 75$.

The position i must be adjusted. If calculation of i results in a fraction of any size, i is rounded up to the next whole number. For example, if $i = 3.1$, i is rounded up to 4. If $i = 3.9$, i is rounded up to 4. If calculation of i results in a whole number, i must be adjusted by adding 0.5. Adding the 0.5 allows the position to fall between two values. For example, if i is 6, adjust i by adding .5 so that $i = 6.5$. Only one of these adjustments occurs. Either i is rounded or .5 is added but not both.

After i is adjusted, count the values of the data to the adjusted position i. If i falls between two values, the quartile or percentile is the value midway between the values. The midway value is determined by adding the values and dividing by two. *Remember that i is only the position where the quartile or percentile is located in the original set of ranked data.*

Steps in Locating Quartiles and Percentiles

1. Rank the data from lowest to highest.
2. Calculate position i.
3. Adjust i:
   a. Add 0.5 if i is a whole number.
   b. Round up to the next whole number if i is a fraction.
4. Count across data to position i.
5. Identify the quartile or percentile.

EXAMPLE 3.14

Experiment   Find the third quartile and the 90th percentile in the examination scores for Professor Miller's class. The scores are 86, 74, 75, 81, 99, 89, 65, 55, 93, 76.

Answer $Q_3 = 89$, $P_{90} = 96$

Solution   There are five steps in identifying quartiles and percentiles. The first step is to rank the data from lowest to highest. The ranked data are 55, 65, 74, 75, 76, 81, 86, 89, 93, 99.

Calculate position i for the quartile and percentile. The calculation of i requires the total number of cases to be multiplied by the quartile value or percentile value, and divided by 100. The value for the third quartile is 75. The value for the 90th percentile is 90.

$$i_{Q_3} = \frac{n(k)}{100} = \frac{10(75)}{100} = \frac{750}{100} = 7.5$$

$$i_{P_{90}} = \frac{n(k)}{100} = \frac{10(90)}{100} = \frac{900}{100} = 9$$

Adjust i as necessary. The i for quartile 3 is 7.5. An i value that is a fraction must be rounded up to the next whole number. Therefore, $i = 7.5$ becomes $i = 8.0$. The value for quartile 3 will be in the eighth position. The i for the 90th percentile is a whole number, 9. An i value that is a whole number is adjusted by adding .5. Therefore, the value for the 90th percentile will be in position 9.5. Count across the data to the eighth position. Quartile three is 89. Count across the data to position 9.5. The 90th percentile is the value midway between 93 and 99. The value midway is determined by adding the values and dividing by 2. The 90th percentile is (93 + 99)/2, or 96.

55, 65, 74, 75, 76, 81, 86, 89, 93, 99
Position 8, Q_3
Position 9.5, P_{90}

A LEARNING AID

Measures of Position

Consider the population of students taking an advanced placement test for college credit. Calculate the standard score of a student receiving a 76, where the mean is 69.83 and the standard deviation is 15.12. Identify the third quartile and the 80th percentile.

45, 50, 52, 61, 64, 72, 76, 79, 81, 83, 84, 91

Step 1   Calculate the standard score. The experiment notes the population is tested; therefore, the z score uses the values of μ and σ. The value of x in question is 76.

$$z = \frac{x - \mu}{\sigma} = \frac{76 - 69.83}{15.12} = \frac{6.17}{15.12} = .41$$

The score 76 is .41 z scores above the standardized mean of 0. It can be used to compare with students' scores from other years.

Step 2   Identify the third quartile. Six steps are required in identifying quartiles. The first step is to rank the data. The data are ranked from lowest to highest. Calculate position i. The value of k for Q_3 is 75.

$$i = \frac{n(k)}{100} = \frac{12(75)}{100} = \frac{900}{100} = 9.0$$

Adjust i. Add .5 to i when it is a whole number. The adjusted value is $9 + .5 = 9.5$. Count across the data to position 9.5. The third quartile falls between the values 81 and 83. The value 82 is the value of the third quartile.

45, 50, 52, 61, 64, 72, 76, 79, 81, 83, 84, 91
Position 9.5, Q_3 ⟶

Step 3   Identify the 80th percentile. Percentiles are determined the same way as quartiles. The data are ranked. Calculate i.

$$i = \frac{n(k)}{100} = \frac{12(80)}{100} = \frac{960}{100} = 9.6$$

Adjust i. Round up to the next whole number when i is a fraction. The value 9.6 is rounded up to 10. The 80th percentile is the value 83, which is in the 10 position.

45, 50, 52, 61, 64, 72, 76, 79, 81, 83, 84, 91
Position 10, P_{80} ⟶

CHAPTER 3 IN REVIEW

3.1   Calculate the mean, mode, and median number of children in the third grade in Monroe County: 31, 28, 25, 24, 35, 31, 32, 22, 20, 28, 28, 29, 30, 22, 30.

3.2   Arrange the data in Problem 3.1 as an ungrouped frequency distribution. Calculate the mean using the formula appropriate for a frequency distribution.

3.3   The following frequency distribution describes the number of patients admitted in the city hospital over the past 30 d.

Class	f
0–4	3
5–9	5
10–14	10
15–19	13
20–24	9
25–29	9
30–34	7
35–39	6
Total	62

a. Calculate the mean number of patients.
b. Calculate the variance.
c. Calculate the standard deviation.
d. What is the class mark of the third class?
e. Which class contains the median?
f. Identify the mode.

3.4   The amounts of time (in minutes) that it took a local ambulance company to reach 16 accidents are:

1.6   5.4   2.8   7.2   3.5   5.4   3.1   2.4
3.0   7.7   2.5   3.9   7.0   5.4   1.9   4.2

a. Find the mean.   e. Find s^2.
b. Find the median.   f. Find s.
c. Find the mode.   g. Find P_{70}.
d. Find the range.   h. Find Q_1.

3.5   The closing prices of AIBI stock on each day during the first week of May were as follows: 27.5, 28.2, 27.5, 28.9, 28.3, 24.5, and 21.1. Find Q_1, Q_3, P_{60}, and P_{20}.

3.6 A class of third-grade students, when given a nationally used standardized examination, was found to have a mean score of 75 with a standard deviation of 4. Each child's score was changed to a standard z score for comparison with his or her classmates.

    a. What is the z score for a child who scored 81?

    b. What is the z score for a child who scored 68?

3.7 The following grouped frequency distribution represents the ages of women marrying in St. Clair County. Find the mean and standard deviation.

Class	Frequency
11–15	8
16–20	10
21–25	16
26–30	7
31–35	4

3.8 You own a potato chip company and are tired of complaints that the bags of chips are not consistently filled with the 1.5 ounces (oz) claimed. You are deciding which new dispensing machine to buy. Machine A dispenses a mean of 1.47 oz with a standard deviation of 0.4. Machine B dispenses a mean of 1.52 oz with a variance of .72. Assuming all other things remain equal, which machine is a better buy?

3.9 Find the mean and the standard deviation of the following distribution of the cholesterol levels of patients visiting Dr. Adam's office.

Cholesterol Level	f
190–194	1
195–199	4
200–204	3
205–209	6
210–214	9
215–219	6
220–224	2
Total	31

3.10 In describing the frequency distribution on cholesterol levels in Problem 3.9, find the following:

    a. Class mark of the fourth class

    b. Class width

    c. Upper class limit of the second class

3.11 A sample of 18 starting salaries for liberal arts college graduates yielded the following results (data in thousands, rounded to nearest hundred):

20.0	28.3	32.7	19.1	19.1	36.8
27.7	20.8	27.2	20.8	29.1	20.8
21.3	28.0	20.8	22.3	20.8	24.4

    a. Find the mean.   **d.** Find the range.

    b. Find the median.   **e.** Find the variance.

    c. Find the mode.   **f.** Find s.

    g. Find Q_1.   **i.** Find P_{40}.

    h. Find Q_2.   **j.** Find P_{79}.

3.12 The following data represent the number of suicides per 10,000 inhabitants in rural areas in Japan. Calculate the mean and standard deviation.

22	10	12	2	10	9	16	11	8	14	11	8	13	10
12	0	10	12	8	11	5	7	10	7	9	9	6	8

3.13 Find the mean and standard deviation of the following frequency distribution of the average age of employees at the local phone company.

Class	Frequency
20–29	46
30–39	32
40–49	31
50–59	24
60–69	20
70–79	5

3.14 The following data represent the number of suicides per 10,000 inhabitants in rural areas in Japan.

22	10	12	2	10	9	16	11	8	14	11	8	13
10	12	0	10	12	8	11	5	7	10	7	9	9
					6	8						

    a. Find Q_1.   **c.** Find P_{30}.

    b. Find Q_3.   **d.** Find P_{37}.

3.15 Water in a local community is tested for various toxins. The average amount of lead in the water is 122 cells per unit, with a standard deviation of 22. The average amount of chlorine is 200 cells per unit, with a standard deviation of 30. The water in Ms O'Kelley's home is tested, and it produces 150 cells of lead and 230 cells of chlorine. Which toxin in Ms O'Kelley's water is highest compared to the average for the community?

3.16 Find the average number of nuclear warheads for the top 10 states.

2258	2090	1650	1365	1248
1085	910	650	595	582

3.17 The average number of computers in the United States per 100 population is 24, with a standard deviation of 4. The average number of microwave ovens is 63, with a standard deviation of 7. A randomly selected neighborhood has 22 computers and 68 microwave ovens. On which item does the neighborhood score closest to the national average?

3.18 The average number of televisions in the United States is 1.9 per household with a standard deviation of .45. What is the z score for a house having only 1 television?

3.19 Find the mean and standard deviation for the cost of rent in the university district.

$365	225	245	325	450
400	410	375	325	395

3.20 What is the z score for a value of x equal to the mean?

4

Descriptive Measures of Two or More Variables

Chapters 1 through 3 describe and condense data from one variable. Most of the questions social and behavioral scientists ask involve the relationships between two or more variables. The techniques for describing a single variable are referred to as univariate analysis. Describing the relationship of two variables is referred to as bivariate analysis, and describing three or more variables is referred to as multivariate analysis. For example, describing the age of students is a form of univariate analysis. Describing the age and sex of students is bivariate, and describing the age, sex, and religious affiliation of students is multivariate.

Multivariate analysis is one of the most important techniques in the social and behavioral sciences. These sciences often depend on statistical techniques to identify the relationships between variables. Social and behavioral sciences generally do not enjoy the luxury of laboratory experiments, where the complete environment is controlled. Understanding that most social problems are very complicated, statistical techniques are developed to isolate the relationships among variables.

It is important to distinguish the difference between explaining relationships and explaining causality. Measures of description, such as correlations, describe the strength and sometimes the direction of the relationship of two variables. Regression analysis predicts and projects movement between two or more variables. Neither directly measures causation. For example, a correlation may exist between turning on the lights and its being night. However, turning on the lights does not cause it to be night.

When working with values for two variables, it is important to keep the values aligned. A value for one variable, X, must be considered with the value for a second variable, Y, for the same case. For example, a soldier's rank must be aligned with the same soldier's years in service. It would not be appropriate to test the relationship of rank and years in service using one soldier's rank with another soldier's years in service. When data are paired across two or more variables, the data are referred to as ordered pairs.

> **Ordered pairs** A pair in which a value for variable X is associated with a corresponding value for variable Y.

SECTION 1

Two Nominal Variables: Contingency Tables/Crosstabs

A nominal variable is one that categorizes or describes the attributes of data. Nominal variables do not specify magnitude, value, or order. Examples of nominal variables include sex, race, religion, marital status, color of hair, and color of car. When two nominal variables are described for the same data, a contingency table shows the relationship between the values of the two variables. A contingency table is a convenient way of reading and describing the relationship between two variables because it is a two-dimensional picture. The outcomes of one variable are overlapped with the outcomes of another variable.

The construction of a contingency table begins with ordered pairs. Ordered pairs give values for two variables for the same case. Each combination of ordered pairs represents a cell. A count determines the value in each cell.

> **Contingency table** A table that represents the relationships of two variables and their events. The outcomes of a variable are overlapped with the outcomes of another variable. The overlaps are referred to as cells.

In most computerized statistical programs, contingency tables are known as crosstabulations, or crosstabs. The cells of the table describe the overlapping information from the two variables. For example, if the gender and ages of students are represented in a contingency table, a cell could be constructed from those students who report being 20 years old and female. Another cell could contain those students who report being 20 years old and male. The outside row and column state the totals for each value of the variable. Table 4.1 is a contingency table reporting gender and

TABLE 4.1 Contingency Table for Gender and Age of Students

Gender	Less than 25	25–34	35–44	More than 44	Total
		Age			
Female	2,900	3,254	1,120	438	7,712
Male	2,460	3,196	1,088	544	7,288
Total	5,360	6,450	2,208	982	15,000

ages of students. The value 2900 in cell 1 indicates that 2,900 females report being less than 25 y old. The value 7,712 at the far right of the first row gives the total number of females in the school. The value 15,000 at the bottom right corner of the table is the total number of students in the school.

The relationship of the variables in a contingency table is determined by comparing the difference between the actual values reported by the sample and the expected values. A measurement known as a chi-square measures the difference between the actual occurrences and the expected frequencies if no relationship exists. That is, if there is no difference, no relationship exists. The actual calculation of the chi-square statistic is presented in later chapters.

EXAMPLE 4.1

Experiment   Construct a contingency table with the following data for party identification and gender. Does there appear to be a relationship? (D = Democrat, I = Independent, R = Republican, M = male, F = female)

Gender	M	M	F	F	M	M	F	F	F	M	M	M	M	F	M	M
	M	F	M	F	F	M										
Party	I	R	D	D	I	R	D	I	R	R	R	I	D	I	D	R
	R	D	R	R	D	I										

Answer   Yes, there appears to be a relationship. Females tend to be Democrats and males tend to be Republicans.

	Party Identification			
Gender	**Democrat**	**Independent**	**Republican**	**Total**
Female	5	2	2	9
Male	2	4	7	13
Total	7	6	9	22

Solution   A contingency table requires each possible combination of ordered pairs to be represented by a cell. Therefore, one cell must represent female Democrats, another female Independents, another female Republicans, and so forth. Gender and party identification are overlaid in a two-by-three table. Keep each ordered pair aligned. Count the number of pairs that fulfill each cell and enter the count in cell. Add across the rows and columns for the totals. Finally, visually determine if there appears to be a relationship between the variables. A trend exists where females tend toward the Democratic side of the table and males tend toward the Republican side of the table. If no relationship exists, each cell would be approximately equal.

EXAMPLE 4.2

Experiment   Describe the following contingency table.

Favor Nonsmoking Rule on Airplane

	Gender		
	Male	**Female**	**Total**
Yes	24	14	38
No	16	6	22
Total	40	20	60

Answer   Although there are fewer women surveyed, proportionately there appear to be more women than men in favor of the nonsmoking policy. Disregarding gender, more people (38) are in favor of the nonsmoking policy than are opposed (22).

A LEARNING AID

Two Nominal Variables: Contingency Table

Construct a contingency table for the following data for a survey questioning whether voters would pay for a new education program through a sales tax increase and/or an income tax increase (Y = yes, N = no).

Sales tax	Y Y N N N Y N N N N
	Y N Y N N Y N N Y Y
	N Y Y Y Y N N Y N N

Income	N Y N Y Y Y N N Y Y
tax	N N Y Y N N N Y Y Y
	Y N N Y Y N N Y N N

Step 1   A contingency table shows the intersection data classified according to two variables. The values in each column must be aligned. There are four combinations of responses. A voter could respond with a yes to the sales tax and a yes to the income tax. A voter could also respond with a yes to the sales tax and a no to the income tax. Another response might be no to the sales tax and no to the income tax, or no to the sales tax and yes to the income tax.

Step 2   Draw a two-by-two table representing the four responses. There are two responses (yes or no) for the first variable and two responses (yes or no) for the second variable.

Step 3   Count the number of answers that fulfill the characteristics of each cell. Place the count in the appropriate cell. Place the row and columns totals on the outside.

		Sales Tax		
		Yes	**No**	**Total**
	Yes	8	7	15
Income Tax	No	5	10	15
	Total	13	17	30

Step 4   Interpret the table. There appears to be a relationship between voters who support a tax increase for both types or oppose a tax increase for both types. Both the yes/yes and no/no cells are the largest. Voters are evenly split on the single issue of income tax, 15 supporting and 15 opposing. However, there are more voters who oppose a sales tax increase than support it, 17 to 13.

Two Ordinal Variables

An ordinal variable ranks or orders data from lowest to highest. Examples of ordinal-level variables include alphabetizing a seating chart, arranging people according to weight or height, or positioning military leaders according to rank. Variables that can be ranked can be compared with a variety of statistical techniques. The most popular technique for describing the relationship of two ordinal variables is the Spearman rank correlation coefficient.

The Spearman rank correlation coefficient, also known as Spearman's r, goes beyond the chi-square description for nominal-level data. Spearman's r describes not only whether a relationship exists, but also the direction of the relationship. Spearman's r reports whether the variables move in the same or different directions: That is, do both variables simultaneously increase and decrease, or does one increase while the other decreases?

> **Spearman's rank correlation coefficient**   Measures the strength and direction of the relationship between two ordinal variables. The notation is r_s.

The calculation of Spearman's r begins with identifying the difference between the paired data. Identify one variable as X and the second as Y. The difference of the ordered pair is $x - y = d$. The value d for each ordered pair must also be squared for the calculation. When working with ranked data, a common problem occurs with rankings that are tied. Ranked data that are tied are assigned the mean of the rankings if they had not been tied. For example, if students are ranked according to height and the second, third, and fourth shortest students are the same height, then all three students are ranked as 3, because the mean is $(2 + 3 + 4)/3 = 3$. If the first and second students are tied, their rankings are 1.5, the mean of 1 and 2.

> **Formula for Calculating Spearman's r**
>
> $$r_s = 1 - \frac{6\Sigma\, d^2}{n\,(n^2 - 1)}$$
>
> where
>
> $d = X - Y$ and d^2 is the squared difference of each ordered pair.
>
> n is the number of ordered pairs.

A correlation coefficient will have a value ranging from -1 to 1. A value of -1 or 1 means there is a perfect relationship between the variables. A -1 is a perfect negative relationship. As the values of one variable increase, there is a corresponding decrease in the values of the second variable. A 1 is a perfect positive relationship. The values of the two variables increase and decrease simultaneously. A value of 0 means there is no relationship.

Values of r_s
$-1 \leq r_s \leq 1$

EXAMPLE 4.3

Experiment   Students at the Phoenix Institute ranked their professors. As part of the tenure process, faculty were also asked to rank other professors. The top five professors (in reverse order, where 5 is the highest and 1 is the lowest) are listed here. Do the students and faculty tend to agree?

	Students (X)	Faculty (Y)
Prof. Dodd	3	1
Prof. Mimick	2	2
Prof. Lee	4.5	4
Prof. Elder	4.5	5
Prof. Pye	1	3

Answer $r_s = .575$; yes, the students and the faculty tend to agree.

Solution   Spearman's r is the measure of association for ranked data. The data are ranked with ties, such as the apparent tie for the fourth and fifth position by the students, reported using the mean of the values of the tied positions. Arrange the table with columns for d, the difference between X and Y, and for d^2. Calculate the coefficient.

	Students x	Faculty y	d $(x - y)$	d^2
Prof. Dodd	3	1	2.0	4.00
Prof. Mimick	2	2	0.0	0.00
Prof. Lee	4.5	4	0.5	0.25
Prof. Elder	4.5	5	−0.5	0.25
Prof. Pye	1	3	−2.0	4.00
				8.50

$$r_s = 1 - \frac{6\Sigma\, d^2}{n(n^2 - 1)} = 1 - \frac{6(8.5)}{5(5^2 - 1)}$$

$$= 1 - \frac{51}{5(24)} = 1 - \frac{51}{120} = 1 - .425 = .575$$

The coefficient .575 implies that there is a positive relationship between the students' and the faculty's rankings. In other words, they tend to agree more than they tend to disagree.

EXAMPLE 4.4

Experiment Is there a relationship between the rankings of the top 10 states with nuclear weapons in 1985 and 1992?

State	1992 Ranking	1985 Ranking
South Carolina	1	1
New Mexico	2	11
North Dakota	3	3
Texas	4	6
Washington	5	5
California	6	4
Louisiana	7	9
Michigan	8	6
Virginia	9	8
Wyoming	10	19

Answer No, $r_s = -.085$.

Solution Spearman's r is the measure of association for ranked data. The data are ranked from lowest to highest or highest to lowest. Arrange the table with columns for d, the difference between x and y, and for d^2. Calculate the coefficient.

State	1992 x	1985 y	d $(x-y)$	d^2
South Carolina	1	1	0	0
New Mexico	2	11	-9	81
North Dakota	3	3	0	0
Texas	4	6	-2	4
Washington	5	5	0	0
California	6	4	2	4
Louisiana	7	9	-2	4
Michigan	8	6	2	4
Virginia	9	8	1	1
Wyoming	10	19	-9	81
				179

$$r_s = 1 - \frac{6\Sigma d^2}{n(n^2-1)} = 1 - \frac{6(179)}{10(10^2-1)}$$

$$= 1 - \frac{1074}{10(99)} = 1 - \frac{1074}{990} = 1 - 1.084 = -.085$$

The coefficient $-.085$ implies that there is a slight negative relationship between the states' rankings in terms of the number of nuclear weapons for 1992 and 1985. Because the coefficient is so small, there does not appear to be a relationship between a state's ranking in the years 1992 and 1985.

A LEARNING AID

Spearman's r

Eight nations report the following data on their infant mortality rate and general mortality rate. Rank the data. Does there appear to be a relationship between the two mortality rates?

	Canada	U.S.	Sweden	U.K.
Infant mortality	8.1	10.5	6.4	9.6
Mortality	7.0	9.0	11.0	11.0

	France	Japan	China	Spain
Infant mortality	10.0	6.2	50	9.6
Mortality	10.7	6.0	8	8.1

Step 1   Rank the data from lowest to highest. The lowest score should be ranked 1 and the highest score, 8. Be sure to use the mean for values that tie. For example, Sweden and the U.K. tie for the worst general mortality rate. Since they tie for the seventh and eighth positions, both are assigned the position 7.5 (7 + 8/2 = 7.5). Rewrite the ranked data.

	Canada	U.S.	Sweden	U.K.
Infant mortality	3	7	2	4.5
Mortality	2	5	7.5	7.5

	France	Japan	China	Spain
Infant mortality	6	1	8	4.5
Mortality	6	1	3	4

Step 2   Rearranging the data in a column, calculate the Spearman rank correlation coefficient.

	Infant Mortality x	Mortality y	d $(x - y)$	d^2
Canada	3	2	1.0	1.00
U.S.	7	5	2.0	4.00
Sweden	2	7.5	−5.5	30.25
U.K.	4.5	7.5	−3.0	9.00
France	6	6	0.0	0.00
Japan	1	1	0.0	0.00
China	8	3	5.0	25.00
Spain	4.5	4	0.5	0.25
				69.50

$$r_s = 1 - \frac{6\Sigma\, d^2}{n(n^2 - 1)} = 1 - \frac{6(69.5)}{8(8^2 - 1)} =$$

$$1 - \frac{417}{8(63)} = 1 - \frac{417}{504} = 1 - .827 = .173$$

Step 3   Interpret the results. A correlation of .173 suggests there is little correlation between the rankings of these nations' infant mortality rates and general mortality rates. The small correlation that does exist is positive, which does suggest that as a nation's infant mortality ranking increases, so does its general mortality rate ranking.

Interval and ratio variables are the highest levels of variables. Both determine the difference or distance between the values of the variable. For example, there is a measurable difference between 1 in. and 2 in. It is the same measurable difference as between 3 in. and 4 in. Ratio-level variables have all the characteristics of interval-level variables, along with a zero starting point. An interval level variable may contain a zero, but the zero does not imply an absolute absence of the variable. Temperature is an interval variable, but 0° does not imply the absence of temperature. However, age is a ratio variable, because 0 y is the absence of age.

The relationships of interval and ratio variables can be diagrammed and calculated. A diagram known as a scatter diagram, scatterplot, or scattergram allows a visual analysis of the relationship of the variables. The scatter diagram plots the values of x and y as a pair of coordinates on coordinate axes. Each ordered pair is

SECTION 3

Two Ratio or Interval Variables: Linear Correlation

represented on the diagram. The values of the variable X are plotted along the horizontal axis, and the values of the variable Y are plotted along the vertical axis. The intervals plotted for the values should be consistent for each value. That is, if x is 0, 10, and 20, do not plot 40, 50, and 60 without an interval for 30. Do not interrupt the intervals unless there will be no distortion to the visual meaning of the diagram. Values on the axes do not necessarily correspond to the reported values. If the reported value of x is 39, the value on the axis may be 40.

   To plot a point, trace *up* from the X axis at the corresponding X value and *across* from the Y axis at the corresponding Y value. Place a dot at the intersection. Continue this process for each ordered pair.

EXAMPLE 4.5

Experiment   Draw a scatterplot for the following ordered pairs:

$$X: \quad 3 \quad 4 \quad 3 \quad 6 \quad 7 \quad 2 \quad 3 \quad 7 \quad 5 \quad 5 \quad 4 \quad 5$$
$$Y: \quad 4 \quad 4 \quad 5 \quad 7 \quad 8 \quad 4 \quad 3 \quad 7 \quad 6 \quad 5 \quad 5 \quad 7$$

Answer

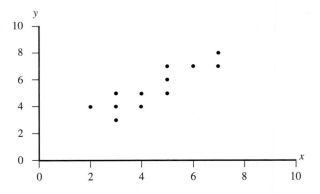

Solution   Draw and label the X and Y axes. Review the values of X and Y to determine the intervals for plotting the values. The variable X ranges from 2 to 7 and the variable Y ranges from 3 to 8. No distortion of the diagram would occur with single-digit intervals from 0 to 10. Begin with the first ordered pair of $x = 3$ and $y = 4$. Trace *up* from the X axis at the value 3 and *across* from the Y axis at the value 4. Place a dot at the intersection of the 3 and 4. For the second ordered pair of $x = 4$ and $y = 4$, trace *up* from the X axis at 4 and *across* from the Y axis at 4. Place a dot at the intersection. Continue this process for the remaining 10 sets of ordered pairs.

   In the scatterplot for Example 4.5, there appears to be a pattern created by the dots. The dots tend to move upward from left to right. As the value of X increases, so, too, does the value of Y. When the plotting of ordered pairs depicts a clear pattern upward, it is referred to as a *positive linear pattern.* If the plotted dots are clustered close together, the pattern depicts a strong positive linear relationship, and if all the dots are exactly in line, the pattern depicts a perfect positive relationship. If the pattern depicts a case where one variable consistently decreases as the other increases, the relationship is referred to as a negative linear pattern. The clustering of a negative pattern also determines if the relationship is strong or perfect. Where no pattern appears, no relationship exists. If a pattern is circular or semicircular, then no linear relationship exists. The most common patterns are shown in Figure 4.1.

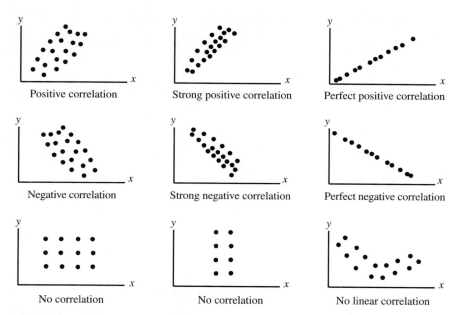

FIGURE 4.1   Most Common Patterns

Scatterplots and scattergrams suggest whether there is a relationship between two variables. But this suggestion is based on a highly subjective, visual inspection of the diagram. A measure of association known as a linear correlation coefficient determines if a relationship exists between two interval or ratio variables.

The most popular technique to describe the relationship of two interval or ratio variables is the Pearson's product moment correlation coefficient, r. As does Spearman's r, Pearson's r measures both the strength and direction of the relationship of two variables. Pearson's r also has values ranging from -1 to 1, as does Spearman's r. A value of -1 represents a perfect negative relationship, whereas a 0 represents no relationship and a $+1$ represents a perfect positive relationship. Any negative r value implies that as the values of one variable increase, the values of the other variable decrease. Any positive *r* value implies that the values of both variables increase or decrease simultaneously. Unlike Spearman's *r*, Pearson's *r* assumes the relationship is linear—that a consistent pattern upward or downward exists. Pearson's *r* should not be applied to nonlinear relationships.

> **Pearson's product moment correlation coefficient** Measures the strength and direction of the relationship between two interval or ratio variables. The notation is *r*.

> **Values of *r***
>
> $$-1 \leq r \leq 1$$

Pearson's *r* represents a sample statistic. The corresponding population parameter is denoted by the Greek letter ρ (pronounced "rhō," like the "ro" in road). Because *r* measures the relationship of ordered pairs from sample data, ρ measures the relationship of all ordered pairs from a population. The calculation of Pearson's *r* is based on the sum of the squares of *x*, *y*, and *xy*. Recall that the sum of the squares is the numerator of the variance formula. The sum of the squares measures the distance of each value from the mean. The distances of the *x* values are measured against the mean of *x*, whereas the *y* values are measured against the mean of *y* and the ordered pairs *xy* are measured against the mean of *xy*. If the distances of the *x* and *y* values are equal to the distances of the ordered pairs, then all values are equal to the means, and a perfect relationship exists.

> **Formula for Calculating Pearson's *r***
>
> $$r = \frac{n\Sigma xy - \Sigma x \Sigma y}{\sqrt{n\Sigma x^2 - (\Sigma x)^2} \ \sqrt{n\Sigma y^2 - (\Sigma y)^2}}$$
>
> where
>
> n is the number of ordered pairs.
> Σxy is each x value multiplied by its y value, summed.
> Σx is the sum of the x values.
> Σy is the sum of the y values.
> Σx^2 is the squares of the x values, summed.
> $(\Sigma x)^2$ is the sum of the x values, squared.
> Σy^2 is the squares of the y values, summed.
> $(\Sigma y)^2$ is the sum of the y values, squared.

To calculate the Pearson's *r*, arrange the data vertically, allowing for the following columns: *x*, *y*, *xy*, x^2, and y^2. Sum and label all columns. Be certain to remember the difference between the various summations, such as Σx^2 and $(\Sigma x)^2$. Σx^2 requires squaring each value of x and then summing the squares. $(\Sigma x)^2$ requires the values of x to be summed and then the summation to be squared.

EXAMPLE 4.6

Experiment   Calculate Pearson's r for the following set of paired data.

$$x:\ \ 3\ \ 4\ \ 3\ \ 6\ \ 7\ \ 2$$
$$y:\ \ 4\ \ 4\ \ 5\ \ 7\ \ 8\ \ 4$$

Answer $r = .922$

Solution   Pearson's r is a measure of association describing the strength and direction of the linear relationship of two interval or ratio variables. Begin by arranging the data with columns representing x, y, xy, x^2, and y^2. Sum and label the columns. Calculate r.

x	y	xy	x^2	y^2
3	4	12	9	16
4	4	16	16	16
3	5	15	9	25
6	7	42	36	49
7	8	56	49	64
2	4	8	4	16
$\Sigma x = 25$	$\Sigma y = 32$	$\Sigma xy = 149$	$\Sigma x^2 = 123$	$\Sigma y^2 = 186$

$$r = \frac{n\Sigma xy - \Sigma x \Sigma y}{\sqrt{n\Sigma x^2 - (\Sigma x)^2}\ \sqrt{n\Sigma y^2 - (\Sigma y)^2}} = \frac{6(149) - (25)(32)}{\sqrt{6(123) - 25^2}\ \sqrt{6(186) - 32^2}}$$

$$= \frac{894 - 800}{\sqrt{738 - 625}\ \sqrt{1116 - 1024}}$$

$$= \frac{94}{\sqrt{113}\ \sqrt{92}}$$

$$= \frac{94}{(10.630)(9.591)}$$

$$= \frac{94}{101.952}$$

$$= .922$$

The interpretation of Pearson's r begins by noting if the relationship is positive or negative as determined by the sign of the calculated value. If the calculated value is negative, then the relationship of the values of the variables is negative. A positive r describes a positive relationship. The strength of the relationship is determined by the size of the value. A value of 1 or -1 implies a perfect relationship. A perfect relationship occurs when all the values of x and y are equal to the mean. A value approaching 1 or -1 implies a strong relationship, whereas a value near 0 implies a very weak relationship and a value of 0 implies no relationship. However, what is considered strong or weak depends on the sample size. As more ordered pairs are sampled, the size of significant r representing a linear relationship decreases. There is an increased risk of committing an error with a small sample versus a large sample. The error in accepting an r of .800 for 5 cases is greater than the error in accepting an r of .800 for 500 cases.

Although the full meaning of statistical significance is described in later chapters, some information about errors should be addressed. In addition to determining the direction and strength, the value of r can be described as statistically significant by comparing the calculated r value with the r values given in Table A1 in Appendix A. The values reported in Table A.1 describe the minimal r values for samples from 4 to 100 and beyond. The r values greater than 100 remain constant. Table A.1 also reports what is called α (alpha). The alpha values reflect the acceptable amount of error. An alpha of .05 suggests that a 5% error is acceptable, whereas an alpha of .01 suggests that a 1% error is acceptable. This means that in 100 occurrences, there is a probability of committing an error either 1 or 5 times. Trace *down* Table A.1 to the sample size n and *across* to the desired alpha. If the calculated value of r is equal to or greater than the table value, then the relationship of the two variables is referred to as statistically significant.

EXAMPLE 4.7

Experiment   Interpret the r value .922 calculated in Example 4.6.

Answer   Strong, positive, and statistically significant relationship

Solution   A .922 r value suggests that the relationship is positive. Since the value is near 1.0, the relationship is very strong. Comparing .922 to the r value for an n of 6 from Table A.1, the relationship is also statistically significant at both the .05 and .01 levels. Move *down* Table A.1 to $n = 6$ and *across* to the r values. The r for $n = 6$ at $\alpha = .05$ is .811 and at $\alpha = .01$, r is .917. The calculated value .922 is greater than both values given in Table A.1.

EXAMPLE 4.8

Experiment   Ten couples are surveyed to determine if there is a relationship between the educational levels of each couple. Given the following data, in years of education, is there a significant relationship?

Couple:	1	2	3	4	5	6	7	8	9	10
Woman's education, x:	12	14	12	13	16	16	18	12	13	14
Man's education, y:	13	16	12	16	17	16	18	17	14	14

Answer $r = .667$; there is a positive, moderately strong relationship between the educational levels of the man and woman in each couple. The relationship is significant at the .05 level.

Solution   Formal education is a ratio-level variable, because there is a measurable difference between 10 years of education and 11 years. Also, 0 years of education means the absence of a formal education. Pearson's r measures the association of ratio-level variables. Pearson's r will describe the direction and strength of the data and whether the relationship is statistically significant. Begin by arranging the data using the columns x, y, xy, x^2, and y^2. Add the column values and label the sums appropriately. Calculate the correlation coefficient. Remember that n is the number of ordered pairs ($n = 10$).

x	y	xy	x^2	y^2
12	13	156	144	169
14	16	224	196	256
12	12	144	144	144
13	16	208	169	256
16	17	272	256	289
16	16	256	256	256
18	18	324	324	324
12	17	204	144	289
13	14	182	169	196
14	14	196	196	196

$\Sigma x = 140$ $\Sigma y = 153$ $\Sigma xy = 2166$ $\Sigma x^2 = 1998$ $\Sigma y^2 = 2375$

$$r = \frac{n\Sigma xy - \Sigma x \Sigma y}{\sqrt{n\Sigma x^2 - (\Sigma x)^2}\ \sqrt{n\Sigma y^2 - (\Sigma y)^2}} = \frac{10(2166) - (140)(153)}{\sqrt{(10(1998) - 140^2}\ \sqrt{10(2375) - 153^2}}$$

$$= \frac{21{,}660 - 21{,}420}{\sqrt{19{,}980 - 19{,}600}\ \sqrt{23{,}750 - 23{,}409}}$$

$$= \frac{240}{\sqrt{380}\ \sqrt{341}}$$

$$= \frac{240}{(19.493)(18.466)}$$

$$= \frac{240}{359.961}$$

$$= .667$$

Interpret the results: An r value of .667 implies that the relationship is positive and moderately strong. A positive relationship suggests that as the woman's educational level increases, the man's increases. Using Table A.1, the calculated r value is significant at the .05 alpha level but not at the .01 level.

A LEARNING AID

Pearson's *r*

Determine if a relationship exists between the age at marriage of a woman and the number of children she bears.

Age at
marriage, *X*: 22 14 18 19 16 26 28 22 23 18 20 21
Number of
children, *Y*:   3 6 5 5 6 3 2 2 4 4 4 4

Step 1 Identify the variables as interval or ratio. Both variables are ratio, because there is measurable distance between age as well as between the number of children.

Step 2 Draw a scatterplot. A scatterplot is one way to determine if a relationship exists between ratio variables. Draw and label the axes. The *X* axis is horizontal and the *Y* axis is vertical. Scan the values of *X* and *Y* to determine the intervals for the diagram. The *X* values range from 14 to 28; therefore, 5-y increments will allow for easy display. The *Y* values range from 3 to 6, so increments of 1 are appropriate. Begin with the first ordered pair, where *x* = 22 and *y* = 3. From the *X* axis, trace up from the value of 22 (which is between the values of 20 and 25) to the *Y* value 3. Place a dot at the point (22, 3). Continue this process for each of the ordered pairs.

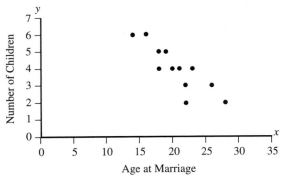

Age at Marriage

The scatterplot displays a negative relationship, where the values of *Y* decrease as the values of *X* increase. If a woman is older when she marries, she tends to have fewer children. The relationship also seems very strong because the dots are clustered close together in a linear pattern.

Step 3 Calculate Pearson's *r*. Pearson's *r* shows the strength and direction of the relationship between two ratio intervals. Begin by arranging the data, using columns *x*, *y*, *xy*, x^2, and y^2. Add the column values and label the sums appropriately. Calculate the correlation coefficient. Remember that *n* is the number of ordered pairs.

x	y	xy	x^2	y^2
22	3	66	484	9
14	6	84	196	36
18	5	90	324	25
19	5	95	361	25
16	6	96	256	36
26	3	78	676	9
28	2	56	784	4
22	2	44	484	4
23	4	92	529	16
18	4	72	324	16
20	4	80	400	16
21	4	84	441	16

$\Sigma x = 247$ $\Sigma y = 48$ $\Sigma xy = 937$ $\Sigma x^2 = 5259$ $\Sigma y^2 = 212$

$$r = \frac{n\Sigma xy - \Sigma x\Sigma y}{\sqrt{n\Sigma x^2 - (\Sigma x)^2}\ \sqrt{n\Sigma y^2 - (\Sigma y)^2}}$$

$$= \frac{12(937) - (247)(48)}{\sqrt{12(5259) - 247^2}\ \sqrt{12(212) - 48^2}}$$

$$= \frac{11{,}244 - 11{,}856}{\sqrt{63{,}108 - 61{,}009}\ \sqrt{2544 - 2304}}$$

$$= \frac{-612}{\sqrt{2099}\ \sqrt{240}}$$

$$= \frac{-612}{(45.815)(15.492)}$$

$$= \frac{-612}{709.764}$$

$$= -.862$$

Step 4 Interpret the results. An *r* value of −.862 implies that the relationship is negative and strong. A negative relationship suggests that as the woman's age at marriage decreases, the number of children she bears increases. Using Table A.1, the calculated *r* value is significant at the .05 and .01 alpha levels. The calculated value, −.862, is greater than the *r* values given in the table for *n* = 12 (.576 and .708). Therefore, the relationship is negative, strong, and statistically significant.

Two or More Ratio or Interval Variables: Linear Regression

Correlation analysis measures the relationship between two variables by describing how the variables vary together. The relationship between X and Y is the same as it is for Y and X. Correlation analysis describes the direction and strength of the relationship, but it does not predict the effects of one variable on another.

The relationship between two or more variables is determined by a regression analysis. Regression analysis predicts or projects the effect of one variable on another. Regression analysis focuses on the linear relationship and is used to predict the effect of the movement of one variable on another variable.

The variable that is to be predicted is known as the *dependent variable, Y*. The dependent variable is the output variable—that is, the one that is affected by the other variable or variables. The variable that is used to predict movement in the dependent variable Y is known as the *independent variable, X*. The case in which one independent variable X predicts Y, is known as a *bivariate regression analysis*. The case in which two or more independent variables predict Y is known as a *multivariate regression analysis*.

The identification of the independent and dependent variable is important. The dependent variable is the variable to be predicted. The independent variable predicts movement in the dependent variable. The independent variables are the inputs, and the dependent variable is the result.

Independent variable, X The variable that predicts a change in the dependent variable.

Dependent variable, Y The variable that is predicted or projected by the independent variable or variables.

Regression analysis assumes linearity. In a bivariate regression, a line could be drawn through the middle of the data displayed on a scatterplot. The regression analysis will define the beginning of the line and the slope of the line as it either ascends or descends through the data. The line is referred to as the line of best fit, least-squares line, or regression line. From this line, a prediction for y can be made given any value of x. The predictions are based on a calculation minimizing the error created by predicting y with sample information, also known as observed values. The most common method of predicting y for regression problems is known as the least-squares method.

The regression line is calculated by determining the y-intercept and the slope of the line. The y-intercept is the place where the predicted y value is when x is zero. The slope determines the increase or decrease in y for every unit increase of x. The predicted value of y is denoted by $\hat{y}$ (y-hat); the y-intercept, by b; and the slope, by m.

Regression line or line of best fit A straight line predicting values of y from values of x using the least-squares method.

$$\hat{y} = b + mx$$

where

       $\hat{y}$ is the predicted value of y.
       b is the y-intercept.
       m is the slope of the regression line.
       x is the given value of x.

The y-intercept value, b, and the slope, m, must be calculated before the predicted value, $\hat{y}$, can be determined. The slope should be determined first. The slope describes how the line ascends or descends through the data. It explains the unit increase or decrease in y for every unit increase in x. For example, if y is weight in pounds, x is age in years, and the slope is .5, y increases ½ pound (lb) for every 1-year increase in age.

Formula for Calculating Slope m

$$m = \frac{n(\Sigma xy) - \Sigma x \Sigma y}{n(\Sigma x^2) - (\Sigma x)^2}$$

where

       m is the slope of the regression line.
       n is the number of ordered pairs.
       Σxy is each x value multiplied by its y value, summed.
       Σx is the sum of the x values.
       Σy is the sum of the y values.
       Σx^2 is the squares of the x values, summed.
       $(\Sigma x)^2$ is the sum of the x values, squared.

Notice the slope formula is similar to the correlation formula. The correlation coefficient also included information about the y value in the denominator. Both formulas attempt to minimize the squares of the deviations. Because it minimizes the squares of the deviations, the slope formula is also referred to as the regression coefficient and as the least-squares formula.

The y-intercept, b, is calculated by using one of two formulas. The first formula uses much of the same information as the formula for the slope. The second formula simplifies the calculation but requires determining the mean of the x values and the mean of the y values.

Formula for Calculating the y-Intercept, b

$$b = \frac{(\Sigma y)(\Sigma x^2) - (\Sigma x)(\Sigma xy)}{n(\Sigma x^2) - (\Sigma x)^2} \quad \text{or} \quad b = \bar{y} - m\bar{x}$$

where

Σy is the sum of the y values.

Σx^2 is the squares of the x values, summed.

Σx is the sum of the x values.

Σxy is each x value multiplied by its y value, summed.

$(\Sigma x)^2$ is the sum of the x values, squared.

$\bar{y}$ is the mean of the y values, $\Sigma y/n$.

m is the value of the slope.

$\bar{x}$ is the mean of the x values, $\Sigma x/n$.

To determine the regression line, calculate the slope and the y-intercept. Place the values in the formula for the line of best fit. The regression line is not solved for one value unless a specific value of x is given; that is, the regression line is given as $\hat{y} = b + mx$, with values inserted for b and m but not for $\hat{y}$ and x. When a value is given for x, the predicted value y is determined. The values b and m can be used to draw the regression line on a scatter diagram.

EXAMPLE 4.9

Experiment **Calculate the regression equation for explaining the cost of passenger airline travel based on the travel distance. (Both values are given in hundreds; that is, \$100 = 1, 100 mi = 1.)**

Travel costs:	2.0	3.5	4.2	2.2	3.1	8.9	6.5	5.9	3.0	2.8
Distance:	2.5	7.0	8.0	2.3	6.0	10.0	8.3	7.3	5.0	4.5

Answer $\hat{y} = -.485 + .771x$

Solution **Begin by noting the dependent variable and independent variable. The dependent variable, y, the variable being explained, is the cost of passenger airline travel. Distance predicts the costs, and therefore distance is the independent variable, x. Arrange the data vertically using the following columns: x, y, xy, and x^2. Sum each column and label the sum.**

x	y	xy	x^2
2.5	2.0	5.00	6.25
7.0	3.5	24.50	49.00
8.0	4.2	33.60	64.00
2.3	2.2	5.06	5.29
6.0	3.1	18.60	36.00
10.0	8.9	89.00	100.00
8.3	6.5	53.95	68.89
7.3	5.9	43.07	53.29
5.0	3.0	15.00	25.00
4.5	2.8	12.60	20.25
$\Sigma x = 60.90$	$\Sigma y = 42.10$	$\Sigma xy = 300.38$	$\Sigma x^2 = 427.97$

$$\text{Slope } m = \frac{n(\Sigma xy) - \Sigma x \Sigma y}{n(\Sigma x^2) - (\Sigma x)^2} = \frac{10(300.38) - (60.90)(42.10)}{10(427.97) - 60.90^2}$$

$$= \frac{3003.80 - 2563.89}{4279.70 - 3708.81}$$

$$= \frac{439.91}{570.89}$$

$$= .771$$

The slope implies that for every unit increase in x, there is a .771-unit increase in y. This means that for every 100-mi increase in distance, there is an increased cost of $77.10 (distance and costs are in hundreds).

$$\text{Intercept: } b = \bar{y} - m\bar{x} = \frac{42.10}{10} - .771 \left(\frac{60.90}{10} \right)$$

$$= 4.21 - .771(6.09)$$

$$= 4.21 - 4.695$$

$$= -.485$$

The intercept is −.485. This means that y is −.485 when x is 0. State the equation with the slope and the intercept:

$$\hat{y} = -.485 + .771x$$

Draw the regression line on the scatterplot. The y-intercept is at −.485. For every increase of 1 in x, there is a .771 increase in y.

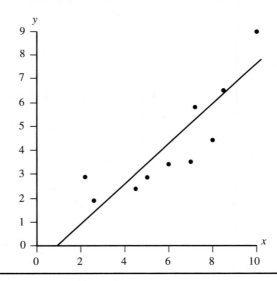

The regression equation not only allows for the identification of the line of best fit for the data displayed in a scatter diagram, it also predicts values of ŷ given values of x. When a value of x is known, an expected value of ŷ can be determined. The expected value is predicted as the average value of y for the specific x value. Place the stated value of x in the regression equation and solve for ŷ. Give the predicted $\hat{y}$ value as the average value expected to occur for the x value. The equation can be solved for any number of x values.

EXAMPLE 4.10

Experiment   Given the regression equation $\hat{y} = -.485 + .771x$, calculate the predicted cost of airline travel based on the travel distance of 200 mi. (Remember that the data are in hundreds, so 200 mi $= 2.0$.)

Answer $105.70

Solution   The predicted value of y is determined by placing the x value in the equation. Calculate $\hat{y}$ and multiply the $\hat{y}$ value by 100 to yield dollars.

$$\hat{y} = -.485 + .771x = -4.85 + .771(2) = -4.85 + 1.542 = 1.057$$

$$1.057(100) = \$105.70$$

EXAMPLE 4.11

Experiment   Predict $\hat{y}$ with the equation $\hat{y} = 2 + 4x$.

a. $x = 3$ b. $x = 10$ c. $x = 5$ d. $x = 20$

Answer

a. $\hat{y} = 14$ b. $\hat{y} = 42$ c. $\hat{y} = 22$ d. $\hat{y} = 82$

Solution   Place each value of x in the regression equation.

a. $\hat{y} = 2 + 4(3) = 2 + 12 = 14$
b. $\hat{y} = 2 + 4(10) = 2 + 40 = 42$
c. $\hat{y} = 2 + 4(5) = 2 + 20 = 22$
d. $\hat{y} = 2 + 4(20) = 2 + 80 = 82$

The basic rules for calculating the line of best fit that predicts one variable from another variable can be extended to allow the predictions to be derived from two or more variables. Predictions based on one variable are known as bivariate linear regressions. Predictions based on two or more variables are known as multivariate, or multiple, linear regressions.

The multiple regression requires a least-squares slope equation for each of the independent variables. If the bivariate equation for one independent variable is $\hat{y} = b + mx$, the multivariate equation for two independent variables is $\hat{y} = b + m_1x_1 + m_2x_2$, and the equation for three independent variables is $\hat{y} = b + m_1x_1 + m_2x_2 + m_3x_3$. Since the calculations for multiple regressions are very complex and time consuming, they are usually performed with a computer software program such as SPSS, SAS, or Minitab.

One independent variable:	$\hat{y} = b + mx$
Two independent variables:	$\hat{y} = b + m_1x_1 + m_2x_2$
Three independent variables:	$\hat{y} = b + m_1x_1 + m_2x_2 + m_3x_3$

Although the calculation of the multiple regression is complex and not detailed in this text, the application of the multiple regression can be addressed. Like the bivariate regression, the predictive power of the multiple regression equation is important.

EXAMPLE 4.12

Experiment   Predict the average number of children born to women who have never lost a child, married at age 35, and are currently 50 y old. Use the following multiple regression equation.

$$\hat{y} = .46 + .42x_1 + (-.292x_2) + .225x_3$$

Number of children — ↑   Child mortality — ↑   ↑ — Age at marriage   ↑ — Current age

Answer $\hat{y} = 1.49$

Solution   A multiple regression equation predicts a dependent variable based on two or more independent variables. The dependent variable is the number of children born to women, which may be partially predicted by the number of deaths of children the women have experienced, the age when they married, and their current age. The equation can be solved by inserting the information from the experiment statement. The value 0 is placed in position x_1 as the number of children's deaths the women have experienced. The value 35 is the second independent variable, the age at which they married. The value of the third independent variable, current age, is 50. Solve the equation.

$$\hat{y} = .46 + .42(0) + -.292(35) + .225(50)$$
$$= .46 + 0 + (-10.22) + 11.25$$
$$= 1.49$$

The equation suggests that, on average, a woman experiencing no death of a child, married at age 35, and currently 50 y old will have 1.49 children.

EXAMPLE 4.13

Experiment   Explain the meaning of each of the terms in the following equation, where y is a job performance rating, x_1 is the number of years of employee experience, x_2 is the number of years of education for the employee, and x_3 is employee's age.

$$\hat{y} = -1.8 + 2.10x_1 + 2.98x_2 + .35x_3$$

Answer   Job performance is predicted by 3 independent variables. The regression line begins at a job rating of -1.8. Job rating increases by 2.10 units for every year increase in experience, 2.98 units for every year increase in education, and .35 units for every year increase in age.

Solution   The equation is a multiple regression equation because it is predicting a y variable with three independent variables. The first value is the y-intercept, denoting job rating is -1.8 where x values are 0. A value describing the slope is reported for each independent variable. A slope value describes the amount of change in y for every unit increase in x. Therefore, the notation $2.10x_1$ describes a positive 2.10 increase in job performance for every year increase in employee experience.

A LEARNING AID

Two Ratio/Interval Variables: Linear Regression

A bagel factory owner wants to predict the number of dozens of bagels an employee produces based on the employee's pay (per hour). Calculate the regression line.

Pay:	5.50	4.50	4.25	6.25	5.10	7.90	6.50	8.00
Productivity:	20	18	17	25	21	28	26	30

Step 1   Begin by noting the dependent variable and independent variable. The dependent variable, y, the variable being explained, is productivity. Pay is predicting productivity, and therefore pay is the independent variable, x. Arrange the data vertically using the following columns: x, y, xy, and x^2. Sum each column and add an appropriate label.

x	y	xy	x^2
5.50	20	110.00	30.25
4.50	18	81.00	20.25
4.25	17	72.25	18.06
6.25	25	156.25	39.06
5.10	21	107.10	26.01
7.90	28	221.20	62.41
6.50	26	169.00	42.25
8.00	30	240.00	64.00

$\Sigma x = 48.00$ $\Sigma y = 185$ $\Sigma xy = 1156.80$ $\Sigma x^2 = 302.29$

Step 2   Calculate the slope m.

$$\text{Slope } m = \frac{n(\Sigma xy) - \Sigma x \Sigma y}{n(\Sigma x^2) - (\Sigma x)^2} = \frac{8(1156.80) - (48.00)(185)}{8(302.29) - 48.00^2}$$

$$= \frac{9254.40 - 8880}{2418.32 - 2304}$$

$$= \frac{3744}{114.32}$$

$$= 3.275$$

The slope implies that for every unit increase in x, there is a 3.275-unit increase in y; that is, for every dollar more an employee is paid, the employee produces 3.275 dozen bagels more.

Step 3   Calculate the y-intercept.

$$\text{Intercept } b = \bar{y} - m\bar{x} = \frac{185}{8} - 3.275\left(\frac{48.00}{8}\right)$$

$$= 23.125 - 3.275(6)$$

$$= 23.125 - 19.65$$

$$= 3.475$$

The intercept is 3.475. This means that y is 3.475 when x is zero.

Step 4   State the equation with the slope and the intercept.

$$\hat{y} = 3.475 + 3.275x$$

Draw the regression line on the scatterplot. The y intercept is at x at 3.475. For every increase of 1 in x, there is a 3.275-unit increase in y. The line should go through the middle of the data.

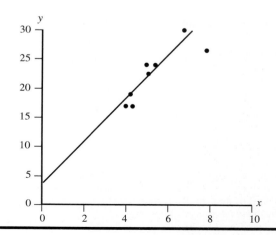

CHAPTER 4 IN REVIEW

4.1   To determine if the amount of money contributed by a city employee affected the number of extra vacation days received, six city employees were surveyed. The results are as follows:

Name	Contribution	Vacation Days
Ms. Ostrom	50	6
Mrs. Demas	0	0
Mr. Kuklinski	25	3
Mr. Kontos	100	12
Mr. Krehbiel	250	30
Mrs. Pantos	125	15

  a. Plot a scatter diagram of the data, and label the axes.
  b. Calculate r.
  c. Is there a linear relationship? Is it significant?
  d. Find the line of best fit.
  e. How many vacation days would we expect for someone contributing $200?

4.2   Indicate whether each of the following variables is measured at the nominal, ordinal, interval, or ratio level:
  a. Religion
  b. Place of birth
  c. High, medium, or low social status
  d. Income
  e. Temperature

4.3   A researcher collects the following data on education and earnings:

Education in years (x):   12   8   10   14   16
Earnings in thousands (y):   25   26   20   25   30

  a. Plot the data on the coordinate axes, and label the axes.
  b. Calculate the correlation coefficient.
  c. Find the linear equation to predict education on earnings.
  d. What income would we expect if a person had only an elementary (6-y) education?

4.4   Note whether the following are nominal, ordinal, interval, or ratio.
  a. Employee production on an assembly line
  b. Political party affiliation
  c. Weight loss after jogging 3 mi
  d. Major in college
  e. Grading scale in school (A, B, C, D, E)
  f. Amount of rainfall
  g. Number of suicides in 1991

4.5   A researcher wants to determine if birth order affects one's likelihood of success in school. The following data are collected, noting birth order as firstborn, second born, third born, and so on. The number of years in higher education is given in the education column.

Student	Birth Order	Education
1	4	2.5
2	3	1.0
3	5	2.0
4	2	1.0
5	3	2.0
6	5	2.5
7	2	0
8	5	3.0
9	2	1.5
10	1	0.5

  a. Plot the data on a scatterplot.
  b. Calculate r.
  c. Interpret r.
  d. Calculate the line of best fit.
  e. If a student is the seventh born, how many years in higher education can be expected?
  f. Repeat part e for the fifth born.

4.6   A survey was taken to determine if the height of an 18-mo-old baby is related to the height at 8 y old. The heights of 10 children are given at 18 mo and 8 y old.

Child	18 mo	8 y
1	36	51
2	39	52
3	30	53
4	23	45
5	28	55
6	41	52
7	29	42
8	27	48
9	28	40
10	28	53

  a. Calculate the Pearson's correlation coefficient.
  b. Interpret the coefficient.
  c. Calculate the line of best fit.
  d. If a child is 21 in. at 18 mo, what height is expected at 8 y old?
  e. If a child is 35 in. at 18 mo, what height is expected at 8 y old?

4.7   Rank the data from Problem 4.6 and calculate the relationship between the ranked data using Spearman's r.

4.8   If $x = 5$, solve for $\hat{y} = -1.96 + .986x$.

4.9   If $x_1 = 3$, $x_2 = 20$, and $x_3 = 60$, solve for $\hat{y} = 1.2 + .823x_1 + (-.248x_2) + .326x_3$.

4.10   A researcher collects the following data to determine if there is a relationship between the lengths of sentences given to convicted criminals (for the same crime) and the ages of the criminals.

Years Sentenced	Age
20	25
25	22
15	47
10	51
21	28
10	60
22	23
25	25
18	45
12	55

a. Plot the data on a scatterplot.

b. Calculate Pearson's r.

c. Calculate the line of best fit.

d. If a criminal is 30 y old, what sentence is expected?

e. If a criminal is 40 y old, what sentence is expected?

4.11 Explain $m = 30$, where x is the production of 1 automobile and y is pay in dollars.

4.12 Explain $m = -2.5$, where x is temperature and y is a heating bill in dollars.

4.13 True or false?

a. The dependent variable predicts the independent variable.

b. The line of best fit is also known as a correlation.

c. If the regression slope is calculated as 1.5, there is a 1.5-unit decrease in y for every unit increase in x.

d. Regression analysis concerning three or more variables is known as bivariate regression analysis.

4.14 True or false?

a. A diagram known as a scatterplot displays the relationship between two ratio- or interval-level variables.

b. The range of values for the calculated r values is 0 to 1.

c. Pearson's r describes the strength and direction of two ratio- or interval-level variables.

d. A negative r implies that the two variables decrease together.

4.15 Determine if there is a correlation between the percentage of births to unmarried women for selected countries between the years 1960 and 1990.

	1960	1990
U.S.	5.2	27.1
Canada	4.4	23.0
France	6.2	28.2
Japan	1.1	1.0
Sweden	11.4	51.9
U.K.	5.1	26.7

4.16 Calculate the Spearman's correlation coefficient for the rankings of the following regions for oil consumption and reserves. Interpret the results.

North America	7	3
Eastern Europe	6	4
Western Europe	5	2
Asia	4	1
Latin America	3	5
Middle East	2	7
Africa	1	6

4.17 Explain the movement of two variables when a correlation coefficient is -1.0.

4.18 Explain the meaning of the following regression equation, where y is child mortality, x_1 is age of a woman, x_2 is the woman's age at marriage, and x_3 the number of years of education for the husband.

$$\hat{y} = .159 + 2.79x_1 - .154x_2 - .103x_3$$

4.19 Calculate the expected age at marriage for a woman whose current age, x_1, is 50, whose education, x_2, is 10 years, and whose husband's education, x_3, is 12 years. Use the following regression equation.

$$\hat{y} = .982 + .210x_1 + .217x_2 + .376x_3$$

4.20 Calculate the expected age at marriage for Problem 4.19 for a woman whose current age is 40, whose education is 16 years, and whose husband's education is 18 years.

5

Probability: Sample Spaces

Students of statistics seem to have unnecessary trouble understanding elaborate and sometimes complicated definitions. Definitions of probabilities top the list on the frustration index. Although the definitions cannot be dispensed with, it is hoped that some of the confusion can. Remember: Probabilities are simply educated guesses. They are the best guesses about what might happen. The person determining the probability usually has some information, background, or experience with what has happened in the past. Guesses are not made blindly.

Because it is the nature of statistics to present variations of themes and formulas, it is always important to keep in perspective the fact that the principles are the same. In other words, as the nature of the data differs, so too will the formulas, but the principles of probability will remain the same: Probabilities are still educated guesses. It is now time to plunge into the definitions of probabilities and their formulas. Do not be led astray about their purpose in making an educated guess.

Most textbooks treat *sample space* and *probability* questions as one and the same. At the other extreme, some textbooks treat them as two separate and distinct concepts. They are neither the same nor totally distinct. The sample space must be known before probabilities can be calculated. This chapter outlines a variety of methods for describing sample space.

SECTION 1

List Method

When confronted with a situation in which a person is trying to predict an outcome of an event, one of the first questions the person might ask is, What can happen? This question usually means, What are all the possible outcomes? It is then followed by the probability part of the question: What is the chance that . . . will happen?

This latter part involves the probability, and it cannot usually be answered without the answer from the first question: What can happen?

Label the first part of the question as the *sample space*. When citing all the outcomes, the *sample space* is defined. A student in class may ask, Will the instructor show up today? The student must ask, What are the possible outcomes? There are only two possible outcomes: The instructor will show up or the instructor will not show up. The student would have to know these two possibilities before asking a second question: What is the chance the instructor will not show up? This is now a probability question that will be answered based on information about past behavior, weather, or any other pertinent information. Calculating the probability is discussed in Chapter 6. This section focuses only on the *sample space*.

> **Sample space** The set of all possible outcomes of an experiment. The sample space is symbolized by: *S*.
>
> Format: $S = \{(\ ), (\ ), (\ ), \ldots\}$
>
> where ( ) represents each outcome. All pairs or combinations form the sample space and are enclosed in braces.

A sample space can be represented by a variety of techniques. This section focuses on the listing method illustrated in the definition. Tree diagrams and Venn diagrams are discussed later.

EXAMPLE 5.1

Experiment   Observe the sex of the next baby born at General Hospital. List the sample space.

Answer $S = \{(M), (F)\}$

Solution   The sex of the baby has two possible outcomes, male or female. There are no other possible combinations.

If there are two parts to an experiment, then the sample space represents all the possible combinations of outcomes. Each combination must be ordered in the same way each time they are listed. These ordered combinations are called *ordered pairs*. The listing format of the sample space given in the definition illustrates the use of ordered pairs: $S = \{(\ ), (\ ), (\ ), \ldots\}$. Each pair of parentheses includes an ordered pair. The sample space is the set of ordered pairs representing all possible combinations.

EXAMPLE 5.2

Experiment   Observe the sex of the next two babies born at General Hospital. List the sample space.

Answer $S = \{(M, M), (M, F), (F, M), (F, F)\}$.

Solution The first baby may be a boy and the second baby may also be a boy. Thus, the first possible outcome can be noted as (M, M). If the first baby is a boy and the second is a girl, a second combination is possible (M, F). However, the reverse is also possible. The first baby may be a girl and the second a boy, giving a third possible combination (F, M). Finally, the first and the second babies may both be girls. This final combination is (F, F). There are no other possible combinations; therefore the set of combinations is enclosed in brackets.

Remember, in this example it is not important where one starts or which combination of the pairs is written first. It is important that the ordering within the pairs remains the same. The first baby's sex is always the first letter and the second baby's sex is always the second letter within each pair of parentheses.

EXAMPLE 5.3

Experiment In a random sample of voters, list the possible outcomes for party identification (Democrat, Independent, and Republican) and gender.

Answer $S = \{$(Democrat, Male), (Democrat, Female), (Independent, Male), (Independent, Female), (Republican, Male), (Republican, Female)$\}$.

Solution The sample space lists each possible combination of outcomes. There are two variables, party identification and gender. List each of the possible answers for party identification with each of the possible answers on gender. There are a total of six combinations.

Event An event is any set of outcomes in a sample space. Each outcome is known as an element of the event. An event is usually a subset of the sample space.

An event is a specified combination of elements that form a subset of the sample space. The event is usually the narrative, such as "two baby boys are born." The elements are the ordered pairs of the sample space that fulfill the criteria of the event, such as (M, M).

EXAMPLE 5.4

Experiment In Example 5.2 the experiment was to observe the sex of the next two babies born at General Hospital. List some of the possible events and elements in those events.

Answer

Event (The Narrative)	Set of Elements in Each Event (The Ordered Pairs)
1. Two boys are born.	{(M, M)}
2. Only one boy is born.	{(M, F), (F, M)}
3. Only one girl is born.	{(M, F), (F, M)}
4. Two girls are born.	{(F, F)}
5. Both babies are the same sex.	{(M, M), (F, F)}
6. The two babies are of opposite sex.	{(M, F), (F, M)}

Solution   The list contains only some of the events that can be identified. Begin by identifying various sets of outcomes known as events: Two boys are born, two girls are born, etc. The second step is to list the elements that make up each event.

A LEARNING AID

Sample Space

You are driving your car and you approach an intersection with a traffic signal. An event is about to occur with the changing of the traffic signal. Put this event into the perspective of what you have learned about sample spaces. List the sample space.

Step 1   Ask yourself, "What can happen?" This question asks, What are all the possible outcomes?

Step 2   Ask yourself, "What are the possible outcomes?" Assuming that the traffic signal is functioning properly, the signal could be red, green, or yellow.

Step 3   List the sample space: The possible outcomes define the sample space. The listing method can be used: $S = \{(R), (Y), (G)\}$

Step 4   Ask yourself, "What is the chance the light will be green? You now have a probability question.

Note: Sample space and probabilities are not the same, but they are not totally separate. The sample space must be known before a probability can be calculated.

SECTION 2

Tree Diagrams

A *tree diagram* is another method of illustrating a sample space. It can be used to represent the same sample space as the listing method. Although sometimes cumbersome to draw, a tree diagram can often provide a clearer picture of sample space. A tree diagram begins with the trunk. The trunk branches to the possible outcomes for the first phase of an experiment. The tree diagram then branches out for the outcomes of the second phase, the third phase, and so forth. Drawing tree diagrams can be helpful when calculating probabilities.

Tree diagram   Another way of illustrating sample space, in which a branch represents each possible outcome or ordered pair.

EXAMPLE 5.5

Experiment   Observe the sex of the next baby born at General Hospital. Illustrate the sample space using a tree diagram.

Answer

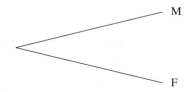

Solution   The diagram illustrates the two branches, which depict two possible outcomes.

EXAMPLE 5.6

Experiment   Observe the sex of the next two babies born at General Hospital. Illustrate the sample space using a tree diagram.

Answer

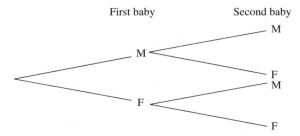

Solution   The trunk of the tree branches are the possible outcomes for the sex of the first baby. From each of these outcomes, extend the branches to show the possible outcomes of the second event. It might look as if there are four possibilities for the second baby; this is not the case. The branches for the second baby represent the combinations based on the sex of the first baby. Looking back at Example 5.2, the listed sample space had four possible outcomes: $S = \{(M, M), (M, F), (F, M), (F, F)\}$. The tree diagram illustrates the same four combinations. The diagram is interpreted as follows: The first baby could be a boy or a girl; if the first baby is a boy then the second baby could be another boy or it could be a girl. If the first baby is a girl (the lower half of the diagram), then the second baby could be a boy or another girl.

Branch   Each ordered pair of a sample space illustrated in a tree diagram. Each branch can be numbered.

To assist in the discussion of a tree diagram, branches are often numbered. Then outcomes that qualify for an event can easily be identified.

EXAMPLE 5.7

Experiment   Observe the sex of the next three babies born at General Hospital. Illustrate the sample space with a tree diagram. Label each branch.

Answer

Answer	First baby	Second baby	Third baby	Branch	Outcome
			M	1	(M, M,M)
		M	F	2	(M,M,F)
	M		M	3	(M,F,M)
		F	F	4	(M,F,F)
			M	5	(F,M,M)
		M	F	6	(F,M,F)
	F		M	7	(F,F,M)
		F	F	8	(F,F,F)

Solution   When reading the solution, a finger may be used to follow along the branches. Branch 1, (M, M, M), is the event that all three babies born at General Hospital are boys. Branch 2, (M, M, F), shows that the first baby is a boy, the second is a boy, and the third is a girl. Branch 3, (M, F, M), shows that the first baby is a boy, the second is a girl, and the third is a boy. Branch 4, (M, F, F) shows the first baby is a boy, the second is a girl, and the third is a girl. Branch 5, (F, M, M) shows the first baby is a girl, the second is a boy, and the third is a boy. Branch 6, (F, M, F) shows the first baby is a girl, the second is a boy, and the third is a girl. Branch 7, (F, F, M) shows the first baby is a girl, the second is a girl, and the third is a boy. Branch 8, (F, F, F), shows that all three babies are girls.

In Example 5.7 a wide range of events occur; they are identified in the following table. The events are further described by the branches and elements.

	Event (The Narrative)	Branch (Number)	Elements (Specific Ordered Pairs)
(a)	No boys	8	{(F, F, F)}
(b)	No girls	1	{(M, M, M)}
(c)	Only one boy	4, 6, 7	{(M, F, F), (F, M, F), (F, F, M)}

A LEARNING AID

Tree Diagrams

You are driving to a friend's house. Along the way, you must proceed through two intersections. Both intersections have traffic signals. Using what you have learned about tree diagrams, illustrate the events of the changing traffic signals of both intersections.

Step 1 First, draw a tree diagram illustrating the sample space for the color changes of the traffic signal at the first intersection.

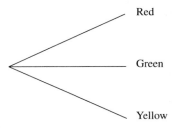

The sample space is written $S = \{(R), (G), (Y)\}$, which contains all the possible outcomes; Red, Green, and Yellow.

Step 2 Extend the tree diagram to include the sample space for all the possible outcomes of the traf-

fic signal changes of both intersections. Number the branches.

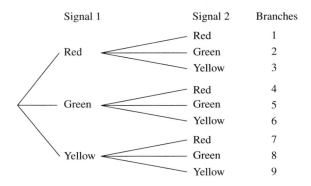

Step 3 Describe the tree. The sample space is written $S = \{(R, R), (R, G), (R, Y), (G, R), (G, G), (G, Y), (Y, R), (Y, G), (Y, Y)\}$. The elements are all the ordered pairs in the sample space. There are nine branches of the tree diagram, each illustrating an ordered pair of the experiment.

	Event (The Narrative)	Branch (Number)	Elements (Specific Ordered Pairs)
(d)	Only two boys	2, 3, 5	{(M, M, F), (M, F, M), (F, M, M)}
(e)	Only one girl	2, 3, 5	{(M, M, F), (M, F, M), (F, M, M)}
(f)	Only two girls	4, 6, 7	{(M, F, F), (F, M, F), (F, F, M)}
(g)	Two or more girls	4, 6, 7, 8	{(M, F, F), (F, M, F), (F, F, M), (F, F, F)}
(h)	Two or more boys	1, 2, 3, 5	{(M, M, M), (M, M, F), (M, F, M), (F, M, M)}
(i)	Exactly 3 girls	8	{(F, F, F)}
(j)	Exactly 3 boys	1	{(M, M, M)}

SECTION 3

Venn Diagrams

Venn diagrams offer a third way of illustrating a sample space (in addition to the listing method and tree diagrams).

> **Venn diagram** A pictorial illustration of subsets of a sample space. A rectangle usually represents the sample space. Subsets are also known as events and are usually represented by capital letters.

The *universal set* is depicted in a Venn diagram as a large rectangle. All other sets are depicted as circles within the rectangle. The universal set is represented by the symbol S (sample space). A *subset* (event) is a set of elements occurring within a universal set. It is depicted in a Venn diagram as a circle. The relationships of the subsets are illustrated by the relationships of the circles.

Universal set   The set of all elements that occur in an overall frame of reference. All other sets occurring within its boundaries are subsets of the universal set.

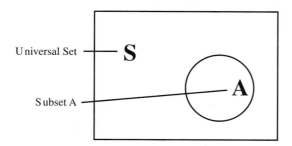

The following definitions illustrate various relationships of subsets in the sample space. The symbols presented (such as ∪, ∩, or ⊆) are used frequently in calculating probabilities. The manner in which the circles in a Venn diagram are presented in regard to the other circles is also important. The circles will be a guide to later calculations.

Union of sets *A* or *B*   The set of all elements in *A or B*, which also includes those in both sets. The union of *A* or *B* is denoted by

$$A \cup B$$

The key word in the definition of union is the word *or.* An element in a *union* of two sets must be in one set *or* the other *or* both. Set union is represented by the shaded areas in the Venn diagram of Figure 5.1.

Venn Diagram

A ∪ B

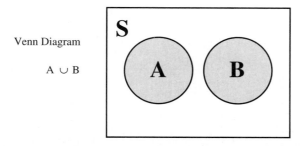

FIGURE 5.1   Venn Diagram: $A \cup B$

Intersection of sets A and B The set of elements in both A and B. It is the area where the two sets overlap. The intersection of A and B is denoted by

$$A \cap B$$

The key word in this definition is the word *and.* An element in an intersection must occur in both A and B; that is, it occurs in set A and it occurs in set B. Thus, it occurs twice; on a Venn diagram, it is in the area where the two sets overlap. It is the shaded area of the Venn diagram in Figure 5.2.

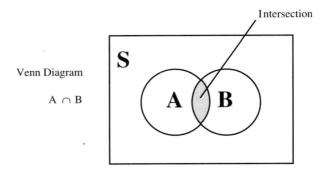

FIGURE 5.2   Venn Diagram: $A \cap B$

Subset When every element of one set is also an element of a second set. "A is a subset of B" is denoted by

$$A \subseteq B$$

Figure 5.3 shows $A \subseteq B$. It is read, "A is a subset of B." Notice that all the elements in A are in B, but not all the elements in B are in A.

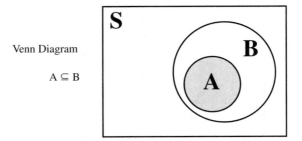

FIGURE 5.3   Venn Diagram: $A \subseteq B$

If all elements of A are in B and every element of B is in A then $A = B$. See Figure 5.4.

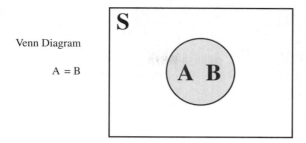

FIGURE 5.4   Venn Diagram: $A = B$

Complement The set of all elements in the universal set that are not in a given set. The complement of set A is denoted by A'.

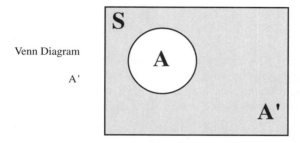

FIGURE 5.5   Venn Diagram: A'

Be careful when defining complementary sets. If there are two subsets in a universal set, then the complement of one set does not necessarily equal the other set. The complement of A is all elements that are not in A. See Figure 5.5. It follows that the union of a set and its complementary set is the universal set. Therefore, $A \cup A' = S$. This relationship is represented by the shaded area in the Venn diagram in Figure 5.6.

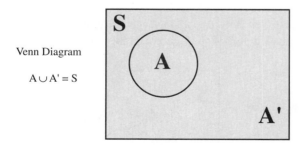

FIGURE 5.6   Venn Diagram: $A \cup A' = S$

Empty set A set with no elements. The empty set is represented by the symbol ϕ.

Mutually exclusive sets When two events cannot happen together.

  If two sets are mutually exclusive, then their intersection is the empty set (there is no overlap of the two events). No element of set A can be an element of set B. Therefore, we can say that $A \cap B = \phi$. *Mutually exclusive* sets A and B are shown in Figure 5.7.

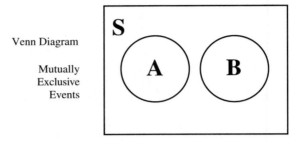

Venn Diagram

Mutually
Exclusive
Events

FIGURE 5.7   Venn Diagram: Mutually Exclusive Events

  Final note: There may be many subsets in a universal set. The rules of unions and intersections hold for more than two sets. For example, $A \cup B \cup C$ is defined as those elements that are in A or B or C. $A \cup B \cup C$ is illustrated for mutually exclusive events by the shaded areas of Figure 5.8.

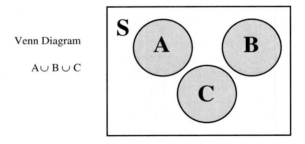

Venn Diagram

$A \cup B \cup C$

FIGURE 5.8   Venn Diagram: $A \cup B \cup C$

  The intersection of $A \cup B \cup C$ for events that are not mutually exclusive is illustrated in the shaded area of the Venn diagram of Figure 5.9.

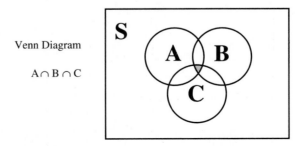

Venn Diagram

$A \cap B \cap C$

FIGURE 5.9   Venn Diagram: $A \cap B \cap C$

EXAMPLE 5.8

Experiment   Let S be the students in class. Let A be the female students and let B be the students who are seniors. Define the following sets, describe them, and illustrate each with a Venn diagram.

   a. $A \cup B'$ **b.** $A \cup B$ **c.** $A \cap B$ **d.** B'

Answer

   a. $A \cup B'$ is the union of A and the complement of B. Therefore, $A \cup B'$ is the set of all female students that are not seniors.

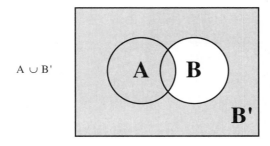

   b. $A \cup B$ is the union of A and B. It is the set of all female students and all seniors. In other words, it comprises all female students and all male seniors.

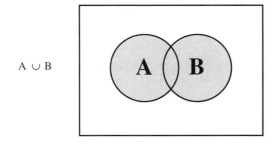

   c. $A \cap B$ is the intersection of A and B. It is the set of female students who are also seniors. It is the area where the two sets overlap.

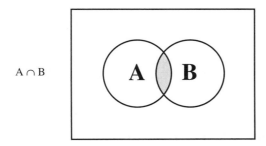

d. *B′* is the complement set of *B*, or all elements that are not in *B*. That is, *B′* is the set of all students that are not seniors.

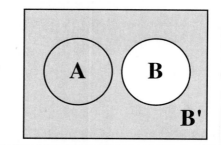

A LEARNING AID

Venn Diagrams

The following Venn diagram illustrates three subsets within the universal set. The regions of subsets *A*, *B*, and *C* are numbered. Describe the following regions using (a) symbols, and (b) words.

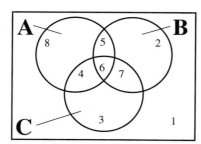

Venn Diagram

Step 1   Describe region 8 of subset *A*.

a. $A \cap B' \cap C'$

b. *A* intersects with *B* prime and intersects with *C* prime (or the complements of sets *B* and *C*).

Step 2   Describe region 7 of subset *B*.

a. $A' \cap B \cap C$

b. *B* intersects with subset *C* and the subset *C* intersects with subset *B* and the complement of subset *A*.

Step 3   Describe region 5 of subset *A*.

a. $A \cap B \cap C'$

b. *A* and *B* intersect with each other and the complement of subset *C*.

CHAPTER 5 IN REVIEW

5.1   A die that has six sides is rolled. Each side has a number, 1 to 6. List the sample space.

5.2   A box contains three marbles. One marble is red, one is black, and one is yellow. One marble is drawn at random. List the sample space.

5.3   A coin is flipped once. The coin may land on heads or tails. List the sample space.

5.4   A young woman has been informed by her doctor that she is expecting triplets. List the sample space with regard to sex.

5.5   A young woman has been informed by her doctor that she

is expecting identical triplets. List the sample space with regard to sex.

5.6   A tack is dropped on a desk top. The tack may land on its top or its side. List the sample space.

5.7   A young man gets into his car with the intent of starting the car. List the sample space.

5.8   If a traffic signal at an intersection is caution, or yellow, list the sample space for the changing color of the traffic signal.

5.9   Three marbles are placed in a box. One is black, one is green, and one is yellow. One marble is drawn at random and then replaced. A second marble is drawn at random and then replaced.

   a. Draw a tree diagram illustrating the exercise.
   b. Describe any four events and their elements.
   c. List the sample space.

5.10 See Exercise 5.9. Repeat the exercise, but this time do not replace the marbles drawn.

   a. Draw a tree diagram illustrating the exercise.
   b. Describe the elements and events.
   c. List the sample space.

5.11 True or false: The complement of set *A* is the set of all elements in the universal set not in *A*. The complement of *A* is denoted by *A'*.

5.12 Define and describe the shaded area of each Venn diagram:

a.

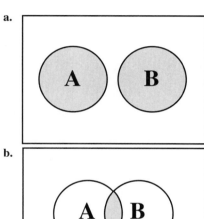

b.

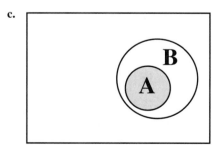

c.

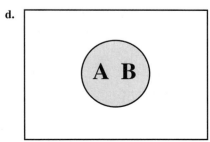

d.

e.

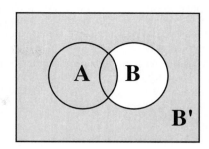

5.13 True or false:

   a. Nonmutually exclusive

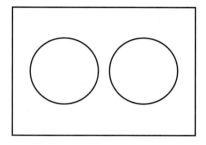

   b. Mutually exclusive

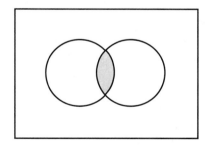

   c. Nonmutually exclusive

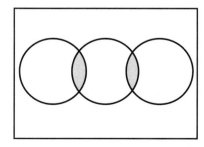

5.14 A box contains three marbles. One marble is red, one is black, and one is yellow. One marble is drawn from the box. Are the events red, black, and green mutually exclusive?

5.15 Three marbles are placed in a box. One is black, one is green, and one is yellow in color. One marble is drawn at random and then replaced. A second marble is drawn at random and then replaced. Does the sample space change?

5.16 Three marbles are placed in a box. One is black, one is green, and one is yellow in color. One marble is drawn at random and not replaced. A second marble is then drawn at random. Does the sample space change?

5.17 What does the rectangle in a Venn diagram represent?

5.18 If the Raiders beat the Lions, the Raiders will then play the Bears, but if they lose to the Lions, they will play the Cardinals. Draw a tree representing the sample space.

5.19 True or false: If two events are mutually exclusive, they share an intersection.

5.20 Draw a tree diagram representing the following sample space: $S = \{(A, A, A), (A, A, B), (A, B, A), (A, B, B), (B, A, A), (B, A, B), (B, B, A), (B, B, B)\}$.

Calculating Probabilities

6

In Chapter 5, sample space is shown to be a means of answering the question What can happen? And understanding sample space is necessary for calculating probabilities. Calculating probabilities gives an answer to the question What is the chance that . . . might happen or has happened?

Probabilities are educated guesses about what might happen or what has happened based on information that we have obtained or observed. It is our best guess about what can happen based on what has happened in the past or what should theoretically happen. For example, suppose a basketball player steps up to the free-throw line. We say he shoots 70% from the line. This means that, on the average, he makes the shot 7 out of 10 times. What is the probability he will make the next shot? The best guess is that he has a 70% chance, since that is what he has been doing in the past. A chance of 70% is a probability of .70.

Probability The relative frequency with which an event can be expected to occur. It is calculated as

$$P(A) = \frac{n(A)}{n(S)}$$

where

P stands for probability.

$n(A)$ stands for the number of outcomes in event A.

$n(S)$ is the total outcomes in the sample space.

The following symbols are used frequently:

P	the probability of
$P(A)$	the probability of event A
$n(A)$	the number of outcomes in event A
$n(S)$	the number of outcomes in the sample space
$<$	less than
$>$	greater than
$\leq$	less than or equal to
$\geq$	greater than or equal to
$\neq$	not equal to
$\cup$	the union of two or more events
$\cap$	the intersection of two or more events

Probability Theory

Probability theory is divided into three different types: experimental, theoretical, and subjective. All probabilities are calculated using the same formula. There are two important properties associated with probabilities. *Property 1* states that probabilities are values greater than or equal to 0 and less than or equal to 1. In other words, a probability is always between 0 and 1, inclusive, where 0 represents no chance of occurrence and 1 represents a certain occurrence. A probability of 0.5 represents a 50–50 chance that something will occur.

Property 1: $0 \leq P(A) \leq 1$

Property 2 states that the sum of the probabilities of all outcomes of the sample space S must equal 1.0. Thus, all outcomes must be known. Each probability must fulfill property 1. The sum of all probabilities must be 1.0.

Property 2: $P(S) = 1$; the sum of the probabilities of all outcomes is 1.

Experimental probabilities Also known as empirical, or observational, probabilities. The observed proportion of times an event occurs in a series of similar experiments. Experimental probability is denoted by P'.

Experimental probabilities are determined by *empirical observation;* that is, an experiment is observed and each outcome is recorded. Then the probability is determined from these observations. For example, suppose a basketball player shoots a ball 5 times. Each shot is observed, whether or not the shot she makes is recorded. Suppose she makes 3 of 5 shots. The probability of her making a shot is then $P(A) = n(A)/n(S)$, or $\frac{3}{5} = .6$. If one were to guess whether she would make her next shot, the best guess would be that she has a 60% chance (or a probability of .6) of making the next shot. The probability of .6 is the best educated guess based on what is known or has been observed from her past record.

EXAMPLE 6.1

Experiment   A basketball player for the Detroit Pistons has made 354 of the 796 field goal attempts up to this point in the season. What is the probability that he will make his next attempt?

Answer $P'(A) = .445$; a 44.5% chance

Solution   The player has a .445 chance of scoring on his next field goal attempt. This probability may change after additional observations. When performing calculations, show all steps.

$$P'(A) = \frac{n(A)}{n(S)}$$

$$= \frac{354}{796}$$

$$= .445$$

Theoretical probabilities   Probabilities in cases where all outcomes are equally likely to occur. Theoretical probability is denoted by P.

Theoretical probabilities differ from *observational probabilities*. With theoretical probability, all possible outcomes must be equally likely. An observed probability contradicting a theoretical probability does not necessarily mean that the theoretical probability is wrong. Consider a typical example. Assuming that a coin is symmetric and its weight is equally distributed, if tossed, there is an equal chance that it will land heads up or tails up. Therefore, since there are only two possible outcomes, following the rules of probability, each event (a head or a tail) has a probability of ½, or .5, or a 50% chance. The theoretical probability of either event is .5. Consider again the examples of babies being born at General Hospital. Assume that there is an equal chance that the next baby born is a boy or girl. What is the probability that it is a boy? Since there are only two possibilities, both with an equal chance of occurring, probability is .5 that the baby will be a boy. What is the chance that, of the next two babies born, both are boys? Look at the sample space, or tree diagram, shown in Figure 6.1. There are four possible outcomes. One is the event

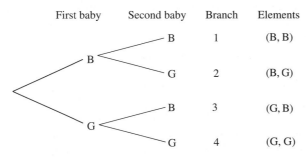

FIGURE 6.1

two boys (see the shaded elements on the tree diagram). Therefore, the probability of two boys equals ¼ (1 outcome of interest divided by the total of 4 possible outcomes). Probabilities are generally not left as fractions: ¼ gives a probability of .25.

EXAMPLE 6.2

Experiment   What is the probability that, of the next two babies born at General Hospital, at least one is a boy?

Answer P(at least one boy) = .75

Solution   Of the four total outcomes, three make up the event. The sample space for all the outcomes is S = {(B, B), (B, G), (G, B), (G, G)}. The first three outcomes each have at least one boy (note that (B, B) also fulfills the event, even though it involves two boys). The probability is found by dividing the 3 outcomes that make up the event by the total number of outcomes, which is equal to 4; 3 divided by 4 equals the probability, .75. When performing calculations, show all steps.

$$P(A) = \frac{n(A)}{n(S)}$$

$$= \frac{3}{4}$$

$$= .75$$

EXAMPLE 6.3

Experiment   In tossing a coin 10 times, what is the probability that on the first toss it will be heads? The second toss? The third toss?

Answer P(heads) = .5 for the first, .5 for the second, and .5 for the third

Solution   Use the formula P(heads) = n(heads)/n(total tosses); the first toss has two possible outcomes and the head is one of the two; therefore, P(heads) = ½, or .5. For the second toss, there is still only 1 chance from 2 possible outcomes; therefore, P(heads) = ½, or .5. The third toss is again the same: P (heads) = ½, or .5. Theoretically, the probability that the result will be heads on any given toss will remain .5. When performing calculations, show all steps.

$$P(A) = \frac{n(A)}{n(S)}$$

$$= \frac{1}{2}$$

$$= .5$$

Observational probabilities do not always match theoretical probabilities. As the number of observations increase, the observational probability will approach the theoretical probability. If a coin is tossed continuously, eventually it will be observed that there are 50% heads and 50% tails. The empirical probability for any one toss will stabilize at about .5 for each subsequent toss. Thus, the observational probability will be approximately the same as the theoretical probability, both at or near .5. This is explained by the *law of large numbers*.

> **Law of large numbers** As the number of times an experiment is done increases, the observed probability will approach the theoretical probability.

If the experiment of tossing a coin 10 times and observing the number of heads is repeated, it will eventually reach a point where the cumulative observational probability of heads will stabilize around the theoretical probability of 0.5. Although it may continue to vary slightly, the variation will continue to decrease as the experiment is repeated.

Although theoretically different, the law of large numbers is analogous to a more familiar idea that may help in understanding the concept. If one wants to find the average age of students in a school, start by asking one student. Is one student's age going to be very representative of the average age of all the students in the school? Probably not. How about asking two students? Three? Four? As more and more students are asked, the average age observed will get closer to the actual average age. Thus, the law of large numbers is similar to the sampling discussed earlier. The larger the number of observations, the closer one gets to the true probability.

A LEARNING AID

Probability Theory

You live in a township that is about to hold an election for the township supervisor. June Smyth is the candidate running on the Republican ticket. Of the registered voters in your township eligible to vote in this election, 80% are Republicans. These same voters have, in the past, voted Republican in the U.S. presidential and congressional races as well as state elections. Based on this information alone, what is the probability that June Smyth will be elected as your next township supervisor?

Step 1 What is a probability?

A probability is an educated guess about what can happen or what is expected to happen based on information that you have obtained or experienced.

Step 2 Is the case presented an experimental, theoretical, or subjective probability?

At this point, it is a subjective probability, because your decision is based on personal judgment about the given information. However, it borders on the experimental by using as the foundation for per-

sonal conclusion a statistic verifiable by past performance, from which you are deriving judgment.

Step 3 What is the probability that June Smyth will win the election?

June Smyth has an 80% chance of winning the election, or a probability of .8 of being elected.

Step 4 Is the probability of .8 a legitimate guess?

Yes; .8 is a legitimate guess. A probability is always between 0 and 1, where 0 represents no chance of an occurrence and 1 represents a certain occurrence.

Step 5 Go one step further. What is the maximum collective vote June Smyth could get? The answer to this question is 100%, which is a probability of 1.0 of being elected. In Property 2 of probability theory, the sum of the probabilities of all outcomes of an event must equal 1. For example, if she has a probability of 0.8 of being elected, the probability she will not be elected is 0.2; $0.2 + 0.8 = 1.0$.

Subjective probabilities Educated guesses based on personal judgment.

Subjective probabilities are educated guesses based on personal judgment. They are neither observed nor theoretical. Subjective probabilities depend on correctly assessing a situation. Weather forecasting is a good example. A weather forecaster predicts what the temperature may be. He or she usually predicts the chance of rain or snow. A forecaster uses personal judgment in assessing weather patterns, radar, barometers, and other equipment. The meteorologist can then make an educated guess when stating, "There is a 30% chance of rain today."

Probability of the Union of Two Events

The union of sets A and B was previously defined as the set of all elements that are in A or in B, which includes those elements in both. The union is represented by $A \cup B$. To find the probability of the union of two sets, add the probability of event A to the probability of event B. If there are elements that are in both A and B, then the probability of the elements in both sets must be subtracted so they are counted only once. To make the calculations easier, first count each set fully, find how many elements have been counted twice, and then subtract the probability of the double-counted elements. This process is known as the *Addition Theorem for Two Events*. The key to remembering that unions involve the *addition theory* is the word *or*.

Addition Theorem for Two Events

$$P(A \cup B) = P(A) + P(B) - P(A \cap B)$$

where

P stands for probability.

A stands for event A.

$\cup$ stands for union.

B stands for event B.

$\cap$ stands for intersection.

EXAMPLE 6.4

Experiment   What is the probability that, on a single roll of a die, the outcome will be either 4 or an even number?

Answer $P(A \cup B) = .5$

Solution   This is a union because it asks for *either* one of two events *or* the other. These events are not mutually exclusive, because in this experiment 4 falls into both events. The following Venn diagram illustrates this situation:

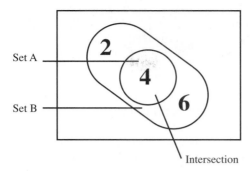

The Venn diagram shows the two sets overlap. Set A, {4}, is completely encased in set B, {2, 4, 6}. Although the answer may be visually obvious, the formula must still be followed. In later experiments the answer will not be so obvious. The probability is calculated using the addition theorem for two events: $P(A \cup B) = P(A) + P(B) - P(A \cap B)$.

Before calculating, recall that $P(A)$ is the probability that the roll of the die is a 4. $P(B)$ is the probability that the roll of the die is an even number. $P(A)$, $P(B)$, and $P(A \cap B)$ are calculated using the formula $P(A) = n(A)/n(S)$ $= \frac{1}{6}$; $P(B) = \frac{3}{6}$; $P(A \cap B) = \frac{1}{6}$, because 4 is in both sets. When performing calculations, show all steps.

$$P(A \cup B) = P(A) + P(B) - P(A \cap B)$$

$$P(4 \text{ or even}) = P(4) + P(\text{even}) - P(4 \text{ and even})$$

$$= \frac{1}{6} + \frac{3}{6} - \frac{1}{6}$$

$$= \frac{3}{6} = \frac{1}{2}$$

$$= .5$$

The addition formula holds true for any pair of events. But in special cases, the formula can be simplified. When sets or events are mutually exclusive, the addition theorem can be shortened as follows: $P(A \cup B) = P(A) + P(B)$. When events are mutually exclusive, they cannot happen together. This means that no elements are found in both sets; therefore, since the intersection is empty, the probability is zero.

Special addition rule Probability of the union of two mutually exclusive events.

$$P(A \cup B) = P(A) + P(B)$$

where

P stands for probability.

A stands for event A.

B stands for event B.

$\cup$ stands for union.

EXAMPLE 6.5

Experiment   What is the probability that on a single roll of a die the outcome will be a 3 or a 4?

Answer $P(A \cup B) = .333$

Solution   This is a union question; the key word is *or*. It asks for the probability of a 3 or a 4. The events are mutually exclusive, because on a single roll you can get a 3 or a 4, but you cannot get them at the same time. Because they are mutually exclusive, use the special addition rule: $P(A \cup B) = P(A) + P(B)$. Before calculating, identify the events. Assign $P(A)$ the probability of rolling a 3. Assign $P(B)$ the probability of rolling a 4. $P(A)$ and $P(B)$ are calculated by the original formula for calculating a probability: $P(A) = n(A)/n(S)$. There is one event in six possible outcomes that is a 3: $P(A) = \frac{1}{6}$. $P(B)$ is found the same way; There is only one way to get a 4 from six possible outcomes, $P(B) = \frac{1}{6}$. The two probabilities are then added together. When performing calculations, show all steps.

$$P(A \cup B) = P(A) + P(B)$$
$$P(3 \cup 4) = P(3) + P(4)$$
$$= \frac{1}{6} + \frac{1}{6}$$
$$= \frac{2}{6} = \frac{1}{3}$$
$$= .333$$

Note: If you are not sure which addition rule to use, remember that the original formula is always correct. Notice what happens if you used the original formula:

$$P(A \cup B) = P(A) + P(B) - P(A \cap B)$$
$$= \frac{1}{6} + \frac{1}{6} - 0$$
$$= \frac{2}{6} = \frac{1}{3}$$
$$= .333$$

Contingency Tables and Unions

Contingency probability table   A table representing probabilities of two variables and their events. The outcomes of a variable are overlapped with the outcomes of another variable. The intersections are referred to as cells.

A *contingency probability table* is another way of representing probabilities of two events. They are a convenient way to determine simple probabilities, unions, and intersections. In most computerized statistical programs, contingency tables are known as *crosstabulations*, or crosstabs. The outcomes of a variable are overlapped with the outcomes of another variable. For example, 100 people were asked their party identification and if they were registered to vote. Table 6.1 is a contingency table that shows these results.

TABLE 6.1   Contingency Table for Party Identification and Voter Registration

		Party Identification			
		Rep.	**Ind.**	**Dem.**	**Totals**
Reg.	Yes	22	28	26	76
	No	2	16	6	24
	Totals	24	44	32	100

Table 6.1 can be turned into a contingency probability table by taking the number in each cell and dividing it by the total. See Table 6.2.

TABLE 6.2   Contingency Probability Table for Party Identification and Voter Registration

		Party Identification			
		Rep.	**Ind.**	**Dem.**	**Totals**
Reg.	Yes	$22/100 = .22$	$28/100 = .28$	$26/100 = .26$	$76/100 = .76$
	No	$2/100 = .02$	$16/100 = .16$	$6/100 = .06$	$24/100 = .24$
	Total	$24/100 = .24$	$44/100 = .44$	$32/100 = .32$	$100/100 = 1.00$

Remember that the numbers on the outside of the contingency probability table are the marginal values, or totals, for the respective events. To obtain the marginal probabilities, the marginal totals are divided by the total number of cases. When the marginal probabilities are added together, they must equal 1.0 (Property 2). The numbers inside the cells show the probabilities for the intersections of two events. For example, the upper left cell represents the intersection of Republicans and people registered to vote. Because there are 22 such people, the probability for the inter-section is $22/100 = .22$. Each cell probability must be between 0 and 1, inclusive. Because the probabilities are so easily obtained, the trick in using such a table is to understand what probability is wanted.

EXAMPLE 6.6

Experiment   Use Table 6.1:

  a. What is the probability that a person is registered to vote?
  b. What is the probability that a person is a Republican?
  c. What is the probability that a person is a Democrat?
  d. What is the probability that a person is a Democrat or a Republican?

e. What is the probability that a person is not registered to vote?

f. What is the probability that a person is a registered voter or a Republican?

g. What is the probability that a person is not a registered voter or a Republican?

Answer

a. P(Reg.) = .76

b. P(Rep.) = .24

c. P(Dem.) = .32

d. P(Dem. $\cup$ Rep.) = .56

e. P(Not Reg.) = .24

f. P(Reg. $\cup$ Rep.) = .78

g. P(Not Reg. $\cup$ Rep.) = .46

Solution

a. This is not a union, because the probability of only one event is desired. The probability of one event is calculated by dividing the number of elements in (A) by the number in the sample space: $P(A) = n(A)/n(S)$. Of the people surveyed, 76 reported they were registered. The probability that a person is registered to vote is 76 divided by the total in the sample space, 100.

$$P(A) = \frac{n(A)}{n(S)}$$

$$P(\text{reg. to vote}) = \frac{n(\text{reg.})}{n(\text{sample space})}$$

$$= \frac{76}{100}$$

$$= .76$$

b. This is not a union, because, as in part a, only one event occurs. It is calculated as in a. Of the 100 people surveyed, 24 reported they were Republican. The probability that a person is Republican is 24 divided by the total in the sample space.

$$P(A) = \frac{n(A)}{n(S)}$$

$$P(\text{Rep.}) = \frac{n(\text{Rep.})}{n(\text{sample space})}$$

$$= \frac{24}{100}$$

$$= .24$$

c. This is not a union, because, as in parts a and b, only one event is involved. The probability is calculated as before. Of the 100 people surveyed, 32 said they were Democrats. The probability that a person is a Democrat is 32 divided by the total in the sample space.

$$P(A) = \frac{n(A)}{n(S)}$$

$$P(\text{Dem.}) = \frac{n(\text{Dem.})}{n(\text{sample space})}$$

$$= \frac{32}{100}$$

$$= .32$$

d. The probability of two events makes this a union. Notice the key word, *or*. The probability of the union of two events is the addition of the probabilities of the events minus the probability of those events that occur in both: $P(A \cup B) = P(A) + P(B) - P(A \cap B)$.

The probability that a person is a Democrat is $P(\text{Democrat}) = n(\text{Democrat})/n(\text{sample space}) = 32/100 = .32$. The probability that a person is a Republican is $P(\text{Republican}) = n(\text{Republican})/n(\text{sample space}) = 24/100 = .24$. There are no people who are both Democrats and Republicans, so the probability of their intersection is 0.

$$P(A \cup B) = P(A) + P(B) - P(A \cap B)$$

$$P(\text{Dem. or Rep.}) = P(\text{Dem.}) + P(\text{Rep.}) - P(\text{both Dem. and Rep.})$$

$$= .32 + .24 - 0$$

$$= .56$$

Notice the events are mutually exclusive. Mutually exclusive events share no elements. A person cannot be a Democrat and a Republican. The union of mutually exclusive events can be calculated with the special addition theorem:

$$P(A \cup B) = P(A) + P(B)$$

$$P(\text{Dem. or Rep.}) = P(\text{Dem.}) + P(\text{Rep.})$$

$$= .32 + .24$$

$$= .56$$

e. As in parts a, b, and c, only one event is desired, so this is not a union. Of the 100 people surveyed 24 reported they were not registered to vote. The probability that a person is not registered to vote is calculated by dividing 24 by the total in the sample space, 100.

$$P(A) = \frac{n(A)}{n(S)}$$

$$P(\text{not reg. to vote}) = \frac{N(\text{not reg. to vote})}{N(\text{sample space})}$$

$$= \frac{24}{100}$$

$$= .24$$

f. The probability of two events is required, so this involves a union. The events are not mutually exclusive, because there are elements in both events. It is similar to part d. But, in this case there are elements common to both events. The probability of the union of two events is the addition of the probabilities of the events minus that of any overlap that occurs: $P(A \cup B) = P(A) + P(B) - P(A \cap B)$.

The probability that a person is registered to vote is P(registered voter) = n(registered voter)/n(sample space) = 76/100 = .76. The probability that a person is a Republican is P(Republican) = n(Republican)/n(sample space) = 24/100 = .24. The overlap occurs because 22 of the 100 people surveyed are registered to vote and are Republicans: 22/100 = .22. When performing the calculation, show all steps.

$$P(A \cup B) = P(A) + P(B) - P(A \cap B)$$

$$P(\text{reg. voter or Rep.}) = P(\text{reg. voter}) + P(\text{Rep.}) - P(\text{reg. voter and Rep.})$$

$$= .76 + .24 - .22$$

$$= .78$$

A LEARNING AID

Contingency Table

A survey was taken in a state representative district in 1990. The district was predominantly Republican and was an area of high socioeconomic status. The purpose of the survey was to determine party identification and position of the voters within this given district on the death penalty for murder. The following contingency table shows the results of this survey.

Death Penalty for Murder

		Yes	Sometimes	No	Total
	Rep.	59	14	10	83
Party I.D.	Ind.	28	4	10	42
	Dem.	8	5	5	18
	Total	95	23	25	143

Step 1   What is a Contingency Table?

A contingency table is a way of representing probabilities of two variables and their events. The cumulative reported survey data are sorted into cells, making it easier to see and calculate simple probabilities, unions, and intersections.

Step 2   What is a simple probability and how do we calculate it?

A simple probability is a number based on data gathered on a single event, which is calculated as $P(A) = n(A)/n(S)$. For example, what is the probability that a respondent to this survey was an independent?

P(Independent) equals n(Independents) divided by n(survey respondents), or the number in the sample space. Calculated, this equals 42 reported respondents divided by 143 surveyed, which gives a probability of .29.

Step 3   What is the probability of the union of two events?

The probability of the union of two events is the probability that event A *or* event B will occur. For example, to find the probability that a survey respondent is a Democrat or a proponent of the death penalty, first use the formula for calculating a simple probability. Determine the probability of event A and then of event B. Then decide if the events are mutually exclusive or if there is an intersection. These events do have elements in common, so they do intersect. Use the addition theorem to calculate this conditional probability: $P(A \cup B) = P(A) + P(B) - P(A \cap B) = P$(Democrat or proponent of death penalty) = P(Democrat) + P(proponent) − P(Democrat and proponent) = 18/143 + 95/143 − 8/143 = .13 + .66 − .06 = .73.

g. As in part f, this is a union of two events that overlap. The events are not mutually exclusive, because there are some people who are not registered to vote and are Republican. Use the formula to calculate the probability of the union of two events, $P(A \cup B) = P(A) + P(B) - P(A \cap B)$.

The probability that a person is not registered to vote is P(not registered to vote) = n(not registered to vote)/n(sample space) = 24/100 = .24. The probability that a person is a Republican is P(Republican) = n(Republican)/n(sample space) = 24/100 = .24. However, 2 of the 100 surveyed report they are Republican and not registered to vote: P(Republican and not registered) = 2/100 = .02. When performing calculations, remember to show all steps.

$$P(A \cup B) = P(A) + P(B) - P(A \cap B)$$

$$P(\text{not reg. or Rep.}) = P(\text{not reg.}) + P(\text{Rep.}) - P(\text{not reg. and Rep.})$$

$$= .24 + .24 - .02$$

$$= .46$$

Conditional Probabilities

The study of *conditional probabilities* begins the transition into the intersection of two events. A conditional probability answers the question, If a given event is already known to have happened, what is the probability that another event will happen at the same time? For example, if identical twins are born and the first baby is a girl, what is the probability that the second baby will be a girl? Because they are identical and one is a girl, the second baby must also be a girl. The probability of the second baby being a girl is 1.0.

Key words in conditional probabilities are *if, since, given, of those, knowing,* and *assuming.* Any question where the probability of the second event is dependent on the conditions of the first event involves a conditional probability.

> **Conditional probability** Where event A has already occurred, the probability that event B will also occur. Conditional probability is denoted by $P(B|A)$:
>
> $$P(B|A) = \frac{P(A \cap B)}{P(A)}$$

In the formula, the probability of the intersection of the events is divided by the probability of event A. The events can be interchanged so the condition is placed on event B. Thus, $P(A|B) = P(A \cap B)/P(B)$. The probability of the event known to have happened is always the denominator. The formula is easily remembered by thinking of the conditional bar as a division or fraction sign; whatever is to the right of it is the event whose probability is in the denominator.

Remember, if events are mutually exclusive, there is no intersection. If there is no intersection, the events cannot occur at the same time. Since they cannot occur at the same time, there cannot be a conditional probability.

EXAMPLE 6.7

Experiment   If $P(A) = .6$, $P(B) = .4$, and $P(A \cap B) = .325$, what is $P(A|B)$?

Answer $P(A|B) = .8125$

Solution   This is a conditional probability because the question asks for a conditional probability (represented by the upright bar). $P(A|B)$ can be read as, "Given that B has occurred, what is the probability that A will occur?" The events A and B are not mutually exclusive, because they intersect with a probability of .325. The conditional probability is determined by dividing the probabilty of the intersection of A and B by the probability of event B: .325/.4 = .8125.

$$P(A|B) = \frac{P(A \cap B)}{P(B)}$$

$$= \frac{.325}{.4}$$

$$= .8125$$

EXAMPLE 6.8

Experiment   If $P(A) = .6$, $P(B) = .4$, and $P(A \cap B) = .325$, what is $P(B|A)$?

Answer $P(B|A) = .542$

Solution   This is a conditional probability, because the question asks for $P(B|A)$. The events are not mutually exclusive, because they intersect. The probability is determined by dividing the probability of the intersection of A and B by the probability of event B: .325/.6 = .542. Notice that the denominator in this problem is $P(A)$, the probability of the event to the right of the conditional bar.

$$P(B|A) = \frac{P(A \cap B)}{P(A)}$$

$$= \frac{.325}{.6}$$

$$= .542$$

Conditional probabilities are easy to calculate using a contingency table. Recall intersections are shown in the cells, where two events overlap. The totals on the outside represent totals for each event. Table 6.3 is a contingency probability table. Note that probabilities, not totals, are given in a contingency probability table.

Conditional probabilities are determined by finding the appropriate cell representing an intersection and dividing by the probability of the event that is already known to have occurred. For example, if it is known that a person is a Democrat, the probability that the person is registered is .26/.32 (the circled values in the table), or .8125. The probability of the intersection of the two events is .26, as shown in the cell where Democrats overlap with all those registered. Since it is known that the person is a Democrat, the probability of the intersection (.26) must be divided

TABLE 6.3   Contingency Probability Table for Party Identification and Voter Registration

		Party Identification			
		Rep.	**Ind.**	**Dem.**	**Total**
Reg.	Yes	$^{22}/_{100} = .22$	$^{28}/_{100} = .28$	$^{26}/_{100} = $ (.26)	$^{76}/_{100} = .76$
	No	$^{2}/_{100} = .02$	$^{16}/_{100} = .16$	$^{6}/_{100} = .06$	$^{24}/_{100} = .24$
	Total	$^{24}/_{100} = .24$	$^{44}/_{100} = .44$	$^{32}/_{100} = $ (.32)	$^{100}/_{100} = 1.00$

by the probability of being a Democrat (.32). Notice that the probability of a Democrat becomes the sample space.

EXAMPLE 6.9

Experiment   Given a person is not registered, what is the probability that the person is an Independent? Use Table 6.3.

Answer $P(\text{Ind.}|\text{not registered}) = .667$

Solution   This is a conditional probability, because information is given that a person is not registered, thus limiting the sample space to only nonregistered people. The events are not mutually exclusive, because there are people who are not registered and who are Independents. When performing calculations, show all steps.

$$P(A|B) = \frac{P(A \cap B)}{P(B)}$$

$$P(\text{Ind.}|\text{not reg.}) = \frac{P(\text{Ind.} \cap \text{not reg.})}{P(\text{not reg.})}$$

$$= \frac{.16}{.24}$$

$$= .667$$

EXAMPLE 6.10

Experiment   Of those registered to vote, what is the probability of a Republican? Use Table 6.3.

Answer $P(\text{Rep.}|\text{reg.}) = .289$

Solution   This is a conditional probability, because a person must first register before being considered a Republican. The sample space is limited to only registered people. The events are not mutually exclusive, because there are people who are registered and are Republicans. Divide the probability of the intersection of those who are registered and those who are Republicans by the probability of being registered. When performing calculations, show all steps.

$$P(A|B) = \frac{P(A \cap B)}{P(B)}$$

$$P(\text{Rep.}|\text{reg.}) = \frac{P(\text{Rep.} \cap \text{reg.})}{P(\text{reg.})}$$

$$= \frac{.22}{.76}$$

$$= .289$$

A LEARNING AID

Conditional Probabilities

From Section 2, recall that the following survey results were obtained from a survey taken in 1990 in a state representative district. The purpose of the survey was to determine the constituents' party identification and their positions on the death penalty for murder. The contingency table shows the results of the survey.

Death Penalty for Murder

		Yes	Sometimes	No	Total
	Rep.	59	14	10	83
Party I.D.	Ind.	28	4	10	42
	Dem.	8	5	5	18
	Total	95	23	25	143

Step 1 What is conditional probability?

Conditional probability refers to the conditions that exist with the intersection of two events. Examining event A and event B, you can determine the probability of event B occurring if you know that event A has already occurred. If the occurrence of event B is dependent on the condition of event A, then it is a conditional probability question.

Step 2 Can the probability of mutually exclusive events be conditional?

No. Mutually exclusive events have no intersection. If there is no intersection, there is no evaluation of dependence between events. If there is no dependence on occurrence between events (no overlap), then there is no condition on their occurrence.

Step 3 Using the given table, what is the probability that a constituent respondent said yes to the death penalty for murder given the fact the constituent is a Republican?

You know the constituent is a Republican. You want to find out, given this fact, the probability that the constituent also said yes in the survey. The formula for calculating this conditional probability is $P(B|A) = P(A \cap B)/P(A)$.

In calculating the conditional probability with this formula, the denominator will be the probability that a person is Republican, because the probability of the event that is known to have occurred is always the denominator. With this known, the calculation is as follows:

$$P(B|A) = \frac{P(A \cap B)}{P(A)}$$

$$P(\text{yes}|\text{Rep.}) = \frac{P(\text{yes and Rep.})}{P(\text{Rep.})}$$

$$= \frac{59/143}{83/143}$$

$$= \frac{59}{83}$$

$$= .711$$

Note: This answer means that given a constituent is a Republican, in this state representative district, the probability of a constituent also being in favor of the death penalty for murder is .711, which is 71.1%. Had the condition shifted from Republican to registered, the formula would be accommodated by adjusting the denominator to registered voters and proceeding with calculations.

In the last section, the conditional probability formula required the probability of the intersection of the events. There are times, however, that the probability of the intersection is not given. The probability of the intersection can be found from other information. The probability of the intersection of two events is known as the joint probability. Joint probability is the probability that two events happen together. The key word for intersection, *and,* is also the key word for joint probabilities. Other key words are *both, together, simultaneously,* or *at the same time.* Another key to remember is that because an intersection does not exist when events are mutually exclusive, mutually exclusive events have a joint probability of 0.

> **Joint probability**   The probability that two events happen at the same time. The joint probability of A and B is represented by $P(A \cap B)$.

Before calculating joint probabilities, some information must be known about the relationship between the events. It must be determined whether the events are dependent or independent. Events are dependent when the occurrence of one event affects the occurrence of the second. If they are independent, they do not affect each other. For example, if someone goes into a store to buy milk, then the purchase depends on whether he or she has any money. If a woman is in labor delivering her second child, the sex of the baby is not dependent on the sex of her first child (unless they are identical twins). Another way to define the difference is to note that the events are dependent if one event precludes another from happening. One cannot buy milk without money. Buying milk depends on having money.

There is a mathematical test to take the guesswork out of deciding if two events are dependent or independent. It combines the idea of a simple probability and the conditional probability. Recall that a conditional probability involves the probability of an event given that something has already happened. If the something that has happened affects the event for which probability is being calculated, then the events are dependent. Thus, one can compare a probability of an event with its conditional probability given the other event. If the two values are equal, then the condition imposed by the conditional probability did not affect the event and they are independent. If the probabilities are not equal, then the events are dependent.

$$P(A) = P(A|B) \quad \text{or} \quad P(B) = P(B|A) \qquad \text{Independent}$$
$$P(A) \neq P(A|B) \quad \text{or} \quad P(B) \neq P(B|A) \qquad \text{Dependent}$$

It is possible that a particular problem will not provide enough information to prove dependency mathematically. However, the researcher needs to make the decision before calculating the probability of the intersection. Once it is clear whether the events are independent or dependent, the probability of the intersection can be determined.

Before preceding with the actual calculation of the probability of joint events, it is important to summarize the decisions that must be made:

1. Determine if the events are mutually exclusive. If they are not mutually exclusive, go to step 2. If they are, no joint probability can be calculated; the result will be 0.

2. Determine if the events are dependent or independent. If the events are dependent, then use the multiplication theorem for two dependent events. If the events are independent, then use the multiplication theorem for two independent events.

Multiplication Theorem for Two Dependent Events

$$P(A \cap B) = P(A) \cdot P(B|A)$$

The *multiplication theorem for two dependent events* requires the multiplication of the probability of event A by the conditional probability of event B given A. The conditional probability is used because it adjusts for the effect of A on B.

EXAMPLE 6.11

Experiment   Seventy percent of the applicants to a law school are accepted into the program. Of those accepted, 40% complete the program. What is the probability that a randomly selected applicant will be both accepted into the program and complete the program?

Answer $P(A \cap B) = .28$

Solution   This is a joint probability; notice the key words *both* and *and*. It asks to find the overlap (intersection) of applicants accepted and completing the program. The events are not mutually exclusive, because some of the applicants are accepted and complete the program. The events are dependent. An applicant must first be admitted before completing the program. Another clue that they are dependent is that the problem gives the conditional probability by using the words *of those accepted*. Therefore, the multiplication theorem for two dependent events is used. (Note that the $P(B|A)$ is already given in the problem). When performing calculations, show all steps.

$$P(A \cap B) = P(A) \cdot P(B|A)$$

$$P(\text{accepted and complete}) = P(\text{accepted}) \cdot P(\text{complete/accepted})$$

$$= (.7)(.4)$$

$$= .28$$

Multiplication Theorem for Two Independent Events

$$P(A \cap B) = P(A) \cdot P(B)$$

When two events are dependent, the conditional probability adjusts for the effect of the first event on the second. When events are independent, the first event has no effect on the second event. Conditional probability is not used. Recall that the mathematical test for dependency showed that if two events are independent, then the conditional probability equals the probability of the event: $P(B|A) = P(B)$. Because this is the case, when events are independent, the simple probability of the event can be substituted for conditional probability in the original formula for joint events.

EXAMPLE 6.12

Experiment   A graduate research assistant was writing her thesis and wanted to determine the probability that a person in the United States receives some form of entitlement program benefits and lives in a consolidated metropolitan statistical area (CMSA). She found that 40% of the population receive some form of entitlement benefits, and 75% live in a CMSA. What is the probability that a person receives benefits and lives in a CMSA?

Answer $P(A \cap B) = .3$.

Solution   This is a joint probability; notice the key word *and*. The question asks to find the overlap (intersection) of those who received benefits and those living in a CMSA. The events are not mutually exclusive, because some people in the United States receive entitlement benefits and live in a CMSA. The events are independent; being an entitlement beneficiary does not affect whether a person lives in a CMSA. Independence can also be determined by comparing the mathematical probabilities of (A) and $(A|B)$:

$$P(A) = P(\text{benefits}) \qquad P(A|B) = P(\text{benefits}|\text{CMSA})$$

$$P(A) = \frac{40}{100} \qquad P(A|B) = \frac{P(\text{benefits and CMSA})}{P(\text{CMSA})}$$

$$P(A) = .4 \qquad P(A|B) = \frac{.4(.75)}{.75}$$

$$P(A|B) = .4$$

Because the events are independent, the multiplication rule for two independent events is used.

$$P(A \cap B) = P(A) \cdot P(B)$$

$$P(\text{benefits and CMSA}) = P(\text{benefits}) \cdot P(\text{CMSA})$$

$$= 40/100 \cdot 75/100$$

$$= (.4) \cdot (.75)$$

$$= .3$$

Note: If it is difficult to determine if the events are independent or dependent and the mathematical test is not applicable, the multiplication rule for two dependent events can always be used. When in doubt, treat the events as dependent.

A LEARNING AID

Joint Probabilities

Using the same contingency table that was used for the Learning Aids in Sections 2 and 3, look at the differences between conditional probabilities and joint probabilities.

Death Penalty for Murder

		Yes	Sometimes	No	Total
	Rep.	59	14	10	83
Party I.D.	Ind.	28	4	10	42
	Dem.	8	5	5	18
	Total	95	23	25	143

Step 1 What is the difference between conditional probability and joint probability?

A conditional probability is the probability that, given the occurrence of event A, event B will occur. The probability of the intersection is known. This is not the case with joint probability. The probability of the intersection is not known. To calculate joint probability is to calculate the probability that two events happen together, or simultaneously.

Step 2 How does the calculation differ for conditional probability and joint probability?

In Section 3, you learned to calculate conditional probability with the formula $P(B|A) = P(A \cap B)/P(A)$. This formula is used because event A is known and you want to find the probability of event B. You also learned that you could shift the condition from event A to event B and proceed with calculation. However, to calculate joint probability you must first test for independence or dependence. Based on these findings, you calculate using either the multiplication theorem for two dependent events, $P(A \cap B) = P(A) \cdot P(B|A)$, or the multiplication theorem for two independent events, $P(A \cap B) = P(A) \cdot P(B)$.

Step 3 What is the joint probability that a constituent will be both a Republican and be a proponent of the death penalty for murder?

This question asks, What is $P(R \cap Y)$? To calculate this joint probability, follow these steps:

a. Are the events dependent or independent?
They are dependent. If it is not obvious, a mathematical test of dependency/independency should be applied:

$$P(A|B) = P(A) \qquad \text{if independent}$$
$$P(A|B) \neq P(A) \qquad \text{if dependent}$$
$$P(A|B) = P(Y|R) \qquad P(A) = P(Y)$$
$$P(A|B) = \frac{59}{83} \qquad P(A) = \frac{95}{143}$$
$$P(A|B) = .711 \qquad P(A) = .664$$

Because .711 does not equal .664, the events are dependent.

b. Use the multiplication theorem for two dependent events.

$$P(A \cap B) = P(A) \cdot P(B|A)$$
$$P(\text{Rep. and yes}) = P(\text{Rep.}) \cdot P(\text{yes}|\text{Rep.})$$
$$= P(\text{Rep.}) \cdot \left[\frac{P(\text{Rep and yes})}{P(\text{Rep})} \right]$$
$$= 83/143 \cdot \frac{59/143}{83/143}$$
$$= .58 \cdot \left(\frac{.413}{.58} \right)$$
$$= .58 \cdot .711$$
$$= .413$$

Joint and Conditional Probabilities Using Tree Diagrams

Joint and conditional probabilities are easily calculated using tree diagrams. Each branch of the tree diagram shows where two events occur simultaneously. The ease of calculating joint probabilities comes from not having to question dependence or independence. If the tree diagram is drawn correctly, dependent effects have already been accounted for by adjustments of the probabilities in each part of the branch. The same is true for conditional probabilities, because conditional effects are also calculated into the branches. Thus, calculations for intersections are made by simply multiplying the probabilities of the parts of a branch.

It is important to understand sample space when drawing tree diagrams. The most crucial issue is understanding changes in the sample space when conducting an experiment. It is always necessary to question what is known as *replacement*.

Replacement   Replacement occurs if, during a phase of an experiment, an element is withdrawn and then replaced in the original sample space. Each event during an experiment with replacement is independent.

No replacement   No replacement occurs if, during a phase of an experiment, an element is removed but is not replaced in the original sample space. The act of not replacing an element results in a change in the sample space of each event. The outcome of the second event is dependent on the outcome of the first event.

With replacement, the sample space remains the same. For example, suppose a person has five coins in his or her pocket. One coin is pulled out. The sample space contains five coins before the person withdraws one coin. If the withdrawn coin is replaced and then a coin is drawn again, the sample space of five coins remains the same for the second draw. But, if the first coin is not replaced, then the sample space does not remain the same. The first experiment has a sample space of five. The second has a sample space of four, reflecting the four coins that remain in the person's pocket.

The changes in the sample space can be reflected in a tree diagram. The changes in the sample space are the adjustments for dependent or conditional effects caused when replacement does not occur. When calculating probabilities using the formula $P(A) = n(A)/n(S)$, the changes in the sample space are reflected in the denominator, although the numerator may also be affected.

EXAMPLE 6.13

Experiment   A bag contains 3 oranges and 4 apples. You pull out a piece of fruit and then pick a second piece of fruit out of the bag without replacing the first. What is the probability you will pick 2 oranges?

Answer $P(\text{O and O}) = .143$

Solution   To approach the solution to this experiment, first draw a tree diagram. Second, calculate the probabilities for the parts of the branches. Finally, label the branches. Adjust the second part of each branch to represent the change in the sample space. The denominator changes to 6 after draw 1; there are only 6 pieces of fruit left in the bag after the first draw. The numerators may change, depending on what was picked on the first draw. For example, for branch 1, the probability for the first part of the branch is 3/7 (fractions are used in the tree diagram to make the calculations easier). There are 3 oranges out of 7 pieces of fruit. The second part of the branch must adjust for what has happened in the first part of the branch. If you had 3 oranges and you drew an orange on the first draw, then you have only 2 oranges left out of a total of 6 pieces of fruit in the bag. The probability for the second part of the branch is 2/6.

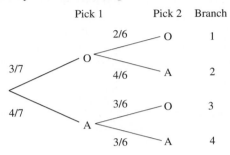

Branch 1 contains the event that both picks result in an orange. The probabilities of the parts of branch 1 are multiplied. The probability of the first part of the branch, 3/7, is multiplied by the probability of the second part of the branch, 2/6. When performing calculations, show all steps.

$$P(\text{O and O}) = P(\text{orange, first draw}) \cdot P(\text{orange, second draw})$$

$$= 3/7 \cdot 2/6$$

$$= (.429) \cdot (.333)$$

$$= .143$$

EXAMPLE 6.14

Experiment   There are 6 yellow marbles and 4 red marbles in a bag. You pick three marbles consecutively without replacement.

  a. What is the probability of picking 3 red marbles?
  b. What is the probability of picking a yellow, a red, and a red marble, in that order?
  c. What is the probability of picking 3 yellow marbles?

Answer

  a. $P(R \text{ and } R \text{ and } R) = .033$
  b. $P(Y \text{ and } R \text{ and } R) = .1$
  c. $P(Y \text{ and } Y \text{ and } Y) = .1665$

Solution   To approach the solution to this experiment, first draw a tree diagram. Second, calculate the probabilities for the parts of the branches. Third, label the branches. In step 2, be sure to adjust the second and third parts of each branch to represent the change in sample space. In the first phase of the experiment, there are 10 marbles in the bag. In the second phase of the experiment, there are 9 marbles left in the bag, because one marble was drawn and not replaced. In the third phase of the experiment, after two marbles are drawn and not replaced, there are only 8 marbles left in the bag. The sample space is the denominator and represents the total number of marbles in the bag at each phase of the experiment. The numerator may also change. Change in the numerator is based on the color of the marble drawn in each phase of the experiment. For example, if you have 6 yellow marbles in the bag and draw a yellow marble on the first draw, you now have 5 yellow marbles left in the bag out of the total of 9 marbles. If you draw a yellow and a yellow in the first and second draws, on the third draw you would have only 4 yellow marbles left out of the 8 marbles still in the bag.

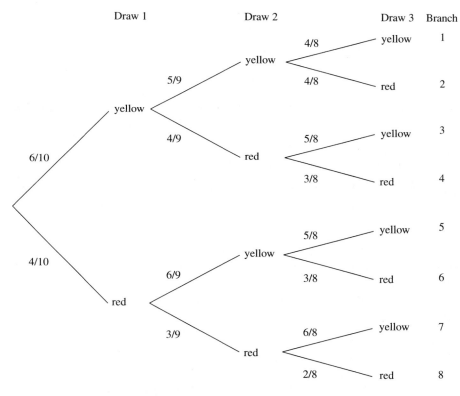

a. Picking three red marbles means that you pick a red marble on the first draw, a red marble on the second draw, and a red marble on the third draw. This event is shown in branch 8. The probability of branch 8 is found by multiplying the probabilities across the branch. That is, multiply the probability of drawing a red marble in the first draw by the probability of drawing a red marble in the second draw and then by the probability of drawing a red marble in the third draw. When performing calculations, show all steps.

$$P(R \cap R \cap R) = P(\text{red}) \cdot P(\text{red}) \cdot P(\text{red})$$

$$= 4/10 \cdot 3/9 \cdot 2/8$$

$$= (.4)(.333)(.25)$$

$$= .033$$

b. The probability of drawing a yellow marble, then a red, and then another red is found by calculating the probability of branch 4. When performing calculations, a student should show all steps and circle the final answer.

$$P(Y \cap R \cap R) = P(\text{yellow}) \cdot P(\text{red}) \cdot P(\text{red})$$
$$= 6/10 \cdot 4/9 \cdot 3/8$$
$$= (.6)(.444)(.375)$$
$$= .100$$

c. Drawing three yellow marbles means you pick a yellow on the first draw, a yellow on the second draw, and a yellow on the third draw. Branch 1 represents this event. When performing calculations, show all steps.

$$P(Y \cap Y \cap Y) = P(\text{yellow}) \cdot P(\text{yellow}) \cdot P(\text{yellow})$$
$$= 6/10 \cdot 5/9 \cdot 4/8$$
$$= (.6)(.555)(.5)$$
$$= .167$$

A LEARNING AID

Joint and Conditional Probabilities Using Tree Diagrams

A friend of yours has 2 pencils, 2 blue pens, and 3 black pens in his school bag. You ask to borrow a writing instrument from your friend. What if he gave you a blue pen, but you need a black pen? If he does not put the blue pen back in the bag, what is the probability that he will pull out a black pen the second time?

Step 1   Draw and label a tree diagram. To draw the tree, begin with the trunk. There are three different events that may occur for any draw from the bag: pencil, blue pen, or black pen. Phase 1 of the experiment is the first time your friend draws from his bag. Phase 2 is the second time he draws from his bag.

Calculate the probability of each part of each branch. To do this you must ask if replacement occurred during the experiment. If not, the sample space and each probability will change for each part of each branch. Replacement does not occur; your friend did not replace the first item drawn from the bag. Note the tree diagram on page 111 and the probabilities for each part of each branch.

Step 2   Find the branch that represents the event that your friend drew a blue pen on his first draw and

a black pen on his second draw. Branch 6 represents the event.

Step 3   This probability is a conditional probability, because replacement did not occur. Because the sample space and probabilities are adjusted in the tree diagram to represent the conditions for each draw, the solution is found by reporting the probability of the second part of the branch.

Step 4   The probability of joint probabilities is found by multiplying across the branch that represents the event. The probability of a conditional probability is the probability of only one part of the branch. The event in question reads: What is the probability that a black pen will be drawn given that a blue pen was drawn?

$$P(A|B) = P(\text{black pen}|\text{blue pen})$$
$$P(\text{black, blue}) = 3/6$$
$$= .5$$

Combining the Addition and Multiplication Theorems

There are times when the addition and multiplication theorems can be combined. Combining the rules of probability allows calculating the probability of two events occurring simultaneously, where at least one event has two or more outcomes or the events happen together several times. Both the addition (Section 2) and multiplication (Section 4) theorems are used. The multiplication rule is applied to the two events as they happen together. If they happen together several times, the multiplication rule for joint probabilities is applied to each as they happen. The addition rule for their union is applied to add together all the joint probabilities.

Combining the theorems is easy when using tree diagrams. Each branch represents the joint occurrences. Joint occurrences, or intersections, require the multiplication rule. If several branches fulfill the outcomes of one or both events, then the union is found by adding the probabilities of the branches. A very simple rule emerges when using tree diagrams for combined events: Multiply across branches and add down branches.

> **Combining theorems using tree diagrams** Multiply across branches to obtain intersections as joint probabilities and add down branches to obtain unions.

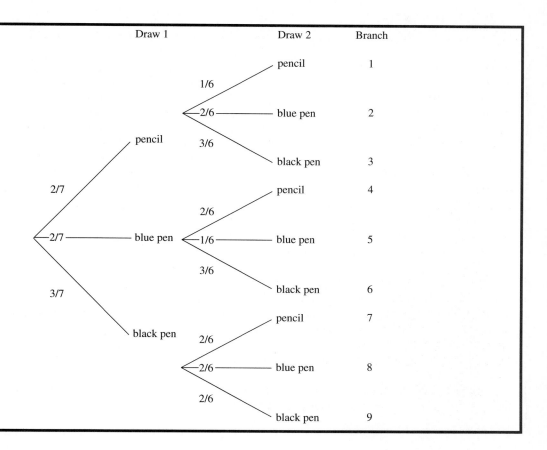

EXAMPLE 6.15

Experiment   Observe the sex of the next two babies born at General Hospital. What is the probability that of the next two babies, only one will be a boy?

Answer   P(only one boy) = .5

Solution   Draw a tree diagram. Assign probabilities to the parts of the branches and label each branch. This experiment happens to be independent. Note that the probabilities of each part of the branch remain the same. For example, for branch 1, the probability that the first baby is a boy is ½. If the first baby is a boy, the probability that the second baby is a boy is still ½. No adjustments are necessary.

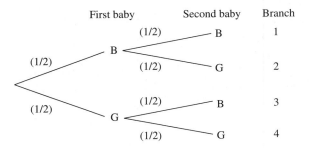

Only on branch 2 and branch 3 is just one boy born. No other branch has exactly one boy. Because two branches fulfill the event in question, the probabilities of each branch must be found by multiplying across the branch and then the probabilities of the two branches must be added together. Multiply across branch 2: (½)(½) = .25. Multiply across branch 3: (½)(½) = .25. Because both branches satisfy the condition that only one boy is born, the probabilities must be added: .25 + .25 = .5. When performing calculations, show all steps.

$$P(\text{only one boy}) = P(\text{B and G}) \text{ or } P(\text{G and B})$$
$$= (1/2 \cdot 1/2) + (1/2 \cdot 1/2)$$
$$= .25 + .25$$
$$= .5$$

One aid in calculating these kinds of probabilities is to remember the rule of multiplying across and adding down branches. The second aid is to draw the tree diagram correctly. Be sure to adjust the second phase of the tree if the sample space changes. Recall that when an experiment is conducted without replacement, the sample space usually changes. This change affects the denominator and possibly the numerator when calculating probabilities using fractions. When replacement does not occur, a conditional probability results. Each phase of an experiment may depend on what happens in prior phases. Adjusting the numerators and denominators controls the conditional probabilities and allows the calculation of branch probabilities as if they are simple joint probabilities. If replacement does occur, the phases of the events are independent, and no adjustment is usually required.

EXAMPLE 6.16

Experiment   A deck of playing cards has 52 cards, of which half are red and half are black. There are two red cards and two black cards for every number 2 through 10 and for every face card (jack, queen, king, and ace). Two cards are drawn without replacement. What is the probability that at least one card will be red?

Answer P(at least 1 red) $= .755$

Solution   Draw and label the tree diagram. Calculate the probabilities for the parts of the branches. Notice that the phases of the experiment are dependent, because there is no replacement of the first card drawn. When there is no replacement, the sample space changes. For the first phase, 52 cards are in hand, 26 red and 26 black. In the second phase, the denominators change to 51, since one card has been drawn. Each numerator is adjusted, depending on the color of the card from the first part of the branch. For example, if, in branch 1, a red card is originally drawn (26/52), in draw 2 there are only 25 red cards left from the total of 51 cards. In branch 2, if a red card was originally drawn in the first phase, all 26 black cards remain, but there are only 51 cards in all. Remember that the numerator and denominator may change when no replacement occurs.

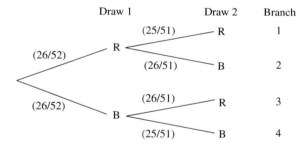

Branches 1, 2, and 3 all satisfy the event of drawing at least 1 red card when drawing 2 cards without replacement. You must find the probabilities of each branch and then add them together. Calculate the probability of each branch by multiplying across. Each of the three branch probabilities must then be added together. When performing calculations, show all steps.

$$P\text{(at least 1 red)} = P(\text{R and R}) + P(\text{R and B}) + P(\text{B and R})$$

$$= (26/52)(25/51) + (26/52)(26/51) + (26/52)(26/51)$$

$$= .245 + .255 + .255$$

$$= .755$$

A LEARNING AID

Addition and Multiplication Theorems

In the Section 5 Learning Aid, a friend of yours has 2 pencils, 2 blue pens, and 3 black pens in his school bag. You need something with which to write. You ask to borrow something from your friend. He pulls one implement from his bag and then pulls another in a second draw. Calculate the probability that your friend drew 2 different-color pens.

Step 1 Draw and label a tree diagram. To draw the tree, begin with the trunk. There are three different events that may occur for any draw from the bag: pencil, blue pen, and black pen. Phase 1 of the experiment is the first time your friend draws from his bag. Phase 2 represents the second time he draws from his bag.

Calculate the probability for each part of each branch. Replacement does not occur, requiring you to adjust the sample space for each part of each branch.

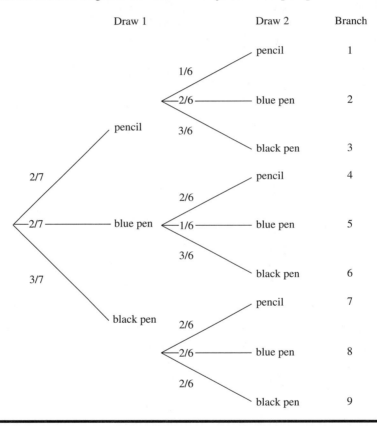

CHAPTER 6 IN REVIEW

6.1 Thirty-five out of 80 people on a police force earned a sharpshooter badge.

    a. What is the probability that on a randomly selected call, the officer would be a sharpshooter?

    b. In answer to 10 consecutive calls, the police officer responding was not a sharpshooter. Is it more likely that the eleventh call will be answered by a sharpshooter?

6.2 Which of the following statements are independent events and which are not independent events? Label the following statements appropriately.

    a. Study and pass an exam

    b. Rolling a pair of dice

    c. Vehicle and flat tire

    d. Draw a card, replace the card, and draw a second card

Step 2   Find the branch or branches representing the event that your friend drew two different-color pens. There are two different branches that represent the event. Branch 6 is the event that your friend pulled out a blue pen then a black pen. Branch 8 is the event he pulled out a black pen then a blue pen. Both branches must be used in calculating the probability that two different-color pens were drawn.

Step 3   This problem begins as a conditional probability treated as a joint probability, because you have already adjusted the probabilities of each part of each branch for the condition that no replacement occurred. But the problem also is a union of two events, since there are two different branches that represent two different-color pens being drawn.

Step 4   The probability of joint and conditional probabilities is found by multiplying across the branch that represents the event. You must do this for branch 6 and branch 8.

$$P(\text{branch 6}) = P(\text{blue pen}) \cdot P(\text{black pen})$$
$$= 2/7 \cdot 3/6$$
$$= (.2857) \cdot (.5)$$
$$= .143$$

$$P(\text{branch 8}) = P(\text{black pen}) \cdot P(\text{blue pen})$$
$$= 3/7 \cdot 2/6$$
$$= (.429) \cdot (.333)$$
$$= .143$$

Step 5   To calculate the union of the two events you must add probabilities. When two branches fulfill an event, add the probabilities of the two branches. Remember the rule to multiply across branches and add down branches. Add the probability of branch 6 to the probability of branch 8. The whole problem would look like this:

$$P[(\text{Blue} \cap \text{Black}) \cup (\text{Black} \cap \text{Blue})]$$
$$= P(\text{bl and bk}) + P(\text{bk and bl})$$
$$= P(\text{branch 6}) + P(\text{branch 8})$$
$$= [(2/7)(3/6)] + [(3/7)(2/6)]$$
$$= [(.2857)(.5)] + [(.429)(.333)]$$
$$= .143 + .143$$
$$= .286$$

---

e. Draw a card, do not replace the card, and draw a second card

6.3   Eighty percent of students must take a statistics course. Of those required to take the course 80% complete the course with a passing grade. What is the probability that a randomly selected student must take statistics and complete the course with a passing grade?

6.4   If $P(A \cap B) = .23$, $P(A) = .7$, and $P(B) = .9$, what is $P(A|B)$? Are these events independent?

6.5   If 36% of bureaucrats are in the Defense Department, 25% are in the Postal Service, 39% are in other agencies, and all agencies are mutually exclusive, what is the probability that a person randomly chosen is in the Postal Service and the Defense Department?

6.6   There are 200 graduates of a school of public administration who were interviewed to find out their employment status. The following contingency probability table shows the results of the graduates interviewed.

Graduates of a School of Public Administration
Employment Status

	Working Full-Time	Working Part-Time	Not Working	Totals
Men	.4	0	.2	.6
Women	.1	.2	.1	.4
Total	.5	.2	.3	1.0

a. What is the probability that a randomly selected person is a male?

b. What is the probability that a person is working full-time?

c. What is the probability that a person will be either a man or working full-time?

d. If a person is a woman, what is the probability that she is working part-time?

e. What is the probability that a person is a woman and is not working?

6.7 In the sample space of single digits 0 to 9 inclusive, what is the probability that a number picked randomly is an odd number or a 5? Are the events mutually exclusive?

6.8 The new transportation bill has a 90% chance of passing if the Democrats win the election. The Democrats have a 60% chance of winning the election. What is the probability that the Democrats will win and the bill will pass?

6.9 The probability of studying for an exam and passing is .82. The probability of studying for the test is .9. Given that you have studied, what is the probability that you will pass the exam?

6.10 If a coin flipped 6 times came up heads each time, what is the probability that on the seventh flip it will come up heads?

6.11 A baseball player has hit 298 times out of the last 500 times at bat. What is the probability that she will hit the ball the next time at bat?

6.12 If a pair of identical twins is born and the first baby is a girl, what is the probability that both babies are girls?

6.13 If a pair of identical twins is born and the first baby is a boy, what is the probability that the second baby is a boy?

6.14 a. Draw a tree diagram showing the probabilities for all outcomes if identical triplets are born.

b. If the first baby is a girl, what is the probability that the second baby is a girl?

c. What is the probability that if the first baby is a girl, the third baby is a boy?

6.15 You have 3 quarters and 3 dimes in your pocket and you select 2 coins without replacement.

a. What is the probability that the first coin you draw is a quarter?

b. What is the probability that you draw 2 quarters?

c. What is the probability that you do not draw a dime?

d. What is the probability that you draw two different coins?

e. What is the probability that you draw two dimes?

6.16 Given $P(A') = .2$, $P(B|A) = .6$, and $P(B|A') = .3$.

a. Draw a tree diagram.

b. What is $P(A \cap B)$?

c. What is $P(A \cup A')$?

d. What is $P(A' \cap B')$?

e. What is $P(B'|A')$?

6.17 A survey of 100 U.S. senators show the following results on a recent vote on a bill and the party identification of the senator.

	Yes	No	Total
Republican	28	12	40
Democrat	50	10	60
Total	78	22	100

a. What is the probability that a senator chosen at random is a Republican.

b. What is the probability that a senator chosen at random is a Democrat who voted for the bill?

c. What is the probability that a senator chosen at random voted against the bill?

d. What is the probability that a senator chosen at random is not a Republican?

e. If the senator chosen is a Democrat, what is the probability he or she voted against the bill?

6.18 Presidents from George Washington to Ronald Reagan have vetoed 15% of the bills passed by Congress. Of those vetoes, only 4% have been overridden by Congress. What is the probability that a bill will be vetoed by the president and overridden by Congress?

6.19 Given $P(A) = .3$, $P(B) = .5$, and $P(A \cap B) = .1$, find:

a. $P(A \cup B)$

b. $P(A|B)$

c. $P(B')$

d. $P(A')$

6.20 The president is about to nominate a justice for the Supreme Court. Let A be the event that the person is African-American, let B be the event that the person is Hispanic, let C be the event that the person is female, and let D be the event that the person is confirmed by the Senate. Describe, in words, the following events.

a. $P(A \cup B)$

b. $P(A \cap C)$

c. $P(A')$

d. $P(A \cap C \cap D)$

e. $P(A \cap C \cap D')$

Probability Distributions of Discrete Variables

7

Now that the fundamentals of probabilities have been mastered, probabilities can be combined with frequency distributions. Recall that a relative frequency distribution (Chapter 2) is a distribution representing the occurrence of a response variable relative to the total number of occurrences. It is a proportional measure: the proportion of the occurrence of the response relative to the total. It is found by dividing the number of occurrences of the response variable by the total number of occurrences of the whole frequency distribution. The response variable is simply a response or a characteristic about a population or sample. In response to the question, What is your religious preference? a person may reply ''Protestant,'' ''Catholic,'' ''Jewish,'' and so on. Each response has a frequency. To determine the relative frequency, the number of responses of a particular type is divided by the total number of responses. Recall a few basic rules that apply to a relative frequency distribution. First, frequency distributions represent discrete variables. Discrete variables are counts. Second, the relative proportion of a response variable in a distribution must be between 0 and 1.00, inclusive. Third, the relative proportions of all responses must have a sum of 1.00. The last two rules are referred to as properties of probabilities.

A relative frequency distribution used in predicting outcomes of an event becomes a probability experiment. The relative frequency distribution is then referred to as a probability distribution. The response variable is referred to as a random variable. The experiment is defined as observing the occurrence of a particular random variable.

Probability Distribution of a Discrete Random Variable

Random variables are equivalent to response variables in a relative frequency distribution. The only difference is that the random variable is assigned a numerical value based on an event that is being observed. For example, instead of asking five people their religious preference, ask how many are Catholic. This way a response is given that has a numerical value. Of the five people asked, the possible number of Catholics could be 0, 1, 2, 3, 4, or 5. There could be no Catholics, one who is Catholic, two who are Catholic, and so forth. Each outcome is referred to as a random variable. Because each outcome represents a discrete count, each count is referred to as a discrete random variable.

> **Discrete random variable** A variable that assumes a numerical value for each outcome or element of the sample space. A random variable is represented by a capital letter, such as X, Y, or Z.

EXAMPLE 7.1

Experiment Observe the next 4 babies born at General Hospital. Note the number of girls born. List all the values of the random variable, a girl is born.

Answer X = girl is born, $x = 0, 1, 2, 3, 4$

Solution This is a discrete variable, because the number of girls being born is a discrete count: 0, 1, 2, 3, ... The random variable is the event defined by the observation looking for the number of girls born. Always check to see if 0 is a valid value. It is possible that no girls are born. The nonoccurrence of an event may be an event, with a value of 0.

A random variable is represented by any capital letter. A person walking down the street can be identified as X, Q, or any other capital letter. The value assigned to a random variable is represented by the corresponding lowercase letter. Thus, X walks down the street and enters house x. Q enters house q, and D enters house d. If the value of a random variable is represented by a number, then it is usually stated with a lowercase letter, equal sign, and the number, such as $x = 0$.

EXAMPLE 7.2

Experiment The random variable is the number of girls being born out of the next four babies born at General Hospital. Describe each value of the random variable.

Answer

$x = 0$: No girls are born.
$x = 1$: One girl is born.
$x = 2$: Two girls are born.
$x = 3$: Three girls are born.
$x = 4$: Four girls are born.

Solution   This is a discrete random variable, because it is a count of the number of girls being born. X = girls being born, and the values of x are 0, 1, 2, 3, 4. This problem differs from Example 7.1 by asking to describe the meaning of the values of x.

___

The probability distribution begins by listing a frequency distribution for the random variable and its values. The frequency distribution can then be converted to a probability distribution. Assigning probabilities to values of a random variable is not always easy. Experiments can involve the three types of probabilities (experimental, theoretical, and subjective). Most of the problems presented in this text use theoretical examples, which allow for easy calculations of probabilities based on the understanding of how to combine sample spaces with frequency distributions. Many problems give enough information to allow easy calculation of the random variable values or their probabilities. The following steps should be used in presenting a probability distribution:

Step 1   State and define the discrete random variable X (or any other letter).

Step 2   Prepare a frequency distribution with a column x and its values below x.

Step 3   List a column for f, the frequency at which each value of x occurs.

Step 4   Calculate the relative frequency by dividing each frequency x by the total number of occurrences found by adding all the f values. That is, for each value of x, determine $f/\Sigma f$.

Step 5   Check to be sure all the rules of probability are met:
a. All values of x are represented.
b. Each probability is greater than or equal to 0 and less than or equal to 1 ($0 \leq x \leq 1$).
c. All probabilities of x sum to 1 ($\Sigma P(x) = 1$).

EXAMPLE 7.3

Experiment   Observe the sex of the next two babies born at General Hospital. List the probability distribution for the number of boys born.

Answer X = number of boys born at General Hospital

x	f	$P(x)$
0	1	.25
1	2	.50
2	1	.25
	—	——
	4	1.00

Solution

Step 1   This is a discrete variable, because the variable is a count of the number of boys born.

Step 2   Prepare the frequency distribution by listing x and its value in the first column. The values of x are 0, 1, and 2, where $x = 0$ represents no boys born; $x = 1$ represents one boy born; and $x = 2$ represents two boys born.

Step 3   List the frequency for each x in a column labeled f. This example is a theoretical example. The sample space has four outcomes: $S = \{(B, B), (G, B), (B, G), (G, G)\}$. The frequency is determined by counting how many boys are in each outcome. There is one outcome with no boys, (G, G). There are two outcomes one boy, (G, B) and (B, G). There is one outcome with two boys, (B, B).

Step 4 Calculate the relative frequency as the probability of each value of x. Divide the frequency of each x by the total number of outcomes. For example: for $x = 0$, with a frequency of 1, the probability is $\frac{1}{4}$, or .25.

x	f	$f/\Sigma f$	$P(x)$
0	1	$\frac{1}{4}$	.25
1	2	$\frac{2}{4}$	.50
2	1	$\frac{1}{4}$	.25
	4	$\frac{4}{4}$	1.00

Step 5 Check to be sure that no rules of probability of distribution have been violated.

a. Are all values of x represented? Yes, there are no other possibilities for x except 0, 1, 2.

b. Are all probabilities between 0 and 1, inclusive? Yes, each x fulfills the requirement.

c. Do the probabilities of x have a sum of 1? Yes, $.25 + .5 + .25 = 1.0$.

A LEARNING AID

Probability Distributions for Discrete Random Variables

Observe the marital status of the next three people you see. List the probability distribution for the number of people who are married.

Step 1 This is a discrete variable, because the variable is a count of the number of people who are married among the next three that you observe. The discrete random variable is the number married. You can identify it as X: the number of people married. The values that X can take on are represented by x.

Step 2 Prepare the frequency distribution by listing each x and its value in the first column of the distribution. List the values of x. The values of x are all the possible number of people who are married. None could be married, one could be married, two could be married and all three could be married. Therefore,

$x = 0$: None is married.
$x = 1$: One is married.
$x = 2$: Two are married.
$x = 3$: All three are married.

x
0
1
2
3

Step 3 List the frequency for each x in a column labeled f. Listing the sample space may help to determine how many times a particular value of x may theoretically occur. Since the random variable is the number of people married, you can identify married and nonmarried people in the listing of the sample space. Represent married by M and nonmarried by N.

$S = \{(M, M, M), (M, M, N), (M, N, M),$
$(M, N, N), (N, M, M), (N, M, N),$
$(N, N, M), (N, N, N)\}$

Now it is possible to count the frequency for each value of x. Looking at the sample space, notice there

Discrete Probability Function

A discrete probability function is a statement that represents a discrete probability distribution. The discrete probability function assigns a probability to each value of the random variable. The rule may state a mathematical formula, which, when applied to each value of x, represents its probability. When the formula is applied to all values of x, a full distribution is represented.

> **Discrete probability function** A rule that assigns a probability to every value of x. such as
>
> $$P(X) = \_\_\_\_ \text{ for } x = 0, 1, 2, \ldots$$

A probability function can be viewed as a shorthand notation that reflects a probability distribution. The rule, or formula, placed in the blank of the definition is any mathematical formula that allows the calculation of the probability for each x cited. The mathematical formula serves no other purpose than for the calculation of the probability. If the formula states to divide each x by 10 ($x/10$), then each value of x is inserted in the numerator and divided by 10. Whatever the formula, each value of x must be inserted to calculate its probability.

Discrete probability functions are tested by calculating the probability of each x and creating a probability distribution. The rules of probability and their distributions must still be met. Each probability must be between 0 and 1, inclusive. The probabilities must have a sum of 1.0. All values of x must be represented.

---

is only one outcome where no one is married, three outcomes where only one is married, three where two are married, and one where all three people are married. The distribution should look like this:

x	f
0	1
1	3
2	3
3	1
Total	8

Step 4 Calculate the relative frequency as the probability of each value of x. Divide the frequency of each x by the sum of f: $f/\Sigma f$. For $x = 0$, divide the frequency of 1 by 8: $\frac{1}{8} = .125$. You must do this for each value of x. The relative frequency is the probability that x occurs, and it is placed in the table under the label $P(x)$.

x	f	f/Σf	P(X)
0	1	⅛	.125
1	3	⅜	.375
2	3	⅜	.375
3	1	⅛	.125
Total	8		1.000

Step 5 Check to be sure that no rules of probabilities have been violated.

a. Are all values of x represented? Yes, the only values of x are 0, 1, 2, and 3.

b. Are all probabilities between 0 and 1, inclusive? Yes, each is greater than or equal to 0 and less than or equal to 1.0.

c. Do the probabilities of x have a sum of 1? Yes, $\Sigma P(x) = 1.000$.

EXAMPLE 7.4

Experiment Is the following a true discrete probability function?

$$P(Y) = \frac{2 + y}{3} \quad \text{for } y = 0, 1$$

Answer No

Solution Insert each value of y into the formula. Calculate the probability and create a probability distribution. Check the distribution to be sure the rules of probability are met. It must be assumed from the rule presented that all values of y are included. Each probability falls between 0 and 1, inclusive. However, the sum of the probabilities is not 1.0; it is 1.667. All three rules must be fulfilled for this rule to be a true probability distribution. If any rule is not fulfilled, then the distribution violates the rules of probabilities. Therefore, the rule is not a true probability function.

y	$\dfrac{2 + y}{3}$	$P(y)$
0	$\dfrac{2 + 0}{3} = \dfrac{2}{3}$	.667
1	$\dfrac{2 + 1}{3} = \dfrac{3}{3}$	1.000
		1.667

A LEARNING AID

Discrete Probability Functions

Determine if the following discrete probability distribution is true. Recall that a function is a mathematical rule that describes a distribution. The formula in the rule may differ for every distribution.

$$P(G) = \frac{g}{10} \quad \text{for } g = 1, 2, 3, 4$$

Step 1 This is a discrete probability function, because it describes a distribution. It is discrete since the values of the random variable represent discrete counts. The rule must be calculated as a distribution to determine if it fulfills the two probability properties.

Step 2 Begin by preparing the distribution. List the values of g in the first column. Label a second column with the function $g/10$. Label a third column as the probability P.

g	$g/10$	P
1		
2		
3		
4		
Total		

Step 3 Insert each value of g into the formula and place the result in the second column.

g	$g/10$	P
1	$\frac{1}{10}$	
2	$\frac{2}{10}$	
3	$\frac{3}{10}$	
4	$\frac{4}{10}$	
Total		

Mean and Standard Deviation of a Discrete Probability Distribution

Now that probabilities have been combined with frequency distributions, add to them the rules of means, variances, and standard deviations. Whereas frequency distributions represent the relative frequency of the response variable x, probability distributions represent the expected relative frequency of a random variable x. The use of the word *expected* implies that the distribution is theoretical. It shows what will happen in the long run. An experiment may be carried out or observed. The observational probability may not equal the theoretical probability. The law of large numbers states that as the number of trials increase, the observational probability will approach the theoretical. This statement is true because theoretical probability represents the universal set, whereas the observational probability represents a sample. Thus, a probability distribution represents a theoretical population. Any descriptive statistic describing that distribution is known as a parameter. Recall that parameters are measures that describe populations and are represented by Greek symbols.

To calculate the mean of a probability distribution, it is important to remember the rules for calculating the mean of a frequency distribution. Recall that the mean of a frequency distribution required as the numerator each value of x multiplied by its frequency. This multiplication was necessary to ensure that each value of x was represented by its relative frequency. The formula can be altered slightly for a probability distribution. Note the adjustment of the formula for the mean of a frequency distribution:

$$\bar{x} = \frac{\Sigma xf}{\Sigma f}$$

Step 4 Calculate the probability for each value of g by rewriting the values. The probability in the second column as decimals. Be sure to perform each calculation separately. Place the calculated value in the third column, labeled P. Sum the third column.

g	$g/10$	P
1	$\frac{1}{10}$	.1
2	$\frac{2}{10}$	.2
3	$\frac{3}{10}$	.3
4	$\frac{4}{10}$	.4
Total		1.0

Step 5 Check that all the rules of probabilities and their distributions are met.

a. Are all values of g included? We must assume so, since no other information is given.

b. Is the probability for each x between 0 and 1, inclusive? Yes, each value in the third column for each g is greater than or equal to 0 and less than or equal to 1.

c. Do the probabilities have a sum of 1.0? Yes, note the total of 1.0.

Since all the rules of probabilities are fulfilled, you can conclude that the probability function describing this distribution is true.

The mean formula of the frequency distribution can be adjusted to represent the mean of a probability distribution. The mean of a probability distribution is found by replacing $f/\Sigma f$ with $P(x)$ and moving the Σ and x. Change the symbol $\bar{x}$ to μ to indicate that the mean is now of a theoretical population.

Mean of a Discrete Probability Distribution

$$\mu = \Sigma[x \cdot P(x)]$$

where

Σ is the summation of the product inside the parentheses for each value of x.

x is each value of the random variable.

$P(x)$ is the probability of x.

The formula for the mean of a discrete probability distribution requires each value of x to be multiplied by its probability. This multiplication occurs for each value. The products of these multiplications are then added together.

EXAMPLE 7.5

Experiment   A coin is tossed three times. Find the mean for the following probability distribution for the random variable x, the number of heads occurring.

x	$P(x)$
0	.125
1	.375
2	.375
3	.125
Total	1.000

Answer $\mu = 1.5$

Solution   The mean is found by multiplying each x by its probability and then adding all the products. The easiest way to solve is to form a column for the multiplication of each x by its probability and then sum the column. The sum of the column is the mean. When performing the calculations, show all steps.

x	$P(x)$	$x \cdot P(x)$
0	.125	.000
1	.375	.375
2	.375	.750
3	.125	.375
Total	1.000	1.500

$$\mu = \Sigma[x \cdot P(x)]$$
$$= 1.5$$

The variance and standard deviation of the probability distribution are also derived from the variance and standard deviation of the frequency distribution. Again, minor adjustments can be made. Recall the variance formula for a frequency distribution:

$$\sigma^2 = \frac{\Sigma x^2 f - \dfrac{(\Sigma xf)^2}{\Sigma f}}{\Sigma f - 1}$$

In the first part of the numerator, $\Sigma x^2 f$, f is replaced by $P(x)$; that is, instead of multiplying x^2 by f, the new formula multiplies x^2 by $P(x)$. Brackets are used to ensure that the multiplication is done before the summation. Thus, $\Sigma x^2 f$ becomes $\Sigma[x^2 \cdot P(x)]$. The second part of the numerator has already been adjusted as the mean formula. The only adjustment to the mean formula is the squared term. Thus, $(\Sigma xf)^2/\Sigma f$ becomes $\Sigma[x \cdot P(x)]^2$. The denominator is dropped and the numerator is put together, subtracting as in the original formula.

> ### Variance of a Discrete Probability Distribution
>
> $$\sigma^2 = \Sigma[x^2 \cdot P(x)] - \Sigma[x \cdot P(x)]^2$$
>
> or
>
> $$\sigma^2 = \Sigma[x^2 \cdot P(x)] - \mu^2$$

Both formulas require that each value of x be squared (x^2) and then multiplied by its probability. These products are then added. Subtracted from this single value is the squared sum of all the products of each x and its probability. Both formulas give the same answer. Since the second part of the first formula equals the mean of a probability distribution, if the mean is already calculated, its value is inserted and squared. The most common mistake in using either formula is forgetting to square the mean.

The standard deviation of a discrete probability distribution is the square root of its variance. Recall that taking the square root of the variance returns to the same unit of analysis that the problem uses in its original form. That is, if a probability distribution describes ages in years, the variance describes ages in squared years, but the standard deviation again uses years.

> ### Standard Deviation of a Discrete Probability Distribution
>
> $$\sigma = \sqrt{\sigma^2} = \sqrt{\Sigma[x^2 \cdot P(x)] - \Sigma[x \cdot P(x)]^2}$$

Example 7.6

Experiment   A coin is tossed three times. Find the variance and standard deviation for the following probability distribution for the random variable x, the number of times a heads occurs.

A LEARNING AID

Means and Standard Deviations of a Probability Distribution

On the basis of the past record of the local electric company, the probability of the number of reported electrical outages on an average day is represented by the following probability distribution. Calculate the mean and standard deviation of the distribution.

x	$P(x)$
0	.01
1	.04
2	.15
3	.25
4	.30
5	.25
Total	1.00

Step 1   This is a discrete probability distribution, because X is the number of reported outages with values (x) of 0, 1, 2, 3, 4, and 5.

This is a true distribution, because you must as-sume all values of x are reported. Each probability of each value of x is between 0 and 1, inclusive. The probabilities have a sum of 1.0.

Step 2   To calculate the mean, begin by creating another column labeled $x \cdot P(x)$. Multiply each value in column 1 by the one in column 2, and place the product in column 3. The sum of column 3 is the mean.

x	$P(x)$	$x \cdot P(x)$
0	.01	.00
1	.04	.04
2	.15	.30
3	.25	.75
4	.30	1.20
5	.25	1.25
Total	1.00	3.54

$$\mu = \Sigma[x \cdot P(x)]$$
$$= 3.54$$

x	$P(x)$
0	.125
1	.375
2	.375
3	.125
Total	1.000

Answer $\sigma^2 = 0.75$; $\sigma = 0.87$

Solution   Start by creating columns that aid in the calculation. Columns for $x \cdot P(x)$, x^2, and $x^2 \cdot P(x)$ are all necessary for the formula. $x \cdot P(x)$ is the value of each x multiplied by its probability (the same as in Example 7.5 for the mean). Sum this column for the second part of the formula. x^2 is the square of each value of x. $x^2 \cdot P(x)$ shows the multiplication of the previous column, x^2, by the probability of x, $P(x)$. Sum this column for the first part of the formula. When performing calculations, show all steps.

x	$P(x)$	$x \cdot P(x)$	x^2	$x^2 \cdot P(x)$
0	.125	.000	0	.000
1	.375	.375	1	.375
2	.375	.750	4	1.500
3	.125	.375	9	1.125
Total	1.000	1.500		3.000

Step 3   Two additional columns are necessary to calculate the standard deviation. Add a fourth column for x^2 and a fifth column for $x^2 \cdot P(x)$. Column 4 requires the original x value from column 1 to be squared. Column 5 requires the value in column 2 to be multiplied by that in column 4. Sum the last column as follows:

x	$P(x)$	$x \cdot P(x)$	x^2	$x^2 \cdot P(X)$
0	.01	.00	0	.00
1	.04	.04	1	.04
2	.15	.30	4	1.20
3	.25	.75	9	6.75
4	.30	1.20	16	19.20
5	.25	1.25	25	31.25
Total		3.54		58.44

Step 4   You are now ready to calculate the standard deviation. Don't forget that the last part of the standard deviation formula is the mean squared. The mean was just calculated as 3.54.

$$\begin{aligned} \sigma &= \sqrt{\Sigma[x^2 \cdot P(x)] - \Sigma[x \cdot P(x)]^2} \\ &= \sqrt{58.44 - 3.54^2} \\ &= \sqrt{58.44 - 12.53} \\ &= \sqrt{45.91} \\ &= 6.78 \end{aligned}$$

Variance is:

$$\begin{aligned} \sigma^2 &= \Sigma[x^2 \cdot P(x)] - \Sigma[x \cdot P(x)]^2 \\ &= 3.0 - 1.5^2 \\ &= 3.0 - 2.25 \\ &= .75 \end{aligned}$$

Standard deviation is:

$$\begin{aligned} \sigma &= \sqrt{\sigma^2} \\ &= \sqrt{.75} \\ &= .866 \\ &= .87 \end{aligned}$$

SECTION 4

Binomial Probability Distribution

A binomial probability distribution is a special kind of probability distribution. A binomial probability distribution of a discrete random variable has only two possible outcomes. Often, a probability distribution represents several outcomes of an experiment. Many times only one of the outcomes of an experiment is of interest. The chance of one thing happening is often asked. In this situation, what is really being asked is the probability that one outcome may happen compared to all the other possible outcomes. By dividing the outcomes into only two categories, a binomial distribution results. For example, in asking people their religious preference, several religions may be reported. There are times that it is important to know only how many people are Catholic. The reported religions could be divided into two groups: Catholic and non-Catholic. The two-group classification represents a binomial random variable.

There are several conditions necessary for using the binomial probability distribution. All the following conditions must be met:

Conditions for Use of the Binomial Probability Distribution

1. There is a fixed number of trials, n.
2. There are only two possible outcomes on each trial, a success and a failure.
3. The probability of success remains constant on all trials and is designated by p. The probability of failure remains constant and is designated by q.
4. The probabilities of success and failure must have a sum of 1.0: $p + q = 1.0$.
5. A success or failure on any trial is independent of a success or failure on any other trial.

Condition 1 requires that there be a fixed number of trials, designated by the symbol n. Trials refer to the number of experiments conducted. Flipping a coin 5 times means there are 5 trials. Watching the outcome of 4 elections means there are 4 trials. With fixed trials, it is known how many trials or experiments will be conducted.

Condition 2 says that only two outcomes are possible on each trial. If several outcomes result in an experiment, they can usually be grouped into two categories. The outcome that is of importance is defined as a success. All other outcomes are combined as the second outcome, or failure.

Condition 3 requires that the probability of success and the probability of failure remain constant on all trials. That is, if the probability of success is .1 on one trial, it must be .1 on all other trials. If q is .4 on one trial, it must be .4 on all others. Success is always represented by the symbol p, and failure is represented by q.

Condition 4 states that $p + q = 1.0$. The binomial distribution, as all probability distributions, must have a sum of 1.0. The probability of each outcome must be between 0 and 1, inclusive: $0 \leq p(x) \leq 1$. All outcomes must be defined as either a success or a failure; therefore, the sum of their probabilities must equal 1.0. The probability of success, p, is often known in a problem. If p is known, then q can be found by subtracting p from 1.0: $1 - p = q$. The opposite is also true where only q is known: $1 - q = p$.

Condition 5 requires that all outcomes be independent. This is determined by asking if the outcome of one trial affects the outcome of another trial. The answer must be no for the trials to be independent. For example, getting heads on a flip of a coin does not affect whether the coin will land heads up again; the results of flipping a coin are independent.

When all the conditions for a binomial distribution are met, the calculations for creating the distribution can be done. The calculations and formula are often intimidating and cumbersome, but once a distribution is determined, a variety of probability questions can easily be answered. Unlike the probability distribution of Section 1, where the probability function or rule differed for every distribution, the binomial probability function always remains the same. The function must be applied to every value of the random variable. That is, the formula must be applied to every value of x. Collectively, the probabilities create the distribution.

Binomial probability function

$$P(x) = \binom{n}{x} p^x q^{n-x}$$

where

$\binom{n}{x}$ is the binomial coefficient, $\dfrac{n!}{x!(n-x)!}$.

p is the probability of success.

q is the probability of failure.

x is the value of the random variable *success*.

n is the number of trials.

The binomial coefficient requires the use of factorials, as indicated by the exclamation point. The factorial of any number is the product of it and all the integers of lesser value, down to 1. Therefore, $4! = 4 \cdot 3 \cdot 2 \cdot 1 = 24$, $3! = 3 \cdot 2 \cdot 1 = 6$, and $1! = 1 \cdot 1 = 1$. It is very important to remember a special factorial that surprises most people: $0! = 1$.

In writing out the factorials involved in the binomial coefficient, identical values in the numerator and denominator can be easily cancelled, allowing a more manageable final calculation. For example, if n is 6 and x is 4, the binomial coefficient is calculated as follows:

$$
\begin{aligned}
\binom{6}{4} &= \frac{6!}{4!(6-4)!} = \frac{6 \cdot 5 \cdot 4 \cdot 3 \cdot 2 \cdot 1}{(4 \cdot 3 \cdot 2 \cdot 1)(2 \cdot 1)} \\
&= \frac{6 \cdot 5}{2 \cdot 1} \\
&= \frac{30}{2} \\
&= 15
\end{aligned}
$$

Cancelling matched values in the numerator and denominator simplifies calculation. The matching values in this case are $4 \cdot 3 \cdot 2 \cdot 1$.

As n increases, the binomial coefficient becomes more difficult to calculate. However, Table A.2 in Appendix A gives the binomial coefficients for any number n up to 20. Remember, the values in Table A.2 are only the coefficients. The coefficient is only the first part of the formula needed when calculating the binomial probability. The coefficient is not a probability.

EXAMPLE 7.7

Experiment   Observe the sex of the next two babies born at General Hospital. What is the probability distribution of the number of boys born?

Answer X = number of boys born at General Hospital

x	$P(x)$
0	.25
1	.50
2	.25
	1.00

Solution   This is a binomial probability distribution, because it meets all the conditions of the binomial distribution.

Condition 1: There are n independent trials. Each baby born is a trial. If two babies are to be observed, $n = 2$.

Condition 2: There are two possible outcomes, as defined by the random variable that a boy is born.

Condition 3: The two outcomes are classified as success (a boy is born) and a failure (a boy is not born).

Condition 4: The probability of success and the probability of failure remain the same across all trials. The probability that the first baby born is a boy is .5. The probability that it is not a boy is also .5. The probabilities are the same for the sex of the second baby. The probability of success and failure add to 1.0, or $p + q = 1$.

Condition 5: The trials are independent. The probability that the first baby is a boy does not affect the probability that the second baby is a boy.

The binomial function may now be applied to each value of X. Where there are 2 babies born, it is possible to have no boys, 1 boy, or 2 boys. Therefore, $x = 0, 1, 2$, where $n = 2$, $p = .5$, and $q = .5$. The probability distribution is calculated as follows:

$$P(0) = \binom{2}{0} (.5)^0 (.5)^{2-0} = \frac{2!}{0!(2-0)!} (1)(.25) = .25$$

$$P(1) = \binom{2}{1} (.5)^1 (.5)^{2-1} = \frac{2!}{1!(2-1)!} (1)(.25) = .50$$

$$P(2) = \binom{2}{2} (.5)^2 (.5)^{2-2} = \frac{2!}{2!(2-2)!} (.25)(1) = .25$$

The binomial probability distribution allows for easy manipulation of the probabilities to determine the probability of a number of events. Events can be defined in such a manner that the probability of one or more values of x fulfills the event. When two or more values of x fulfill an event, their probabilities are added. Some key words to look for are *less than, less than or equal to, more than, more than or equal to, not greater than,* and *not more than.* These key words usually require the addition of two or more probabilities.

If a binomial probability distribution has a random variable with values of 0, 1, 2, and 3 and one wishes to find the probability that an event occurs at 2 or more times, the probability of x at 2 and of x at 3 are added together. The notation for such an event is written $P(x \geq 2)$. Be careful with the definitions. If *greater than x* is sought, then the value cited as x is not included in the calculation. For example, to find the probability of x *greater than* 2, $P(x > 2)$, requires adding the probability of $x = 3$ and all probabilities of x values greater than 3. But if $P(x \geq 2)$ is sought, then the probability of $x = 2$ is also included, adding the probabilities of x values of 2, 3, and all others greater. Recall the addition theorem (Chapter 6). When two or more outcomes make up an event, the probability of their union is the addition of the two (or more) probabilities minus the probability of their intersection. Binomial distributions do not involve intersections, because the outcomes are mutually exclusive events. The probability of unions is, thus, the sum of all the outcomes' probabilities.

EXAMPLE 7.8

Experiment   The probability of a given number of boys born at General Hospital when the sex of the next two babies born are observed as follows:

x	$P(x)$
0	.25
1	.50
2	.25
	1.00

a. What is the probability that no more than one boy is born?
b. What is $P(x > 1)$?
c. What is the probability that x is greater than or equal to 1?
d. What is the probability that both babies are boys or neither are boys?

Answer

a. $P(x \leq 1) = .75$
b. $P(x > 1) = .25$
c. $P(x \geq 1) = .75$
d. $P(0 \cup 2) = .50$

Solution

a. The probability that there is no more than one boy means we want the probability that one boy or no boys are born. Two outcomes fulfill the event, one boy born or no boys are born. The notation is $P(x \leq 1)$. The calculation involves the addition of the two probabilities that fulfill the event. When performing calculations, show all steps.

$$P(x \leq 1) = P(0) + P(1)$$
$$= .25 + .50$$
$$= .75$$

b. $P(x > 1)$ is the probability of more than one boy being born. Having only one boy *does not* fulfill the event. Since there is only one value of x greater than 1, the probability of the event is the probability of that one outcome. That outcome is that two boys are born. When performing calculations, show all steps.

$$P(x > 1) = P(x = 2)$$
$$= .25$$

c. The probability that x is greater than or equal to 1 is the probability that one or more boys are born. The probability of one boy and the probability of two boys must be added. When performing calculations, show all steps.

$$P(x \geq 1) = P(1) + P(2)$$
$$= .50 + .25$$
$$= .75$$

d. Finding the probability that both are boys or neither are boys requires the addition of the two outcomes. When performing calculations, show all steps.

$$P(0 \cup 2) = P(0) + P(2)$$
$$= .25 + .25$$
$$= .50$$

EXAMPLE 7.9

Experiment   Six members of congress are up for reelection. Each election is a toss-up. What is the probability distribution for the number of members winning reelection?

Answer X = number of members winning reelection

x	$P(x)$
0	.016
1	.093
2	.236
3	.313
4	.236
5	.093
6	.016
	1.00

Solution   This is a binomial distribution, because all the conditions are fulfilled.

Condition 1: There are six elections. Each election represents a trial, so $n = 6$.

Condition 2: There are two possible outcomes: Success is winning the election, and failure is losing the election.

Condition 3: The probabilities of success and failure remain the same. Since each election is a toss-up (50/50 chance for each candidate in each election), $p = .5$ and $q = .5$.

Condition 4: $p + q = 1.0$. Here, $.5 + .5 = 1.0$.

Condition 5: Each election is independent. No election affects the outcome of any other election (this is assumed, because no other information is given). The binomial function must be applied to each value of x.

The random variable has values of 0, 1, 2, 3, 4, 5, and 6; $p = .5$, $q = .5$, $n = 6$.

$$P(0) = \binom{6}{0}(.5)^0(.5)^{6-0} = \frac{6 \cdot 5 \cdot 4 \cdot 3 \cdot 2 \cdot 1}{1(6 \cdot 5 \cdot 4 \cdot 3 \cdot 2 \cdot 1)}(1)(.0156) = 1(1)(.0156) = 0.16$$

$$P(1) = \binom{6}{1}(.5)^1(.5)^{6-1} = \frac{6 \cdot 5 \cdot 4 \cdot 3 \cdot 2 \cdot 1}{(1)(5 \cdot 4 \cdot 3 \cdot 2 \cdot 1)}(.5)(.031) = 6(.5)(.031) = .093$$

$$P(2) = \binom{6}{2}(.5)^2(.5)^{6-2} = \frac{6 \cdot 5 \cdot 4 \cdot 3 \cdot 2 \cdot 1}{(2 \cdot 1)(4 \cdot 3 \cdot 2 \cdot 1)}(.25)(.063) = 15(.25)(.063) = .236$$

$$P(3) = \binom{6}{3}(.5)^3(.5)^{6-3} = \frac{6 \cdot 5 \cdot 4 \cdot 3 \cdot 2 \cdot 1}{(3 \cdot 2 \cdot 1)(3 \cdot 2 \cdot 1)}(.125)(.125) = 20(.125)(.125) = .313$$

$$P(4) = \binom{6}{4}(.5)^4(.5)^{6-4} = \frac{6 \cdot 5 \cdot 4 \cdot 3 \cdot 2 \cdot 1}{(4 \cdot 3 \cdot 2 \cdot 1)(2 \cdot 1)}(.063)(.25) = 15(.063)(.25) = .236$$

$$P(5) = \binom{6}{5}(.5)^5(.5)^{6-5} = \frac{6 \cdot 5 \cdot 4 \cdot 3 \cdot 2 \cdot 1}{(5 \cdot 4 \cdot 3 \cdot 2 \cdot 1)(1)}(.031)(.5) = 6(.031)(.5) = .093$$

$$P(6) = \binom{6}{6}(.5)^6(.5)^{6-6} = \frac{6 \cdot 5 \cdot 4 \cdot 3 \cdot 2 \cdot 1}{(6 \cdot 5 \cdot 4 \cdot 3 \cdot 2 \cdot 1)1}(.0156)(1) = 1(.016)(1) = .016$$

EXAMPLE 7.10

Experiment   Using the binomial probability distribution from Example 7.9, congressional reelections, find the following:

a. The probability that three members will win reelection
b. The probability that no more than three will win reelection
c. The probability that more than four will win reelection

Answer

a. $P(x = 3) = .313$
b. $P(x \leq 3) = .658$
c. $P(x > 4) = .109$

Solution

a. The probability that three members will win reelection means that only the probability that $x = 3$ is sought. From the binomial probability distribution presented in Example 7.9, the probability is .313. When performing calculations, show all steps.

$$P(x = 3) = .313$$

b. The probability that no more than three will win reelection means that the probability of three or fewer is sought. This problem requires the use of the addition theorem. The probabilities of the values for x, where x is three or less, must be added. When performing calculations, show all steps.

$$P(x \leq 3) = P(0) + P(1) + P(2) + P(3)$$
$$= .016 + .093 + .236 + .313$$
$$= .658$$

c. The probability that more than four will win also requires use of the addition theorem. The value of four is not asked for, because more than four is sought. When performing calculations, show all steps.

$$P(x > 4) = P(5) + P(6)$$
$$= .093 + .016$$
$$= .109$$

A LEARNING AID

Binomial Probability Distributions

The governors of five states are meeting in Washington, D.C., to go before a congressional committee on crime problems across the nation. Each governor arrives separately by plane, and all planes arrive independently at 9 A.M. If the probability that each plane arrives on time is 0.4, what is the probability that at least three of the planes arrive on time?

Step 1 This a binomial probability, because a binomial is a special kind of probability distribution that defines outcomes as one of two categories. These categories can be described as success and failure. In this example, success occurs when a plane arrives on time. Check to see that all the conditions for the binomial probability are met.

Condition 1: There is a fixed number of trials, n. In this example, n is equal to 5. There are five governors arriving in Washington, so the arrival of each governor represents a trial.

Condition 2: There are only two outcomes, defined as success and failure. Success is a governor arriving on time. Failure is a governor not arriving on time.

Condition 3: The probabilities of p and q must remain constant. The probability of arriving on time is the same for each governor. The probability of not arriving on time is also the same for each governor.

Condition 4: Success (p) is stated as .4. Since $p + q = 1.0$, subtract p from 1.0 to find q: $1 - .4 = .6$, so $q = .6$.

Condition 5: The outcomes of each trial must be independent of those of all other trials. Each governor is arriving independently of all others. Therefore, arriving on time for any one governor does not affect any other governor's arrival time.

Step 2 State the random variable, X, and its values, x. X is "a governor arrives on time"; its values, x, are 0, 1, 2, 3, 4, and 5. No governors could arrive on time, or one, two, three, four, or five could arrive on time.

Step 3 Apply the binomial probability function to each value of x. Recall the information given in the problem necessary for the calculations:

$$n = 5 \qquad x = 0, 1, 2, 3, 4, 5 \qquad p = .4 \qquad q = .6$$

The probability function is:

$$P(x) = \binom{n}{x} p^x q^{n-x}$$

$$P(0) = \binom{5}{0} (.4)^0 (.6)^{5-0} = \frac{5 \cdot 4 \cdot 3 \cdot 2 \cdot 1}{1(5 \cdot 4 \cdot 3 \cdot 2 \cdot 1)} (1)(.078)$$

$$= (1)(1)(.078) = .078$$

As all probability distributions represent theoretical populations, so too does the binomial distribution. Remember, the binomial probability distribution is simply a special kind of probability distribution, and all statistics representing populations are known as parameters and are usually represented by Greek letters.

Binomial probability distributions also lend themselves to description by parameters. With all probability distributions, means and standard deviations of binomials represent theoretical populations. The mean of the binomial is also represented by the Greek letter μ. The standard deviation of the binomial is represented by the Greek letter σ. The mean and standard deviation for a binomial probability distribution are easily calculated.

The formula for the mean of a binomial distribution is very easy to use. Recall the formula in Section 3 of this chapter for the mean of a probability distribution. It was quite lengthy and required each value of x to be multiplied by its probability. Then all products were summed. The formula for the mean of a binomial probability distribution does not require each value of x to be identified. Both the formula just presented and the formula presented in Section 3 calculate means for probability

The Mean and Standard Deviation of the Binomial Distribution

$$P(1) = \binom{5}{1}(.4)^1(.6)^{5-1} = \frac{5 \cdot 4 \cdot 3 \cdot 2 \cdot 1}{1(4 \cdot 3 \cdot 2 \cdot 1)}(.4)(.13)$$
$$= (5)(.4)(.13) = .260$$

$$P(2) = \binom{5}{2}(.4)^2(.6)^{5-2} = \frac{5 \cdot 4 \cdot 3 \cdot 2 \cdot 1}{(2 \cdot 1)(3 \cdot 2 \cdot 1)}(.16)(.216)$$
$$= (10)(.16)(.216) = .346$$

$$P(3) = \binom{5}{3}(.4)^3(.6)^{5-3} = \frac{5 \cdot 4 \cdot 3 \cdot 2 \cdot 1}{(3 \cdot 2 \cdot 1)(2 \cdot 1)}(.064)(.36)$$
$$= (10)(.064)(.36) = .230$$

$$P(4) = \binom{5}{4}(.4)^4(.6)^{5-4} = \frac{5 \cdot 4 \cdot 3 \cdot 2 \cdot 1}{(4 \cdot 3 \cdot 2 \cdot 1)(1)}(.026)(.6)$$
$$= (5)(.026)(.6) = .078$$

$$P(5) = \binom{5}{5}(.4)^5(.6)^{5-5} = \frac{5 \cdot 4 \cdot 3 \cdot 2 \cdot 1}{(5 \cdot 4 \cdot 3 \cdot 2 \cdot 1)(1)}(.01)(1)$$
$$= (1)(.010)(1) = .010$$

Step 4   Present the information in the form of a probability distribution. Column 1 should be labeled x and column 2 should be labeled $P(x)$. Check to see that all the rules of probability are met.

x	$P(x)$
0	.078
1	.260
2	.346
3	.230
4	.078
5	.010
	1.000

It is not always necessary that the values for the whole distribution be calculated to find the probability of only a few values of x.

Step 5   Now you can go back to the original problem and state the event being asked. You were asked to find the probability that at least 3 of the planes arrived on time. At least 3 means 3 or more planes arrive on time. Therefore, the event you are looking for is the union of 3, 4, and 5 on-time arrivals. Unions of independent events require the addition theorem:

$$P(x \geq 3) = P(3) + P(4) + P(5)$$

These probabilities are easily obtained from the distribution presented in Step 4.

$$P(x \geq 3) = P(3) + P(4) + P(5)$$
$$= (.230) + (.078) + (.010)$$
$$= .318$$

There is a probability of .318 that at least three of the planes will arrive in Washington, D.C., on time.

> **Mean for a Binomial Probability Distribution**
>
> $$\mu = n \cdot p$$
>
> where
>
> n is the number of independent trials.
> p is the probability of success.

distributions. They will both result in the same answer any time the random variable x fulfills the conditions of a binomial distribution. In fact, many of the examples in Section 2 were binomials. It may be wise to look back at Section 3 and calculate the means with the new formula to see that the same answers are obtained.

The mean for the binomial probability distribution requires that the number of independent trials, n, be multiplied by the probability of success, p. The only catch with this formula is to identify success correctly. Sometimes a question defines a problem in such a way that the probability of failure is sought. Be careful not to define failure as success when calculating the mean.

EXAMPLE 7.11

Experiment Using the information from Example 7.5, calculate and compare the mean using the formula for a probability distribution given in Section 3 and the formula for a binomial probability distribution given here. A coin is tossed three times. Find the mean for the random variable x, the number of heads occurring.

Answer $\mu = \Sigma[x \cdot P(x)] = 1.5$, $\mu = n \cdot p = 1.5$

Solution The mean for a probability distribution is found by multiplying each x by its probability then adding all the products. Recall that the probability of each x in a distribution must be found. Using the probability distribution from Example 7.5, the mean was found to be 1.5. When performing calculations, show all steps.

x	$P(x)$	$x \cdot P(x)$
0	.125	0.000
1	.375	.375
2	.375	.750
3	.125	.375
		1.500

$$\mu = \Sigma[x \cdot P(x)]$$
$$= 1.5$$

However, tossing a coin and observing heads is a binomial, and the mean for a binomial is much easier to calculate. All conditions of a binomial distribution are met: There are three trials ($n = 3$); there are only two possible outcomes, heads or no heads; the probability of heads is .5 and remains constant; the probability (p) of success (heads) is .5 and the probability of failure (q) is .5; .5 + .5 = 1.0; and each toss is independent of the other tosses. The binomial mean requires n to be multiplied by p. The number of trials is 3, representing each toss. The probability of success on any one toss is .5:

$$\mu = n \cdot p$$
$$= 3 \cdot (.5)$$
$$= 1.5$$

The formula for the standard deviation of a binomial distribution is also easily calculated. It is the square root of the product of the number of trials, the probability of success, and the probability of failure.

Standard Deviation for a Binomial Probability Distribution

$$\sigma = \sqrt{n \cdot p \cdot q}$$

where

   n is the number of trials.
   p is the probability of success.
   q is the probability of failure.

The standard deviation is the square root of the number of trials multiplied by the probability of success and the probability of failure. As in the calculation of the mean for a binomial distribution, the standard deviation of a binomial distribution does not require the calculation of the full probability distribution. This makes their calculations easier and faster. The ease of these calculations makes the mean and standard deviation formulas preferred over the formulas in Section 3 when a probability distribution can be defined as a binomial probability distribution.

EXAMPLE 7.12

Experiment   Six members of congress are up for reelection. Each election is a toss-up. What are the mean and standard deviation of the number of members winning reelection?

Answer $\mu = 3$, $\sigma = 1.225$

Solution   This is a binomial. To summarize the conditions for a binomial, this problem has two possible outcomes: winning and not winning. There are six independent trials, representing the six members and their individual elections. The probability of success is a toss-up in any one election, which is a probability of .5 of success. The mean requires the product of n, the number of trials, and p, the probability of success. There are six independent trials. The chance of any one member winning has a probability of .5. Thus, $\mu = n \cdot p = 6(.5)$, or 3. The standard deviation is the square root of npq. The probability of q is $1 - p$.

Because $p = .5$, q is also $.5$ ($1 - .5 = .5$). Thus, $\sigma = \sqrt{6(.5)(.5)} = 1.225$. When performing calculations, show all steps.

$$n = 6 \qquad p = .5 \qquad q = .5$$

$$\mu = n \cdot p$$
$$= 6(.5)$$
$$= 3$$

$$\sigma = \sqrt{n \cdot p \cdot q}$$
$$= \sqrt{6(.5)(.5)}$$
$$= \sqrt{1.5}$$
$$= 1.225$$

A LEARNING AID

Mean and Standard Deviation of Binomial Distributions

Use the same information in the Learning Aid for Section 4 to find the mean and the standard deviation of the number of planes that can be expected to arrive on time.

To summarize the information, five governors are meeting in Washington, D.C. Each arrives separately and each arrival is independent of other arrivals. The probability that each plane will arrive on time is .4.

Step 1 This is a binomial, because there are only two outcomes defined as success and failure. Success occurs when a plane arrives on time. Success (p) is set at .4. Failure is 1 minus success, or $1 - .4 = .6$. There are five trials ($n = 5$), and each is independent of the others.

Step 2 To find the mean, multiply the number of trials to the probability of success:

$$\mu = n \cdot p$$
$$= (5)(.4)$$
$$= 2$$

The mean for a binomial distribution is much easier to find than the mean for other probability distributions. The full probability distribution is not necessary.

Step 3 To find the standard deviation, first multiply the number of trials by the probability of success and the probability of failure. Second, take the square root of the product.

$$\sigma = \sqrt{n \cdot p \cdot q}$$
$$= \sqrt{(5)(.4)(.6)}$$
$$= \sqrt{1.2}$$
$$= 1.095$$

CHAPTER 7 IN REVIEW

7.1 Which of the following fulfill the requirements for a discrete probability function?

a. $P(X) = \dfrac{x}{2 - x}$ for $x = 0, 1$

b. $P(G) = g - 1$ for $g = 0, 1, 2$

c. $P(H) = \dfrac{h}{4}$ for $h = -2, 0, 2, 4$

d. $P(Q) = \dfrac{q + 2}{6}$ for $q = -1, 0, 1$

7.2 Given the probability function

$$P(X) = \frac{x - 1}{15} \qquad \text{for } x = 2, 3, 4, 5, 6$$

a. Find the probability distribution.

b. Is it a true probability distribution?

c. Find $P(x \geq 5)$.

d. Find $P(x \leq 4)$.

e. Find $P(x = 5)$.

7.3 Find the mean, variance, and standard deviation of the probability function described in Exercise 7.2.

7.4 A consulting firm submits five independent proposals to the city council for the building of several new sports complexes, and each proposal has a probability of .4 of getting approved.

    a. What is the probability distribution of the number of successful proposals?

    b. What is the probability that no more than two proposals are successful?

    c. What are the mean and standard deviation of the number of proposals expected to pass?

7.5 In a recent year 36% of bureaucrats worked in the Defense Department, 25% worked in the Postal Service, and 39% worked in all other agencies. In a random sample of six employees, what is the probability that three work in the Defense Department?

7.6 Former President Reagan's appointments to the federal district courts consisted of 61% Protestant, 30% Catholic, and 8% Jewish appointees. In a random sample of 10 justices, list the probability distribution for the random variable of a Catholic being appointed.

7.7 If 75% of the public favors the death penalty for murderers, then what are the expected mean and standard deviation who favor the death penalty in a random sample of 20 people?

7.8 Sixty percent of the criminal cases coming before Judge Harris result in convictions. The judge will hear five independent cases tomorrow. What is each probability?

    a. Exactly 3 convictions

    b. No more than 3 convictions

    c. At least 3 convictions

    d. No convictions

    e. All convictions

7.9 Mr. Matthews drives to work everyday. He passes four traffic lights. If each light is independent of the others and each has a probability of .5 of being green what is each probability on any given day?

    a. All the lights will be green

    b. All the lights will be red or yellow

    c. More than two will be green

7.10 Of the babies born out of wedlock, 64% are born to African American females. In a random sample of 10 babies born out of wedlock, what is the probability that at least 6 were born to African American females?

7.11 In 1990, 30.5% of Americans lived in central cities, 47.2% lived in the suburbs, and 22.3% lived in nonmetropolitan areas. A random sample of 8 people is taken.

    a. What is the probability that at least 6 lived in the central city

    b. What is the probability that at least 6 lived in a suburb

    c. Find the mean and standard deviation of the number of people expected to be in the suburbs.

7.12 If n is 8 and p is .42, find the binomial mean and standard deviation.

7.13 If 85% of homes in the United States have a video-game player, what is the average number of homes that should have a video-game player in a random sample of 20 homes? What is the standard deviation?

7.14 If 44.6% of violent crimes in the country are solved by the police, what is the average number of crimes expected to be solved in a random sample of 15 crimes? What is the standard deviation?

7.15 If $n = 5$ and $p = .32$, what is $P(x \geq 3)$?

7.16 Eighteen percent of women say they've been physically abused by a husband or a boyfriend. In a random sample of eight women, what is the probability that none have been physically abused?

7.17 Eighty percent of Americans claim that they are middle class. In a random sample of 14 Americans, what is the average number claiming to be middle class?

7.18 If the probability of on-time arrivals for Trans Airlines is .92, what is the probability that all the next 10 flights will arrive on time?

7.19 Thirty-five percent of children in juvenile court receive probation. Of the next four cases, what is the probability that at least half will receive probation?

7.20 Find μ for $n = 25$ and $p = .25$.

8 Normal Probability Distributions

Chapter 7 combined the concepts of frequency distributions of discrete variables with probabilities, creating discrete or binomial probability distributions. Discrete variables were described as counts. Recall that there is another kind of variable, which uses measurements instead of counts. Variables that use measures instead of counts are called continuous variables. Continuous variables typically measure distance, time, or temperature. Many of the social sciences also measure continuous concepts, such as the degree of support for a candidate, the income level of a group of people, or the degree of racial integration of a community. Any variable that uses measures instead of counts is a continuous variable.

This chapter combines the concept of a frequency distribution of a continuous variable with probabilities. The probability distribution of a continuous variable can take many shapes. One of the most common shapes of a continuous probability distribution is the bell-shaped distribution. The bell-shaped distribution is also known as the Gaussian, or normal, distribution.

SECTION 1

Continuous Random Variable

A continuous random variable is a random variable whose values are usually found by measuring. The probability distribution of the continuous random variable can take on many shapes. The most commonly described distribution is the normal, or bell-shaped, distribution. Although the calculations of the normal distribution are very difficult, the use of a table to determine probabilities for any normally distributed random variable is relatively easy.

140

> **Continuous random variable** A variable that describes a measurement. It can take on an infinite number of values. When describing intervals, a continuous random variable can take on an infinite number of possible values in the interval.

Continuous random variables use measures instead of counts. They also can take on an infinite number of values. That is, the number of values a *continuous random variable* can have is limited only by the measuring device. For example, if a digital scale measures whole pounds, a person may weigh 175 lb. However, another scale may measure in tenths of pounds, and the same person may weigh 175.4 lb. On yet another scale, the person may weigh 175.49 lb. It is obvious that weight is a continuous measurement whose values are limited only by the measuring device.

Continuous random variables often describe a measurement between two designated points. The interval between the points is continuous if the number of possible values is infinite. If the number of values between two points is infinite, then the random variable is continuous. If the number of values is finite, then the random variable is discrete. For example, counting the number of desks in a classroom between the first row and the last row is a discrete count between two designated points. The count is finite, because the number of values is clearly represented by the number of desks. However, the distance between the desks in the first row and the desks in the second row is a continuous measurement. The distance between the two designated points is viewed as infinite, because the measuring device used can always be improved to give an infinite number of possibilities. A ruler marked in inches can be used, as well as one marked in quarter inches. A ruler can be improved to measure in smaller and smaller increments. Thus, it is said to have an infinite number of values.

EXAMPLE 8.1

Experiment   Determine if the following are discrete or continuous random variables:

   a. Number of students in class with black hair
   b. Time necessary to get from home to school
   c. Change in the temperature of the room during 1 h
   d. Number of pencils sold in the bookstore in 1 d

Answer

   a. Discrete
   b. Continuous
   c. Continous
   d. Discrete

Solution   a. The number of students in class with black hair is discrete, because it is a count. The values are represented by counting the number of students in the class with black hair.

b. The time necessary to get from home to school is continuous. Time is a continuous random variable, because it requires a measurement. Its measuring instrument is typically a watch, and the values the random variable can take on are limited only by the instrument.

c. As is time, temperature is a continuous random variable. The change in the temperature of a room must be measured with some sort of thermometer, whose values are limited by the thermometer itself. As technology is developed, thermometers will have fewer limitations.

d. The number of pencils sold in a day is discrete. To determine the number, one simply counts the number of pencils sold.

A LEARNING AID

Continuous Random Variable

You are asked to measure the change in your body's temperature between morning and night. Identify the three continuous variables involved in this experiment.

Step 1 Identify the events. There are three different events occurring: (1) measuring your temperature in the morning, (2) measuring your temperature at night, and (3) measuring the change in the temperature readings from morning to night.

Step 2 Address each event as a variable, noting whether the variable is continuous or discrete.

Variable 1: *Temperature in the morning.* Temperature is a measurement and is, therefore, continuous. Continuous variables measure; discrete variables count. Suppose your temperature is 98.0 in the morning. Your thermometer is the traditional type marked with .2° increments. In reality, you visually estimated your temperature; it looked closer to the 98.0 marking. But if you had a digital thermometer, it might have revealed your temperature to be closer to 98.1. Yet a third digital thermometer measuring in hundredths might reveal your temperature is 98.08. Every time the measuring device is improved, the measurement might

change. Thus, the measurement is limited only by the measuring device.

Variable 2: *Temperature at night.* Again, temperature is a continuous measurement limited by the measuring device. Your traditional thermometer now reads 98.8, but the digital thermometer reads 98.7, and the other digital thermometer reads 98.77.

Variable 3: *Change of temperature from morning to night.* This variable is a measurement between two points. It is referred to as an interval. Not only are the two temperature readings continuous, so, too, is the distance between them. It is easy to comprehend the mathematical difference between 98.0 and 98.8 (an increase of .8°). It may be a little more difficult to comprehend the continuous interval between these points, which is limited only by the measuring device. There are infinitely many possibilities in measuring intervals. One measuring device may be in tenths; another may be in hundredths. The distance between two points is a continuous variable.

Normal Probability Distributions

The normal probability distribution is yet another kind of probability distribution. Unlike those discussed in Chapter 7, the normal probability distribution describes the theoretical distribution of continuous data. Although the distribution could be described by a probability function, the calculations are much more difficult than the functions describing other probability distributions. However, there is a relatively easy way of calculating various probabilities using what is known as a standard z score and a probability table found in Appendix A.

Normal probability distribution A probability distribution describing continuous random variables. The distribution is plotted as a bell-shaped curve that is symmetric, with the mean, mode, and median in the center. It is also know as a normal curve.

The *normal probability distribution* can be plotted as a bell-shaped curve. The bell-shaped curve is a symmetric curve with its maximum height in the center and what are known as tails at either end. See Figure 8.1.

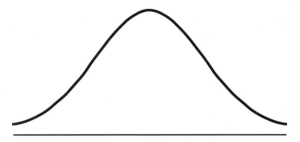

FIGURE 8.1   The normal curve

Many of the phenomena that social scientists study approximate the *normal curve.* For example, most Americans are ideologically middle of the road, or moderate. Americans pretty evenly disperse themselves around the middle, becoming more liberal on one side and more conservative on the other side. Both sides then almost consistently taper off equally in both directions as the numbers of people with increasingly liberal or conservative views diminish. This is illustrated in Figure 8.2.

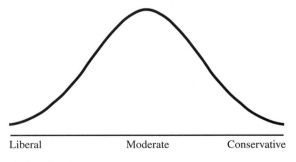

Liberal   Moderate   Conservative

FIGURE 8.2

The *normal probability distribution* has two parameters, μ and σ. Recall that the mean describes central tendency. All measures of central tendency are equal to the mean in a *normal probability distribution.* As expected by looking at the bell-shaped curve, the mean, mode, and median all occur in the center (Figure 8.3). Since the distribution is a probability distribution and is, therefore, theoretical, the mean represents a population and is represented by the symbol μ.

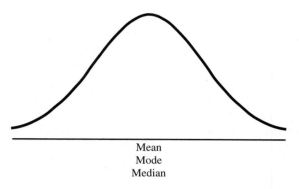

Mean
Mode
Median

FIGURE 8.3

The standard deviation, σ, describes dispersion around the mean. Recall that the standard deviation describes how far the average value of *x* deviates from the mean. Standard deviations in a *normal probability distribution* may deviate both to the left and to the right of the mean.

EXAMPLE 8.2

Experiment The mean height of students at a university is 5 ft 8 in., or 68 in., and the standard deviation is 2 in. On a normal probability curve, place the mean value in its appropriate place and also show three standard deviations above and below the mean.

Answer

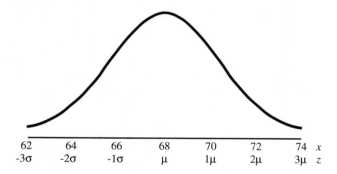

62	64	66	68	70	72	74	*x*
-3σ	-2σ	-1σ	μ	1μ	2μ	3μ	*z*

Solution Begin by drawing the curve. Place the mean in the center. Because the standard deviation is 2 in., one standard deviation above the mean must be 68 + 2, or 70, in. Two standard deviations above the mean is 72, and three is 74. To find the values corresponding to the standard deviations below the mean, repeatedly subtract 2 in. One standard deviation below the mean equals 68 − 2, or 66, in. Two standard deviations below the mean is 64, and three below the mean is 62. Notice that the distribution is normal; the heights of most students cluster around the mean, with other student heights deviating almost equally in both directions. The highest point in the center of the curve represents where most people are clustered.

It would be very cumbersome to calculate a probability distribution for each population and for each mean and standard deviation. To make the task much easier, the random variable that the distribution describes can be transformed into a standard normal variable known as a standard score, standard *z* score, or, simply, a *z* score.

> **Standard normal variable (standard score, *z* score)** A standard score that transforms any normally distributed random variable into a distribution that has an expected mean (μ) of 0 and whose standard deviation is 1. The formula for the transformation is
>
> $$z = \frac{x - \mu}{\sigma}$$

This formula allows the transformation of any random variable *X* into a *standard score*. The actual values of the mean and standard deviation are not important on the distribution itself. The transformation adjusts all means to a standard score, 0, and all standard deviations to a standard score of 1. This transformation allows the comparison of several values of *x* either from the same population or from different populations.

The standard score, *z*, can be either negative or positive. A negative *z* score falls below the mean, whereas a positive *z* score falls above the mean. Remember, the mean has a *z* score of 0. Standard *z* scores are simply standardized standard deviations.

Typically, *z* scores are rounded to two decimal places. The scores should be determined to at least three decimal places and rounded to two. A calculated score of 1.234 should be rounded to a *z* score of 1.23.

EXAMPLE 8.3

Experiment   Describe the probability distribution in Example 8.2 as a normal probability distribution. Example 8.2 states that the mean height of students at a university is 68 in. and the standard deviation is 2 in.

Answer

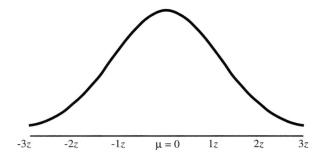

$$-3z \qquad -2z \qquad -1z \qquad \mu = 0 \qquad 1z \qquad 2z \qquad 3z$$

Solution   Begin with the curve. Unlike Example 8.2, the normal curve does not use the original values described in the problem. Normal probability distributions have the mean in the center and *z* scores at specific intervals around the mean. The mean is always 0. The other values can be transformed with the *z* score calculation. Begin with the value 70 (it does not matter with which value you start). In the formula, $\mu = 68$, $\sigma = 2$, and $x = 70$. When performing calculations, show all work.

$$z = \frac{x - \mu}{\sigma}$$
$$= \frac{70 - 68}{2}$$
$$= \frac{2}{2}$$
$$= 1$$

Because the values 70 and 66 are 1 standard deviation away from the mean, both will have a value of 1. The value of 70 is transformed into a z score of positive 1, as shown in the preceding calculation. The value 66 has a z score of negative 1. The next two values, 72 and 64, were originally two standard deviations away from the mean. Both will be transformed into z scores with absolute value 2, with 64 as negative 2, and 72 as positive 2. Notice the calculation for 64:

$$z = \frac{x - \mu}{\sigma}$$
$$= \frac{64 - 68}{2}$$
$$= \frac{-4}{2}$$
$$= -2$$

The same calculation must be done for the values 62 and 74. Recall these values are three standard deviations away from the mean. Three standard deviations are equivalent to z scores of -3 and 3. Note the calculations for the value 62.

$$z = \frac{x - \mu}{\sigma}$$
$$= \frac{62 - 68}{2}$$
$$= \frac{-6}{2}$$
$$= -3$$

EXAMPLE 8.4

Experiment   If the mean height of students in your school is 68 in. with a standard deviation of 2 in., what z score would a student have if the student is 63 in. tall?

Answer $z = -2.5$

Solution   This is a normal probability distribution, because height is a continuous random variable (it is a measurement). Begin by calculating the z score. The value of μ is given as 68 in., and σ is given as 2. The value of x that you are given is 63. When performing calculations, show all work.

$$z = \frac{x - \mu}{\sigma}$$
$$= \frac{63 - 68}{2}$$
$$= \frac{-5}{2}$$
$$= -2.5$$

Be sure not to drop the negative sign. The negative sign means that the z score is to the left of the mean. It may help to visualize the answer on the following distribution:

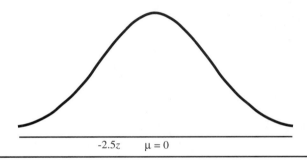

One of the most important uses of the standard z score is in describing the probabilities associated with intervals between specific values of z. This is accomplished by first dividing the distribution in half and then calculating probabilities from the center of the distribution out to a specific point. The full distribution has a probability of 1, with each half having a probability of .5.

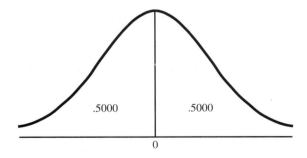

Before learning to translate z scores into probabilities, it is important to summarize a few key points:

1. z scores are not probabilities, but they can be translated into probabilities.

2. z scores can be negative or positive. The sign indicates on which side of the curve a value falls relative to the mean, which is adjusted to 0.
3. z scores are simply standardized standard deviations
4. Probabilities can only be positive, ranging from 0 to 1.
5. The full curve represents a probability of 1. Each half is .5000.

A LEARNING AID

Normal Probability Distributions

If the mean body temperature is 98.6° with a standard deviation of .4, what z score would a person have if her body temperature is 98.1?

Step 1 Determine if this is a continuous variable. Temperature is a continuous variable since it measures instead of counts.

Step 2 Decide if this is a normal probability distribution. Although you cannot be sure, continuous variables are typically described using a normal curve. Also, the question implies it is normally distributed, because it asks for the standard z score.

Step 3 Calculate the z score. The calculation requires an x value representing the person's temperature; here, $x = 98.1$. The calculation also requires the mean and standard deviation. These values are given: $\mu = 98.6$, $\sigma = .4$. Therefore,

$$z = \frac{x - \mu}{\sigma}$$
$$= \frac{98.1 - 98.6}{.4}$$
$$= \frac{-.5}{.4}$$
$$= -1.25$$

Step 4 Interpret the result. The answer tells you the person's body temperature is below the mean at -1.25 standard z scores. A standard z score is a standardized standard deviation. It can be used to calculate probabilities or to compare values across populations with different means and standard deviations. The following curve, represents the z score in relation to the mean.

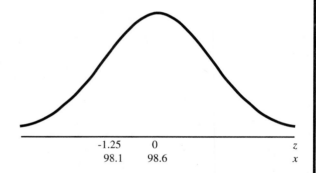

SECTION 3

The Normal Probability Table

Table A.3 in Appendix A describes the probabilities associated with standard z scores. It is important to become familiar with Table A.3, because it will also be used in several forthcoming chapters. Notice the curve at the top of Table A.3. The curve is a normal probability distribution that shows the mean, 0, at the center. The shaded area of the curve represents the area of the curve between the mean, 0, and z. This shaded area could be enlarged, reduced, or placed on the left of the curve, depending on the actual z score. Notice the values of z down the left of the page beginning with 0 and ending with 3.0. These values are given to one decimal place. To have two decimal places, the scores are combined with the z scores across the top row of the table that represent second decimal places. For example, to find the probability for a z score of 1.22, begin by going down the first column to 1.2. Then move over that row to the column corresponding to the second decimal place, .02 (see Table 8.1). The probability .3888, found at the intersection of the column and row, represents the z score 1.22 (1.2 + .02 = 1.22).

TABLE 8.1   Excerpt from Appendix Table A.3

z	0.00	0.01	0.02	...
0.0				
⋮				
1.2			.3888	
⋮				

The numbers in the body of the table are probabilities associated with the area of the curve from the mean 0 to a specific z score. All probabilities read from the mean out to a specific place. Negative z scores are found by symmetry. The negative sign of a z score represents the side of the curve on which the probability falls; it does not make the probability itself negative.

EXAMPLE 8.5

Experiment   Find and interpret the area of the curve associated with a z score of 2.12.

Answer $P(0 \leq z \leq 2.12) = .4830$. The probability associated with the area from μ to 2.12 is .4830.

Solution   Begin with Table A.3. Find $z = 2.1$ in the first column and 0.02 across the top row. The value at the intersection of the column and row is .4830. Placing the value on a curve helps visualize the area found.

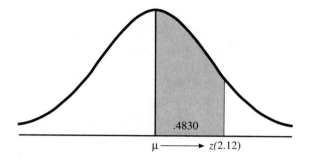

EXAMPLE 8.6

Experiment   Find and interpret the probability associated with the area of the curve for a z score of −3.06.

Answer $P(0 \leq z \leq -3.06) = .4989$; the probability associated with the area of the curve from the mean to the z score -3.06 is $.4989$.

Solution   Beginning with Table A.3, find the z score of 3.0 in the first column and 0.06 in the top row. Find their intersection, which is the probability $.4989$. Remember that the curve is symmetric. The negative z score value shows that the area of the curve is to the left of the mean. The z score can be negative but a probability is never negative. Find the probability of a negative z score in the same way you find that of a positive one. However, place the negative score and its probability to the left of the mean, as in the following curve:

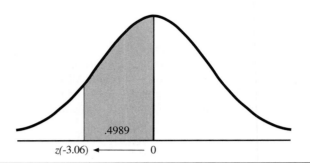

Remember, the table describes the probability associated with the area of the curve from 0 to a z score. To find the probability of the area of the curve beyond a specified point, subtraction is required. Remember, each side of the curve is associated with a probability of .5. If the probability of the area of the curve from the mean 0 to a specific point is known and if the probability of the whole curve is known, the probability beyond a specified point can be found by subtraction. Since the probability distribution of the normal curve is based on two symmetric halves of the curve, most answers can be found by subtracting from .5. For example, if the probability associated with the area from the mean 0 to a z score of 1.52 is $.4357$ (see Table A.3), the probability associated with the area beyond the z of 1.52 is found by subtracting $.4357$ from .5. That is, the probability associated with the area beyond 1.52 is $.5 - .4357 = .0643$. The notation for this probability is $P(z \geq 1.52) = .0643$.

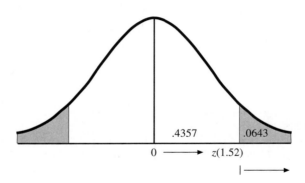

EXAMPLE 8.7

Experiment   Find $P(z \leq -.38)$

Answer $P(z \leq .38) = .3520$

Solution   Begin by looking up .3 in the left column of Table A.3. Read across the top row to .08 to find the second decimal place. You should find the value .1480 at the intersection. Remember, the negative sign shows that you are concerned with the left of the curve. Also notice that you are looking for the area of the curve to the left of the z score $-.38$. Because the probability .1480 is from 0 to $-.38$ and you know that the whole side of the curve is .5, you can subtract .1480 from .5 to find the probability associated with the remaining portion of the area. It is the probability associated with the following shaded area of the curve that you are asked to find.

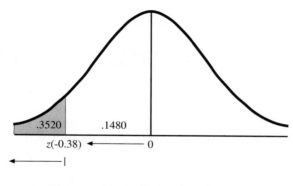

$$P(z \leq -.38) = .5000 - .1480$$
$$= .3520$$

A question involving combinations of areas could be asked. It is usually helpful to draw and shade the area of the curve under consideration. The visual helps place negative signs and decide whether it is necessary to subtract the probability from .5 or make any other adjustments. There are times when it may be necessary to add a probability to .5 or to add two probabilities together. Remember, even when adding probabilities, the final probability is always between 0 and 1, inclusive.

EXAMPLE 8.8

Experiment   Find $P(z \geq -.38)$

Answer $P(z \geq -.38) = .6480$

Solution   Find the probability associated with $-.38$ from Table A.3. The value at which .30 and .08 intersect is .1480. Placing the information on the curve and shading the desired area allows you to see whether you need to do any subtractions or additions. Notice that part of what you want is the area associated with the curve from the mean, 0, to $-.38$. This area has a probability of .1480. But you also want all the area of the curve to the right of $-.38$. This includes the whole second half of the curve. The probability associated with half of the curve is .5000. In this case, you want to add .1480 to .5000 to obtain the probability of .6480.

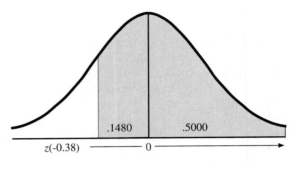

$$P(z \geq -.38) = .1480 + .5000$$
$$= .6480$$

EXAMPLE 8.9

Experiment   Find $P(.60 \leq z \leq 1.5)$

Answer $P(.60 \leq z \leq 1.5) = .2075$

Solution   You must treat the two z scores separately before finding the probability between them. First, find the probability from 0 to .60. Table A.3 shows a probability of .2257 for $z = .60$. The z score of 1.5 has a probability of .4332. You are asked to find the probability associated with the area between these two z values. To do this, subtract the smaller probability from the larger. The logic of this is that since both probabilities read from the mean to a specific point, you can subtract the smaller probability from the larger to leave only the area between them. Again, it is always recommended that you illustrate the area of the curve that you want to find.

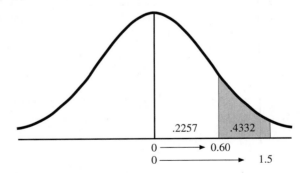

$$P(.60 \leq z \leq 1.5) = .4332 - .2257$$
$$= .2075$$

There are times that a probability is known or sought and the actual z score or original value x is not known. For example, a student may want to know what score on a final exam will yield a certain grade in the course. In this situation, the actual score is desired. If information about the class is available and a particular percentile ranking is known (the percentage that will give the desired grade), then it is possible to work backward using the normal curve. Algebraically, the z score formula is rewritten so that the value x is isolated on one side of the formula.

> **To Find the Value of x When Information About the Population Is Known**
>
> $$x = \mu + \sigma z$$
>
> where
>
> > x is the random variable value.
> > μ is the population mean.
> > σ is the population standard deviation.
> > z is the standard z score.

To find the value x, the z score must first be determined. It is usually easiest to translate the desired probability into a z score by drawing and shading the normal curve and reading Table A.3. For example, for a student to be in the top 10% of the class, the probability can be found by rewriting 10% as a probability and then working with the normal curve and Table A.3. Percentages are rewritten as probabilities by moving the decimal to the left two places. Thus, 10% gives a probability of .1000. The top .1000 of a normal curve is seen in the shaded area of the curve in Figure 8.4.

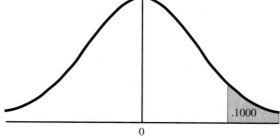

0

FIGURE 8.4

Because the normal curve is symmetric, with 0 in its center, the probability associated with the right half of the curve is .5. If .1000 is the value of the area outside of the curve near the tail, .4000 must be the value of the area under the remaining inner portion of the right half of the curve. See Figure 8.5.

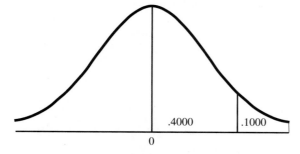

0

FIGURE 8.5 $.5000 - .1000 = .4000$

The probability reported in Table A.4 for the normal curve reads from the mean to a specific point. To find the point that is associated with the probability .4000, find .4000 in the body of Table A.3. The closest probability in the table is .3997. Read across the row and up the column to find the z score. The z score associated with the probability .3997 is 1.28.

The following steps summarize the procedure in finding a z score when a probability or percentile is given:

1. Draw and shade a curve to visualize the area desired.
2. Rewrite the percent or percentile as a probability.
3. Adjust the probability if necessary.
4. Use Table A.3 to find the probability or the nearest probability reported.
5. Use Table A.3 to find the z score associated with the probability.

Once the z score is obtained, the value can be inserted into the formula $x = \mu + \sigma z$ to find the value of x.

EXAMPLE 8.10

Experiment   The local cable company is installing cable in your neighborhood. You are told that the time required is a normally distributed random variable, $\mu = 24.6$ d, and $\sigma = 3$ d. You are planning to buy a new TV. You don't want to buy the TV until you are 95% sure that the installation is completed. How many days should you wait before buying the TV?

Answer $x = 30.48$ d

Solution   This is a normal distribution, because time is a continuous variable and thus is normally distributed. Also, the problem states that the variable is normally distributed. The problem asks you to find the value of x, the number of days to wait before buying a TV. To find the value of x you must find the mean and add to it the standard deviation multiplied by z.

Begin by finding z. The z score can be found by using Table A.3 to translate the probability given in the problem into a z score. The problem states that you want to be 95% sure that the installation is completed before buying the TV. 95% yields a probability of .9500. Using the normal probability distribution, the probability of .9500 is split on the left and right of the mean. This is done, because it is possible that the installation is done before normally expected or after normally expected. Half of the .9500, or .4750, is to the right of the mean, and the other half of .9500, or .4750, is to the left of the mean.

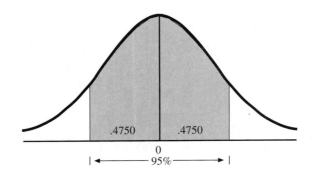

The probability .4750 is associated with the z score of 1.96. Using Table A.3, $z = 1.96$ is found by looking through all the probabilities and finding the probability closest to .4750. After locating the closest probability, read up and over to the columns to find the associated z score.

The equation for x requires the mean and standard deviation: μ was given as 24.6 and σ, as 3.

$$x = \mu + \sigma z$$
$$= 24.6 + 3(1.96)$$
$$= 24.6 + 5.88$$
$$= 30.48$$

A LEARNING AID

Normal Probability Table

If the average body temperature is 98.6° with standard deviation .4°, what is the probability that a person randomly chosen has a body temperature lower than 98.1°?

Step 1 Determine if this is a continuous variable and if it is normally distributed. Temperature is a measurement and is therefore continuous. Continuous variables can be represented by the normal curve.

Step 2 State the probability of interest. The question asks the probability of a person having a temperature lower than 98.1°. The statement is written:

$$P(x \le 98.1)$$

Step 3 Calculate the z score to enable you to use the normal probability table. The calculation requires an x value representing the person's temperature, 98.1°. It also requires the mean and standard deviation. These values are given: $\mu = 98.6$, $\sigma = .4$.

$$z = \frac{x - \mu}{\sigma}$$
$$= \frac{91.8 - 98.6}{.4}$$
$$= \frac{-.5}{.4}$$
$$= -1.25$$

Step 4 Find the probability associated with the z score $-$ 1.25. Table A.3 shows the probability for 1.25 is .3944. The negative z score also has the same probability but denotes the area of the curve to the left of center.

Step 5 Adjust the probability to represent the portion of the curve desired. This is easiest done by drawing and shading the normal curve. Remember the probability statement. The statement $P(x \le 98.1)$ can now be written using the z score. The adjusted statement now reads $P(z \le -1.25)$. This means you want the area of the curve from -1.25 to the left. However, the probability given in Table A.3 represents the curve from 0 to -1.25. The remaining portion of the curve can be found by subtracting the table probability from .5000. This subtraction is done because it is known that half of the curve has a probability of .5000. Therefore, the area of the curve to the left of -1.25 is .5000 $-$ .3944 = 1.056.

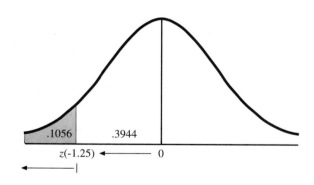

$$P(z \le -1.25) = .5000 - .3944$$
$$= .1056$$

Step 6 Restate the final answer. The probability that a person has a body temperature below 98.1° is .1056.

$$P(x \le 98.1) = .1056$$

Normal Approximation of the Binomial Distribution

The binomial probability distribution was introduced in Chapter 7. Recall that the binomial probability distribution describes probabilities for discrete variables. Also recall that the calculations for binomial probabilities become very difficult as n increases. In fact, calculating the binomial coefficient is difficult if n is much larger than 8 or 9. Table A.2 in Appendix A gives binomial coefficients up to $n = 20$. Rarely would one want to continue using the binomial formula for large samples. Fortunately, there is a method of approximating binomial probability by the normal probability distribution. The normal approximation of the binomial becomes closer to the actual binomial probability as n increases.

The approximation is based on two principles. The first principle is the law of large numbers. As the number of trials increases, the observational probability approaches the theoretical. Although the binomial distribution is theoretical, the distribution differs for each random variable and is very much affected by n. The effect that the sample size has on the probability is signified by the inclusion of n in the binomial probability function.

The second principle that explains why the normal distribution can approximate the binomial is that all samples taken repeatedly from a population will appear to be normally distributed regardless of the original appearance of the population. This principle is discussed in more detail in Chapter 9. The important idea here is that repeated observations of a discrete variable will appear normal even though the original population may not be normally distributed.

Figure 8.6 shows a binomial distribution illustrated as a histogram. For this distribution, $n = 8$ and $p = .5$. The histogram resembles a normal distribution. If the corners of the bars were smoothed, the distribution would resemble a normal distribution even more.

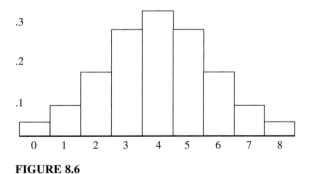

FIGURE 8.6

Now notice the distribution in Figure 8.7, in which a normal curve is superimposed over a binomial distribution. There are portions of the bars of the histogram that fall outside the normal curve, but other portions of the bars fall inside the curve. An adjustment must occur that will balance the overestimation with the underestimation. This adjustment is needed because of the two types of random variables. The binomial distribution represents a discrete random variable, whereasthe normal probability distribution represents a continuous random variable.

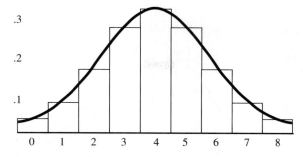

FIGURE 8.7

The actual process of approximating the binomial distribution with the normal distribution begins with an adjustment of the value of the random variable. Pay special attention to the bars of the histogram. The value of a discrete random variable actually occurs in the center of the bar. Because of the approximation, any probability needed that includes a bar must be adjusted to include the whole bar. For example, if the probability for the bar representing the value of 6 is required, the bar includes the values from 5.5 to 6.5. Because the normal curve describes the probability associated with areas of the curve, the probability of a discrete value 6 must include the area of the curve from 5.5 to 6.5.

When Using the Normal Distribution as an Approximation of the Binomial Distribution, the Value x Must Always Be Adjusted by $\pm$ .5.

The value of x may be adjusted in several different ways. If the probability of a specific value x is desired, two probabilities must be calculated, one for the lower edge of the bar and one for the higher edge of the bar. See Figure 8.8.

$$P(x = 6) = P(5.5 < x < 6.5)$$

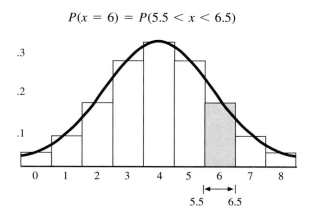

FIGURE 8.8

If the area in question is greater than or equal to a specific value, the value x must be adjusted to include the lower edge of the bar. This is accomplished by subtracting .5 from x. See Figure 8.9.

$$P(x \geq 6) = P(x \geq 5.5)$$

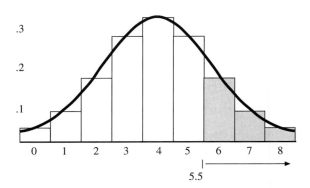

FIGURE 8.9

Alternatively, if the area in question is less than or equal to a specific value, the value x must be adjusted to include the higher edge of the bar. This is accomplished by adding .5 to the value x. See Figure 8.10.

$$P(x \leq 6) = P(x \leq 6.5)$$

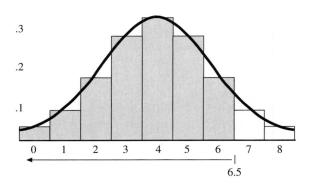

FIGURE 8.10

The rule is that if any portion of a bar is desired, then the whole bar must be included. This also means that when a value x is excluded, such as in cases where the probability of an area is greater than or less than some value, the whole bar must be excluded. Again, drawing and shading a curve usually helps visualize the necessary adjustment.

EXAMPLE 8.11

Experiment Restate the following discrete probabilities as required by the normal approximation of the binomial.

   a. $P(x \leq 2)$
   b. $P(x > 1)$

c. $P(x = 2)$

d. $P(x < 2)$

Answer

a. $P(x \leq 2.5)$

b. $P(x > 1.5)$

c. $P(1.5 < x < 2.5)$

d. $P(x < 1.5)$

Solution

a. The discrete probability for $x \leq 2$ means that the area includes 2 and below. To include 2 means that the whole bar representing 2 must be included in the calculation. The value 2 is adjusted by adding .5 so the upper edge of the bar is included. Because any distribution can be used to represent this, the distribution presented earlier is used. Notice the shaded area is the area in question.

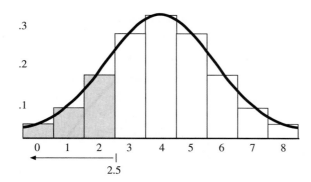

b. The probability for the area greater than 1 does not include the bar representing 1. Greater than means everything larger than 1, which means 2 or more. The bar representing 2 begins at 1.5. Notice the shaded area of the curve.

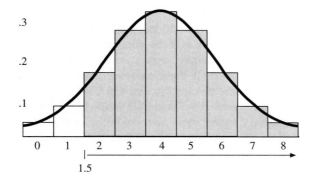

c. The probability that x is equal to 2 requires only the probability of the bar representing 2. The bar representing 2 has two edges; the lower edge begins at 1.5, and the upper edge ends at 2.5. These two values are used in any calculations for the area of the curve representing the value of 2.

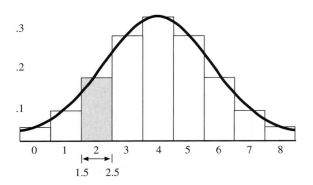

d. The probability of the area of the curve less than 2 does not include the bar representing 2. To have included the bar for 2, the problem would have read "less than or equal to 2." Because the bar representing 2 must be excluded, the desired area begins at 1.5.

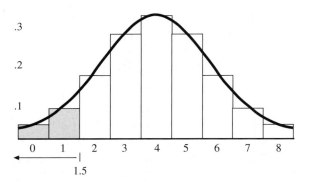

Once the adjustment of the random variable has been completed, the calculation of its probability proceeds as if the random variable were continuous. Recall that the calculation for the standard score z requires the population mean and the population standard deviation. If these parameters are not readily available, they must be calculated using the process discussed in Chapter 7.

The mean of the binomial is found by multiplying the number of trials by the probability of success. Caution about how the problem defines success is required. If the problem states what appears to be a failure and asks for the probability of the apparent failure, the failure is usually treated as a success.

The Mean and Standard Deviation of the Binomial Probability Distribution

$$\mu = n \cdot p$$
$$\sigma = \sqrt{n \cdot p \cdot q}$$

where

n stands for the number of cases.

p stands for the probability of success.

q stands for the probability of failure.

The *standard deviation* is the square root of the product of the number of trials, the probability of success, and the probability of failure.

After the adjustment is made for the random variable and the *mean* and *standard deviation* are known or calculated, the z score can then be calculated just as it was in the last section. The z score is calculated by subtracting the population mean from the value x (adjusted) and then dividing by the population standard deviation.

Calculation of the z Score for the Normal Approximation of the Binomial

$$z = \frac{x - \mu}{\sigma}$$

where

x is the adjusted random variable.

μ is the population mean.

σ is the population standard deviation.

EXAMPLE 8.12

Experiment   A government agency reported that 10% of all recipients are not truthful on their applications. What is the probability that in a random sample of 20 applicants, no more than 3 were not truthful on their applications?

Answer $P(x \leq 3.5) = .8686$

Solution   This is a discrete random variable. The random variable is a count of people. Counts are discrete variables. This is a binomial random variable, because all the conditions of the binomial exist. Briefly, only two outcomes are possible, success and failure. The sample is random, allowing for independent trials. However, an n value of 20 complicates the binomial calculations. Binomials can be approximated using the normal distribution.

The first step is to state the problem and adjust x. The normal approximation of the binomial always requires x to be adjusted by $\pm.5$. Drawing a histogram usually helps visualize the adjustment. The problem asks for everything lower than a value of 3 but not more than 3. Three itself is a valid value. The bar in the following partial histogram representing 3 illustrates that .5 must be added to 3 to obtain the whole bar. The probability statement is also stated after the histogram.

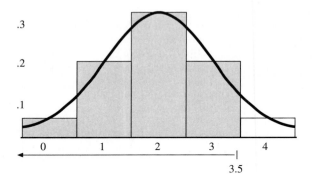

$$P(x \leq 3) = P(x \leq 3.5)$$

The next step is to find the mean and the standard deviation of the binomial distribution in order to calculate the z score. The mean is the number of cases multiplied by the probability of success. Even though the experiment seems to state a failure (not being truthful on an application), it also asks for the probability of that same event. Therefore, not being truthful will be looked at as the success. The number of cases, n, is stated as 20. A random sample of 20 people is taken. The probability of success, not being truthful, is .1, because 10% of people are reported not to be truthful. A percentage is rewritten as a probability by moving the decimal to the left two places, so 10% = .1. The mean is then calculated as follows:

$$\mu = n \cdot p$$
$$= 20(.1)$$
$$= 2$$

The standard deviation is the square root of the product of the number of cases, the probability of success, and the probability of failure. The probability of failure is found by subtracting the probability of success from 1.0. The probability of failure is $1 - .1 = .9$. The standard deviation is

$$\sigma = \sqrt{n \cdot p \cdot q}$$
$$= \sqrt{20(.1)(.9)}$$
$$= \sqrt{1.8}$$
$$= 1.34$$

A LEARNING AID

Normal Approximation of the Binomial Distribution

At the present time, incumbency advantage for House members seeking reelection is 92%. This means that a member is 92% certain of winning reelection. What is the probability that in a random sample of 50 House members, 44 or more will win reelection?

Step 1   Determine if this is a discrete or continuous variable. Counting the number of members winning reelection is a discrete variable. Discrete variables are counts, whereas continuous variables are measures.

Step 2   This discrete variable is also a binomial variable, because the conditions for a binomial discrete variable exist. Briefly, there are two outcomes, winning or losing; 50 independent trials; a probability of success of .92 (92% = .92); and a probability of failure of .08 ($q = 1 - p$). Because the binomial experiment requires a large n (50), it is possible to approximate the distribution using the normal curve.

Step 3   State the probability of interest. The question asks for the probability that 44 or more members will win. But when using the normal approximation of the binomial, you must adjust x to represent the inclusion or exclusion of the whole bar. In this case, 44 is desired as a possible value. To include 44, the lower edge of the bar representing 44 must be used. The lower edge of the bar for 44 is 43.5. Therefore,

$$P(x \geq 44) = P(x \geq 43.5)$$

Step 4   To calculate z, first calculate the mean and standard deviation. These parameters of the binomial are easily calculated. Note the information needed: $n = 50$, $p = .92$, and $q = .08$.

$$\mu = n \cdot p \qquad \sigma = \sqrt{n \cdot p \cdot q}$$
$$= 50(.92) \qquad = \sqrt{50(.92)(.08)}$$
$$= 46 \qquad\qquad = \sqrt{3.68}$$
$$\qquad\qquad\qquad = 1.92$$

Step 5   Calculate z. Note the information needed: $x = 43.5$, $\mu = 46$, and $\sigma = 1.92$.

$$z = \frac{x - \mu}{\sigma}$$
$$= \frac{43.5 - 46}{1.92}$$
$$= \frac{-2.5}{1.92}$$
$$= -1.30$$

Step 6   Find the probability associated with -1.30. Table A.3 gives the probability .4032 for a z of -1.30. The negative z score denotes the area of the curve to the left of center.

Step 7   Adjust the probability to represent the portion of the curve desired. Drawing the normal curve may help visualize the adjustment. The probability statement $P(x \geq 43.5)$ can now read as a z statement $P(z \geq -1.30)$. The probability associated with -1.30 involves the area of the curve from 0 left to -1.30 as well as the entire right half of the curve. The right half of the curve has a probability .5000, which must be added to .4032.

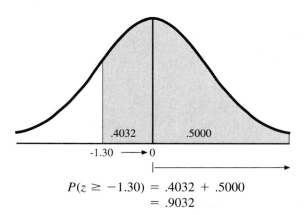

$$P(z \geq -1.30) = .4032 + .5000$$
$$= .9032$$

Step 8   Restate the final answer. The probability that 44 or more House members in a sample of 50 will win reelection is .9032.

$$P(x \geq 43.5) = .9032$$

The next step is to calculate the z score; z is calculated by subtracting the mean from x and dividing by the standard deviation.

$$z = \frac{x - \mu}{\sigma}$$
$$= \frac{3.5 - 2}{1.34}$$
$$= \frac{1.5}{1.34}$$
$$= 1.12$$

The final step is to transform the z score into a probability and make any adjustments necessary. The transformation is done by looking up the z score in Table A.3 and finding its associated probability. If you look up the z score 1.12, you will find the probability .3686. The adjustment necessary is to add .5 to the probability to represent the area of the curve to the left of 1.12 and the entire left side of the curve. Visualizing the area by using a curve usually helps.

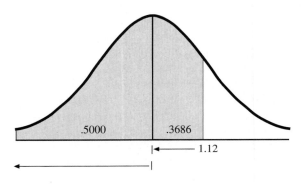

$$P(x \leq 3.5) = P(z \leq 1.2)$$
$$= .5000 + .3686$$
$$= .8686$$

CHAPTER 8 IN REVIEW

8.1 Find the area of the normal curve that lies between the following z scores.

    a. $z = 0$ to $z = 1.94$ **d.** $z = 0$ to $z - .49$
    b. $z = 0$ to $z = 2.42$ **e.** $z = 0$ to $z - .80$
    c. $z = 0$ to $z = .49$ **f.** $z = 0$ to $z - 1.96$

8.2 Find the area of the normal curve that lies between the following z scores.

    a. $z = -1.94$ to $z = 1.94$ **d.** $z - 2.00$ to $z = 2.00$
    b. $z = -1.12$ to $z = 3.00$ **e.** $z - .40$ to $z = .49$
    c. $z = -.89$ to $z = 3.56$ **f.** $z - 1.96$ to $z = 1.96$

8.3 Find the following probabilities:

    a. $P(z > 1.96)$ **d.** $P(z < 1.96)$
    b. $P(z > .96)$ **e.** $P(z < .49)$
    c. $P(z > 3.00)$ **f.** $P(z < -.49)$

8.4 Find the following probabilities:

    a. $P(-2.59 < z < -1.81)$ **d.** $P(.75 < z < 1.79)$
    b. $P(-2.57 < z < -.75)$ **e.** $P(1.0 < z < 2.00)$
    c. $P(-.95 < z < -.12)$ **f.** $P(1.96 < z < 2.45)$

8.5 What is the probability that $z = 0$?

8.6   What is the probability that z is greater than 0?

8.7   What is the probability associated with the area of the curve between the following z scores?

    a. −1 and 1

    b. −2 and 2

    c. −3 and 3

8.8   What is the z score associated with the middle 50% of the normal curve?

8.9   Find the z score associated with the shaded area of each curve.

a.

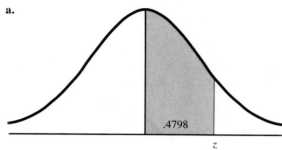

.4798

z

b.

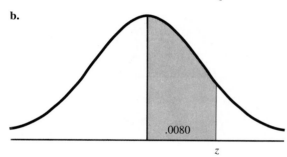

.0080

z

c.

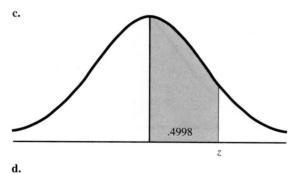

.4998

z

d.

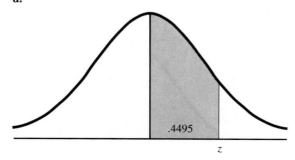

.4495

z

8.10   Find the z score associated with the shaded area of each curve.

a.

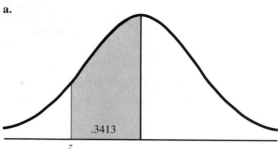

.3413

z

b.

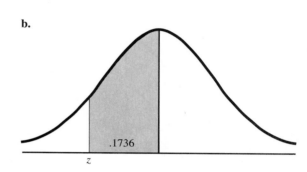

.1736

z

c.

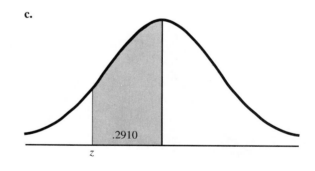

.2910

z

d.

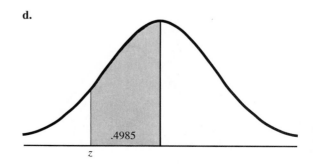

.4985

z

8.11   Find the z score associated with the shaded area of each curve.

a.

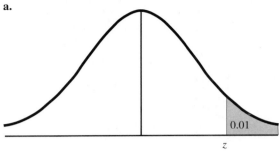

b.

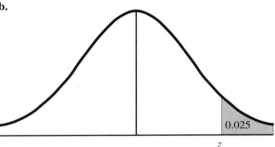

c.

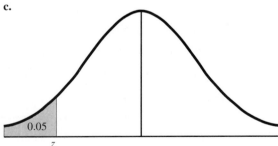

d.

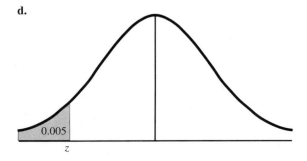

8.12   Find the z score associated with the shaded area of each curve.

a.

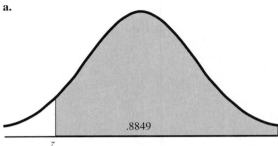

b.

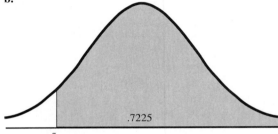

c.

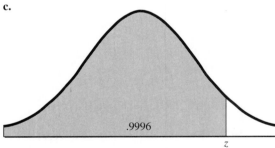

d.

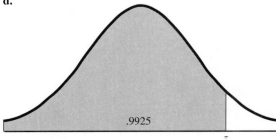

8.13   The amount of time a patient waits in the waiting room of a doctor's office is normally distributed with parameters $\mu = 15$ and $\sigma = 10$. Find the probability that a randomly selected patient will be in the waiting room

    a. Less than 10 minutes.

    b. Between 10 and 30 minutes.

    c. More than 20 minutes.

8.14   The number of crimes in a month in the central city is approximately normally distributed with $\mu = 550$ and $\sigma = 20$. What is the probability that the number of crimes in a randomly selected month will be greater than 570?

8.15   The percentage of eligible voters voting in presidential elections is normally distributed with a mean 52 and standard deviation of 2. In a randomly selected election, what is the probability that the percentage of eligible voters is

    a. Between 50 and 53?   **c.** Less than 50?

    b. Greater than 52?   **d.** Greater than 53?

8.16   The price of grapes in the farmers' market is a normally distributed random variable with a mean of 99¢ and a standard deviation of 5¢. Find the probability that on a randomly selected day the price of grapes is

    a. 99¢.   **c.** Between 90¢ and $1.10.

    b. Greater than $1.10.   **d.** Between 80¢ and 90¢.

8.17   If 40% of the employees of the university favor going on strike, what is the probability that at least 5 of the 8 employees in the registrar's office will favor going on strike?

8.18   A study was conducted on the effects of incarceration in state prisons. It was found that 10% of prisoners are helped by their prison experience, 60% of prisoners are harmed, and 30% are unaffected. Out of 100 prisoners, what is the probability that more than 15 are helped by their prison experience?

8.19   If 30% of urban youth are arrested before they reach the age of 18, what is the probability that in a family of 8 children, fewer than 3 children will be arrested before they are 18?

8.20   The average length of a bill passed by Congress is now 10.8 pages, with a standard deviation of 1.8. Find the probability that a randomly selected bill is between 11 and 12 pages.

8.21   In planning a no-smoking section of a room with a capacity of 240, what are μ and σ for the expected number of smokers?

8.22   Of college graduates, 18.4% smoke cigarettes. What is the probability that more than 56 smoke from a sample of 280 graduates?

8.23   If the average amount of caloric intake for a region is normally distributed with a mean of 2,189 calories, a standard deviation of 138, and a z score of 1.96, what is the value of x?

8.24   What is the value of z equal to the mean?

8.25   If a brand of low-fat popcorn has a mean of 3 grams of fat with a standard deviation of .65, what is the probability that a randomly selected bag contains less than 2 grams of fat?

9

Sampling Distributions

One of the most important aspects of doing research is obtaining data. Although the ideal situation may be to observe every element of a population, there are times when every element cannot or should not be used. When the whole population cannot or should not be studied, samples are usually taken. It is possible to describe a population after studying a sample drawn from that same population. For example, a light bulb manufacturer would not test every bulb in the factory to determine the average bulb's life. If he or she did, there would be no bulbs left to sell. Instead, the manufacturer would probably take a sample and use the sample to infer information about the whole population.

Sampling thus becomes very crucial in data analysis. To enable inference from a sample to a population, a sample must be representative of the population. A representative sample must reflect the characteristics of the population the researcher deems relevant. Many situations call for a specific kind of sampling technique, such as intentionally overcounting or undercounting an element in a population.

One of the most common goals in sampling is to produce an unbiased sample. This usually means that a good unbiased sample mirrors the population. Mirroring suggests that every element in the population is represented in the same proportion in the sample. For example, if in your school there are more males (55%) than females (45%), a sample should comprise the same proportions.

SECTION 1

Random Sampling

The most common sampling technique that results in a representative sample mirroring the population is known as a *random sample.*

> **Random sample** A sample in which every element of the population has an equal probability of being included in the sample.

Random sampling is also referred to as simple random sampling or probability sampling. Random sampling occurs when every element or object of a population has an equal chance of being chosen for the sample. The result should be an unbiased sample that mirrors the population.

Random sampling cannot usually be accomplished by simply choosing elements appearing to be representative of a population. A haphazard selection of samples tends to be overrun with biases. For example, standing at a street corner to interview people walking past will be biased against those driving or those passing a different corner. Also, although family members and neighbors may seem to be "average," using family members and neighbors creates a definite bias. Several acceptable procedures reduce the risk of bias in using a sample to infer to a population.

One procedure for simple random sampling requires a list of all the elements of the population and a random number table. The procedure usually begins by listing and numbering each element of the population. A random number table is used to decide which elements from the population list should be selected. The numbers on the table of random numbers correspond to the numbers assigned to the elements of the population.

Another procedure for selecting sample elements is to use the random number generator available on many calculators and computers. Again, the elements of the population must first be listed and numbered. The numbers on the list of elements can then be drawn upon by matching the number on the randomly generated list.

A third method for simple random sampling is to enter the list of elements of the population in a computer and allow the computer to generate a sample list. Some computer software programs can produce a number of sample lists, each different from the other but all considered random samples.

Another form of sampling that can usually achieve the same goal as simple random sampling—but with less time and effort—is known as systematic sampling.

> **Systematic sample** A sample determined by choosing every kth element after having begun by choosing the first element randomly.

In conducting a systematic sample, only one random number k is needed to get started. All other elements are chosen by systematically selecting every kth element thereafter. For example, if 5000 citizens vote at a particular precinct and a sample of 100 is needed, after randomly choosing the first voter, choosing every 50th thereafter will result in a random sample of 100. This is a much easier procedure than simple random sampling, which requires a full list and numbering of voters. Systematic sampling should not be used when a population is cyclical or repetitive with any distinct pattern. Systematic sampling would cause a serious error if used to select months of the year to determine unemployment. Unemployment tends to be cyclical—higher in certain times of the year and lower in others.

There are times when a characteristic of interest is not common among all elements of the population (for example, wanting only men, people with blonde hair, or students who are seniors). When this occurs, a stratified random sample is a practical way to partition the population, saving time and effort as well as reducing the sampling error.

> **Stratified random sample** A simple random sample taken from each subset or strata of the population.

A stratified sample can be used when testing whether hospital patients have had a cesarean delivery or a normal delivery. A random sample would require a list of all patients in a hospital, including men. It would be much easier, would require less time and effort, and would lead to fewer errors to stratify patients by sex and take a random sample of women, because only women deliver babies. Or better yet, only women in the maternity ward could be sampled. Another way to stratify is to identify patients in the various departments of the hospital and select a random sample of women in each department.

Another way of saving time and money is to use cluster sampling. Cluster sampling also partitions the data into subsets or clusters but then limits sampling to only a few of the subsets.

> **Cluster sampling** A technique that limits sampling to a few subsets of the population considered to be representative of the population.

Cluster sampling requires the subsets to mirror the population. Thus, information about the subset is necessary to determine if it is representative of the population. The subsets or clusters are first chosen randomly; then elements within the selected subsets are chosen randomly. One of the most common examples of cluster sampling occurs in public opinion polling. Because the country is too large to survey efficiently and the population of the country as a whole is similar to the population of certain states, sampling a few states may produce the sample results with a great savings of time and money. For example, 10 states may be randomly selected from the 50 states, followed by a random sample of perhaps 500 people in each of the 10 states. Each state represents a cluster and must have characteristics similar to the whole country.

Cluster sampling differs from stratified sampling in that cluster sampling requires the subset to be fully similar to the population, whereas stratified sampling is based on specific characteristics of interest to the researcher. Cluster sampling samples only a few of the subsets, whereas stratified sampling samples from every subset. Both require prior knowledge of the population and must be followed by simple random sampling once the subsets are identified.

Sampling is done to reduce the time and cost of observing every element of the population. The goal is to obtain a sample with minimum error attributed to the sampling procedure. Each sampling technique is not practical for every purpose. A researcher must choose a sampling technique carefully.

A LEARNING AID

Random Samples

Consider the population of a class of 99 students. Obtain a random sample of 20 students using a random number table.

Step 1 List all the students by name and assign each a number beginning at 01 and ending at 99. Each student must be listed to allow each the same chance of being selected for the sample. A list of the whole population is obtained with each element assigned a number. For example:

01 Smith
02 Valdez
⋮
50 Williams
⋮
99 Jones

Step 2 Obtain a random numbers table (see Table A.7). To use the table, begin anywhere on the table; then systematically read down, across, or diagonally. Numbers on the table correspond to numbers on the list of students. Since the list of students is numbered with two-digit numbers (01–99), Table A.7 should be read with two digits. (The table can always be adjusted for as many digits as needed by crossing over the columns.)

Step 3 Select the numbers from Table A.7. For example, a segment may read:

92 63 07 82
40 19 26 79
54 57 53 49

Reading across the table, the following 10 numbers are chosen: 92, 63, 07, 82, 40, 19, 26, 79, 54, and 57.

Step 4 Using the numbers just listed, select the corresponding numbers representing students. This list becomes the random sample and should represent the class, because no direct biases were created in the selection process.

92	Kahn	19	Todd	82	Jackson
40	Lane	57	Wright	79	Lin
54	Miller	07	McFarland		
63	Carter	26	Edwards		

SECTION 2

Sampling Distributions

Although the key to sampling is to make the sample representative of the population, it is unrealistic to believe that every sample will yield information that perfectly matches the population. One way of reducing the possible error resulting in using a sample is to increase the size of the sample. Recall that the law of large numbers states that as the number of cases increase, the observational probability approaches the theoretical probability. A researcher must determine the cost and benefit of increasing the sample size to achieve a reduction in the sampling error. There are times when it may not be possible or may be too costly.

Another way to reduce the error resulting from using a sample is to conduct several samples. Also, based on the law of large numbers, collecting several small samples may balance any biases found in any one sample. Information such as means and standard deviations of one sample can be compared to those of other samples. Conducting several samples is referred to as *repeated sampling*.

Repeated sampling Obtaining several samples from the same population.

EXAMPLE 9.1

Experiment   Using a Venn diagram, illustrate a repeated sample of the average age of students at your school. Use four samples of 10 students, and arbitrarily assign means to each sample.

Answer

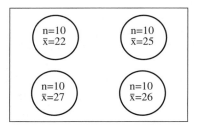

Solution   Draw the rectangle representing the sample space. Each sample is equivalent to an event and is represented by a circle. The experiment requires you to represent four samples; therefore, there are four circles. Each sample mean is arbitrarily set and noted in each circle.

Because the goal remains selecting a sample that represents the population, repeated sampling helps to create a set of unbiased samples that can be compared and combined to represent the population. The mean of one sample can be calculated and then compared to the mean of another sample. When all possible samples are taken, their means can be recorded and presented in a frequency distribution. This frequency distribution is transformed into a probability distribution. The probability of a specific sample mean occurring can be calculated and presented in a probability distribution, along with the probabilities of other means of samples of the same size. For example, if a class of five has students of age 18, 19, 20, 21, and 22, a sample of two would not necessarily be representative of the whole class and might cause a large error in inferring about the population. However, several samples of two could be taken and compared to each other to better decribe the population. A list of all possible combinations of two can be made, along with the mean for each sample.

Sample	Mean	Sample	Mean
(18, 19)	18.5	(21, 18)	19.5
(18, 20)	19.0	(21, 19)	20.0
(18, 21)	19.5	(21, 20)	20.5
(18, 22)	20.0	(21, 22)	21.5
(19, 18)	18.5	(22, 18)	20.0
(19, 20)	19.5	(22, 19)	20.5
(19, 21)	20.0	(22, 20)	21.0
(19, 22)	20.5	(22, 21)	21.5
(20, 18)	19.0		
(20, 19)	19.5		
(20, 21)	20.5		
(20, 22)	21.0		

A distribution of the sample means can be created by counting the number of times each of the sample means occurs. Because there are 20 possible sample combinations, the probability of each sample mean can be determined by dividing the number of occurrences of each mean by 20. This is referred to as a sampling distribution. See Table 9.1.

TABLE 9.1   Sampling Distribution of Mean Ages for Sample Size = 2

Sample Mean	Frequency	Probability
18.5	2	$\frac{2}{20} = .1$
19.0	2	$\frac{2}{20} = .1$
19.5	4	$\frac{4}{20} = .2$
20.0	4	$\frac{4}{20} = .2$
20.5	4	$\frac{4}{20} = .2$
21.0	2	$\frac{2}{20} = .1$
21.5	2	$\frac{2}{20} = .1$

Sampling distribution of the mean Probability distribution of the values of the sample mean from all possible samples of the same size.

As with all probability distributions, sampling distributions of the mean must meet the conditions required to make the distribution true. Recall from previous chapters that all probabilities must be no less than 0 and no more than 1 ($0 \leq p \leq 1$), and all probabilities associated with an event must have a sum of 1.0 ($\Sigma p = 1.0$). The sample statistic is known as $\mu_{\bar{x}}$ (sometimes written $\overline{X}$).

EXAMPLE 9.2

Experiment Using a sample of size three, illustrate the sampling distribution of the mean for {1, 2, 3, 4}.

Answer

Sampling Distribution, Sample Size = 3

Sample Mean	Frequency	Probability
2.0	6	.25
2.33	6	.25
2.67	6	.25
3.0	6	.25

Solution   All combinations of three digits must be listed so that the mean of each sample combination can be calculated.

Combination	Mean, $\bar{x}$	Combination	Mean, $\bar{x}$
(1, 2, 3)	2.00	(3, 1, 2)	2.00
(1, 2, 4)	2.33	(3, 1, 4)	2.67
(1, 3, 2)	2.00	(3, 2, 1)	2.00
(1, 3, 4)	2.67	(3, 2, 4)	3.00
(1, 4, 2)	2.33	(3, 4, 1)	2.67
(1, 4, 3)	2.67	(3, 4, 2)	3.00
(2, 1, 3)	2.00	(4, 1, 2)	2.33
(2, 1, 4)	2.33	(4, 1, 3)	2.67
(2, 3, 1)	2.00	(4, 2, 1)	2.33
(2, 3, 4)	3.00	(4, 2, 3)	3.00
(2, 4, 1)	2.33	(4, 3, 1)	2.67
(2, 4, 3)	3.00	(4, 3, 2)	3.00

There are 24 sample combinations. As the mean of each combination is calculated, only four different values appear: 2, 2.33, 2.67, and 3.0. A count of each of these values reveals each mean occurs six times. The sampling distribution presented as the answer records only the four different values of the mean, the number of times each occurred (usually omitted but presented for learning purposes), and the probability of that mean occurring. The probability is calculated by dividing the number of times each mean occurred by 24 total occurrences. Recall the probability formula, $P(A) = n(A)/n$. In this example, since each of the four means occurs 6 times, the probability of each is 6/24, or .25. The conditions of a probability distribution exist: Each probability of .25 is between 0 and 1 and the sum of all the probabilities is 1.0.

Something interesting happens when the theory of sampling distributions is combined with the theory of random sampling. A sampling distribution of sample means of a random sample has characteristics of the normal distribution. The mean of the sample means of the same sample size n approaches a normal distribution as sample size increases. Notice the distributions in Figure 9.1. As a sampling distribution of the mean moves from a sample size of 2 to a sample size of 5, the distribution begins to look like a normal distribution.

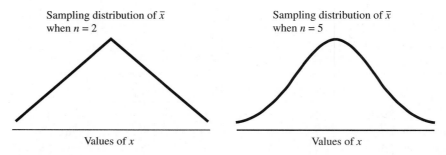

Sampling distribution of $\bar{x}$ when $n = 2$
Values of x

Sampling distribution of $\bar{x}$ when $n = 5$
Values of x

FIGURE 9.1

The sampling distribution will always approach a normal distribution regardless of the shape of the probability distribution of the original population. If the random variable X of the population is itself normally distributed (as in the case of heights of an adult population), then the means of a sample of any size, including 1, will be normally distributed. If the distribution of the random variable X of a population is skewed or even U-shaped, sample means of size 20 or more will approach the normal distribution. The general rule is that a sample of size 30 is nearly always considered large enough to use the normal distribution.

The sampling distribution of the mean is a theoretical probability distribution and, as such, has an expected mean value and standard deviation. Because the distribution is characteristic of the normal distribution, the expected value of the mean can be estimated by the mean value of the population; that is, the mean of the sample means is estimated by the mean of the population. The estimate is referred to as the *sampling mean,* or the mean of the means.

> **Sampling mean** The expected value of the mean of the sample means if random samples of size n are drawn from a population.
>
> $$\mu_{\bar{x}} = \mu$$
>
> where
>
> $\mu_{\bar{x}}$ is the sampling mean (mean of the sample means).
> μ is the population mean.

The Greek letter μ, a population parameter, represents the theoretical distribution. The subscript $\bar{x}$ represents the sample means. Putting the two together, $\mu_{\bar{x}}$ represents the mean of the sampling distribution of the sample means, which is known as the sampling mean.

EXAMPLE 9.3

Experiment   Suppose the average age of patients seeing Dr. Martinez is 35 with a standard deviation of 6. What is the expected value of sample means when the ages of five patients are sampled?

Answer $\mu_{\bar{x}} = 35$

Solution   The mean of the sample means, or the sampling mean, is always estimated to be equal to the mean of the population. This is true of all populations. Because the original population mean is given as 35, the mean of samples is likely to be 35.

The variability of the sampling distribution is more complicated than the mean. Variances and standard deviations are not normally distributed and become difficult to estimate when a sample size is small. Recall that the standard deviation depends on sample size. Repeated sampling increases the dependency on sample size. Any estimation of the standard deviation of the sample mean requires an adjustment when samples are small. The adjusted standard deviation becomes known as the standard error of the mean.

Standard error of the mean   Standard deviation of the sampling distribution of the sample means. It is calculated as

$$\sigma_{\bar{x}} = \frac{\sigma}{\sqrt{n}}$$

where

$\sigma_{\bar{x}}$ represents the standard error.
σ represents the population standard deviation.
$\sqrt{n}$ is the square root of the sample size, n.

Greek letters are used, because these parameters represent a theoretical probability distribution. The Greek letter σ represents the standard deviation of the population, and the subscript $\bar{x}$ represents a sample mean; thus, $\sigma_{\bar{x}}$ is the standard deviation of the sample mean, which is known as the standard error.

EXAMPLE 9.4

Experiment   Suppose the average age of patients seeing Dr. Martinez is 35 with a standard deviation of 6. What is the standard error of the sample means when the ages of five patients are sampled?

Answer $\sigma_{\bar{x}} = 2.68$

Solution   The standard error is the standard deviation of the sample means—that is, the variability between the sample means. Because the standard deviation depends on sample size, it must be adjusted to compensate for the repeated sampling of size 5. Although the mean of the means is simply equal to the population mean, the standard deviation of the means is the standard deviation of the population divided by the square root of the sample size. The population standard deviation is given as 6 ($\sigma = 6$) whereas the sample size is given as 5 ($n = 5$). The standard error is

$$
\begin{aligned}
\sigma_{\bar{x}} &= \frac{\sigma}{\sqrt{n}} \\
&= \frac{6}{\sqrt{5}} \\
&= \frac{6}{2.24} \\
&= 2.68
\end{aligned}
$$

A LEARNING AID

Sampling Distributions

The numbers 2, 3, 4, 5, 6, and 7 have a mean of 4.5 and a standard deviation of 1.71. Find the probability distribution of samples of size 2. What is the expected mean of the sample means and the expected standard error?

Step 1   A probability distribution for sample means is known as a sampling distribution. A sampling distribution lists all possible sample means of a specific size with the probability of each occurring. Begin by finding all the possible samples of size 2. Listing each and finding the sample mean of each will help create the sampling distribution. The following is a list of each possible sample of size 2, with the mean of each sample.

Sample $\bar{x}$		Sample $\bar{x}$		Sample $\bar{x}$	
(2,3)	2.5	(4,2)	3.0	(6,2)	4.0
(2,4)	3.0	(4,3)	3.5	(6,3)	4.5
(2,5)	3.5	(4,5)	4.5	(6,4)	5.0
(2,6)	4.0	(4,6)	5.0	(6,5)	5.5
(2,7)	4.5	(4,7)	5.5	(6,7)	6.5
(3,2)	2.5	(5,2)	3.5	(7,2)	4.5
(3,4)	3.5	(5,3)	4.0	(7,3)	5.0
(3,5)	4.0	(5,4)	4.5	(7,4)	5.5
(3,6)	4.5	(5,6)	5.5	(7,5)	6.0
(3,7)	5.0	(5,7)	6.0	(7,6)	6.5

Step 2   There are 30 different samples of size 2 that can be found. The 30 samples produce 9 different sample means: 2.5, 3.0, 3.5, 4.0, 4.5, 5.0, 5.5, 6.0, and 6.5. The frequency of each sample mean can be listed in a frequency distribution, which can then be redone as a probability distribution. List each possible sample mean and the number of times it occurred. Divide each frequency by 30 (the total number of occurrences) to obtain its probability.

Sample Mean	Frequency	Probability
2.5	2	.067
3.0	2	.067
3.5	4	.133
4.0	4	.133
4.5	6	.200
5.0	4	.133
5.5	4	.133
6.0	2	.067
6.5	2	.067

Step 3   The expected mean of the sample means is known as the sampling mean and is estimated to be equal to the population mean. The original problem stated that the population mean is 4.5; therefore, the estimated sampling mean is 4.5. The standard error is really the standard deviation of the sampling means and is equal to the standard deviation of the population divided by the square root of the sample size, n. Thus, the estimated mean and the standard error are

$$\mu_{\bar{x}} = \mu \qquad \sigma_{\bar{x}} = \sigma/\sqrt{n}$$
$$= 4.5 \qquad = 1.71/\sqrt{2}$$
$$= 1.71/1.41$$
$$= 1.21$$

Combining the information from the previous sections results in a theorem known as the central limit theorem. The central limit theorem is applied to sampling distributions approaching the normal distribution, where the mean of the sample means equals the population mean and the standard deviation of the sample means is the standard error.

Central Limit Theorem

Central limit theorem If random samples are taken from a population with a mean μ and a standard deviation σ, the sampling distribution approaches the normal probability distribution.

1. samples must be of equal size.
2. $\mu_{\bar{x}} = \mu$.
3. $\sigma_{\bar{x}} = \dfrac{\sigma}{\sqrt{n}}$.

The central limit theorem combines sampling distributions with the z score of the normal distribution. Because the central limit theorem requires that a sampling distribution approach the normal distribution, with the means equal and a standard error based on the standard deviation, the z score representing the normal distribution can be adjusted to reflect a sampling distribution.

z Score for Sampling Distributions

$$z = \frac{\bar{x} - \mu_{\bar{x}}}{\sigma_{\bar{x}}} \quad \text{or} \quad z = \frac{\bar{x} - \mu}{\sigma/\sqrt{n}}$$

The central limit theorem is of great use because it describes all types of sampling distributions, regardless of the shape of the original population. Because the mean from a large sample will have a normal probability distribution, the adjusted z calculation becomes one of the most common tests of sample means.

EXAMPLE 9.5

Experiment Suppose the probability distribution of incomes in the United States is skewed to the right with a mean of $20,000 and a standard deviation of $8,000. If a random sample of 100 people is taken from the U.S. population, what will be the shape of the sampling distribution of the sample means?

Answer A normal, bell-shaped distribution.

Solution According to the central limit theorem, the probability distribution of sample means will be a normal probability distribution. This is true regardless of the fact that the original population is skewed. Notice the two distributions:

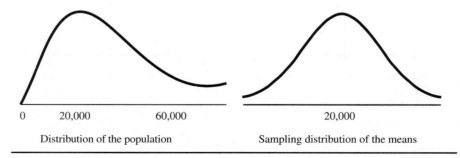

0 20,000 60,000	20,000
Distribution of the population	Sampling distribution of the means

It is very important to understand the difference between the z score calculation presented in Chapter 8 and the adjusted calculation presented for sampling distributions. The z score calculation of Chapter 8 is applied when finding the probability of one element of a population. For example, finding the probability of a cantaloupe in a farmer's field (one cantaloupe from a whole field) having a specific weight is to find the probability of one element of a population. In the calculation $(x - \mu)/\sigma$, the population mean is subtracted from one element or value of the random variable. The adjusted z score calculation, $(\bar{x} - \mu_{\bar{x}})/\sigma_{\bar{x}}$, using a sampling distribution gives the probability of a value of a sample mean (not one element) from all possible sample means. The value of the mean of means must be subtracted from a value of one specific sample mean. For example, to find the probability of a mean of a sample of 10 cantaloupes after the mean of all samples of 10 has been estimated is to find the probability of a value of a sample mean from the sampling mean.

The process of applying the new z score calculation is the same as in Chapter 8. The first step is to identify the probability statement. The probability statement requires the notation of the sample mean and a value. For example, a problem may require finding the probability that a sample mean is less than 10. The statement is written $P(\bar{x} < 10)$. The second step is to calculate the z score using its adjusted formula. The z score formula when a sample mean is involved is the adjusted formula $(\bar{x} - \mu_{\bar{x}})/\sigma_{\bar{x}}$. Use the value from the probability statement as the value represented by $\bar{x}$. The mean of the means is estimated as the population mean. Thus $\mu_{\bar{x}} = \mu$. The standard error requires the population standard deviation to be divided by the square root of n, the number of cases in the sample. The actual computational formula is

$$z = \frac{\bar{x} - \mu}{\sigma/\sqrt{n}}$$

The third step is to transform the calculated z score into a probability using Table A.3. The value related to the z score is written as a probability by rounding the z score to two decimal places. The value found by reading the intersection of the appropriate left column and top row represents the probability of the z score. The final step is to place the probability on a normal curve and make any adjustments the problem may require. Drawing and shading a curve usually helps visualize whether adjustments are required. To find the area on the outside tails of the curve, the probability found in Table A.3 must be subtracted from .5000. To find the area in the center of the curve that overlaps parts of both sides, the probabilities found in Table A.3 must be added. There are times when adding and subtracting may be required. Interpreting the probability is the same as in earlier chapters. A probability approaching 1.0 is very strong and means an event is likely to occur. A probability approaching 0.0 is very weak and means the event is not likely to occur. Probabilities range from 0.0 to 1.0, inclusive. Probabilities are never negative.

Remember that the z score itself is the standardized value of the random variable. It measures the number of standardized standard deviations a value is from the mean, where the mean is adjusted to 0. Watch for checks that may signal errors. For example, if a sampling mean is 5 and a sample value is 7, the z score must be positive and the score is placed on the right side of the curve. A negative z score is placed on the left side of the curve, but its probability is still positive. Also remember that there may be times when the area needed involves both sides of the curve. A probability statement may ask for the area between two sample means (for example, $P(10 \leq \bar{x} \leq 15)$). A calculation for each sample value is needed before each z score is transformed into a probability and is placed on a curve. Shading the areas of the curve or using arrows helps visualize how probabilities need to be adjusted.

EXAMPLE 9.6

Experiment   Suppose the probability distribution of incomes in the United States is skewed to the right with a mean of $20,000 and a standard deviation of $8000. What is the probability that a sample of 10 would produce a sample mean less than $25,000?

Answer $P(\bar{x} \leq 25,000) = .9756$

Solution   Begin by asking if this is a normal distribution. Income is a continuous variable and its sampling distribution approximates a normal distribution regardless of the shape of the original population. The key words in the problem implying this is a sampling distribution are "a sample of 10." The process begins by stating the probability question. The problem requires the probability that a sample mean is less than 25,000. A sample mean is represented by $\bar{x}$; therefore, the probability statement is $P(\bar{x} \leq 25,000)$.

The calculation of the z score involves the adjusted formula that reflects the use of a sampling distribution. Remember $\mu_{\bar{x}} = \mu$ and the standard error equals the standard deviation divided by the square root of the sample size. The following information is found in the wording of the original problem: $\bar{x} = 25,000$, $\mu = 20,000$, $\sigma = 8,000$, and $n = 10$.

$$
\begin{aligned}
z = \frac{\bar{x} - \mu}{\sigma/\sqrt{n}} &= \frac{25,000 - 20,000}{8000/\sqrt{10}} \\
&= \frac{5,000}{8,000/3.16} \\
&= \frac{5000}{2532.65} \\
&= 1.97
\end{aligned}
$$

A calculated z score transforms the original sample value to standard scores. It shows that a sample mean of 25,000 is 1.97 standardized standard deviations above the sampling mean of 20,000. The z score must be transformed into a probability using Table A.3. The z score 1.97 yields a probability of .4756. This may not be the final answer. The probability must be considered in terms of the curve to determine if any adjustments are needed. In the following curve, the area needed is not only that represented by .4756 but also the entire other half of the curve. Half of the curve has a probability of .5000. The probability of the curve from 1.97 to 0 must be added to the probability of the left half of the curve. Therefore, the probability from 1.97 through the left half of the curve is .4756 + .5000, or .9756. A probability of .9756 is very high and suggests that a sample of incomes producing a mean of less than $25,000 is very likely.

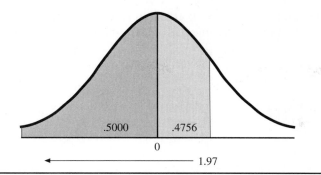

.5000   .4756

0

1.97

EXAMPLE 9.7

Experiment   Suppose the average number of points scored in a football game is normally distributed with $\mu = 44$ and $\sigma = 4$. What is the probability that a sample of 12 games would produce a mean between 42 and 47 points?

Answer $P(42 \leq \bar{x} \leq 47) = .9524$

Solution   This is a normal distribution, because the problem states that it is normally distributed, even though scores of a game are not a continuous variable. Also, since the problem asks for the probability of a sample of 12 games, the central limit theorem states that sampling distributions approach the normal distribution. The probability statement requires two values instead of the usual one. The problem asks the probability that a sample mean will be between 42 and 47. The statement is written $P(42 \leq \bar{x} \leq 47)$. Although the problem does not state these values as inclusive, a normal distribution treats all variables as continuous and as being included in the probability statement. The adjusted z formula is used for sample means. The calculations are needed for each value in the statement. The basic information is given in the problem: $\bar{x} = 42$, $\bar{x} = 47$, $\mu = 44$, $\sigma = 4$, and $n = 12$. The calculations are as follows.

$$\text{For } \bar{x} = 42: \quad z = \frac{\bar{x} - \mu}{\sigma/\sqrt{n}} \qquad \text{For } \bar{x} = 47: \quad z = \frac{\bar{x} - \mu}{\sigma/\sqrt{n}}$$

$$= \frac{42 - 44}{4/\sqrt{12}} \qquad\qquad = \frac{47 - 44}{4/\sqrt{12}}$$

$$= \frac{-2}{4/3.46} \qquad\qquad = \frac{3}{4/3.46}$$

$$= \frac{-2}{1.16} \qquad\qquad = \frac{3}{1.16}$$

$$= -1.72 \qquad\qquad = 2.58$$

The z scores must be transformed into probabilities using Table A.3. The z score -1.72 has a probability of .4573. The z score -1.72 is placed on the left of the curve. Its associated probability, .4573, is not negative, because probabilities are never negative. The other z score must also be transformed into a probability. Using Table A.3, the z score 2.58 has a probability of .4951. These probabilities should be placed on a curve to help visualize the adjustment needed.

The shaded area of the curve is the area requested by the original probability statement. The probabilities must be added to find the area from −1.72 to 2.58:

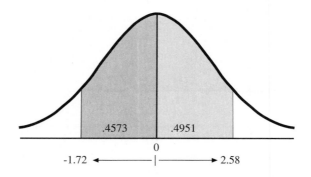

$$.4573 + .4951 = .9524$$

Therefore, the probability that a sample of 12 games produces a sample mean score from 42 to 47 is .9524, which is very likely to occur. Remember, a probability approaching 1.0 means the event is very likely.

A LEARNING AID

Central Limit Theorem

Suppose the daily sales at the local delicatessen average $600, with a standard deviation of $50. What is the probability that a sample of 10 randomly selected days produces a sample mean above $650?

Step 1   Identify the problem as a sampling distribution. The variable, money, is a continuous variable with a normal distribution whose sampling distribution is also normally distributed. The central limit theorem states that the distribution will approach the normal distribution when samples are taken in the case where the mean of the means is equal to the population mean and the standard error is equal to the population standard deviation divided by the square root of the number of cases sampled. This problem asks about the probability of a sample mean, thus qualifying as a sampling distribution.

Step 2   Identify the probability statement. The problem asks for the probability of a sample mean above (greater than) 650. The statement is written $P(x > 650)$.

Step 3   Calculate the z score using the adjusted z formula representing sampling distributions. The population mean, μ, is given as 600, the standard deviation is $\sigma = 50$, the number of cases is $n = 10$, and the sample mean is $\bar{x} = 650$.

$$z = \frac{\bar{x} - \mu}{\sigma/\sqrt{n}} = \frac{650 - 600}{50/\sqrt{10}} = \frac{50}{50/3.16}$$

$$= \frac{50}{15.82} = 3.16$$

Step 4   Transform the z score into a probability by using Table A.3. The table reveals the z score 3.16 yields a probability of .4992.

Step 5   Place the probability on a curve to visualize any needed adjustments. The desired area is not the area of the curve represented by the probability .4992. Table A.3 gives probabilities associated with the area of the curve from the mean 0 out to a z score. The area desired in this problem is to the right of the z score. Because half of the curve has a probability of .5000, the area from .4992 out to the tail is found by subtracting .4992 from .5000:

$$.5000 - .4992 = .0008$$

Step 6   Interpret the results. The probability .0008 represents the probability that a sample of 10 daily sales would produce a mean greater than $650. Because .0008 is very small, it can be said that such a sample mean is very unlikely to occur.

Table A.3 reports the probability associated with the area of the curve from the mean 0 to a *z* score. The shaded areas on the normal curves in Figure 9.2 illustrate the possible adjustments needed to the reported probability values from Table A.3. The *z* scores 1.0 and −1.0 are used as illustration.

Shading and Adjusting Probabilities on the Normal Curve

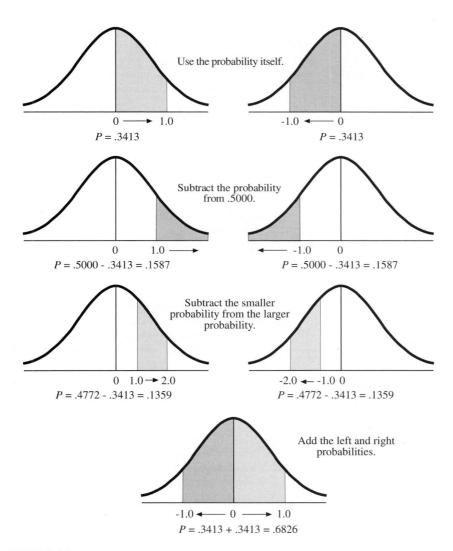

$P = .3413$

Use the probability itself.

$P = .3413$

$P = .5000 - .3413 = .1587$

Subtract the probability from .5000.

$P = .5000 - .3413 = .1587$

$P = .4772 - .3413 = .1359$

Subtract the smaller probability from the larger probability.

$P = .4772 - .3413 = .1359$

Add the left and right probabilities.

$P = .3413 + .3413 = .6826$

FIGURE 9.2

CHAPTER 9 IN REVIEW

9.1   Find the sampling distribution of samples of size 2 from the population 1, 3, 5, 7. Does it meet the requirements of a true probability distribution?

9.2   The ages of employees in the secretarial pool are 20, 25, 30, and 40. Find the probability distribution of samples of size 2.

9.3   Find the probabilities associated with the following z scores.

    a. $z = 1.25$ **c.** $z = 0.67$
    b. $z = -1.25$ **d.** $z = -3.12$

9.4   Find the probabilities associated with the area of the curve between the following z scores.

    a. $-.67$ to $.67$ **c.** -2.00 to 2.00
    b. -2.12 to 1.34 **d.** -1.50 to 1.29

9.5   Find the probabilities associated with the area of the curve between the following z scores.

    a. $-.67$ to -2.12 **c.** 0 to -2.00
    b. 1.34 to 2.00 **d.** 1.29 to 1.99

9.6   In studying areas of a city in order to determine voter attitudes toward a proposal to establish casino gambling, what type of sample would be most appropriate?

9.7   Subscribers in a health care plan visited the clinic on average 4.6 times a year, with a standard deviation of 2.0. An interview sampled 36 subscribers on a specific day. What is the probability that these subscribers had a sample mean of fewer than 5 visits a year?

9.8   What kind of sample is appropriate to determine the mean number of children under 12 y of age for the 2500 employees in an auto plant in Detroit, Michigan?

9.9   What kind of sample is appropriate in selecting voters in an exit poll?

9.10   Business travelers are on the road an average of 10 d a month, with a standard deviation of 3 d. What is the sampling mean and standard error for a sample of 40 business travelers?

9.11   A cigarette company claims that smokers smoke a mean of 35 cigarettes a day, with a standard deviation of 6 cigarettes.

    a. What is the expected sampling mean of a sample of 25 smokers?

    b. What is the standard error of the sample?

    c. What is the probability that the sample of 25 will produce a mean of smoking not more than 33 cigarettes a day?

9.12   How many samples of size 2 can be obtained from a population containing the numbers 1, 3, and 5?

9.13   Explain the advantages of random sampling.

9.14   If Ms. Young spends an average 44.1 h a week in her office, with a standard deviation of 4.2, what is the probability that a sample of a 10 wk will produce a mean less than 40 h?

9.15   The mean weight of employees at the oil-distribution center is 178 lb, with a standard deviation of 12.5.

    a. What is the probability that Mr. Bauer, an employee at the company, weighs more than 180 lb?

    b. What is the probability that a random sample of 30 employees will produce a sample mean greater than 180 lb?

    c. Explain why the answers in a and b are not the same.

9.16   A population is normally distributed with a mean 100 and a standard deviation 16. What is the probability that a sample of 40 will produce a sample mean between 95 and 105?

9.17   Students spend on average 12.5 h a week studying for a statistics course, with a standard deviation of 4.

    a. What is the expected mean of a sample of 30 students?

    b. What is the standard error of the mean for the sample?

    c. What is the probability that students in the sample of 30 spend more than 12.5 h studying?

    d. What is the probability that students in the sample of 30 spend less than 12.5 h studying?

    e. What is the probability they would spend less than 13 h studying?

    f. What is the probability they would spend more than 13 h studying?

9.18   Explain the meaning of a probability of 1.0.

9.19   The expected number of absences in a school year for college students is 8.9 and the standard deviation is 2.0 d.

    a. What is the expected sampling mean for absences of a randomly selected group of 40 college students?

    b. What is the standard error for absences of the sample?

    c. What is the probability that the mean of the random sample of 40 college students will be more than 9.4 d?

9.20   A professor believes students cheat on average 5 times a semester, with a standard deviation of 3. What is the probability that your class of 30 students will have a sample mean for cheating less than 6 times a month?

9.21   True or false?

    a. Probabilities are never negative.

    b. To find the area of the normal curve on the outside of the tail, the probability is added to .5000.

    c. A z score represents standardized means.

    d. The calculation of the standard error is equal to the population standard deviation.

9.22   True or false?

    a. A sampling distribution of means approaches a normal curve regardless of the shape of the distribution of the original population.

    b. The sampling mean equals the population mean.

    c. One way of reducing sampling error is to conduct several samples.

    d. Random samples should never mirror the population.

Inferential Statistics

SECTION 1   The Null and Alternative Hypotheses

SECTION 2   Hypothesis Testing Using the Classical Approach

SECTION 3   Hypothesis Testing Using *P*-Values

SECTION 4   Confidence Intervals

Probabilities and sampling distributions, as presented in previous chapters, determine the likelihood of an event occurring when information is known about the population. However, information about the population may not be known or be able to be determined. For example, can all the fish in Lake Michigan be measured to determine their average length? Though some may answer yes, such a project seems almost impossible, and the consequences would be severe. Sampling distributions require that every fish be measured and that the mean of several samples be estimated by the population mean. But if the population mean cannot be determined, a sampling mean has little use.

Inferential statistics works in the opposite fashion. Instead of predicting sample information from a population, inferential statistics predicts population information from a sample. More importantly, decisions can be made about various hypotheses that may lead to accepting or discarding policies, behavior, and even theories.

The goal is to make inferences (thus the name inferential statistics) about a population using sample data. Most inferences are based on one or two samples, usually concerning the mean, variances, and the binomial probability *p*.

SECTION 1

The Null and Alternative Hypotheses

Inferential statistics allow testing of hypotheses, which leads to theory building. The nature of theory building does not allow a theory to be proven absolutely; such is also the case with hypotheses. The rule is that theories and hypotheses can be disproved but cannot be proven. Hypotheses must be accepted as true until such time that they are proven false. A theory or hypothesis cannot be proven at all times in all situations. But when tested, if the theory fails, it is clear that it is not true.

Consider, for example, the theory that the sun will rise in the east and will set in the west. There is no way to test today what will happen tomorrow; a scientist cannot guarantee the theory that the sun will rise in the east tomorrow and every day for eternity. Yet, the theory that the sun will rise tomorrow in the east and set in the west remains an accepted theory until such time that it can be proven to be false—until it does not rise in the east and set in the west.

Another example of testing hypotheses involves the theory that the world was flat. By the laws of theory and hypothesis testing, the theory must be accepted as true until proven otherwise. Christopher Columbus, among others, doubted the theory and set out to prove that the world was not flat. It was only when Columbus presented irrefutable proof that the world was not flat that the theory could be rejected for the new theory—the world is round.

Inferential statistics usually begins with testing hypotheses about the differences between the value of samples and the estimated value of the population. It is the science of making decisions about the descriptive statistics that have been collected from a population or from a sample. A population parameter is usually hypothesized and compared to a sample statistic. Hypotheses are divided into two categories: null and alternative.

> **Null hypothesis** A statement that there is no difference between the hypothesized value of the population parameter and a sample statistic. It carries the benefit of the doubt. It is denoted by H_0.

The null hypothesis states that there is no difference between the hypothesized population parameter and the value of a sample statistic. It is the hypothesis that is tested and is denoted by H_0. It gets its name from the fact that it states there is no difference between the population and the sample other than what can be reasonably attributed to chance. It is also the hypothesis that must be proven false before it can be rejected. This means that the null hypothesis must be favored in the case of doubt. It must be accepted as true until there is definite evidence showing it to be false.

> **Alternative hypothesis** A statement that the value of the population parameter is different from that specified by the null hypothesis. It carries the burden of proof and is denoted by H_1 or H_a.

The alternative hypothesis is a statement that the value of the population parameter is different than that stated in the null hypothesis. The alternative hypothesis carries the burden of proof. It is denoted by H_1 or H_a. If the alternative hypothesis is found to be true, then the null hypothesis can be rejected.

In verifying scientific hypotheses, the burden of proof falls on the alternative hypothesis. It is the one that must be proven. The null hypothesis is accepted as true until such time that an alternative hypothesis disproves it. Again, the null hypothesis is given the benefit of the doubt and must be disproved. It can be rejected only when an alternative hypothesis is used to disprove it.

In the example of the theory about the sun rising every day, the null hypothesis is that the sun will rise in the east and set in the west. It must be accepted as true until tested and proven false. An alternative hypothesis must challenge the theory. It could state that tomorrow the sun will not rise in the east and set in the west. If, in the test, the sun does not rise in the east and set in the west, then the null hypothesis can be rejected in favor of the alternative. If the test supports the original theory set out in the null hypothesis, then the theory again passes the test; although not proven false, it is not proven that it will always be true. It has passed only this particular challenge.

In the theory about the earth, the null hypothesis states that the earth is flat. The alternative hypothesis states that the earth is not flat, it is round. The null hypothesis was tested, and it failed. The alternative hypothesis then replaces the null hypothesis as the theory until such time that a new challenge can prove otherwise.

EXAMPLE 10.1

Experiment It is a premise of the U.S. legal system that a person is innocent until proven guilty. A person is being brought to trial for first-degree murder. What are the null and alternative hypotheses?

Answer

H_0: The person is innocent

H_1: The person is not innocent

Solution The premise that all are innocent until proven guilty is a claim for the population. That this particular person is innocent until proven guilty is then the sample from the population. The null hypothesis makes a comparison between the sample and the population and states that there is no difference. Therefore, the person must be said to be innocent until proven guilty. The alternative hypothesis must challenge the null hypothesis. The alternative states that there is a difference between the sample and the population. Therefore, the person is not innocent; the person is guilty.

Hypotheses are usually stated with symbols and values as opposed to words. Usually a value of a parameter is in question. For example, the director of fisheries claims that the average length of fish in Lake Michigan is 3.5 in. An angler thinks the average length of fish is not 3.5. The parameter in question is the population mean μ, the length of all fish in Lake Michigan. The value in question is 3.5. The null hypothesis is the statement from the director of fisheries, H_0: $\mu = 3.5$. The null hypothesis always contains an equal sign (including $\leq$ and $\geq$). The angler questions the null hypothesis; this claim becomes the alternative hypothesis and is written H_1: $\mu \neq 3.5$.

There are only three possible symbols for the null hypothesis and three for the alternative hypothesis (Table 10.1). When in doubt, the symbols can be used as a cue in determining which statement is the null hypothesis. Note that symbols are also paired. For example if the H_0 contains $\leq$, H_1 uses $>$.

TABLE 10.1

Hypothesis	Symbols	Parameters
H_0	$=, \leq, \geq$	$\mu, \sigma^2, \sigma, \rho$
H_1	$\neq, <, >$	$\mu, \sigma^2, \sigma, \rho$

Another requirement in determining the null and alternative hypotheses is to question the authority of the person making a claim. When a claim is offered by someone of authority, there is usually no reason to doubt that claim. The claim usually becomes the null hypothesis, based on the idea that the null hypothesis carries the benefit of the doubt. Since the null hypothesis always shows equality between the sample statistic and the population parameter, any claim involving equal to ($=$), greater than or equal to ($\geq$), or less than or equal to ($\leq$) becomes the null hypothesis. Any other claim, involving not equal to ($\neq$), less than ($<$), or greater than ($>$), becomes the alternative hypothesis.

EXAMPLE 10.2

Experiment   The owner of the local cable television company claims the average cable bill is $24.95, with a standard deviation of 2.50. A cable subscriber believes the mean may be correct but thinks the standard deviation is greater than 2.50. State the null and alternative hypotheses.

Answer H_0: $\sigma \leq 2.50$, H_1: $\sigma > 2.50$

Solution   Begin by identifying the parameter. There are four choices for the parameter: μ, σ^2, σ, p. The mean is stated but is not in question. The subscriber is questioning the standard deviation, σ. Next, the null hypothesis must be identified. There are two ways of identifying the null statement. The first is to consider the authority of the two individuals. The owner has the information needed to calculate the standard deviation for cable subscribers. There is probably no reason to doubt the owner. Also, the owner's claim includes an equal sign. The owner claims the standard deviation is (is equal to) 2.50. The null hypothesis carries the benefit of the doubt until someone can prove it false. The subscriber's claim becomes the alternative hypothesis and must prove the information from the owner is incorrect. The subscriber carries the burden of proof. The subscriber does not just think the owner's claim of 2.50 is wrong; the subscriber thinks it is wrong in a particular direction, greater than 2.50. The greater than sign ($>$) is needed with the alternative hypothesis, so the null hypothesis symbol must be equal to or less than ($\leq$). Thus, a test may be conducted to determine if the subscriber's challenge is correct. He or she would be correct only if a value greater than 2.50 is found. If a value equal to or less than 2.50 is found, then the original null hypothesis still stands.

As important as stating the hypotheses correctly is making the correct decision to accept the null hypothesis or to reject it when a test is conducted. For example, suppose a hypothesis is really true, but the test is not conducted correctly (perhaps the sample is not a random sample). The decision to reject the hypothesis because of the sample test would be an error. There are four different decisions that can be made, two correct decisions and two incorrect decisions. The two correct decisions are to accept the null hypothesis when it is true or to reject it when it is false. There are two kinds of errors that can occur in incorrectly deciding the status of the hypotheses, type I error and type II error.

A type I error is committed when the researcher incorrectly rejects the null hypothesis based on a test when the null hypothesis is actually true. A type II error occurs when the null hypothesis is incorrectly accepted to be true based on a test when it is actually false. The seriousness of each error changes from hypothesis to hypothesis. Which error is more serious must be decided by the researcher. Because the null hypothesis is the one to favor in case of doubt, it should be stated in such a way as to make the more serious error avoidable. Table 10.2 summarizes the situation.

TABLE 10.2

	H_0 is True	H_0 is False
Test results in accepting H_0	Correct decision I No error	Type II error Error β
Test results in rejecting H_0	Type I error Error α	Correct decision II No error

EXAMPLE 10.3

Experiment   A woman is diagnosed by her doctor as having breast cancer. State the null and alternative hypotheses in words (not symbols). Describe the errors. Which error is more serious?

Answer

H_0:   Woman does not have cancer

H_1:   Woman does have cancer

Type I error: She does not have cancer but a test incorrectly shows she does.

Type II error: She has cancer but a test incorrectly shows she does not.

Most serious error: Type II

Solution H_0 states that she does not have cancer, because that was her condition prior to going to the doctor. Theoretically, there is no difference in her health prior to or after she goes to the doctor. Although she may have questioned her health before she visited the doctor, there is no proof that anything specifically is wrong. The benefit of the doubt goes to the null hypothesis. The H_1 states that she has cancer, a claim by the doctor that requires conclusive proof. The type I correct decision is that she does not have cancer; further tests correctly support this by being negative. The type II correct decision is that further tests show correctly that she has cancer and she accepts treatment. The type I error is that she does not have cancer but for some reason further tests incorrectly suggest she does. The type II error is that she does have cancer but further tests suggest that she does not. The most serious error must, therefore, be the type II error, because its consequences are fatal. That is, in a type I error she would be treated as if she has cancer—perhaps with surgery or chemotherapy. As severe as unnecessary treatment is for a nonexisting disease, more severe is no treatment at all for a patient who has a fatal disease. **The type II error, in this case, would probably result in the death of the woman; therefore, it is the more severe error that needs to be avoided.**

In a world of certainty, errors would not be of concern. Statisticians would always predict accurately what would or would not happen. But the world is not one of certainty. In the real world people make mistakes. These mistakes can be costly, even deadly. The only way errors can be reduced is to observe the whole universe of events. Generally speaking, testing every object in a universe cannot, and sometimes should not, be done. Large samples increase the cost of doing research. Smaller samples are often as useful and are more manageable but can increase the chance of error. A solution is to assign a probability to the error, which can be adjusted to avoid the more serious error. For example, often a person wants to be 95% sure he or she is correct, which means there will be a 5% chance he or she is incorrect. Adjusting the risks of being correct and incorrect may reduce the chance of serious error. Most researchers attempt this balance by using smaller samples and assigning probabilities to errors by defining the hypotheses in such a way that the more serious error is the type I error. The error is then controlled by adjusting the acceptable level of significance associated with the type I error. This means the level of significance is the probability of committing a type I error when testing the null hypothesis.

> **Level of significance** The probability of committing a type I error (the probability of rejecting H_0 when it is actually true). The level of significance is represented by the greek letter α (alpha).

The most common levels set for α are .01, .05, .025, and .1. When the type I error is not so grave, a higher α level, such as .05, is acceptable. This would mean that 95% of the benefit of doubt would rest upon the null hypothesis, and 5% would go to the probability of being wrong. If the consequence of the type I error is critical, then a smaller α would add extra certainty that an incorrect hypothesis would not be mistakenly accepted as correct.

The probability of committing a type I error is represented by the first letter in the Greek alphabet, alpha (α). The probability of committing a type II error is represented by the second letter in the Greek alphabet, beta (β). Alpha and beta can be thought of as opposites. As one increases, the other decreases. This text will not directly use or calculate beta but will avoid type II errors by increasing or decreasing alpha appropriately. When a type II error is the more serious error, alpha is set large so that beta is reduced. When the type I error is more serious, alpha is set low.

EXAMPLE 10.4

Experiment An electrician is told by the building manager that the electrical power to the building is off. Which error is more serious, type I or type II? At what level should alpha be set?

Answer Type II error; α should be large, perhaps .05.

Solution A type I error may occur if the electrical power is off but the electrician believes it is on. Nothing serious would occur by making this mistake.

A type II error occurs if the electrical power is on but the electrician believes it is off. This is a serious error, because the electrician may be electrocuted if he or she attempts to repair any wiring. Alpha represents the probability of committing a type I error; if α is set high, the probability of a type II error is reduced. A type II error should be avoided.

A LEARNING AID

The Null Hypothesis

Suppose the local bakery claims that the mean weight of a loaf of bread is 14 oz. A customer believes that the mean weight is less than 14 oz. State the hypotheses and describe the errors.

Step 1   State the null hypothesis. The null hypothesis is found by considering the authority of the bakery claiming the mean weight of bread is 14 oz. The bakery has access to information about weight, and the customer probably does not. Also, the bakery's claim includes an equal sign. The null hypothesis is affected by the customer's claim that the mean weight is less than 14. The challenge of less than 14 forces the null hypothesis to become not only equal to 14 but also greater than 14. The null hypothesis is believed to be true until proven false and reads

$$H_0: \quad \mu \geq 14$$

Step 2   State the alternative hypothesis. The alternative hypothesis challenges the null hypothesis and carries the burden of proof. The customer's claim must prove the bakery's claim false. The customer is not viewed as the authority, nor does the claim contain an equal sign. The customer's claim is that the mean is less than 14 and reads

$$H_1: \quad \mu < 14$$

Step 3   Describe the errors. A type I error is incorrectly rejecting a null hypothesis. This would be the case if a test of the weights of a sample leads to a decision that the mean weight of all the bread is less than 14 oz. A type II error is incorrectly accepting a null hypothesis when really it is false. A type II error would occur if a test of weights of the bread leads to a decision to accept the bakery's claim when the claim is really false. Neither errors are extremely serious. The type I error may result in losing a customer because he or she might think the bakery is overcharging for the bread. The type II error could result in a complaint to the Department of Agriculture and other government agencies that, one hopes, would conduct further tests to discover if the bakery does indeed sell 14-oz loaves. The type II error could be the more serious error and should be avoided.

Hypothesis Testing Using the Classical Approach

The process of testing and deciding whether to reject hypotheses can be very systematic. A series of five steps is detailed and then reviewed and integrated at the end of this section. Each step is important and cannot be overlooked. These steps are applicable to many types of data and to testing of different parameters. Therefore, they must be followed, with slight alterations, for most of the rest of the text.

The first step is to state the hypotheses. The null and alternative hypotheses must be stated in appropriate form. Recall that the null hypothesis must carry the benefit of the doubt and must be assumed to be true until the alternative hypothesis proves it wrong. The null hypothesis always involves an equal sign ($=$), less than or equal to sign ($\leq$), or greater than or equal to sign ($\geq$). The alternative hypothesis carries the burden of proof and directly challenges the null hypothesis. The alternative hypothesis never involves an equal sign, but instead may be written with $\neq$, $<$, or $>$.

The second step in hypothesis testing is to establish the test criteria. The test criteria allow one to determine the level of significance, the type I error. The criteria also determine the exact test to be performed that will challenge the null hypothesis and the values of a test that may result in the rejection of the null hypothesis. The test criteria have four specific concerns. The first concern is to specify the level of significance, alpha, or the probability of committing a type I error. The second is to determine the test statistic that will be applied to the sample information. The third concern of the test criteria is to determine the critical region, which will specify the range of values that will not fall within an acceptable distance of the population parameter. The fourth and final concern is to determine the critical value that will note the decision line dividing the critical region from the noncritical region. Each concern is further discussed in the following text.

Test criteria Four considerations leading to the actual test of the null hypothesis:

1. Setting the level of significance.
2. Identifying the test statistic.
3. Determining the critical region.
4. Determining the critical value.

The level of significance, alpha, is the probability of committing a type I error. Typically, a problem states the alpha level as part of a claim challenging a null hypothesis. The alpha level specifies how much error is acceptable. If alpha is not stated, then one must decide how much risk will be allowed by rejecting a potentially true hypothesis. If a type I error appears more severe than a type II error, then alpha should be set low. If a type II error is more serious, then alpha should be set high so that beta is reduced.

The test statistic is the random variable, and its probability distribution is used to compare the sample statistic to the hypothesized population parameter. Thus far, only the test statistic z has been described with its normal probability distribution. In later sections and chapters, different test statistics will be used to calculate means of very small samples, variances between one and two samples, and proportions representing the binomial distribution. Probability distributions representing t, F, and χ^2 will be added to the choice of the test statistic. When the z score is used for means of large samples, the central limit theorem is applied in the same fashion as in Chapter 9.

Test statistic The random variable used to calculate and compare the sample statistic to the hypothesized population parameter. The test statistics used in this book are z, t, χ^2, and F.

The critical region is an area of the probability distribution that will lead to rejecting the null hypothesis if the calculated test statistic value falls within it. A sample rarely results in a value exactly equal to the value specified in the null hypothesis. A value ''close enough'' to the specified is usually accepted. For example, suppose that the average age of students at school is 27 y. The null hypothesis would state that the mean of a sample of student's ages must be 27. If a sample mean results in 26.5, should it be accepted as close enough to 27 to be considered correct? The answer is probably yes. If the sample produces a mean of 27.5, should it also be accepted as close enough? Again, the answer is probably yes. But what if the sample produces a mean of 20? Should 20 be considered close enough? The answer is probably not. One of the considerations in hypothesis testing is the acknowledgment that a specified value of the null hypothesis will have a range of values that will be considered close enough to be correct. Determination of how large the range will be is a critical question. The allowed range is referred to as the *noncritical region,* whereas the name for the values outside the range is the *critical region.*

The process of establishing the critical region begins by drawing the appropriate distribution for the test statistic. For example, the bell-shaped normal distribution is drawn for the test statistic z. The next step is to review the null and alternative hypotheses. Most people concentrate on the alternative hypothesis in determining where to draw the critical region. If the alternative hypothesis states the parameter is not equal to a hypothesized value, the critical region will be divided in half and appropriately placed on the two ends of the distribution. That is, if an alternative hypothesis states a mean is not equal to 27 (H_1: $\mu \neq 27$), an accepted range of values below and above the mean will be identified, as shown in Figure 10.1. Any values beyond those values will be considered in the critical region. When the critical region is divided, falling in both tails of the curve, it is referred to as a two-tailed test.

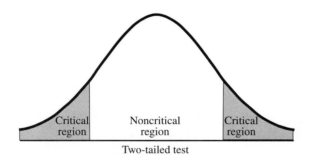

Two-tailed test

FIGURE 10.1

Two-tailed test   A test used when a critical region is divided, with half of its area on both ends of the probability distribution. This test occurs when H_1 indicates a parameter is not equal to a hypothesized value.

EXAMPLE 10.5

Experiment   A candy company claims an average box of jelly beans contains 40 candies. A disgruntled consumer claims the mean is incorrect. If H_0 is $\mu = 40$ and H_1 is $\mu \neq 40$, identify the location of the critical region.

Answer

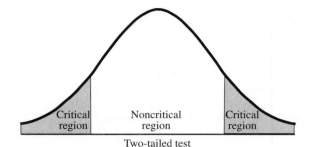

Two-tailed test

Solution   Draw the normal curve, which represents the test statistic *z*. The critical regions are indicated by the alternative hypothesis, because it contains a not equal to (≠) sign. The critical region must be divided, with half of its area in the left tail and half in the right tail. This is a two-tailed test situation.

There are times when the critical region may fall in only one tail of a probability distribution. Sometimes a concern arises that the hypothesized value is underestimated. The alternative hypothesis then would contain a greater than sign (>). Sometimes the hypothesized value is overestimated, which results in an alternative hypothesis containing a less than sign (<). In either case, the critical area falls on one side, the side that the alternative hypothesis indicates. When the critical region falls to only one side, the related test is called a one-tailed test. See Figure 10.2.

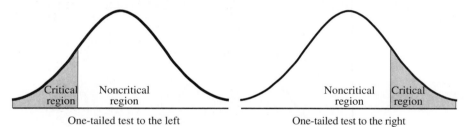

One-tailed test to the left   One-tailed test to the right

FIGURE 10.2

One-tailed test   The test used when a critical region falls on only one side of a probability distribution. This occurs when H_1 involves less than (<) or greater than (>).

Because many statistics books write the null hypothesis only with an equal sign, the alternative hypothesis can best indicate whether a test is one-tailed or two-tailed. The following chart should be used to determine the placement of the critical region.

Sign in H_1		
<	≠	>
One-tailed	Two-tailed	One-tailed
left	half/half	right
α on left	α/2	α on right

EXAMPLE 10.6

Experiment   A candy company claims an average box of jelly beans contains 40 candies. A disgruntled consumer not only believes the mean is incorrect but thinks it is less than 40. He claims that his boxes are always short of 40 candies. If H_0 is $\mu \geq 40$ and H_1 is $\mu < 40$, draw and identify the location of the critical region.

Answer

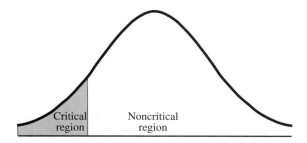

Solution   Draw a normal curve, which represents the test statistic z. The alternative hypothesis states the mean is less than 40. When H_1 is less than ($<$), the critical region is in the left tail of the distribution. If, when tested, a mean is found to be greater than 40, perhaps even as high as 100, the null hypothesis would stand, because the consumer challenges the mean only as being less than 40. The area to the left of the mean is the only area with values that could result in rejecting the null hypothesis.

The fourth consideration of the test criteria is the critical value. Thus far, the critical region has been drawn only to illustrate where the critical region falls, with no values assigned to the dividing line. The critical value is the value in the critical region that divides the critical from the noncritical areas. Its value will be compared with the calculated value, which is found in the next step. The critical value is included in the critical region. When a two-tailed test is conducted, there is a critical value representing each critical region.

Critical value The value of the critical region used to compare with the calculated test statistic.

The critical value reflects values that are not considered close enough to the hypothesized mean. For example, what sample mean of ages of students in one class would be acceptable as close enough if the population mean is hypothesized at 27? Is 26 close enough? Is 25 close enough? The critical value not only reflects what is close enough, but it does so as a value of the test statistic. Thus far, it does so as a z score after the hypothesized mean is transformed into the standard z score 0.

To find the critical value, begin by noting the level of significance. Place the alpha on the curve in its appropriate tail. If the critical region is one-tailed, simply place the probability of alpha in the critical region. If the test is two-tailed, alpha must be divided by 2 before placing each half in the separate critical regions. For example, if alpha is .05, in a one-tailed test the value .05 is placed in the critical region; for a two-tailed test, .05 must be divided by 2, and .025 (.05/2 = .025) is placed in the left critical region and .025 is placed in the right critical region. See Figure 10.3.

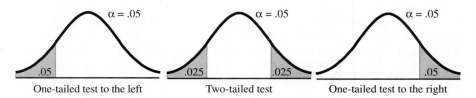

One-tailed test to the left   Two-tailed test   One-tailed test to the right

FIGURE 10.3

If alpha notes the probability of the critical region, then the area of the curve not represented by alpha is that of the noncritical region. For the normal curve, the probability of half of the curve is .5000. The value associated with the noncritical region is easily found by subtracting the probability of the critical region from .5000. That is, .5000 − α is the value of the noncritical region for one-tailed tests and .5000 − α/2 is the value for two-tailed tests. For example, if alpha for a one-tailed test is .05, then probability associated with the noncritical region is .5000 − .05, or .4500. See Figure 10.4.

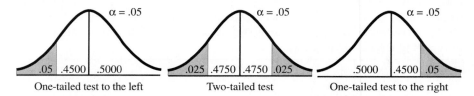

One-tailed test to the left   Two-tailed test   One-tailed test to the right

FIGURE 10.4

Finally, the critical value itself is found by using Table A.3 in Appendix A and finding the z score that corresponds to the probability of the noncritical region. Table A.3 is now read in reverse, as compared to its use in earlier chapters. The probability of the noncritical region is matched as closely as possible to a probability in the body of the table. The critical value is found by tracing over and up to the z score on the outside of the table. For example, if a one-tailed noncritical region is represented by .4900 (thus, α is .01, and .5000 − .01 = .4900), .4900 is closest to the probability of .4901 in Table A.3:

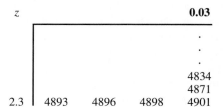

To the left of .4901 is the z score 2.3, and at the top of the column is the z score 0.03. These two scores are added, reflecting a z score of 2.33 associated with the probability .4901. The z score 2.33 is the critical value dividing the critical region from the noncritical region. Any calculated value falling in the critical region will

lead to a decision to reject the null hypothesis. Remember: When working specifically with z scores, z critical values to the left of the mean are negative numbers.

EXAMPLE 10.7

Experiment   Find the critical value for the alternative hypothesis if the mean
is less than 10; $\alpha = .025$.

Answer -1.96

Solution   The critical value cannot be determined until the critical region is set.
The critical region is guided by the alternative hypothesis, which requires only
values less than the mean, 10. The test is a one-tailed z test to the left, because
the alternative hypothesis questions the mean and denotes less than ($<$). The
normal curve is drawn. Alpha is placed in the critical region in the left tail.
Because .025 is the probability of the alpha, the area of the noncritical region is
found by subtracting .025 from .5000, the probability of half a normal curve.
The probability associated with the noncritical region is .5000 $-$ .025 or .4750.

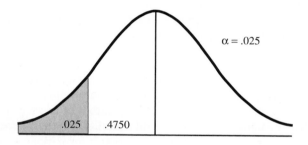

Using Table A.3, .4750 is found in the middle of the table. Across the row from
.4750 is the z score 1.9; up the column from .4750 is the score 0.06. The critical
value is the z score of -1.96 (the negative sign is needed because the area falls
to the left of the mean).

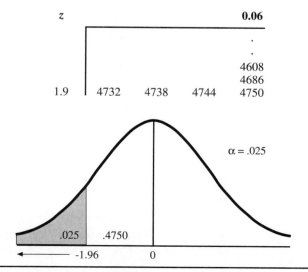

Once the hypotheses are stated and all test criteria are found, the calculation of the test statistic occurs. The test involves the calculation of the sample information offered as a challenge to the null hypothesis. In other words, the information from a sample is transformed into the form taken by the probability distribution so that it can be compared to the test criteria. The calculated value is placed on the curve. If it falls in the critical region, it is said to have provided sufficient proof to reject the null hypothesis. The calculation used is specific to the test statistic. So far only the test statistic z has been used, but later sections will use other tests, including t, F, and χ^2. The value of z is calculated using the formula given in Chapter 9.

The Calculation of z When Testing Means Are Normally Distributed

$$z = \frac{\bar{x} - \mu}{\sigma/\sqrt{n}}$$

EXAMPLE 10.8

Experiment   The registrar of State University reports the mean age of students as 29 with a standard deviation of 4. A random sample of 32 students produces a mean 27. Calculate the test statistic.

Answer -2.83

Solution   The test statistic is calculated by subtracting the population mean from the sample mean and then dividing by the product of the standard deviation divided by the square root of n, the number of cases in the sample. The problem clearly identifies the sample information, where the sample of 32 students produces a mean of 27. The population information is contained in the first phrase, stating that the mean of all students at the college is 29 with a standard deviation of 4. The calculation is:

$$z = \frac{\bar{x} - \mu}{\sigma/\sqrt{n}} = \frac{27 - 29}{4/\sqrt{32}}$$

$$= \frac{-2}{4/5.66}$$

$$= \frac{-2}{.707}$$

$$= -2.83$$

The final stage of hypothesis testing involves the decision and interpretation process. There are only two decisions that can be made. The decision is either to reject the null hypothesis or to fail to reject the null hypothesis. The decision is based on the placement of the calculated value.

Decision

Reject H_0 when the calculated test statistic falls in the critical region or fail to reject H_0 when the calculated test statistic falls in the noncritical region.

The calculated value of the test statistic must be placed on the probability curve. If the calculated value is in the critical region, then the decision must be to reject the null hypothesis. The null hypothesis is rejected only when the sample information falls outside the area defined as noncritical. That is, if the sample information is not close enough to the hypothesized value, then the null hypothesis cannot be accepted as true. Although the null hypothesis is said to have been proven false, the alternative hypothesis is not necessarily proven true. The null hypothesis can be rejected in favor of the alternative, but then the alternative will itself eventually be tested.

If the value of the test statistic is found to be within the noncritical region, then the decision is to fail to reject the null hypothesis. The understanding of this decision is that the test of the sample produced values considered to be close enough to the hypothesized value to be viewed as the same. The sample test does not necessarily prove the null true, but at least it does not prove it false. Perhaps another test will prove the null hypothesis wrong. Perhaps a different level of significance would also prove the null hypothesis wrong. But until such time as the null hypothesis is proven wrong, it is assumed to be true. Notice the words ''fail to reject the null hypothesis.'' The null hypothesis is not accepted or proven correct; it is only not proven false. Do not use different wording.

The interpretation is the final step in hypothesis testing. Once the decision is made, it must be applied to the original problem. Recall that the testing process transformed all information into the standardized values using z scores or other test statistics. The original values must be recalled to understand the application of the decision. The decision to reject the null hypothesis or to fail to reject the null hypothesis should be interpreted by restating the null hypothesis, using the words in the original problem. Because the decision is based on a specific level of significance, the alpha should also be restated. For example, the answer might be: there is sufficient proof to reject the null hypothesis that the mean length of fish in the river is equal to 3 in. at the .05 level of significance.

To review, there are several steps in testing hypotheses using the classical approach. The specific test statistic will differ from problem to problem, but the other steps remain very similar.

Steps in Hypothesis Testing Using the Classical Approach

1. State H_0 and H_1.
2. Identify the test criteria.
   a. Level of significance, α
   b. Test statistic (z, t, χ^2, F)
   c. Critical region
      (1) One-tailed test
      (2) Two-tailed test
   d. Critical value
3. Calculate the test statistic.
4. Place the calculated value on a distribution curve.
5. Make a decision.
   a. Fail to reject H_0.
   b. Reject H_0.
6. Interpret the results.

EXAMPLE 10.9

Experiment   A farmer claims that the mean weight of the turkeys on the farm is 10.2 lb, with a standard deviation of 2. An employee believes the mean weight is more than 10.2 lb. To test this claim, a random sample of 100 turkeys is taken. The sample produces a mean of 10.6. Does the sample provide sufficient evidence to reject the null hypothesis at the .05 level of significance?

Answer   Yes, there is sufficient evidence at the .05 level of significance to reject the farmer's claim that the mean weight of the turkeys is 10.2 lb.

Solution   Step 1 is to state the hypothesis. The null hypothesis is the claim from the farmer. This claim carries the benefit of the doubt and includes an equal sign. The null assumes there is no difference between a sample and a population until a difference can be proven. The employee's claim is the alternative hypothesis, since the employee is challenging the farmer's claim. The employee claims the mean is greater than 10.2. If a sample produces a mean equal to or less than 10.2, the null hypothesis will stand and the employee's claim falls. Writing these claims in symbols produces the following:

$$H_0: \quad \mu \leq 10.2$$
$$H_1: \quad \mu > 10.2$$

Step 2 requires the identification of the test criteria. Begin by identifying the level of significance. The problem clearly states to use a level of significance, alpha, of .05. The test statistic that should be used is the z distribution, which represents normally distributed means. The critical region must be set in the right tail, so a one-tailed test is used. This choice is guided by the alternative hypothesis, because the area of concern in the employee's challenge involves only values greater than the mean. The critical value is found by placing the alpha level on the normal curve in the critical region and finding the probability of the noncritical region. When using the normal curve, this is done by subtracting alpha from .5000. The noncritical probability can be transformed into a z score by using Table A.3. Therefore, .5000 − .05 = .4500. The probability .4500 is the z score 1.645 (reading from Table A.3.) The z score 1.645 is the value at the beginning of the critical region.it will fall in the critical region.

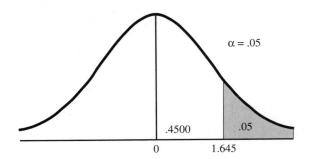

Step 3 is to calculate the test statistic, which is identified as z. Using the following information, the z score is calculated: $\bar{x} = 10.6$, $\mu = 10.2$, $\sigma = 2$, and $n = 100$.

$$z = \frac{\bar{x} - \mu}{\sigma/\sqrt{n}} = \frac{10.6 - 10.2}{2/\sqrt{100}}$$

$$= \frac{.4}{2/10}$$

$$= \frac{.4}{.2}$$

$$= 2.00$$

In Step 4, the calculated z score is placed on the normal curve and compared to the critical value.

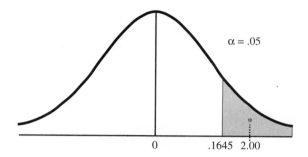

Step 5 involves the decision concerning the null hypothesis. Notice that the calculated value 2.0 is within the critical region, which begins at 1.645. The decision to reject H_0 is made whenever the calculated value falls within the critical region.

$$\text{Reject } H_0$$

Step 6 is the interpretation of the decision. To reject the null hypothesis is interpreted as follows: There is sufficient proof, at the .05 level, to allow us to reject the null hypothesis. Therefore, the farmer's claim that the mean weight of turkeys is 10.2 lb is not accepted as true. The employee provides sufficient evidence that the mean weight of turkeys is greater than 10.2 lb.

EXAMPLE 10.10

Experiment   The New York Stock Exchange reported that it had an average closing value of 2067 for the previous year with a standard deviation of 42. A broker believes the average is not the 2067 the exchange reports and conducts a survey of 75 d, which produces a mean of 2053. Is there sufficient evidence to reject the null hypothesis ($\alpha = .01$)?

Answer   Yes, there is sufficient proof at the .01 level of significance to reject the null hypothesis that the average closing value of the stock exchange was 2067.

Solution   State the hypotheses. The null hypothesis contends that the mean equals 2067. The New York Stock Exchange should be viewed as the authority, having access to the information. Also, the statement includes the equal sign that must be placed in the null hypothesis. The alternative hypothesis is the challenge presented by the broker who believes the exchange is wrong. Because the broker does not specify whether the mean is too high or too low, the statement implies the average is simply not equal to 2067. It is the broker's burden to prove the exchange wrong. Writing the hypotheses in symbols gives

$$H_0: \quad \mu = 2067$$
$$H_1: \quad \mu \neq 2067$$

Identify the test criteria by beginning with the level of significance. Alpha is given at .01. The test statistic is again the z score, which tests means that are normally distributed. The critical region is guided by the alternative hypothesis. When the alternative contains the not equal sign, the test will be two-tailed, with half of the critical region in the left tail and half in the right tail. Alpha is divided by 2, so that half of the probability of error is represented by the critical region in each tail. The right critical value is found by placing half of the alpha in the right tail and subtracting it from .5000:

A LEARNING AID

Hypothesis Testing—Classical Approach

A commuter college claims that the average travel time is normally distributed with a mean of 32 min and a standard deviation of 4.6 min. Does a sample of 40 students producing a mean of 34 min provide sufficient evidence to reject the college's claim? Use $\alpha = .01$.

Step 1   State the hypothesis. The null hypothesis must carry the benefit of the doubt and must contain an equal sign. The college's claim asserts the mean is equal to 32 min. The sample of travel times for 40 students challenges the college's claim, suggesting the mean is not equal to 32 min.

$$H_0: \quad \mu = 32$$
$$H_1: \quad \mu \neq 32$$

Step 2   Identify the test criteria. The level of significance is represented by alpha and is set at .01. The test statistic z is used in testing normally distributed means. The critical region falls in both tails of the curve, as determined by the alternative hypothesis, which contains a not equal to sign. The critical values are found by dividing alpha by 2, placing it on the curve, calculating the probability of the curve from α to the mean, and transforming the probability to a z score using Table A.3. Alpha is .01; dividing it by 2

(.01/2) yields .005. If the area of the curve from $\alpha/2$ to the tail is .005, then the area from the mean to $\alpha/2$ is found by subtracting .005 from .5000, which is .4950. Because the normal curve is symmetric, .4950 is the probability of the curve from 0 to $\alpha = .005$ for both the left and right halves of the curve. The probability .4950 must be transformed into a z score using Table A.3. The probability values closest to .4950 are the values .4949 and .4951. The associated z scores are 2.57 and 2.58, respectively. Because the probability .4950 falls between these two z scores, the critical value for the right tail of the curve becomes the adjusted value 2.575. The score 2.575 is placed on the right side of the curve. The curve is symmetric, so the z score to the left of center is found simply by adding a negative sign to 2.575. The left critical value is -2.575.

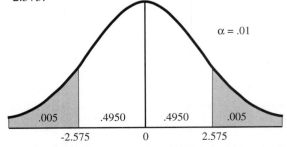

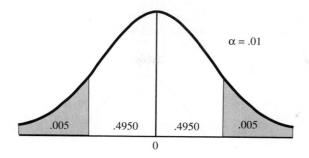

$$.5000 - \frac{.01}{2} = .5000 - .005 = .4950$$

Table A.3 is used to find the z score associated with the probability of .4950. Looking at Table A.3, the probability .4950 is between .4949 and .4951. The z score for .4949 is 2.57. The z score for .4951 is 2.58. Because .4950 is exactly between, the z score can be written as 2.575. The critical value for the right tail is 2.575. The left critical value is found the same way. Since the normal curve

Step 3 Calculate the test statistic. The z score is already identified as the test for normally distributed means. The calculation requires the following information derived from the original problem: $\bar{x} = 34$, $\mu = 32$, $\sigma = 4.6$, and $n = 40$.

$$z = \frac{\bar{x} - \mu}{\sigma/\sqrt{n}}$$

$$= \frac{34 - 32}{4.6/\sqrt{40}}$$

$$= \frac{2}{4.6/6.32}$$

$$= \frac{2}{.73}$$

$$= 2.74$$

Step 4 Place the calculated test statistic on the distribution curve. The calculated value 2.74 is placed on the normal curve to the right of the critical value 2.575.

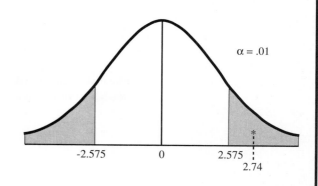

Step 5 Make a decision. The decision is to reject H_0, because the calculated value falls in the critical region.

Reject H_0

Step 6 Interpret the results. The decision must be applied to the original problem. The null hypothesis states the average travel time to school is 32 min. Rejecting this hypothesis suggests that the mean travel time is something other than 32 min. More appropriately, the interpretation may be worded as follows: There is sufficient evidence, at the .01 level of significance, to reject the null hypothesis that the mean travel time to school is 32 min.

is symmetric, adding a negative sign to the z score 2.575 will represent the same area but in the left tail, left of the mean. The critical value for the left tail is -2.575.

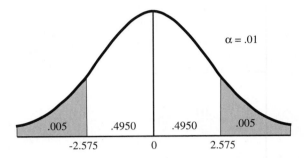

The next step is to calculate the test statistic z. The information from the problem is $\bar{x} = 2053$, $\mu = 2067$, $\sigma = 42$, and $n = 75$.

$$z = \frac{\bar{x} - \mu}{\sigma/\sqrt{n}} = \frac{2053 - 2067}{42/\sqrt{75}}$$

$$= \frac{-14}{42/8.66}$$

$$= \frac{-14}{4.85}$$

$$= -2.89$$

Place the calculated test statistic on the curve. Note the calculated score is a negative number and must be placed to the left of the mean.

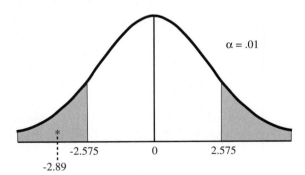

The calculated value of -2.89 falls in the left critical region, which leads to the decision to reject the null hypothesis.

Reject H_0

Rejecting the null hypothesis is interpreted as follows: There is sufficient proof at the .01 level of significance that the mean closing value for the New York Stock Exchange was not 2067.

With the invention of the computer came a new approach to hypothesis testing. Computers go one step further than the classical approach by computing the test statistic as a value known as a *P*-value. The *P*-value is a probability representing the level of significance at which the test statistic becomes significant provided the null hypothesis is true. In other words, the *P*-value is the probability of obtaining a sample value at least as extreme as the value reported in the sample challenging the null hypothesis.

> ***P*-value or prob-value** The smallest level of significance for the sample test statistic at which it becomes significant, provided the null hypothesis is true. *P* is considered significant when it is less than or equal to the type I error.

The *P*-value is the point at which a sample statistic is more extreme, toward the tails of a probability curve, than the sample information challenging the null hypothesis. It is the point at which the test statistic is considered significant, leading to rejecting the null hypothesis. If the type I error value, alpha, is in the region representing the *P*-value, then the null hypothesis must be rejected.

One-Tailed Left	Two-Tailed	One-Tailed Right
$P(z < z^*)$	$P(z < z^*) + P(z > z^*)$	$P(z > z^*)$

where

z represents values that are more extreme than the calculated z^* value.

z^* is the calculated value.

Hypothesis testing using the *P*-value begins much like the classical approach. Step 1 is to identify the null and alternative hypotheses. Step 2 is to identify two aspects of the test criteria, the level of significance and the test statistic. The level of significance is usually offered as α in the problem. The test statistic must be determined by reviewing the parameter noted in the hypotheses (so far, only normally distributed means have been tested using z scores). The critical value and the critical region are not needed in the *P*-value approach. Step 3 is to calculate the test statistic exactly as done in the classical approach:

$$z = \frac{\bar{x} - \mu}{\sigma/\sqrt{n}}$$

Step 4 is the calculation of the *P*-value. The calculated value of the test statistic is transformed into a probability and adjusted as needed. For the normal curve, a calculated z score is transformed into a probability using Table A.3. The adjustment needed is to find the area of the curve from the calculated z to the tail of the curve. This adjustment is accomplished by subtracting the z score's probability from .5000, the probability of half of the normal curve. The probability for the tail is the *P*-value if the test is a one-tailed test. For example, a one-tailed test to the right for a calculated z score 2.12 produces a *P*-value of .0170. Referring to Table A.3, the z score 2.12 has a probability of .4830. The probability .4830 is the area of the curve from 0 to

2.12. The area from 2.12 to the end of the tail is needed. Because half of the curve is associated with a probability .5000, subtracting .4830 produces a *P*-value .0170. See Figure 10.5.

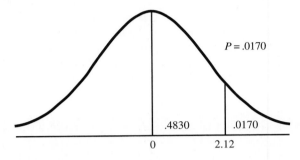

FIGURE 10.5

A two-tailed test requires that the probabilities of both tails be calculated and added to produce the *P*-value. Because the normal curve is symmetric, the test statistic *z* is placed on both sides of the mean, with the left value carrying a negative sign. The probability of the *z* score is found in Table A.3 and adjusted to represent the area from *z* out to the end of the tails. The probabilities of the tails are then added. For example, a two-tailed test with a calculated *z* score 2.12 produces a *P*-value .0340. The *z* score 2.12 must be read as 2.12 and −2.12. Table A.3 gives the probability of all *z* scores regardless of sign. The *z* scores 2.12 and −2.12 represent the probability .4830. For the right tail, the area from 2.12 is found by subtracting .4830 from .5000, which gives .0170. For the left tail, the area from −2.12 is also found by subtracting .4830 from .5000, which gives .0170. Thus, the probability that a test statistic is significant is found by adding .0170 to .0170. The *P*-value is .0340. See Figure 10.6.

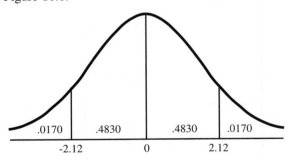

FIGURE 10.6

$$P = \text{value} = .0170 + .0170$$
$$= .0340$$

Step 5 is the decision concerning the null hypothesis. The decision requires the comparison of the *P*-value to the alpha level. If the probability of committing a type I error is in the tail whose values are considered significant, then the decision is to reject the null hypothesis. If the point where values are significant is greater than the probability of a type I error, the decision is to fail to reject the null hypothesis. In other words, if the *P*-value is less than or equal to alpha, then the null hypothesis must be rejected. If the *P*-value is greater than alpha, then the decision is to fail to reject the null hypothesis.

$$P \leq a \quad \text{Reject } H_0.$$
$$P > a \quad \text{Fail to reject } H_0.$$

Step 6 is the interpretation of the decision using the original information from the problem. The decision to reject the null hypothesis implies there is sufficient evidence to reject the null hypothesis at a specified level of significance. A decision to fail to reject the null hypothesis also depends on the specific level of significance.

Steps in Hypothesis Testing Using the *P*-Value Approach

1. State H_0 and H_1.
2. Identify the test criteria.
   a. Level of significance
   b. Test statistic
3. Calculate the test statistic.
4. Calculate the *P*-value.
   a. One-tailed test
   b. Two-tailed test
5. Make a decision.
   a. Fail to reject H_0.
   b. Reject H_0.
6. Interpret the results.

EXAMPLE 10.11

Experiment   A farmer claims that the mean weight of turkeys on the farm is 10.2 lb, with a standard deviation of 2. An employee believes the mean weight is more than 10.2 lb. To test this claim, a random sample of 100 turkeys is taken. The sample produces a mean of 10.6. Using the *P*-value approach, does the sample provide sufficient evidence to reject the null hypothesis at the .05 level of significance?

Answer   Yes, there is sufficient evidence at the .05 level of significance to reject the farmer's claim that the mean weight of the turkeys is 10.2 lb.

Solution   State the hypothesis. Notice the farmer's claim contains an equal sign, as required by the null hypothesis. The employee believes the mean weight of turkeys is more than 10.2 lb. The employee's challenge is a one-directional alternative hypothesis, concerned only with values greater than 10.2. If a sample produces a mean equal to or less than 10.2, then the null hypothesis will stand, and the employee's challenge will fail. Writing these claims symbolically gives:

$$H_0: \quad \mu \leq 10.2$$
$$H_1: \quad \mu > 10.2$$

The second step is to identify the level of significance and the test statistic. The level of significance is given as .05. The test statistic for means of sampling distributions normally distributed is the z score. The test is a one-tailed test to the right, as determined by the alternative hypothesis challenging the mean, which contains greater than ($>$).

Step 3 is to calculate the test statistic, z. The z score is calculated using the information $\bar{x} = 10.6$, $\mu = 10.2$, $\sigma = 2$, and $n = 100$.

$$z = \frac{\bar{x} - \mu}{\sigma/\sqrt{n}} = \frac{10.6 - 10.2}{2/\sqrt{100}}$$

$$= \frac{.4}{2/10}$$

$$= \frac{.4}{.2}$$

$$= 2.00$$

Step 4 requires the calculation of the P-value. The P-value is found by transforming the test statistic into a probability using Table A.3 and adjusting the probability to represent the area of the right tail of the curve (if this were a two-tailed test, both tails would be calculated and then added). Table A.3 gives a probability of .4772 for the z score of 2.00. The probability .4772 is from the mean 0 to the z score 2.00. To find the probability from 2.00 out to the tail, subtract .4772 from .5000. For a one-tailed test, this subtracted value is the P-value. The P-value is .0228.

$$P\text{-value} = .5000 - .4772 = .0228$$

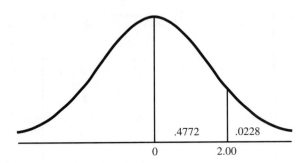

The next step is to compare the P-value to alpha and make a decision about the null hypothesis. If P is greater than α, then the decision is to fail to reject the null hypothesis. If P is less than or equal to α, the decision is to reject the null hypothesis. P at .0228 is less than α at .05, so the decision is reject the null hypothesis.

$$P_{(.0228)} \leq \alpha_{(.05)} \qquad \text{Reject } H_0$$

The final step is the interpretation of the decision. Rejecting the null hypothesis is interpreted using the original problem: There is sufficient proof, at the .05 level, to allow rejecting the null hypothesis; therefore, the farmer's claim that the mean weight of turkeys is 10.2 lb is not accepted as true. The employee provides sufficient evidence that the mean weight of turkeys is greater than 10.2 lb.

EXAMPLE 10.12

Experiment The New York Stock Exchange reports that the exchange had an average closing value of 2067 for the previous year, with a standard deviation of 42. A broker believes the average is not the 2067 the exchange reports and conducts a survey of 75 d, which produces a mean of 2053. Using the *P*-value approach, is there sufficient evidence to reject the null hypothesis for $\alpha = .01$?

Answer Yes, there is sufficient proof at the .01 level of significance to reject the null hypothesis that the average closing of the stock exchange was 2067.

Solution State the hypotheses. The null hypothesis contends that the mean equals 2067. The New York Stock Exchange should be viewed as the authority, having access to the information. Also, the statement includes an equal sign, which must be placed in the null hypothesis. The alternative hypothesis is the challenge presented by the broker who believes the exchange is wrong. Because the broker does not specify whether the mean is too high or too low, the statement simply implies the average is not equal to 2067. It is the broker's burden to prove the exchange wrong. Writing the hypotheses in symbols gives

$$H_0: \quad \mu = 2067$$
$$H_1: \quad \mu \neq 2067$$

Identify the level of significance and the test statistic. The level of significance is alpha, given at .01. The test statistic is again the *z* score, which tests means that are normally distributed. The test is two-tailed, as determined by the alternative hypothesis, which contains a not equal to sign.

The next step is to calculate the test statistic *z*. The information from the problem is $\bar{x} = 2053$, $\mu = 2067$, $\sigma = 42$, and $n = 75$.

$$z = \frac{\bar{x} - \mu}{\sigma/\sqrt{n}} = \frac{2053 - 2067}{42/\sqrt{75}}$$
$$= \frac{-14}{42/8.66}$$
$$= \frac{-14}{4.85}$$
$$= -2.89$$

The *P*-value is found by transforming the test statistic -2.89 into a probability. A negative *z* score represents a value below the mean, but its probability is not negative. Table A.3 gives a probability of .4981 for the *z* score 2.89. The probability .4981 must be subtracted from .5000 to give the probability of the curve

A LEARNING AID

P-Value

A potato chip factory packages bags of chips that weigh an average of 4 oz, with a standard deviation of .62 oz. The Bureau of Weights and Measures randomly selects 30 bags, measures their contents, and reports a sample mean of 4.2. Using the *P*-value approach, does the sample provide sufficient evidence to conclude that the potato chip company cheats its customers ($\alpha = .02$)?

Step 1   State the hypotheses. The potato chip company claims the mean is 4 oz. A claim including an equal sign ($=$) becomes the null hypothesis. The bureau challenges the factory's claim. Since the bureau does not specify where the mean may be, its challenge is simply that the mean is not equal to ($\neq$) 4 oz.

$$H_0: \quad \mu = 4 \qquad H_1: \quad \mu \neq 4$$

Step 2   Identify the level of significance and the test statistic. The level of significance is the alpha (α) value of .02 reported. The test statistic z must be used for normally distributed means. The test is a two-tailed test, because the alternative hypothesis contains a not equal to sign ($\neq$).

Step 3   Calculate the test statistic. The z score must be calculated given the information provided: $\bar{x} = 4.2$, $\mu = 4$, $\sigma = .62$, and $n = 30$.

$$z = \frac{\bar{x} - \mu}{\sigma/\sqrt{n}} = \frac{4.2 - 4}{.62/\sqrt{30}}$$

$$= \frac{.2}{.62/5.48}$$

$$= \frac{.2}{.113}$$

$$= 1.77$$

Step 4   Calculate the *P*-value. The calculated z score, 1.77, is transformed into a probability using Table A.3. In a two-tailed test, the calculated z score must be read as negative and positive, representing both tails of the normal curve. Begin by calculating the right tail. The z score 1.77 carries the probability .4616 (from Table A.3). The probability .4616 is the area of the curve from 0 to 1.77. To find the area from 1.77 to the end of the tail, subtract .4616 from .5000. The

remaining portion (.0384) is the probability associated with the right tail of the curve.

$$.5000 - .4616 = .0384$$

The probability of the left tail is calculated in the same way as the right tail. A negative z score, -1.77, also carries the probability of .4616. Subtracting from .5000, the area of the curve from -1.77 out to the end of the left tail is found to be associated with a probability .0384.

$$.5000 - .4616 = .0384$$

The *P*-value for a two-tailed test is the sum of the probabilities of the two tails. Add .0384 to .0384:

$$P\text{-value} = .0384 + .0384 = .0768$$

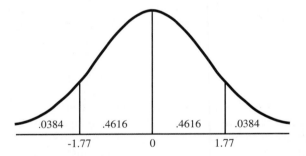

Step 5   Compare the *P*-value to alpha and make a decision about the null hypothesis. If the *P*-value is less than or equal to alpha, the decision is to reject the null hypothesis. If P is greater than alpha, then the decision is to fail to reject the null hypothesis. The *P*-value of .0768 is greater than the alpha. The decision must be to fail to reject H_0.

$$P_{(.0768)} > \alpha_{(.02)} \qquad \text{Fail to reject } H_0$$

Step 6   Interpret the results. Failing to reject the null hypothesis implies the bureau's check on the weights of potato chip bags produced a mean close enough to confirm the factory's claim. In other words, there is no sufficient evidence at the .02 level of significance to reject the factory's claim that the mean weight of a bag of potato chips is 4 oz.

from $z = 2.89$ out to the end of the tail: $.5000 - .4981 = .0019$. This value would be the P-value if this were a one-tailed test; however, as a two-tailed test, the area of the right tail must also be calculated. Because the normal curve is symmetric, the test statistic -2.89 for the left tail becomes 2.89 for the right tail. Again, 2.89 has a probability $.4981$ representing the area of the curve from 0 to the z score. The area of the curve from the z score out to the end of the tail is found by subtracting its probability from $.5000$. The right tail carries a probability $.5000 - .4981$, or $.0019$. Adding the probabilities of the two tails results in the P-value. Therefore, the P-value for this two-tailed test is

$$P\text{-value} = .0019 + .0019 = .0038$$

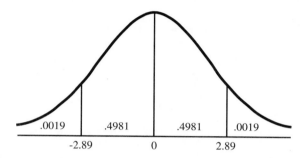

The P-value must be compared to the original alpha to make a decision about the null hypothesis. Compare the P-value $.0038$ to the alpha, $.01$. Because P is less than α, we must reject the null hypothesis.

$$P_{(.0038)} \leq \alpha_{(.01)} \qquad \text{Reject } H_0$$

Rejecting the null hypothesis suggests there is sufficient proof at the $.01$ level of significance that the mean closing for the New York Stock Exchange was not 2067.

Confidence Intervals

The introduction explains that inferential statistics predict population parameters from sample information. Sections 1 through 3 showed how to test population information using sample statistics. However, there are times that the population information is not known. For example, a light bulb manufacturer would not test every bulb to determine the average life of a bulb. There would not be bulbs left to sell. Even testing repeated samples may be very costly. But whether one or several samples are tested, the manufacturer really has no definite population mean. Sample data can be used to predict population parameters. A population parameter can be estimated from sample data by establishing a range of values where the parameter may lie. The range of values is called a confidence interval.

> **Confidence interval** Estimating a population parameter from sample statistics given a specified level of confidence.

Recall how, in Chapter 9, one estimated the sampling mean given a population mean. A standard error was also estimated given a standard deviation and the sample size. Turning the rules around and combining information from the earlier sections of this chapter, one has the ability to estimate the population mean given a sample mean. An interval in which the population mean will fall can be calculated based on sample information. The term confidence interval implies there is an interval or range of values where the mean will fall given a particular degree of confidence. The interval is estimated using the sampling information and the degree of certainty that seems adequate given the risk of error.

The central limit theorem describes a distribution where the mean of a sampling distribution is equal to the population mean ($\mu_{\bar{x}} = \mu$). If this statement is true, then it is possible to reverse the rule allowing the mean to be estimated by the sampling mean ($\mu = \mu_{\bar{x}}$).

Logically, if the mean is not determined, then the mean of all sample means is also not likely to be determined. Using one sample to estimate the population mean increases the chance of error. However, one sample mean is a good place to begin. The estimate using a sample mean as the point of departure to determine a range of values in which the population mean will fall is referred to as a point estimate.

> **Point estimate** The sample statistic used to estimate the population parameter. When estimating the parameter μ, the point estimate is the sample statistic $\bar{x}$.

The point estimate can be used for any sample statistic estimating a population parameter. When estimating μ, $\bar{x}$ is the point estimate. When estimating σ, s is the point estimate. For example, if the length of all fish in Lake Michigan cannot be determined and repeated sampling is impractical, one sample mean may be sufficient as a starting place. If a sample mean is 3.5 in., then the point of estimation begins at 3.5 in.

An interval encasing the point estimate can be determined. The population mean can be expected to occur within this interval. The interval is split, with half of the range of values to the right of the point estimate and half to the left. The size of the range depends on the level of confidence that is to be allowed. The level of confidence establishes the probability that the population parameter will fall inside the range of values set by the sample statistic. The level of confidence is also referred to as the degree of confidence reflecting the level of certainty desired.

> **Level of confidence** The probability that a parameter is contained in the confidence interval established around a sample statistic. It is also known as a confidence coefficient and is
>
> $$1 - \alpha$$

The level of confidence can be understood as the probability of being correct. It is the opposite of alpha, which is the probability of being wrong. Therefore, because alpha is often given in a problem, the degree of confidence is determined by subtracting alpha from 1.0. Because the most common alpha levels are .05, .01, and .1, the most common degrees of confidence are .95, .99, and .90. In other words, one typically wishes to be 95%, 99%, or 90% sure the population parameter will be in the estimated range.

Calculating the probability for the level of confidence is similar to finding the critical value in a hypothesis test. Whether alpha (α) or a confidence level percentage is given, the probability must be found for the normal curve from 0 out to where the confidence ends and the alpha level begins. Since a range of values below and above the point estimate is required, all confidence intervals can be understood as two-tailed. See Figure 10.7.

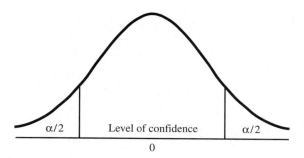

FIGURE 10.7

The level of confidence must be transformed into a probability and then into a z score. Confidence levels are reported as percentages, which are easily transformed into probabilities by dropping the percent sign (%) and moving the decimal to the left two places. For example, a 95% confidence interval becomes a probability of .95. Half of .95 (.95/2 = .4750) is above the point estimate, and half is below. The probability of half the level, .4750, is transformed into a z score using Table A.3 in Appendix A. The z value 1.96 is denoted by $z_{(\alpha/2)}$, which will be the upper limit of the curve, setting the boundary for the range of values in the interval. The left limit has a negative sign, reflecting the area of the curve below the point estimator. The probability .4750 left of the center is associated with the negative z score -1.96. The subscript $\alpha/2$ is used to reflect the two-tailed alpha level, indicating that α must be divided by 2 to find the z value for the half of the range above the mean and the half of the range below. Alpha is the opposite of the confidence level; thus, either can be found when the other is given. See Figure 10.8.

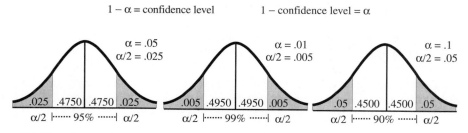

FIGURE 10.8

Combining the concepts of the point estimator and the level of confidence results in an interval, or range of values, where the parameter should fall. Precision is lost when using an interval instead of a point estimator, but confidence is gained.

The calculation of the confidence interval for normally distributed means with large sample size is an algebraic manipulation of the z score calculation for the central limit theorem. Instead of finding the probability of the z score, the probability of the z score is inserted in the formula and the population mean is estimated.

$$z = \frac{\bar{x} - \mu}{\sigma/\sqrt{n}} \qquad E_\mu = \bar{x} \pm z_{(\alpha/2)} \frac{\sigma}{\sqrt{n}}$$

Formula for a Confidence Interval with a Normally Distributed Mean and a Large Sample Size

$$E_\mu = \bar{x} + z_{(\alpha/2)} \frac{\sigma}{\sqrt{n}} \quad \text{and} \quad E_\mu = \bar{x} - z_{(\alpha/2)} \frac{\sigma}{\sqrt{n}}$$

where

E_μ is the estimate of the population mean.
$\bar{x}$ is the sample mean, also known as the point estimator.
$z_{(\alpha/2)}$ is the z value reflecting the level of confidence.
$\sigma/\sqrt{n}$ is the standard error.

The point estimate is understood as the sample mean, where half of the interval is to the right and half is to the left. The values in the right half of the interval are calculated using the formula that involves adding to the sample mean. The values to the left of the interval are calculated using the formula that involves subtraction from the sample mean.

The formula for calculating the confidence interval requires the multiplication of $z_{(\alpha/2)}$ (found in the earlier stage) by the standard error $\sigma/\sqrt{n}$. The value $z_{(\alpha/2)}$ reflects the probability of being correct. The value is inserted into the formula without any further manipulation (that is, it is not multiplied by $\alpha/2$). The product of z and the standard error $\sigma/\sqrt{n}$ is added to the sample mean $\bar{x}$ and is the upper limit of the interval. The lower limit is found by subtracting the product of z and the standard error from the sample mean. The final interval is noted by stating the values with the parameter in the middle:

$$\text{Lower limit} < \mu < \text{upper limit}$$

It is important to understand that an interval depends on a specific sample. If a different sample mean is used as a point estimate, then the range of values estimating the population mean will change. Also, if the degree of confidence or the alpha level changes, so will the range of values in the interval. Decreasing the level of confidence decreases the range of values.

EXAMPLE 10.13

Experiment   In order to determine the mean grocery store bill for shoppers at Big Market Warehouse Grocers, a random sample of 50 shoppers is selected and analyzed. The mean bill is $47.80. Assuming the standard deviation of the population is $16.91, find the 95% confidence interval for the mean grocery bill.

Answer $\$43.11 < \mu < \$52.49$

Solution   The problem requires a 95% confidence interval for the population mean. The sample size is relatively large at 50 and money, as a continuous variable, is normally distributed. The z score is the test statistic for normally distributed means of large samples. Begin by identifying the point estimate. The point estimate is the sample mean $47.80 used to estimate the range of values encasing the population mean. The level of confidence must be identified and transformed into a z score. A confidence of 95% is given. Dividing 95% by 2 gives 47.50%. Drop the percent sign and move the decimal to the left two places, and 47.50% becomes the probability of .4750. Using Table A.3 in Appendix A shows the probability .4750 is associated with a z score of 1.96. The value 1.96 represents the boundary of values above the point estimate. The lower z score is -1.96, representing the area of the curve below the point estimate. The value 1.96 will be used in the calculation of the interval to represent $z_{(\alpha/2)}$.

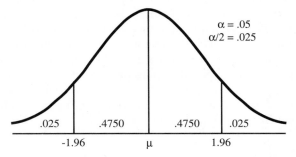

$\alpha = .05$
$\alpha/2 = .025$

.025   .4750   .4750   .025
-1.96 μ 1.96

The next step is to calculate the interval. The calculation of the interval requires the following information: $\bar{x} = 47.80$, $\sigma = 16.91$, $n = 50$, and $z_{(\alpha/2)} = 1.96$

$$E_\mu = \bar{x} + z_{(\alpha/2)} \frac{\sigma}{\sqrt{n}} \qquad\qquad E_\mu = \bar{x} - z_{(\alpha/2)} \frac{\sigma}{\sqrt{n}}$$

$$= 47.80 + 1.96 \frac{16.91}{\sqrt{50}} \qquad\qquad = 47.80 - 1.96 \frac{16.91}{\sqrt{50}}$$

$$= 47.80 + 1.96 \frac{16.91}{7.07} \qquad\qquad = 47.80 - 1.96 \frac{16.91}{7.07}$$

$$= 47.80 + 1.96(2.39) \qquad\qquad = 47.80 - 1.96(2.39)$$

$$= 47.80 + 4.69 \qquad\qquad = 47.80 - 4.69$$

$$= 52.49 \qquad\qquad\qquad = 43.11$$

43.11 ← μ → 52.49

The confidence interval estimating the range of values where the population mean should fall has a lower boundary of 43.11 and an upper boundary of $52.49. Therefore, with 95% confidence, the mean grocery bill is between $43.11 and $52.49.

$$\$43.11 < \mu < \$52.49$$

EXAMPLE 10.14

Experiment   Repeat Example 10.13 using a confidence interval of 99%.

Answer $41.63 < \mu < 53.97$

Solution   The difference between this problem and the previous is the level of significance. This problem requires a 99% confidence interval. A larger confidence interval increases the range of values, because you want to be more sure that the range includes the population mean. Begin by identifying the sample mean, $47.80, as the point estimate. The next step is to transform the level of confidence into a probability and then a z score. Dividing the 99% by 2 gives 49.50%. Moving the decimal and dropping the percent sign gives a probability of .4950. Table A.3 reveals the probability .4950 is associated with a z score of 2.58. The value 2.58 is used in the equation representing the symbol $z_{(\alpha/2)}$. The left boundary will carry a negative sign: -2.58.

A LEARNING AID

Confidence Interval for the Mean

Considering the difficulty of finding the average body temperature of the world's population, construct a 90% confidence interval for the mean body temperature using a sample of 50 people that produces a sample mean of 98.7. (Assume a population standard deviation of .4.)

Step 1   The problem asks for a confidence interval that estimates the mean body temperature of all the people in the world. The central limit theorem allows estimating a population mean using a sample mean known as the point estimator. The sample size is considered large (50), and the variable *temperature* is a continuous variable. The test statistic for continuous means of large samples is the z score.

Step 2   Identify the level of confidence and transform it into a probability and then a z score. The level of confidence is the probability that a parameter is contained in the confidence interval. The problem identifies the confidence level as 90%. A 90% value involves a probability of .90 that the parameter is in-

cluded in the interval. The probability .90 is transformed into a z score by dividing by two and using Table A.3. The division allows half of the interval to be above the point estimator and half of the interval to be below; .90 divided by 2 is .4500. A probability of .4500 above the mean on the normal curve carries a z score 1.65, whereas .4500 below the mean is associated with -1.65. These values are represented by the symbol $z_{(\alpha/2)}$.

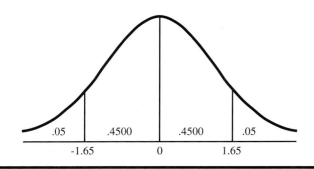

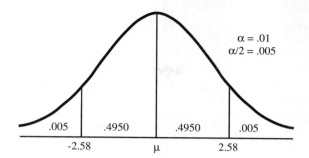

The next step is to calculate the interval. The calculation of the interval requires the following information: $\bar{x} = 47.80$, $\sigma = 16.91$, $n = 50$, and $z_{(\alpha/2)} = 2.58$.

$$E_\mu = \bar{x} + z_{(\alpha/2)} \frac{\sigma}{\sqrt{n}} \qquad\qquad E_\mu = \bar{x} - z_{(\alpha/2)} \frac{\sigma}{\sqrt{n}}$$

$$= 47.80 + 2.58 \frac{16.91}{\sqrt{50}} \qquad\qquad = 47.80 - 2.58 \frac{16.91}{\sqrt{50}}$$

$$= 47.80 + 2.58 \frac{16.91}{7.07} \qquad\qquad = 47.80 - 2.58 \frac{16.91}{7.07}$$

$$= 47.80 + 2.58(2.39) \qquad\qquad = 47.80 - 2.58(2.39)$$

$$= 47.80 + 6.17 \qquad\qquad = 47.80 - 6.17$$

$$= 53.97 \qquad\qquad\qquad = 41.63$$

Step 3   Calculate the confidence interval. The calculation of the interval requires the following information: $\bar{x} = 98.1$, $\sigma = .4$, $z_{(\alpha/2)} = 1.65$, and $n = 50$. The calculation is a confidence interval representing the z statistic for normally distributed means.

Upper Limit   Lower Limit

$$E_\mu = \bar{x} + z_{(\alpha/2)} \frac{\sigma}{\sqrt{n}} \qquad E_\mu = \bar{x} - z_{(\alpha/2)} \frac{\sigma}{\sqrt{n}}$$

$$= 98.7 + 1.65 \frac{.4}{\sqrt{50}} \qquad = 98.7 - 1.65 \frac{.4}{\sqrt{50}}$$

$$= 98.7 + 1.65 \frac{.4}{7.07} \qquad = 98.7 - 1.65 \frac{.4}{7.07}$$

$$= 98.7 + 1.65(.057) \qquad = 98.7 - 1.65(.057)$$

$$= 98.7 + .093 \qquad\qquad = 98.7 - .093$$

$$= 98.8 \qquad\qquad\qquad = 98.6$$

Step 4   Identify and interpret the interval. The lower limit of the interval begins at 98.6; the upper limit ends at 98.8. Thus, with 90% certainty, the mean body temperature for the world's population should fall between 98.6 and 98.8.

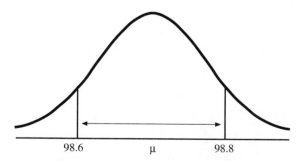

99% confidence interval ($98.6 < \mu < 98.8$)

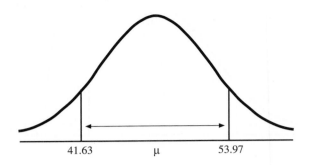

The confidence interval estimating the range of values in which the population mean should fall has a lower boundary of 41.63 and an upper boundary of 53.97. Therefore, with 99% confidence, the mean grocery bill is between $41.63 and $53.97.

| 99% confidence interval | $41.63 < \mu < $53.97 |
| 95% confidence interval | $43.11 < \mu < $52.49 |

CHAPTER 10 IN REVIEW

10.1 Find the critical z value associated with the shaded area of each curve.

a.

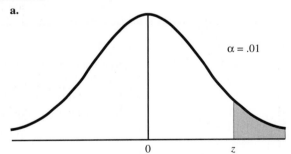

$\alpha = .01$

c.

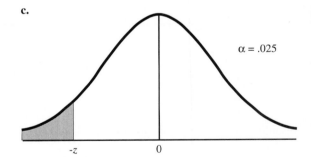

$\alpha = .025$

b.

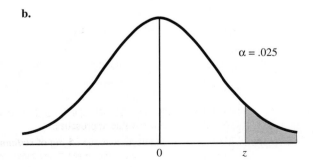

$\alpha = .025$

d.

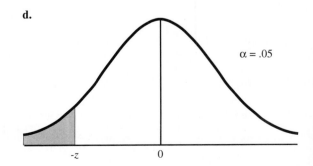

$\alpha = .05$

10.2   Find the critical z values associated with the shaded areas of each curve.

a.

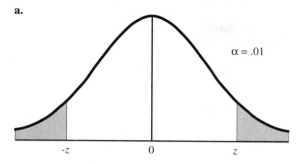

$\alpha = .01$

b.

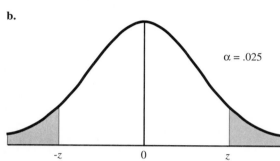

$\alpha = .025$

c.

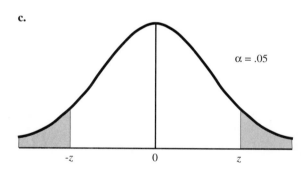

$\alpha = .05$

d.

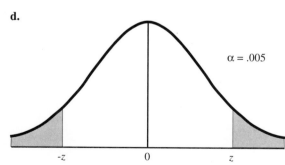

$\alpha = .005$

10.3   Using the correct format, state the null and alternative hypotheses.

a. The mean age of students is 27 y.

b. The mean commute for employees is less than 30 min.

c. The mean mortgage is more than $75,000.

d. The mean weight of babies is 7.2 lb.

e. The mean cost of a new car is $13,560.

10.4   Narratively describe the type A correct decision, type B correct decision, type I error and type II error for the null hypothesis that a man does not have cancer.

10.5   Identify whether the following hypotheses are one-tailed to the left, one-tailed to the right, or two-tailed.

a. H_0: $\mu \le 3$, H_1: $\mu > 3$
b. H_0: $\mu = 275$, H_1: $\mu \ne 275$
c. H_0: $\sigma \le 2.1$, H_1: $\sigma > 2.1$
d. H_0: $\sigma \ge .4$, H_1: $\sigma < .4$
e. H_0: $\sigma^2 = 19$, H_1: $\sigma^2 \ne 19$
f. H_0: $\mu \ge 2$, H_1: $\mu < 2$

10.6   Test the null hypothesis $\mu = 25$ given a sample mean 23.6 and a sample size 100. Use the classical approach with $\sigma = 5$ and $\alpha = .05$.

10.7   Test, using the classical approach, the claim that a population mean exceeds 52 using a sample of 50 producing a mean 54; $\sigma = 6$, $\alpha = .05$.

10.8   A randomly selected group of 200 students in Mrs. Brown's fifth grade class produces a score of 60.3 on a standardized test. Test whether their score significantly exceeds the national average of 58.01 with a standard deviation of 13.2. Use the classical and P-value approach; $\alpha = .01$.

10.9   The average weight of burgers sold at a fast-food chain is ¼ lb, with a standard deviation of .2. An employee wants to test whether a sample of 50 burgers producing a mean of .22 is significantly less than the claimed mean. Test using the P-value approach with a 5% level of significance.

10.10   An ulcer medicine claims that each tablet contains an average of 300 milligrams (mg), with a standard deviation of 11 mg. Test whether a sample of 60 tablets producing a mean of 304 mg significantly exceeds the claimed mean. Use the classical approach with a level of significance of .01.

10.11   Describe the errors involved in a car manufacturer's claim that the driver's side airbag was tested and approved. Which error is the most serious?

10.12   Describe the decision concerning the following P-values.

a. $P = .024$, $\alpha = .05$ **d.** $P = .013$, $\alpha = .01$
b. $P = .01$, $\alpha = .02$ **e.** $P = .05$, $\alpha = .01$
c. $P = .005$, $\alpha = .005$ **f.** $P = .215$ $\alpha = .025$

10.13   Describe the decision concerning the following one-tailed z critical values.

a. calculated $z = 1.29$,   critical $z = 1.96$
b. calculated $z = 2.47$,   critical $z = -1.96$
c. calculated $z = 1.96$,   critical $z = 1.645$
d. calculated $z = 2.09$,   critical $z = 2.58$
e. calculated $z = -3.09$, critical $z = -2.58$
f. calculated $z = -2.85$, critical $z = 2.58$

10.14   Test the claim $\mu \le 100$, with $\sigma = 12$, $n = 43$, $\bar{x} = 104$, $\alpha = .05$. Use the classical and P-value approaches.

10.15   A bottle of soda contains an average 35 mg of sodium with a standard deviation of 4.5 mg. Test to see if the mean is accurate based on a sample of 40 bottles with a mean of 33 mg. Use the classical approach with a level of significance of .01.

10.16   Estimate with 90% certainty the mean amount of stream pollution in the Rouge River using a sample of 100 units producing 122 milliliters (mL) of pollution; $\sigma = 14$.

10.17   Calculate a confidence interval for the mean amount of credit-card spending per year given a sample of 100 customers with a sample mean of $1756. The population standard deviation is 843 and $\alpha = .05$.

10.18   Conduct a 90% confidence interval for the average monthly apartment rent using a sample of 32 apartments with a mean of $375; $\sigma = 32.5$.

10.19   True or false?

    a. Increasing the percentage for the confidence interval decreases the range of values of the interval.

    b. If $P \le \alpha$, the decision is to reject the null hypothesis.

    c. The critical region is determined by the sign in the null hypothesis.

    d. A two-tailed test has one critical region to the right.

10.20   True or false?

    a. The level of significance is represented by alpha.

    b. Theories must be accepted as true until proven false.

    c. The null hypothesis carries the burden of proof.

    d. The probability of a type I error is failing to reject the null hypothesis when it is really false.

Inferences Concerning One Population

11

The central limit theorem presented in previous chapters is used when testing means of large samples when the population standard deviation σ is known. It is very unusual to have access to the population standard deviation when a population mean must be estimated. Samples are often small or not normally distributed. When a random variable is not fully normally distributed, when sample size is small, or when the population standard deviation is unknown, a *z* test cannot be performed. If any of the conditions for the normal distribution are absent when testing a mean, a *Student t distribution* can be used. The *Student t* distribution is a common test used in statistical analysis. Social scientists, behavioral scientists, and health scientists are often confronted with testing situations where samples are small and where the population standard deviation is unknown.

The *t* Distribution

The *Student t* distribution is a probability distribution similar to the normal curve. The *t* distribution is a probability distribution that depicts sampling means. It has several characteristics similar to the normal *z* distribution. The *t* distribution is symmetric, its mean is 0, and its variance is greater than 1 but decreases towards 1 as *n* increases. The *t* distribution looks very much like the *z* distribution, but if overlaid, *t* appears less peaked (flatter) than *z*. The tails of *t* are thicker than those for *z*. In other words, *t* is shorter and fatter than *z*. See Figure 11.1.

As with *z*, *t* values to the left of the mean 0 are negative, whereas *t* values to the right are positive. Unlike *z*, the table in Appendix A for *t* values gives actual critical values instead of probabilities.

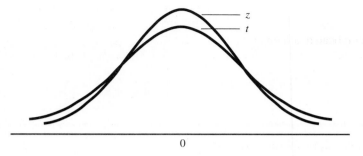

FIGURE 11.1

***Student t* distribution (*t* test)** A distribution representing means of one population, where

1. The random variable is not normally distributed.
2. Sample size is small, $n \leq 30$.
3. The population standard deviation σ is unknown.

Although there are several differences between *z* and *t*, some differences require special emphasis. A major difference lies in the calculation of the test statistic. The *t* test statistic is calculated by substituting the sample standard deviation for the unknown population standard deviation in the standard error estimate. Note the *z* and *t* formulas:

$$z = \frac{\bar{x} - \mu}{\sigma/\sqrt{n}} \qquad t = \frac{\bar{x} - \mu}{s/\sqrt{n}}$$

Another difference between *z* and *t* relates to the sample size. The *t* distribution estimates the population standard deviation σ with the sample standard deviation *s*. Because *s* is subject to sampling error and depends on sample size, the *t* distribution becomes a *series* of distributions. The distribution applied to any population depends on the sample size. A different distribution exists for every *n* from 2 through infinity. The smaller the *n*, the shorter the *t* curve. As sample size increases, the *t* curve resembles the *z* curve. For sample sizes greater than 30, the *t* distribution approximates the *z* curve. See Figure 11.2.

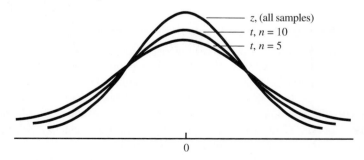

FIGURE 11.2

To find the appropriate t distribution for a given population, the sample size is used to find the number of *degrees of freedom*. The concept of degrees of freedom is very complicated, although it can be partially understood as the number of values in a sample that are independent of others. For the purpose of the t test, the number of degrees of freedom (denoted by df) is $n - 1$, and it determines which of the several t distributions should be used.

> **Degrees of freedom (df)** Determines which t distribution represents a particular population.
>
> $$df = n - 1$$
>
> where n equals the sample size.

In addition to being used to find the appropriate distribution, degrees of freedom and the level of significance, α, are used to find critical values for hypothesis testing and confidence intervals. Recall that alpha is the probability of committing a type I error, rejecting a true hypothesis. Table A.4 represents critical values of t. Table A.4 must be read using the degrees of freedom, the level of significance, alpha, and information about whether the distribution is one-tailed or two-tailed. Alpha levels appear across the top row, and degrees of freedom appear down the left column. The t notation representing the critical value is written with a subscript showing df and α. For example, if $n = 30$ and $\alpha = .05$, df $= 30 - 1$, or 29, and t is denoted by

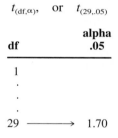

$$t_{(df, \alpha)}, \quad \text{or} \quad t_{(29, .05)}$$

df	alpha .05
1	
.	
.	
.	
29	→ 1.70

Figure 11.3 shows right-tailed notations and critical values.

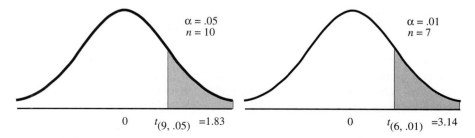

$\alpha = .05$
$n = 10$

$\alpha = .01$
$n = 7$

$0 \qquad t_{(9, .05)} = 1.83$

$0 \qquad t_{(6, .01)} = 3.14$

FIGURE 11.3

Left-tailed t values are indicated in two different ways. Some people use $1 - \alpha$ to imply left-tailed t values. For example, if $\alpha = .05$ and df = 20, then a right-tailed test would be indicated by $t_{(20,.05)}$, and a left-tailed value would be indicated as $t_{(20,.95)}$. In this text left-tailed t values are shown using right-tailed notations preceded by a negative sign. The negative sign is a reminder that the t value must also be negative, representing values less than the mean, 0. For example, a right-tailed notation is shown as $t_{(20,.05)}$, and the corresponding left-tailed notation is $-t_{(20,.05)}$. As with z, left-tailed t critical values are negative. See Figure 11.4.

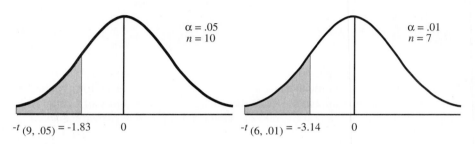

$-t_{(9,.05)} = -1.83$ 0 $-t_{(6,.01)} = -3.14$ 0

FIGURE 11.4

EXAMPLE 11.1

Experiment   Find the t critical values for the following notations.

a. $t_{(27,.025)}$ **b.** $t_{(14,.05)}$ **c.** $t_{(16,.01)}$
d. $-t_{(8,.025)}$ **e.** $-t_{(12,.05)}$ **f.** $-t_{(29,.10)}$

Answers

a.   2.05   **b.** 1.76   **c.** 2.58
d. -2.31 **e.** -1.78 **f.** -1.31

Solution   Table A.4 gives t critical values using degrees of freedom and levels of significance. The t notations are in the form of $t(\text{df}, \alpha)$. The values in a, b, and c are for right-tailed tests, because no alteration of the notation occurred. Right-tailed values require moving *down* to the appropriate number of degrees of freedom and then *across* to the appropriate alpha level. The values reported in the table are the critical values and need no adjustments. The values in d, e, and f are for the left side of the curve because all three have a negative sign. The critical values are found the same way as the right-tailed values—by tracing *down* to the appropriate number of degrees of freedom and then *across* to the appropriate alpha. The only difference is that the answers in d, e, and f must also be preceded by a negative sign, because they represent an area below the mean.

EXAMPLE 11.2

Experiment   Find the *t* critical values for the following two-tailed tests.

a.

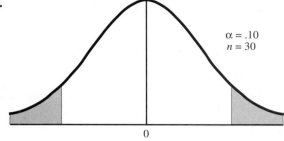

$\alpha = .10$
$n = 30$

c.

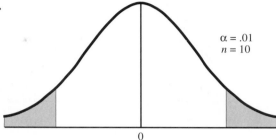

$\alpha = .01$
$n = 10$

b.

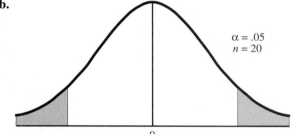

$\alpha = .05$
$n = 20$

d.

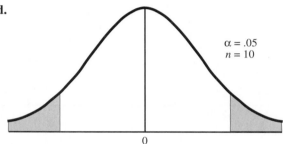

$\alpha = .05$
$n = 10$

Answers

a. −1.70 and 1.70   **c.** −3.25 and 3.25
b. −2.09 and 2.09   **d.** −2.26 and 2.26

Solution   All four curves are two-tailed and contain half of the critical region to the right of the mean and half to the left. Critical values for *t* are found by determining the degrees of freedom and alpha. Degrees of freedom are equal to $n − 1$. All four curves report the sample size *n*; thus, the degrees of freedom for the first curve are $30 − 1$, for the second, $20 − 1$, and for the third and fourth, $10 − 1$. Alpha in a two-tailed test must be divided by 2 before finding the critical values. Therefore, the notations describing the curves are as follows.

a. $-t_{(29,.1/2)}$ and $t_{(29,.1/2)}$ **c.** $-t_{(9,.01/2)}$ and $t_{(9,.01/2)}$
b. $-t_{(19,.05/2)}$ and $t_{(19,.05/2)}$ **d.** $-t_{(9,.05/2)}$ and $t_{(9,.05/2)}$

Once the notations are found, the critical values are determined by reading Table A.4. For part a, $-t(29, .1/2)$ and $t(29, .1/2)$, trace *down* to 29 and *across* to .1/2, or .05. The value 1.70 is found. Because the *t* distribution is symmetric, a value of −1.70 represents the left tail in a two-tailed test. For b, $-t(19, .05/2)$ and $t(19, .05/2)$, the value is found by tracing *down* to 19 and *across* to .05/2, or .025. The value 2.09 represents the right tail and −2.09 represents the left tail. In the third case, $-t(9, .01/2)$ and $t(9, .01/2)$ the value is found by tracing *down* to 9 and *across* to .01/2, or .005. Both values, 3.25 and −3.25, must be used for a two-tailed test. Finally, $-t(9, .05/2)$ and $t(9, .05/2)$ are found by tracing *down* to 9 and *across* to .05/2, or .025. The values 2.26 and -2.26 are used.

a.

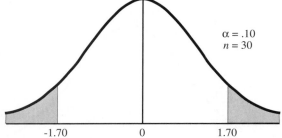

$\alpha = .10$
$n = 30$

-1.70   0   1.70

c.

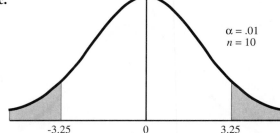

$\alpha = .01$
$n = 10$

-3.25   0   3.25

b.

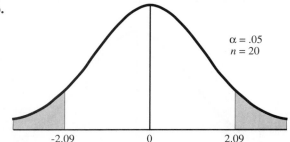

$\alpha = .05$
$n = 20$

-2.09   0   2.09

d.

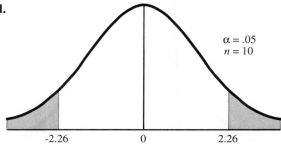

$\alpha = .05$
$n = 10$

-2.26   0   2.26

A LEARNING AID

t Distribution

Find the critical value for a two-tailed test of a mean with a sample of 21 and an alpha of .05.

Step 1 Identify the test statistic. A test for a mean has two possible test statistics, z and t. Student t is used when the sample size is small ($n \leq 30$) or the population standard deviation σ is unknown. The sample is given as 21, which requires the use of t. Also, σ is not given.

Step 2 Identify the test statistic notation. The t notation includes a subscript for the degrees of freedom and alpha. As a two-tailed test, there will be two notations, which means alpha must be divided by 2. The left-tailed value must carry a negative sign. The degrees of freedom are determined by subtracting 1 from the sample size.

$$df = n - 1 = 21 - 1 = 20$$

Where df $= 20$ and alpha $= .05$, the notations are as follows

Left-tailed notation: $-t_{(df, \alpha/2)} = -t_{(20, .05/2)} = -t_{(20, .025)}$
Right-tailed Notation: $t_{(df, \alpha/2)} = t_{(20, .05/2)} = t_{(20, .025)}$

Step 3 Determine the critical values. Table A.4 is read by moving *down* to the degrees of freedom, 20, and *across* to alpha, .025. The value 2.09 is given in the intersection. 2.09 is the critical value for the right tail of a t distribution with 20 degrees of freedom and an alpha at .05/2, or .025. Because t is a symmetric curve with a mean of 0, the left-tail value is determined by appending a negative sign to 2.09. Only z and t left-tail values are found by affixing negative signs to the values reported in Appendix A.

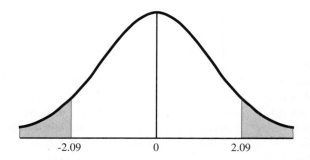

-2.09   0   2.09

The classical approach for testing means of small samples using t follows the same steps presented in Chapter 10 for z. The t distribution will be used for testing means for small samples where n is less than or equal to 30 ($n \leq 30$) or where the population standard deviation σ is unknown. The first step requires stating the null and alternative hypotheses. The statement of the hypotheses for t is the same as in testing for z. That is, the null hypothesis, H_0, requires the notation of the parameter μ, a mathematical symbol $=$, $\leq$, or $\geq$, and a specified value. The alternative hypothesis, H_1, includes the same parameter and value but uses a contrasting mathematical symbol, $\neq$, $>$, or $<$. That is,

Hypothesis Test: Classical Approach for *t*

If H_0 is $\mu = 0$, then H_1 is $\mu \neq 0$.

If H_0 is $\mu \leq 3$, then H_1 is $\mu > 3$.

If H_0 is $\mu \geq 27$, then H_1 is $\mu < 27$.

The second step in hypothesis testing is to identify the test criteria. The test criteria include the level of significance, the test statistic, the critical region, and the critical value. The level of significance is usually given in the problem as alpha (α). If alpha is not known, then the level of significance is determined based on the seriousness of a type I error. The test statistic is determined by deciding which test to conduct. The test statistics include z, t, χ^2, F. Thus far, only z and t have been described. The z test statistic is used when sample means are normally distributed, the sample size is greater than 30, and σ is known. The t test statistic is used when sample size is less than or equal to ($\leq$) 30 or σ is unknown. The critical region is determined by considering the alternative hypothesis to decide if the test is one-tailed to the left, two-tailed, or one-tailed to the right. Recall that a one-tailed test to the left requires an alternative hypothesis involving less than. A two-tailed test requires the alternative hypothesis to involve not equal to, and a right-tailed test requires the alternative hypothesis to involve greater than.

Test	Sign in H_1
One-tailed left	$<$
Two-tailed	$\neq$
One-tailed right	$>$

The critical values are found in Table A.4. To find the critical value, the degrees of freedom and alpha level must be known. One-tailed values are found simply by reading *down* Table A.4 to the appropriate number of degrees of freedom (calculated as $n - 1$) and *across* to alpha. Values for one-tailed to the left are negative. Two-tailed tests require alpha to be divided by 2 ($\alpha/2$) before Table A.4 can be used. The right tail in a two-tailed test is the value reported with the appropriate df and $\alpha/2$. Because t is symmetric, the left-tail value is the same value as used for the right tail, but it is negative to reflect its position below (to the left of) the mean 0.

The third step in hypothesis testing using the classical approach is to calculate the test statistic. The calculation of the t statistic is similar to z, but the sample standard deviation s replaces the unknown population standard deviation σ.

Calculation of the Test Statistic t

$$t = \frac{\bar{x} - \mu}{s/\sqrt{n}}$$

where

$\bar{x}$ is the sample mean.

μ is the population mean.

s is the sample standard deviation.

n is the square root of the sample size.

Step 4 in hypothesis testing requires the placement of the calculated value on the curve to compare it to the critical value. Step 5 is the decision to reject the null hypothesis or to fail to reject the null hypothesis. Rejection of the null hypothesis must occur when the calculated value falls within the critical region. Failing to reject the null hypothesis should occur when the calculated value does not fail within the critical region. The critical regions are determined in step 2. See Figures 11.5–11.7.

The final step in hypothesis testing is to apply the decision to the problem. The decision to reject H_0 or fail to reject H_0 must be interpreted using the information in the original problem. The rejecting of H_0 means that the sample data provided sufficient evidence at the tested level of significance to reject the claim of the null hypothesis. Failing to reject H_0 means the sample did not provide sufficient evidence to disprove the null hypothesis. *Failing to reject H_0 does not prove the null hypothesis correct. It simply does not prove it false.*

Recall the steps in hypothesis testing as reviewed here and as presented in Chapter 10. Each step must be completed. The only major differences thus far are

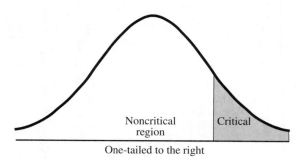

One-tailed to the right

FIGURE 11.5

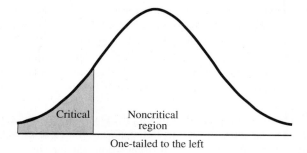

One-tailed to the left

FIGURE 11.6

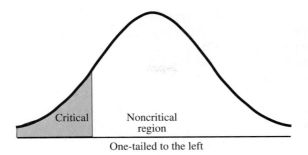

One-tailed to the left

FIGURE 11.7

in calculating the test statistic t and using the t distribution table in Appendix A for the critical value.

Steps in Hypothesis Testing Using the Classical Approach

1. State H_0 and H_1.
2. Identify the test criteria.
   a. Level of significance, α
   b. Test statistic (z, t, χ^2, F)
   c. Critical region
      (1) One-tailed test
      (2) Two-tailed test
   d. Critical value
3. Calculate the test statistic.
4. Place calculated value on a distribution curve.
5. Make a decision.
   a. Fail to reject H_0.
   b. Reject H_0.
6. Interpret the results.

EXAMPLE 11.3

Experiment   The camp coordinators at the ABC summer camp program claim the average age of students attending their camp is 12 y. A teenage boy thinks the average age is something less than that and hopes to prove the camp coordinators wrong so he can convince his parents not to send him to summer camp. The boy conducts a survey of the ages of 30 boys at camp last year. The sample mean is 10.9 with a standard deviation of 1.4. Conduct a hypothesis test using the classical approach with an alpha of .05.

Answer   Reject H_0. The sample provides sufficient evidence at the .05 level of significance to reject the claim that the average age of children at the summer camp is 12 y old.

Solution   The problem clearly asks for a classical hypothesis test. The first step in hypothesis testing requires stating the null and alternative hypotheses. The null hypothesis is the claim by the camp coordinators that the mean age of children is 12 y. The alternative hypothesis is the challenge by the teenage boy, who claims the mean age of children at camp is less than 12 y. Because the alternative hypothesis is less than, the null hypothesis becomes not only equal to but also greater than. The parameter in question is the mean, and the value challenged is 12 y. The hypotheses are

$$H_0: \quad \mu \geq 12$$

$$H_1: \quad \mu < 12$$

Step 2 is the identification of the test criteria. The test criteria include the level of significance, test statistic, critical region, and critical value. The level of significance is given as alpha = .05. The test statistic is the *t* test, because the sample size is small at 30 (*t* is used when $n \leq 30$) and the population standard deviation σ is unknown. Either of these conditions (small sample size or σ unknown) is sufficient reason to use *t*. The critical region is to the left, because the < sign in the alternative hypothesis denotes a one-tailed test to the left. The critical value is found using Table A.4. Critical values for *t* require the degrees of freedom and alpha. The degrees of freedom are equal to $n - 1$. Table A.4 is read by going *down* the left column to the appropriate number of degrees of freedom and *across* to the appropriate alpha level. This is a left-tailed test in which $n = 30$, df $= 30 - 1$, or 29, and alpha = .05. The notation and critical value are:

Critical value $t_{(29,.05)} = -1.70$

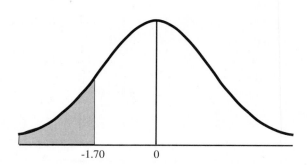

$$-1.70 \qquad 0$$

Step 3 is the calculation of the test statistic. The information needed for the calculation is: $n = 30$, $\mu = 12$, $\bar{x} = 10.9$, and $s = 1.4$. The *t* calculation is as follows:

$$t = \frac{\bar{x} - \mu}{s/\sqrt{n}} = \frac{10.9 - 12}{1.4/\sqrt{30}}$$

$$= \frac{-1.1}{1.4/5.48}$$

$$= \frac{-1.1}{.255}$$

$$= -4.31$$

Step 4 involves placing the calculated value, −4.31, on the curve representing the distribution. Notice −4.31 falls to the left of the critical value, −1.70.

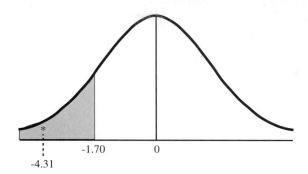

Step 5 is the decision to reject H_0 or fail to reject H_0. The decision is to reject H_0, because the calculated value −4.31 falls in the critical region, left of the critical value, −1.70.

Step 6 is the interpretation of the decision using the original problem. Rejecting the null hypothesis suggests that the sample provides sufficient evidence that the mean age of children at the camp is not equal to 12 y. There is sufficient proof at the .05 level of significance that the mean age of children is less than 12 y. It would seem that the teenage boy may have a pretty good argument not to go to the camp.

EXAMPLE 11.4

Experiment An employee at a credit card company claims the holders of its card spend more than $1500 per year. A survey of 25 cardholders produces a mean of $1756 and a standard deviation of $843. Is the company's claim justified at the .025 level of significance?

Answer No, there is not sufficient evidence at the .025 level of significance to justify the credit card company's claim that the average bill is greater than $1500.

Solution The first step in hypothesis testing requires stating the null and alternative hypotheses. The employee's claim is that the bills are greater than $1500. The symbol > represents greater than and can be placed only in the alternative hypothesis. The null hypothesis must be the opposite. The opposite of > (more than) is ≤ (less than or equal to). The parameter in question is the mean, and the value challenged is $1500. The hypotheses are written as follows:

$$H_0: \quad \mu \leq 1500$$

$$H_1: \quad \mu > 1500$$

Step 2 is the identification of the test criteria. The test criteria include the level of significance, test statistic, critical region, and critical value. The level of

A LEARNING AID

Classical Testing for *t*

The admissions officer at a university believes that recent applicants have lower mean scores on the English placement test than past students. The mean of past students is 65. Twenty-five students were selected; their mean was 60 and standard deviation was 9. Can it be concluded that today's students have lower test scores? Use $\alpha = .05$.

Step 1 State the hypothesis. The classical approach for all test statistics begins by stating the null and alternative hypotheses. The null hypothesis carries the benefit of the doubt. A challenge to the null hypothesis carries the burden of proof. The mean of past students becomes the parameter used in the hypotheses. The admissions officer challenging the mean claims the mean is less than 65. A claim challenging a null hypothesis that also carries a less than ($<$) sign must be placed in the alternative hypothesis. A less than ($<$) sign in the alternative hypothesis requires a greater than or equal to ($\geq$) sign in the null hypothesis. The parameter is a population mean (μ) with a value 65. State the hypotheses.

$$H_0: \quad \mu \geq 65 \qquad H_1: \mu < 65$$

Step 2 Determine the test criteria. The first test criteria is the level of significance, alpha. Alpha is stated as .05. Select a test statistic from z, t, χ^2, and F. Choose the t distribution because the sample size is small ($n \leq 30$) and the population standard deviation σ is unknown. Either of these conditions is sufficient to require the use of t.

The test is a left-tailed test, as determined by the direction of the sign in the alternative hypothesis. When the alternative hypothesis is less than ($<$), the test is one-tailed to the left. Add a negative sign to left-tailed t critical values. Write the critical value using degrees of freedom and alpha. Degrees of freedom (df) for t are calculated as $n - 1$. The sample of 25 students produces df $= 25 - 1$, or 24. Alpha is .05. Alpha does not need to be divided in this problem, because it is not a two-tailed test. State the notation:

$$t_{(df, \alpha)} = t_{(24, .05)}$$

Using Table A.4, trace *down* to 24 degrees of freedom and *across* to .05. The value in the intersection is the critical value. You should find a value of 1.71. Add a negative sign to represent the left tail of the curve. The critical value separating the critical region from the noncritical region is -1.71.

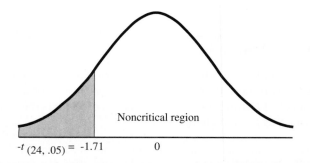

$$^{-}t_{(24, .05)} = {-}1.71 \qquad 0$$

significance is given as alpha $= .025$. The test statistic is the t test, because the sample size is small at 25 (t is used when $n \leq 30$) and the population standard deviation σ is unknown. Either of these conditions (small sample size or σ unknown) is sufficient reason to use t. The critical region is to the right, because the $>$ sign in the alternative hypothesis denotes a one-tailed test to the right. The critical value is found using Table A.4. Critical values for t require the degrees of freedom and alpha. The degrees of freedom are equal to $n - 1$. Table A.4 is read by going *down* the left column to the appropriate number of degrees of freedom and *across* to the appropriate alpha level. This is a right-tailed test where $n = 25$, df $= 25 - 1$, or 24, and alpha $= .025$. The notation and critical value are:

Step 3   Calculate the test statistic. The test statistic for t uses the sample standard deviation instead of the unknown population standard deviation. The sample of 25 produced a sample mean of 60 and a sample standard deviation of 9; calculate t: $\mu = 65$, $\bar{x} = 60$, $s = 9$, and $n = 25$.

$$t = \frac{\bar{x} - \mu}{s/\sqrt{n}} = \frac{60 - 65}{9/\sqrt{25}}$$

$$= \frac{-5}{9/5}$$

$$= \frac{-5}{1.8}$$

$$= -2.78$$

Step 4   Place the calculated test statistic on the distribution curve. The calculated value -2.78 is placed to the left of the critical value, -1.71.

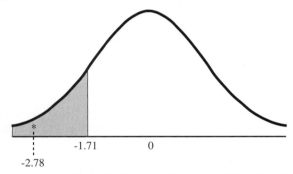

Step 5   Make a decision. Reject the null hypothesis, because the calculated value -2.78 falls within the critical region.

Reject H_0

Step 6   Interpret the results. Apply the decision to the original question presented in the experiment. The question is to determine if it can be concluded that today's students have lower test scores than past students. The decision to reject the null hypothesis suggests that the answer to the question is yes. Based on this sample of 25 students at the .05 level of significance, there is sufficient evidence to suggest that the scores of today's students are significantly lower than scores of past students. The test only suggests the scores are significantly lower than 65. It does not indicate the average of the scores is 60. The rejection of the null hypothesis merely indicates it is false, not that any other assertion is correct.

Critical value $t_{(24,.025)} = 2.064$

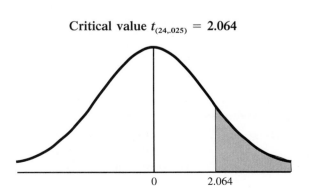

Step 3 involves the calculation of the test statistic. The information needed for the calculation is: $n = 25$, $\mu = 1500$, $\bar{x} = 1756$, and $s = 843$. The t calculation is as follows:

$$t = \frac{\bar{x} - \mu}{s/\sqrt{n}} = \frac{1756 - 1500}{843/\sqrt{25}}$$

$$= \frac{256}{843/5}$$

$$= \frac{256}{168.6}$$

$$= 1.518$$

Step 4 is to place the calculated value 1.518 on the curve representing the distribution. Notice that 1.518 falls to the left of the critical value 2.064.

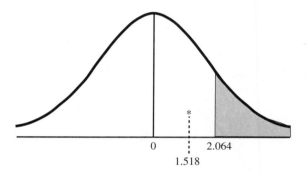

Step 5 involves the decision to reject H_0 or fail to reject H_0. The decision is to fail to reject H_0, because the calculated value does not fall in the critical region.

Step 6 is the interpretation of the decision using the original problem. Failing to reject the null hypothesis suggests that the sample does not provide sufficient evidence that the mean bill of cardholders is less than or equal to $1500. There is not sufficient proof at the .025 level of significance that the mean bill for cardholders is less than or equal to $1500. It would seem that the employee is wrong; the bills are not more than $1500.

SECTION 3

t Testing Using P-Values

The prob-value, or *P*-value, approach to hypothesis testing takes the classical approach one step further by transforming the calculated value into a probability and comparing the probability to an alpha level. *P*-values, whether for *z*, *t*, or other test statistics, are probabilities that measure the level of significance at which the test statistic becomes significant provided the null hypothesis is true. Because *P*-values and alphas are probabilities, each compared to the other leads to decisions about the null hypothesis.

Computerized statistical programs typically report calculated *t* values with an associated *P*-value. The calculated *t* value may be used to conduct a classical hypothesis test, and the *P*-value may be used to conduct a *P*-value hypothesis test. The classical approach requires identification of the test criteria, including the critical region and critical value. Usually a statistics book or *t* distribution table is necessary to determine the critical value. When such tools are not readily available, the *P*-value test allows the same conclusions to be drawn.

When a *P*-value is offered by a computerized program or by another source, a comparison of the *P*-value with the alpha level is necessary. If the *P*-value is less than or equal to α, then the null hypothesis should be rejected. If the *P*-value is greater than α, the null hypothesis should fail to be rejected.

A complete hypothesis test using the *P*-value approach is much like the classical approach for *t* and the *P*-value approach for *z*. The six steps identified for *z* in Chapter 10 are repeated here for *t*. Step 1 is to identify the null and alternative hypotheses. Step 2 is to determine two aspects of the test criteria, the level of significance and the test statistic. The level of significance is either given as α in the problem or must be determined by considering the seriousness of a type I error—that is, rejecting a true hypothesis. The test statistic must be determined by reviewing the parameter in the hypotheses. The only parameter used in testing so far is the population mean, μ, allowing for the use of only *z* or *t* test statistics. The *t* statistic is used with samples having an *n* of 30 or less or when σ is unknown. Step 3 is to calculate the test statistic. The calculation for the *t* test statistic is

$$t = \frac{\bar{x} - \mu}{s/\sqrt{n}}$$

Step 4 is the rewriting of the calculated test statistic as a probability. The transformation of *t* is slightly different than for *z*. The *z* score requires finding a probability in the *z* table, subtracting it from .5000, and adjusting it as necessary. The *t* score also requires consulting the *t* table for a probability. To find the probability for *t*, the degrees of freedom for the sample are also necessary. The *P*-value for *t* is determined by noting the calculated value from step 3 with the degrees of freedom from step 2. Using Table A.4, trace *down* to the appropriate number of degrees of freedom. Read *across* all the values of that row, finding the value closest to the calculated value. The value in the table nearest to the calculated value serves as a guide to the probability used as the *P*-value. The *P*-value is the alpha level associated with the column where the value closest to the calculated value is found. For example, if the calculated value in step 3 equals 1.76 for a sample of 17 with df $= 16$ ($17 - 1 = 16$), the *P*-value is .05. Find the *P*-value of .05 by moving *down* to the number of degrees of freedom, 16, *across* to the value 1.746, which is nearest to the calculated value 1.76, and *up* to the alpha value of .05 associated with the column where 1.746 is found at 16 degrees of freedom.

Degrees of Freedom		Alpha			
	.01	.025	.05		←
1	. . .	. . .	. . .	. . .	
2	. . .	. . .	. . .	. . .	
. . .	. . .	. . .	. . .		
16	. . .	. . .	. . .	1.746	

$$P\text{-value}_{(1.76,\ df\ 16)} = .05$$

If the calculated value falls between two critical values, use both alpha values to denote the range of values where the P-value lies. For example, if the calculated value in step 3 equals 2.32 for a sample of 17, with df $= 16$, then the P-value lies in a range from .01 to .025. Both values are noted and compared to the original alpha in making a decision about the hypothesis. Find the P-value for a calculated value of $t = 2.32$ by tracing *down* the t table to 16 degrees of freedom, *across* to the closest values, and *up* to the alpha levels. The values closest to 2.32 at 16 df are 2.584 and 2.120. Tracing up the columns, 2.584 is associated with an alpha of .01, whereas 2.120 is associated with .025. The P-value falls between .01 and .025.

Degrees of Freedom		.01	Alpha	.025	.05
1		. . .	↑	. . .	. . .
2		. . .		. . .	. . .
. . .		. . .		. . .	. . .
16	. . .	2.584		2.120	1.746

$$P\text{-value}_{(2.32, df16)} = .01 < P < .025$$

The next step in P-value testing requires comparing the P-value to alpha and making a decision about the hypothesis. The rule for the decision using P-values remains constant for all test statistics. If the P-value is less than or equal to alpha, then reject the null hypothesis. If the P-value is greater than alpha, then fail to reject the null hypothesis.

$P \le \alpha$ Reject H_0.
$P > \alpha$ Fail to reject H_0.

The final step is to interpret the decision. Rejecting the null hypothesis suggests that the sample provided sufficient statistical proof that the null hypothesis is not true. It is important to remember that rejecting the null hypothesis does not suggest that the sample information is true or that the new parameter is represented by the sample statistic. Likewise, failing to reject the null hypothesis suggests only that the sample does not provide sufficient evidence to challenge the null hypothesis. Failing to reject the null hypothesis does not prove it to be correct or true but shows only that it withstood this specific test.

Steps in Hypothesis Testing Using the *P*-Value Approach

1. State H_0 and H_1.
2. Identify the test criteria.
   a. Level of significance
   b. Test statistic
3. Calculate the test statistic.
4. Calculate the *P*-value.
   a. One-tailed test
   b. Two-tailed test
5. Make a decision.
   a. Fail to reject H_0.
   b. Reject H_0.
6. Interpret the results.

EXAMPLE 11.5

Experiment   It is argued that the risk of complications in pregnancy is increased as the age of the mother increases. The mean age of mothers for all pregnancies is 27.8 y. Case histories of 25 pregnancies where complications occurred at Mercy Hospital reveal the mean age of mothers to be 29.75 y, with a standard deviation of 3.2. Using the *P*-value approach, does the sample provide sufficient evidence to support the assertion that the risk of complications in pregnancy increases with the age of the mother? Use $\alpha = .025$.

Answer   Yes, there is sufficient evidence to suggest that complications in pregnancy increase with the age of the mother.

Solution   There are six steps in hypothesis testing using the *P*-value approach: State the hypothesis, identify the test criteria, calculate the test statistic, calculate the *P*-value, make a decision, and interpret the results. The hypothesis concerns the mean age of pregnancy. The mean is the parameter for the population, with a value of 27.8 y. The mathematical symbol referred to in the experiment is greater than ($>$), which is found in the statement that the risk of complications increases as the age of the mother increases. The symbol $>$ is allowed only in the alternative hypothesis. Also, the statement about the relationship of complications to age is suggested as an argument. The alternative hypothesis argues or challenges the null hypothesis. If the alternative symbol is $>$, then the null symbol must be $\leq$. State the hypotheses.

$$H_0: \quad \mu \leq 27.8 \qquad H_1: \quad \mu > 27.8$$

The test criteria for *P*-value testing require identification of the test statistic and level of confidence. The test statistic is *t*. Use the *t* distribution for a sample of 25 where the population standard deviation is unknown. The level of significance is given as .025.

The third step in using the *P*-value approach is to calculate the test statistic. The calculation of t requires the following information derived from the experiment: $\mu = 27.8$, $\bar{x} = 29.75$, $s = 3.2$, and $n = 25$.

$$t = \frac{\bar{x} - \mu}{s/\sqrt{n}} = \frac{29.75 - 27.8}{3.2/\sqrt{25}} = \frac{1.95}{3.2/5} = \frac{1.95}{.64} = 3.04$$

Transform the calculated value into a probability using Table A.4. The P-value for the t statistic is determined by moving *down* the degrees of freedom column, *across* to the value closest to the calculated value, and *up* to the alpha associated with that column. The degrees of freedom equal $n - 1$; for a sample of 25, df $= 24$. The calculated value is 3.04. Move *down* to df 24. Reading *across* this row only, notice the value closest to 3.04 is 2.797. Move *up* the column containing 2.797 and find alpha, .005. The alpha value of .005 is the P-value associated with the calculated value 3.04 at 24 degrees of freedom.

Degrees of Freedom	Alpha .005
1	. . .
2	. . .
. . .	. . .
24	2.797

$$P\text{-value}_{(3.04, \text{df}24)} = .005$$

Compare the P-value to the original alpha given in the experiment. If $P \leq \alpha$, then reject the null hypothesis. If $P > \alpha$, then fail to reject the null hypothesis. P at .005 is less than α at .025; therefore, reject the null hypothesis.

$$P\text{-value}_{(.005)} \leq \alpha_{(.025)} \qquad \text{Reject } H_0$$

The final step in P-value testing is interpreting the results. Rejecting the null hypothesis suggests there is sufficient evidence provided by this sample of 25 at the .025 level of significance that the risk of complications in pregnancies is related to the age of the mother. As the age of the mother increases, so, too, does the risk of complications.

EXAMPLE 11.6

Experiment   A computer software program gives a calculated t value of 1.325 with a P-value of .10. What decision can be made for a one-tailed hypothesis test at $\alpha = .05$?

Answer   Fail to reject H_0

Solution   Computer software programs often give P-values representing the level of significance at which the test statistic becomes significant. When a P-value is reported, proceed directly to step 5 in hypothesis testing. The identification of the calculated value and its transformation into a probability is already represented in the P-value. Simply compare the P-value to alpha and make a decision. If the P-value is less than or equal to ($\leq$) alpha, reject the null hypothesis. If P is greater than alpha, fail to reject the null hypothesis. In this experiment, $P = .10$ is greater than $\alpha = .05$. Fail to reject the null hypothesis.

$$P\text{-value}_{(.10)} > \alpha_{(.05)} \qquad \text{Fail to reject } H_0$$

A LEARNING AID

t Testing Using *P*-Values

A random sample of nine students who used a computer to type a term paper showed that the mean number of typing errors was 7.8, with a standard deviation of 3.0. It had been predicted that the average number of errors would be 9.0. Using the P-value approach, do these results show, at the .05 level of significance, that the mean number of errors is actually different from 9.0?

    Step 1 State the hypotheses. The null hypothesis is contained in the sentence asking whether the mean number of errors is different from the predicted 9.0. If the mean is different, it is not equal to the given value. The not equal to symbol ($\neq$) is allowed only in the alternative hypothesis. Because the mathematical symbols in hypotheses are paired, if the alternative is not equal to, then the null must be equal to. State the hypotheses.

$$H_0: \quad \mu = 9.0 \qquad H_1: \quad \mu \neq 9.0$$

    Step 2 Identify the test criteria. The test criteria for P-value testing include the level of significance and test statistic. The level of significance is given as .05. The test statistic is t. Use t when testing for means with small sample sizes or when the population standard deviation is unknown.

    Step 3 Calculate the test statistic. The following information is derived from the problem: $n = 9$, $\bar{x} = 7.8$, $s = 3.0$, and $\mu = 9.0$.

$$t = \frac{\bar{x} - \mu}{s/\sqrt{n}} = \frac{7.8 - 9.0}{3.0/\sqrt{9}} = \frac{-1.2}{3.0/3} = \frac{-1.2}{1} = -1.2$$

    Step 4 Transform the calculated value into a P-value. Use Table A.4. Note that degrees of freedom are necessary for the t statistic. Degrees of freedom are equal to $n - 1$; in this case, $9 - 1 = 8$. Using the table, move *down* to 8 degrees of freedom. Read

across this row until the value closest to the calculated value -1.2 is found. Because the t distribution is symmetric, a negative value is treated exactly like a positive value. The closest value to -1.2 is 1.397. Read *up* the column containing 1.397 to the alpha value of .10. The value of .10 is for a one-tailed test. This experiment is two-tailed, because the alternative hypothesis includes the $=$ sign. Multiply the alpha by 2 to obtain a two-tailed alpha value. The P-value is .10 $\times$ 2 = .20.

Degrees of Freedom	Alpha .10
1	
2	
. . .	
8	1.397

$$P\text{-value} = .10 \times 2 = .20$$

    Step 5 Make a decision. Compare the P-value to the original alpha presented in the problem. If P is less than or equal to alpha, then reject the null hypothesis. If P is greater than alpha, then fail to reject the null hypothesis. The P-value of .20 is greater than alpha (.05); therefore, fail to reject the null hypothesis.

$$P\text{-value}_{(.20)} > \alpha_{(.05)} \qquad \text{Fail to reject } H_0$$

    Step 6 Interpret the results. Due to the decision to fail to reject the null hypothesis, there is not sufficient evidence at this particular level of significance to reject the mean. Applying this interpretation to the problem, the sample of nine students does not provide sufficient evidence at the .05 level of significance that the mean number of errors is different than the predicted 9 errors.

Confidence Interval for t

Testing population parameters using sample information is only one aspect of inferential statistics. A second aspect of inferential statistics is estimating population parameters from sample statistics. Testing and estimating can be viewed as opposite sides of the same coin. Testing allows a researcher to determine if a sample statistic is within a given range around the parameter. Estimating allows a researcher to determine the parameter within a given range around a sample statistic. A population parameter can be estimated from sample data using the technique known as confidence intervals. Recall the definition of a confidence interval presented in Chapter 10.

> **Confidence interval** Estimating a population parameter from sample statistics given a specified level of confidence.

A confidence interval establishes a range of values around the sample information where the population parameter will fall given a particular degree of confidence. The sample statistic used as the point of departure to determine the range of values for the interval is known as the point estimate.

> **Point estimate** The sample statistic used to estimate the population parameter. When estimating the parameter μ, the point estimate is the sample statistic $\bar{x}$.

The degree of confidence, or level of confidence, establishes the probability that the population parameter will fall inside the range of values set by the point estimate. Recall that Chapter 10 presents the concept of the level of confidence as the opposite of alpha. Alpha is the probability of committing an error; the level of confidence is the probability of being correct. The level of confidence is usually stated as a percentage. To be 90% sure the population parameter falls within a range around the point estimate, the level of confidence must be .90 and alpha must be .10. Alpha and the level of confidence must have a sum of 1.0.

Unlike Chapter 10, where the level of confidence is transformed into a probability and then into a z score, confidence intervals for t require transforming the level of confidence directly into a t value by using the degrees of freedom and alpha divided by 2. *Remember that all confidence intervals are two-tailed, requiring dividing alpha by 2.* Also remember that t values are dependent on sample size, described as degrees of freedom and equal to $n - 1$. Identify the degrees of freedom and the alpha level, $\alpha/2$. Use Table A.4. Go *down* to the appropriate degrees of freedom and *across* to the value under the correct alpha level. The critical value found in the intersection is denoted by $t_{(\text{df},\alpha/2)}$. Use this value to calculate the confidence interval.

EXAMPLE 11.7

Experiment Find the critical value associated with a 95% confidence interval for t where $n = 30$.

Answer $t_{(29,.025)} = 2.045$.

Solution Critical values for t are found in Table A.4. Alpha and the number of degrees of freedom are required for t critical values. If a 95% (.95) confidence level is necessary, then alpha must be 5%, or .05. All confidence intervals are two-tailed. Divide alpha, .05, by 2 so that half of the probability of an error is on both sides of the point estimate. The alpha to use is .05/2, or .025. The degrees of freedom are $n - 1 = 30 - 1 = 29$. Using Table A.4, go *down* the degrees of freedom to 29 and *across* to the $\alpha/2$ value .025. The value 2.045 is found in the intersection and is the critical value to be placed in the calculation of the interval.

The calculation of the confidence interval for means normally distributed with small samples ($n \leq 30$) is similar to z, but the population standard deviation, σ, is substituted for the sample standard deviation s.

The Formula for a Confidence Interval with a Mean Normally Distributed and a Small Sample Size (30 or Less)

$$E_\mu = \bar{x} + t_{(df,\alpha/2)} \frac{s}{\sqrt{n}} \quad \text{and} \quad E_\mu = \bar{x} - t_{(df,\alpha/2)} \frac{s}{\sqrt{n}}$$

where

E_μ is the estimate of the population mean.

$\bar{x}$ is the sample mean, known as the point estimate.

$t_{(df,\alpha/2)}$ is the critical value found in Table A.4.

$s/\sqrt{n}$ is the estimate of the sample error for t.

As in the case of other procedures, there are several steps that help organize the calculation and interpretation of the confidence interval.

Steps in Calculating a Confidence Interval for a Population Parameter

1. Identify the level of confidence.
2. Identify the test statistic (z, t, χ^2, or F).
3. Determine the critical value with $\alpha/2$.
4. Calculate the interval.
5. State the interval.

Step 1 identifies the problem as a confidence interval and the level of confidence. Key words are *interval, confidence,* or *estimate.* The level of confidence is also usually cited within the statement as "estimate with 90% confidence" or "calculate a 90% interval." Questions asking for a confidence interval for the mean would not cite a population mean, or μ value.

Step 2 is to identify the test statistic. Thus far, z and t have been described. Use z for normally distributed means with large samples and where the standard deviation of the population is known. Use t for normally distributed means with small samples ($n \leq 30$) or when the population standard deviation is unknown.

The third step is to determine the critical value. The t statistic requires the degrees of freedom and alpha. Degrees of freedom are equal to $n - 1$. Alpha is determined by subtracting the level of confidence from 1. If a 90% level of confidence is desired, then alpha is $1 - .9$, or .10. *All alphas must be divided by 2 when calculating a confidence interval.* Use Table A.4. Go *down* to the degrees of freedom and *across* to the alpha column. The value in the intersection is the critical value. Use this value for the calculation in step 4.

The fourth step is to calculate the confidence interval. The calculation must be performed twice to establish the lower and upper limits of the range. The formulas are essentially the same; one formula subtracts a value from the point estimate and the other formula adds a value to it. The t calculation is

$$E_\mu = \bar{x} + t_{(df,\alpha/2)} \frac{s}{\sqrt{n}} \quad \text{and} \quad E_\mu = \bar{x} - t_{(df,\alpha/2)} \frac{s}{\sqrt{n}}$$

The final step is restating the calculated values in the appropriate format. The notation for an interval places the parameter inside the lower and upper limit of the values calculated in step 4. The parameter μ is used for the t statistic.

$$\text{lower limit} < \mu < \text{upper limit}$$

EXAMPLE 11.8

Experiment   Find the 90% confidence interval for the mean age of the members of the U.S. Congress using a sample of 25 whose mean age is 54 y, with a standard deviation of 2.5 y.

Answer   90% confidence interval: $53.15 < \mu < 54.86$

Solution   Begin by identifying the experiment as a confidence interval. The statement clearly asks for a confidence interval. The level of confidence is given at 90%. A 90% level of confidence means that the true population parameter should fall in the range of values 90% of the time. Stated another way, the probability of being correct is .9.

Use the t statistic for the problem, because the sample size is small and the population standard deviation is unknown. Either of these conditions is sufficient to require the use of t. A critical value for t requires the degrees of freedom and alpha. The degrees of freedom are equal to $n - 1$, or $25 - 1 = 24$. Alpha must be determined by subtracting the level of confidence from 1: $1 - .9 = .10$. Divide alpha by 2 before using the t table. Remember, all confidence intervals require $\alpha/2$. Alpha divided by two is $.10/2$, or .05. Using Table A.4, go *down* to 24 degrees of freedom and *across* to an alpha ($\alpha/2$) of .05. The value 1.711 is found in the intersection. Retain this value for the calculation of the interval.

To calculate the interval, the following information is necessary: $\bar{x} = 54$, $s = 2.5$, $n = 25$, and $t_{(df,\alpha/2)} = 1.711$.

$$E_\mu = \bar{x} + t_{(df,\alpha/2)} \frac{s}{\sqrt{n}} \quad \text{and} \quad E_\mu = \bar{x} - t_{(df,\alpha/2)} \frac{s}{\sqrt{n}}$$

$$= 54 + 1.711 \frac{2.5}{\sqrt{25}} \qquad = 54 - 1.711 \frac{2.5}{\sqrt{25}}$$

$$= 54 + 1.711 \frac{2.5}{5} \qquad = 54 - 1.711 \frac{2.5}{5}$$

$$= 54 + 1.711(.5) \qquad = 54 - 1.711(.5)$$

$$= 54 + .8556 \qquad = 54 - .8556$$

$$= 54.86 \qquad = 53.15$$

A LEARNING AID

Confidence Intervals for t

A sample of 30 teenage mothers shows that they have a lifetime average of 5.4 children, with a standard deviation of 1.2. Find the 95% confidence interval for the mean number of children born to all teenage mothers.

Step 1   Identify the level of confidence. The problem requires a 95% confidence interval. The level of confidence estimates the probability that the parameter will be contained in the range established around the sample statistic.

Step 2   Identify the test statistic. The t statistic is necessary, because the mean is estimated using a sample of 30 where the population standard deviation is unknown. If the sample size were larger and the population standard deviation were known, then the test statistic would be z.

Step 3   Determine the critical value, remembering to divide alpha by 2 when calculating a confidence interval. The critical value for t is determined with degrees of freedom $(n - 1)$ and alpha. With an n of 30, df = 29. An alpha for a 95% confidence interval is found by subtracting the level of confidence from 1; that is, alpha is $1 - .95$, or .05. The alpha must be divided by 2 before reading critical values from Table A.4. Read *down* Table A.4 to 29 degrees of freedom and *over* to .05/2 (.025). The value in the intersection, 2.05, is the critical value for $t_{(29,.05/2)}$. Retain this value for the calculation.

$$t_{(29,.05/2)} = 2.05$$

Step 4   Calculate the confidence interval. The t confidence interval uses the sample mean as the point estimate for the population mean. The necessary information for the calculation is $\bar{x} = 5.4$, $s = 1.2$, $n = 30$, and $t_{(29,.05/2)} = 2.05$.

$$E_\mu = \bar{x} + t_{(df,\alpha/2)} \frac{s}{\sqrt{n}} \qquad \text{and} \quad E_\mu$$

$$= \bar{x} - t_{(df,\alpha/2)} \frac{s}{\sqrt{n}}$$

$$= 5.4 + 2.05 \frac{1.2}{\sqrt{30}} \qquad = 5.4 - 2.05 \frac{1.2}{\sqrt{30}}$$

$$= 5.4 + 2.05 \frac{1.2}{5.477} \qquad = 5.4 - 2.05 \frac{1.2}{5.477}$$

$$= 5.4 + 2.05(.219) \qquad = 5.4 - 2.05(.219)$$

$$= 5.4 + .449 \qquad = 5.4 - .449$$

$$= 5.85 \qquad = 4.95$$

Step 5   State the interval. The lower limit of the interval is 4.95 and the upper limit is 5.85. This suggests that, based on this sample, with 95% confidence, the mean number of children born to all teenage mothers ranges from 4.95 to 5.85.

$$4.95 < \mu < 5.85$$

The lower limit of the interval is 53.15, and the upper limit is 54.86. Based on this sample, with 90% confidence, the mean age of all members of Congress ranges from 53.15 y to 54.86 y.

$$53.15 < \mu < 54.86$$

CHAPTER 11 IN REVIEW

11.1 Find the t critical values associated with the shaded area of each curve.

a.

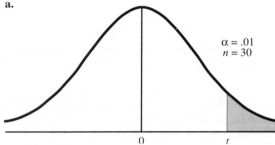

$\alpha = .01$
$n = 30$

c.

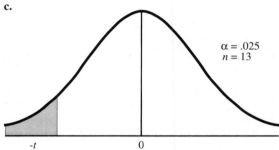

$\alpha = .025$
$n = 13$

b.

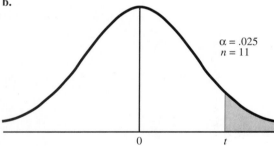

$\alpha = .025$
$n = 11$

d.

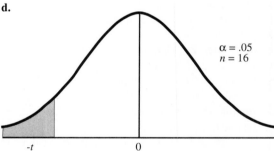

$\alpha = .05$
$n = 16$

11.2 Find the t critical values associated with the shaded areas of each curve.

a.

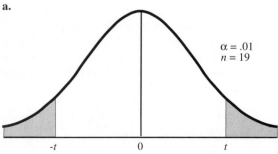

$\alpha = .01$
$n = 19$

b.

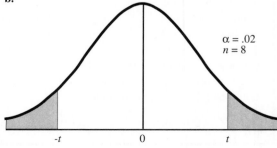

$\alpha = .02$
$n = 8$

c.

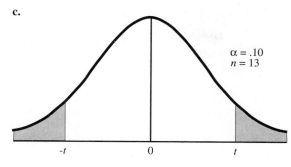

$\alpha = .10$
$n = 13$

d.

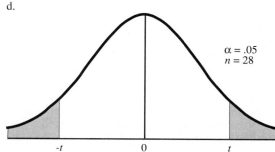

$\alpha = .05$
$n = 28$

the claim of a patient who complains that the mean costs for all such surgeries exceeds $1800.

11.10   A random sample of 31 countries produces a mean per capita GNP of $3760, with a standard deviation of 870. At the .02 significance level, use the *P*-value approach to test a researcher's claim that the mean per capita GNP is significantly less than $4225.

11.11   An airport supervisor randomly selects 20 planes of the same model and tests them to determine the distance they require for takeoff. The 20 planes produce a sample mean of 678 m and a standard deviation 30 m. At the .01 level of significance, test the claim that the mean distance for all such planes is more than 650 m. Use the classical and *P*-value approaches.

11.12   Calculate the 90% confidence interval for the mean number of years to finish a Ph.D. after a baccalaureate degree. A sample of 30 professors produces a mean time of 11.2 y with a standard deviation 1.6.

11.13   Test the null hypothesis $\mu = 26$ given a sample mean of 24.6, a sample standard deviation of 5, and a sample size of 100. Use the classical approach with $\alpha = .05$.

11.14   Test, using the classical approach, the claim that a population mean exceeds 52 using a sample of 30 producing a mean of 54 and a standard deviation of 6; let $\alpha = .05$.

11.15   A randomly selected group of 20 fifth graders produces a mean score of 60.3 and a standard deviation of 13.4 on a standardized test. Test whether their score significantly exceeds the national average of 58.01. Use the classical and *P*-value approaches with $\alpha = .01$.

11.16   Describe the decision concerning the following *P*-values.

   a. $P = .04, \alpha = .05$
   b. $P = .05, \alpha = .02$
   c. $P = .005, \alpha = .005$
   d. $P = .013, \alpha = .01$
   e. $P = .025, \alpha = .01$
   f. $P = .015\ \alpha = .025$

11.3   Using the correct format, state both the null and alternative hypotheses.

   a. The mean age of patients is less than 7 y.
   b. The mean temperature is no less than 30°.
   c. The mean price of bread is mroe than $1.25.
   d. The mean weight of babies is different than 7.2 lb.
   e. The mean travel time is 32 min.

11.4   Find the *t* critical values suggested by the given data.

   a. $H_0: \mu = 12; H_1: \mu \neq 12; n = 27, \alpha = .05$
   b. $H_0: \mu \leq 500; H_1: \mu > 500; n = 17, \alpha = .10$
   c. $H_0: \mu \geq 10.75; H_1: \mu < 10.75; n = 29, \alpha = .01$
   d. $H_0: \mu = 75; H_1: \mu \neq 75; n = 24, \alpha = .05$
   e. $H_0: \mu \geq 98.4; H_1: \mu < 98.4; n = 12, \alpha = .05$

11.5   Using the appropriate format, state both the null and alternative hypotheses.

   a. The mean weight of students is not less than 150 lb.
   b. The average length of pencils is 9.5 in.
   c. The mean cost of textbooks is greater than $30.00.
   d. The mean height of students is 5 ft 8 in.
   e. The mean IQ of students is greater than 110.

11.17   Describe the decision concerning the following one-tailed *t* critical values.

   a. Calculated $t = 1.57$, critical $t = 1.58$
   b. Calculated $t = -2.47$, critical $t = -2.96$
   c. Calculated $t = 1.96$, critical $t = 1.45$
   d. Calculated $t = 2.09$, critical $t = 2.08$
   e. Calculated $t = -3.09$, critical $t = -1.58$
   f. Calculated $t = -2.85$, critical $t = -3.98$

11.6   Test the claim that $\mu \leq 10$, given a sample of 9 for which $\bar{x} = 11$ and $s = 2$. Use a significance level of .05.

11.7   Test the claim that $\mu \leq 32$, given a sample of 27 for which $\bar{x} = 33.5$ and $s = 3$. Use $\alpha = .10$.

11.8   Test the claim that $\mu \geq 100$, given a sample of 22 for which $\bar{x} = 95$ and $s = 18$. Use a 5% level of significance.

11.9   For each of 12 hospitals, the cost of a surgery per patient was found. The 12 hospitals have a mean cost of $2133 and a standard deviation of $345. At the .01 level of significance, test

11.18   Find the *P*-values for the following calculated values.

   a. -2.52; df $= 19$
   b. 1.84; df $= 10$
   c. 3.00; df $= 7$
   d. -1.85; df $= 22$
   e. -1.0; df $= 10$

11.19   Estimate, with 95% certainty, the average infant mortality rate of the world given a sample of 25 countries whose mean infant mortality rate is 91.2, with standard deviation 15.7.

11.20   Estimate, with 90% certainty, the mean number of pounds of household garbage produced per week using a sample of 24 houses whose mean is 15.9 lb, with standard deviation 2.34.

11.21   True or false?

  a. If the alpha level is .05, the level of confidence is 90%.

  b. The t confidence interval is used when estimating a population with a sample less than or equal to 30 when the population standard deviation is unknown.

  c. If $P > \alpha$, then the decision is to reject the null hypothesis.

  d. If df = 29 and a calculated value is 1.7, the P-value is 2.054.

11.22   True or false?

  a. The degrees of freedom are based on the standard deviation.

  b. If the calculated value falls to the right of a right-tailed critical value, the decision is to reject the null hypothesis.

  c. The t distribution is symmetric, with positive values greater than 0.

  d. The t test can be used for testing variances and standard deviations.

11.23   A local cable company claims that the average cost of a cable bill is no more than $18.00 per month. A consumers' advocacy group challenges this, claiming the bills are, on average, higher. Test at the .1 level of significance with the following information:

$$n = 33, \qquad \bar{x} = \$8.329, \qquad s = \$2.147.$$

11.24   Calculate the 95% confidence interval for the percent change in apartment rent over a 1-y period using a sample of 32 with a mean change of 1.5 and a standard deviation of 1.69.

11.25   The average number of years a country takes to double its population is 41. Test the claim that the mean is greater than 41 using a sample of 20 countries whose mean is 45 and standard deviation is 22.35. Let $\alpha = .05$.

The Chi-Square Distribution

12

So far means have been tested and estimated. There are many situations when a variance or a standard deviation must be tested or estimated. For example, a potato chip company purchasing a new machine to fill bags with chips is concerned with the mean weight of each bag and the consistency with which the machine fills each bag with the desired weight. Although mean weight is important, the manufacturer does not want customers in stores shaking bags to feel the fullness of the bag of chips. The consistency of the fill is measured by the variance and standard deviation. Recall that the variance and standard deviation measure dispersion—that is, the variability of the data around the mean. Although means that are normally distributed are represented by a symmetric, bell-shaped curve, variances are not. The curve representing variances and standard deviations is skewed to the right.

SECTION 1

The Chi-Square Distribution

Variances are represented in a distribution curve that is skewed to the right. A right-skewed distribution has extreme values to the right, pulling the tail of the distribution toward the right. See Figure 12.1.

The right-skewed distribution representing variances is known as the chi-square distribution. Chi is the Greek letter χ (pronounced as "ki," as in the ki in kite). The square represents the square of the variance. Thus, chi-square is written as χ^2.

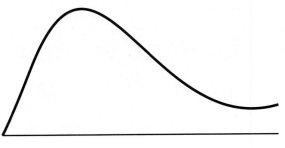

FIGURE 12.1

Chi-square distribution, χ^2 A distribution representing variances of one population

1. χ^2 is nonsymmetrical, skewed to the right.
2. χ^2 is nonnegative, greater than or equal to 0.

The chi-square distribution has several characteristics that differ from the symmetric z and t distributions. Chi-square is not symmetric but is skewed to the right. The mean, mode, and median are neither centered nor placed together. The mode is to the left, the median is slightly to the right of the mode, and the mean is pulled further to the right. Recall that extreme values pull the mean in their direction. With extreme values to the right, the mean is pulled to the right. See Figure 12.2.

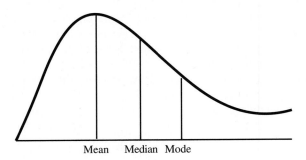

Mean   Median   Mode

FIGURE 12.2

Because chi-square is nonsymmetric, the values lower than the mean are not found by adding a negative sign to right-tailed values. Chi-square values are *never* negative. Chi-square begins at 0. A value less than 0 is impossible, because χ^2 is a distribution representing variances. Variances are never less than 0. Recall that variance measures the dispersion of values around the mean. If all values are equal to the mean, then the variance is 0.

The chi-square distribution is dependent on sample size. As does t, χ^2 has a different distribution for every sample size. Each distribution represents the sample size through the concept of the degrees of freedom. The degrees of freedom for χ^2 are found as $n - 1$.

> ## Degrees of Freedom for χ^2
> $$df = n - 1$$

The χ^2 critical values for hypothesis testing and confidence intervals are found in Table A.5 of Appendix A. Critical values for χ^2 require degrees of freedom and alpha. Notice there are alphas reported in Table A.5 with values such as .99 and .95. Since χ^2 is not symmetric, critical values for the left tail are not negative right-tailed values. Left-tailed χ^2 values are reported under alphas adjusted for the left side of the distribution curve. The adjustment is made by subtracting alpha from 1.0 when the critical region is in the left tail. That is, if alpha is .05, a left-tail value is reported in Table A.5 under the column alpha .95 $(1 - .05 = .95)$. An alpha of .025 is reported as a left-tail value under alpha $= .975$ $(1 - .025 = .975)$. For a two-tailed test at alpha $= .05$, .05 is divided by 2, with critical values found under the alphas .025 for the right tail and .975 for the left $(.05/2 = .025; 1 - .025 = .975)$.

The χ^2 notation uses the subscripts (df, α) for one-tailed tests and $(df, \alpha/2)$ for two-tailed tests. To read Table A.5, move *down* the left column to the appropriate number of degrees of freedom and *across* to the appropriate alpha. The value found in the intersection of the number of degrees of freedom and alpha is the critical value.

EXAMPLE 12.1

Experiment Find the critical values for the following notations:

a. $\chi^2_{(12,.05)}$ d. $\chi^2_{(40,.99)}$

b. $\chi^2_{(21,.025)}$ e. $\chi^2_{(6,.95)}$

c. $\chi^2_{(8,.005)}$ f. $\chi^2_{(16,.90)}$

Answer

a. 21.026   d. 22.164

b. 35.479   e. 1.635

c. 21.955   f. 9.312

Solution Table A.5 in the appendix gives χ^2 critical values using degrees of freedom and levels of significance. The χ^2 notations in a, b, and c are for right-tailed tests, because no alteration of the notation occurred. Right-tailed values require tracing *down* to the appropriate number of degrees of freedom and then *across* to the appropriate alpha level. The values reported in the table are the critical values. Notations d, e, and f are values for the left side of the curve, because all three have large alpha values. These alpha values were obtained by subtracting a typical alpha, such as .01, .05, or .10, from 1.0. Left-tailed critical values are found the same way as right-tailed values—by tracing *down* to the appropriate number of degrees of freedom and then *across* to the appropriate alpha.

EXAMPLE 12.2

Experiment Find the χ^2 critical values for the following two-tailed tests:

a.

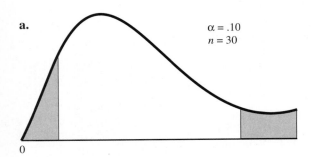

$\alpha = .10$
$n = 30$

c.

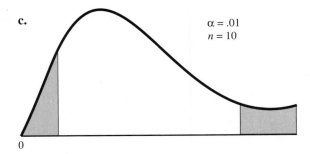

$\alpha = .01$
$n = 10$

b.

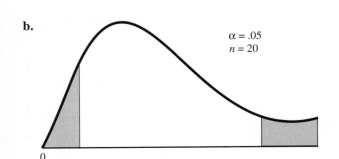

$\alpha = .05$
$n = 20$

d.

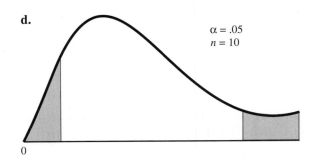

$\alpha = .05$
$n = 10$

Answer

a. $\chi^2_{(29,.95)}$ and $\chi^2_{(29,.05)} = 17.708$ and 42.557
b. $\chi^2_{(19,.975)}$ and $\chi^2_{(19,.025)} = 8.907$ and 32.852
c. $\chi^2_{(9,.995)}$ and $\chi^2_{(9,.005)} = 1.735$ and 23.589
d. $\chi^2_{(9,.975)}$ and $\chi^2_{(9,.025)} = 2.700$ and 19.023

Solution Chi-square critical values are found in Table A.5. Chi-square distributions differ for every sample size. Therefore, degrees of freedom ($n - 1$) are needed in addition to the alpha level. The four curves presented are all two-tailed. As with all two-tailed distributions, alpha must be divided by 2 before reading from the tables in the appendix. Right two-tailed values are indicated by df and $\alpha/2$. Read *down* to the appropriate number of degrees of freedom and *over* to the divided alpha value. Left two-tailed values require df and $1 - \alpha/2$. Because the chi-square distribution is not symmetric, left-tail values require a separate set of alpha columns representing the left side of the curve.

On these problems, notice that n is given, not df. Find the degrees of freedom by subtracting $n - 1$. The first curve has a sample of 30, so df $= 29$. Divide alpha by 2. The right-tailed alpha is .05. The left-tailed alpha is $1 - .05 = .95$. Reading from Table A.5, move *down* to 29 degrees of freedom, *across* to alpha $= .95$, and *across* to alpha $= .05$. The left-tailed critical value is 17.708, and the right-tailed value is 42.557. Part b asks for a sample of 20 with an alpha .05. Df = 20 − 1, or 19. Alpha divided by 2 is .05/2, or .025. The left-tailed alpha is 1 − .025 = .975. Move *down* Table A.5 to 19 df, *across* to alpha = .975, and *across* to alpha = .025. Note both 8.907 and 32.852 as critical values. Part c has 10 − 1 = 9 degrees of freedom. Alpha values are .01/2 = .005 with 1 − .005 = .995. Chi-square critical values at 9 degrees of freedom with alphas at .995 and .005 are 1.735 and 23.589. The last curve also is for a sample of 10; df = 9 and alpha = .05. Divide alpha by two. The right-tailed alpha is .025, with a left-tailed value at 1 − .025 = .975. Chi-square critical values at 9 degrees of freedom with alphas at .975 and .025 are 2.700 and 19.023.

A LEARNING AID

The Chi-Square Distribution

Find the critical chi-square values for a two-tailed test for a sample of 31 with an alpha .10.

Step 1 Note the distribution. Chi-square is a nonsymmetric distribution skewed to the right. Critical values for chi-square are found by noting the degrees of freedom and alpha. The experiment states the test is two-tailed. Both tails of the curve must be shaded, with critical values found for each.

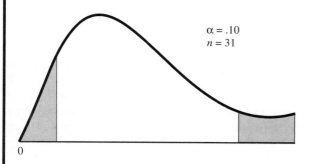

$\alpha = .10$
$n = 31$

Step 2 Calculate the degrees of freedom. The degrees of freedom for chi-square is $n − 1$. The sample size, n, is 31. Degrees of freedom are $31 − 1 = 30$.

Step 3 Adjust alpha for a two-tailed test. Alpha must always be divided by 2 for two-tailed tests. Alpha is .10. Alpha divided by 2 is .10/2 = .05. The area in the right tail is .05. The area in the left tail is also .05 but is noted as 1 − .05, or .95. Alpha for left tails of the chi-square curve is subtracted from 1, because chi-square is not symmetric. The alpha .95 must be used

in finding the left-tailed critical value. The following notations reflect the needed critical values:

Left-tail notation: $\chi^2_{(30,.95)}$

Right-tail notation: $\chi^2_{(30,.05)}$

Step 4 Determine the critical values using Table A.5. Move *down* the table to 30 degrees of freedom and *across* to alpha at .95. The value in the intersection, 18.493, is the critical value for the left tail. The rightG-tail value is found by moving *down* to 30 df and *across* to the alpha value of .05. The value 43.773 is the critical value for the right tail.

Degrees of Freedom	Alpha	
	.95	.05
. . .	. . .	. . .
. . .	. . .	. . .
30 ⟶	18.493 ⟶	43.773

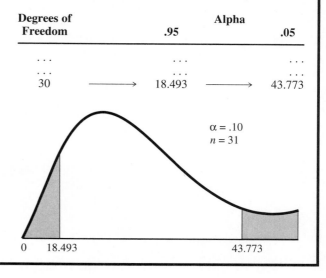

$\alpha = .10$
$n = 31$

0   18.493   43.773

Hypothesis Test: Classical Approach for Chi-Square

The classical approach for testing a variance using χ^2 follows the same steps as for z and t. The six steps in the classical approach begin with stating the hypotheses. Recall that hypotheses include a population parameter, a mathematical symbol, and a numerical value. Chi-square tests variances and standard deviations. The parameter for the population variance, σ^2, or the parameter for the population standard deviation, σ, must be included in the hypotheses. Do not use the mean symbol, μ, when testing for χ^2.

The three choices of the mathematical symbol for the null hypothesis are $=$, $\leq$, and $\geq$. The null hypothesis carries the benefit of the doubt and must be proven false before it can be rejected. The alternative hypothesis carries a contrasting symbol, $\neq$, $>$, or $<$. That is, if the null hypothesis is $=$, then the alternative hypothesis must be $\neq$. The alternative hypothesis carries the burden of proof and challenges the null hypothesis.

The value included in the hypothesis is determined by the experiment. It is either the stated or expected population variance or population standard deviation. Be careful to observe if the experiment tests the variance or the standard deviation.

If H_0 is $\sigma^2 = 0$, then H_1 is $\sigma^2 \neq 0$.

If H_0 is $\sigma^2 \leq 4$, then H_1 is $\sigma^2 > 4$.

If H_0 is $\sigma^2 \geq 30$, then H_1 is $\sigma^2 < 30$.

If H_0 is $\sigma = 2$, then H_1 is $\sigma \neq 2$.

If H_0 is $\sigma \leq 4$, then H_1 is $\sigma > 4$.

If H_0 is $\sigma \geq 6$, then H_1 is $\sigma < 6$.

The second step in hypothesis testing is to identify the test criteria. The test criteria include the level of significance, the test statistic, the critical region, and the critical value. The level of significance, or alpha, is usually given in the problem. If alpha is not stated, it must be determined based on the seriousness of a type I error—that is, rejecting a true hypothesis. The test statistic is determined by deciding which test to conduct. Thus far, three test statistics have been described: z, t, and χ^2. Both z and t are for testing normally distributed means. Chi-square is used for testing a variance or standard deviation. The critical region is determined by considering the alternative hypothesis to decide if the test is one-tailed to the left, two-tailed, or one-tailed to the right. Remember to use the following symbols found in the alternative hypothesis to determine the placement of the critical region.

Sign in H_1	Test
$<$	One-tailed left
$\neq$	Two-tailed
$>$	One-tailed right

The critical values are found in Table A.5. To find the critical value, the degrees of freedom and alpha level must be known. One-tailed values are found simply by tracing *down* Table A.5 to the appropriate degrees of freedom value (calculated as $n - 1$) and *across* to alpha. Remember to subtract alpha from 1 when looking for a left-tailed critical value. Two-tailed critical values require dividing alpha by 2. The divided alpha value is used for the right-tailed value, and it is subtracted from 1 to find the left-tailed value. For example, the critical value for χ^2 with 28 degrees of freedom at the .01 level of significance is found by moving *down* to 28 and *over* to the alpha column for .01. The value found in the intersection, 48.279, is the critical value.

Degrees of Freedom		Alpha		
		.05	.025	.01
.				
.				
.				
28	$\longrightarrow$	. . .	. . .	48.279

EXAMPLE 12.3

Experiment   Find the critical χ^2 values for the following.

a. $\chi^2_{(10,.05)}$ **c.** $\chi^2_{(40,.95)}$

b. $\chi^2_{(13,.005)}$ **d.** $\chi^2_{(18,.995)}$

Answer

a. 18.307   **c. 26.509**

b. 29.819   **d. 6.265**

Solution   Chi-square critical values are reported in Table A.5. Table A.5 gives alpha levels across the top row and degrees of freedom along the left column. Critical values are found by moving *down* to the degrees of freedom and *across* to the alpha level. In part a, the degrees of freedom are 10 for an alpha at .05. Move *down* to 10 degrees of freedom and *across* to the alpha column for .05. The critical value 18.307 is found in the intersection. In part b, move *down* to 13 degrees of freedom and *over* to the alpha column for .005. The critical value is 29.819. Parts c and d request critical values for the left side of the curve, because the alphas are .95 and .995. Chi-square is not symmetric like z and t; therefore, critical values for the left are found by using alpha subtracted from 1.0. A .95 means that the alpha given in the problem is .05, but the test according to the alternative hypothesis is left-tailed $(1 - .05 = .95)$. The critical value is found by using the .95 alpha value. For c, the critical value, tracing down to 40 degrees of freedom and over to alpha of .95, is 26.509. For d, move down to 18 degrees of freedom and over to .995. The critical value is 6.265.

The third step in hypothesis testing using the classical approach is the calculation of the test statistic. In the calculation of the χ^2 statistic, the sample variance is multiplied by $n - 1$ and then divided by the population variance. Be sure to note whether an experiment gives a variance or a standard deviation. If a variance is given, then place the value in the formula. If a standard deviation is given, then the value must be squared. The standard deviation squared equals the variance.

Calculation of the Test Statistic χ^2

$$\chi^2 = \frac{(n-1)s^2}{\sigma^2}$$

where

n is the sample size.
s^2 is the sample variance.
σ^2 is the population variance.

EXAMPLE 12.4

Experiment   Calculate the χ^2 test statistic for a sample of 20 if the sample variance is 5 and the population variance is 8.

Answer $\chi^2 = 11.88$

Solution   Identify the information given in the experiment. Chi-square requires n, s^2, and σ^2. Sample size, n, is 20. The sample variance, s^2, is 5, and the population variance, σ^2, is 8. Place these values in the formula and calculate χ^2.

$$\chi^2 = \frac{(n-1)s^2}{\sigma^2} = \frac{(20-1)5}{8} = \frac{(19)5}{8} = \frac{95}{8} = 11.8$$

EXAMPLE 12.5

Experiment   Calculate the χ^2 test statistic for a sample of 30 if the sample standard deviation is 9 and the population standard deviation is 11.

Answer $\chi^2 = 19.41$

Solution   Determine the information given in the experiment. Chi-square requires n, s^2, and σ^2. Sample size, n, is 30. The sample variance is not given, but it can be calculated by squaring the sample standard deviation. Squaring standard deviation gives variance. Therefore, the sample standard deviation, 9, and the population standard deviation, 11, must be placed in the formula wih the square notation.

$$\chi^2 = \frac{(n-1)s^2}{\sigma^2} = \frac{(30-1)9^2}{11^2} = \frac{(29)81}{121} = \frac{2349}{121} = 19.41$$

The fourth step in hypothesis testing using the classical approach is to place the calculated value on the curve and compare it to the critical value. Step 5 involves deciding whether to reject or not to reject the null hypothesis. Reject the null hypoth-

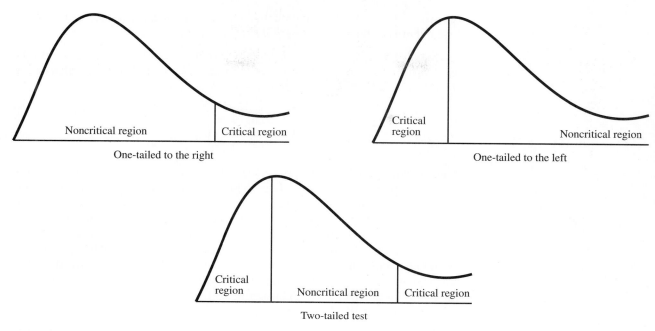

FIGURE 12.3

esis when the calculated value falls in the critical region. Fail to reject the null
hypothesis when the calculated value falls in the noncritical region. See Figure 12.3.

The final step in hypothesis testing is to apply the decision to the problem.
Narratively interpret the information provided in the original experiment as the decision is applied. That is, restate the null hypothesis narratively with explanation as to
failing to reject or rejecting it.

Steps in Hypothesis Testing Using the Classical Approach

1. State H_0 and H_1.
2. Identify the test criteria.
  a. Level of significance, α
  b. Test statistic (z, t, χ^2, F)
  c. Critical region
  d. Critical value
3. Calculate the test statistic.
4. Place the calculated value on distribution curve.
5. Make a decision.
6. Interpret the results.

EXAMPLE 12.6

Experiment   Test the null hypothesis $\sigma = 5$ using a sample of 25 with a sample
standard deviation 3; $\alpha = .10$.

Answer Reject the null hypothesis. There is sufficient evidence to reject the null hypothesis that the standard deviation is equal to 5.

Solution The null hypothesis is already stated: $\sigma = 5$. The alternative hypothesis must include the contrasting mathematical sign; therefore, the alternative hypothesis is $\sigma \neq 5$. State the hypotheses.

$$H_0: \quad \sigma = 5$$

$$H_1: \quad \sigma \neq 5$$

The test criteria begin with identifying the level of significance, alpha. Alpha is given as .10. The test statistic is χ^2. The z and t distributions cannot be used when testing a standard deviation or a variance. Chi-square represents the skewed distribution of variances and standard deviations. The critical region is two-tailed. A two-tailed test occurs when the alternative hypothesis includes the $\neq$ sign. All two-tailed tests require dividing alpha by 2, placing half of the critical region on each side of the distribution. Because $\alpha = .10$, alpha divided by 2 is .05. The .05 is the area for the right tail. Since χ^2 is not symmetric, the area for the left tail is determined by subtracting .05 from 1. The critical area for the left tail is $1 - .05$, or .95. The degrees of freedom are $n - 1$, or 24. The χ^2 notations are:

$$\chi^2_{(24,.05)} \quad \text{and} \quad \chi^2_{(24,.95)}$$

Use Table A.5 to find critical values for χ^2. For the right tail, read *down* to 24 degrees of freedom and *across* to alpha = .05. The 36.415 value found in the intersection is the critical value for the right tail. The left-tail value is found by reading *down* to 24 degrees of freedom and *across* to alpha = .95. The critical value for the left tail is 13.848.

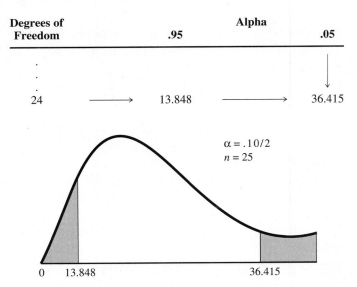

Degrees of Freedom	Alpha	
	.95	.05
.		
.		
.		
24	13.848	36.415

$\alpha = .10/2$
$n = 25$

0   13.848   36.415

Calculate the test statistic. The calculated χ^2 value requires the following information: $n = 25$, $\sigma = 5$, and $s = 3$. Notice that 5 and 3 are values representing standard deviations and not variances. The χ^2 formula requires the variance, which is obtained by squaring the standard deviation.

$$\chi^2 = \frac{(n-1)s^2}{\sigma^2} = \frac{(25-1)3^2}{5^2} = \frac{(24)9}{25} = \frac{216}{25} = 8.64$$

Place the calculated value 8.64 on the distribution curve. Its placement is determined by comparing 8.64 to the critical values already placed on the curve.

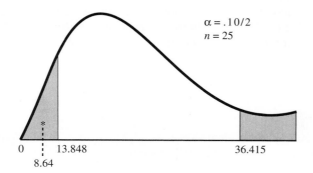

$$\alpha = .10/2$$
$$n = 25$$

0   13.848   36.415
8.64

The next step is to decide to reject or not to reject the null hypothesis. If the calculated value falls in the critical region, as it does here, the decision is to reject the null hypothesis.

$$\text{Reject } H_0$$

The final step is to interpret the decision. Rejecting the null hypothesis suggests that there is sufficient proof based on this sample at this level of significance that the null hypothesis is incorrect. Because the original experiment did not explain what the test is, the interpretation is limited to the following: There is sufficient evidence at the .10 level of significance to reject the null hypothesis that the standard deviation is equal to 5.

EXAMPLE 12.7

Experiment   Test the claim that the variance in body temperature is no greater than 1.2° using a sample of 51 patients producing a sample variance of 1.9; use $\alpha = .10$.

Answer   Reject the null hypothesis. There is sufficient evidence at the .10 level of significance to reject the null hypothesis that the variance in body temperature is no greater than 1.2°.

Solution   State the hypotheses. The null hypothesis is already derived from the statement that the variance in body temperature is no greater than 1.2°. The key words are *no greater than*. The symbol for not greater than is ≤, and it must be placed in the null hypothesis. The symbol for the alternative hypothesis is the contrasting mathematical sign; therefore, the alternative hypothesis involves $>$. The parameter is σ^2, the population variance.

$$H_0: \quad \sigma^2 \leq 1.2$$
$$H_1: \quad \sigma^2 > 1.2$$

The test criteria begin with identifying the level of significance, alpha. Alpha is given as .10. The test statistic is χ^2. Chi-square represents the skewed distribution of variances and standard deviations. The critical region is one-tailed to the right as guided by the $>$ sign in the alternative hypothesis. The degrees of freedom for chi-square are $n - 1$, or 50. At alpha $= .1$ and 50 degrees of freedom, the χ^2 notation is

$$\chi^2_{(50,.1)}$$

Use Table A.5 to find critical values for χ^2. Move *down* to 50 degrees of freedom and *over* to alpha $= .1$. The 63.167 value found in the intersection is the critical value for the right tail.

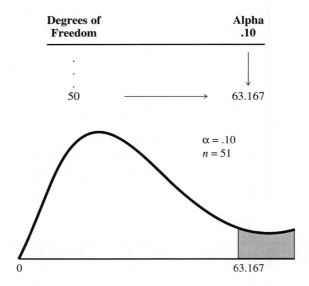

Calculate the test statistic. The calculated χ^2 value requires the following information: $n = 51$, $\sigma^2 = 1.2$, and $s^2 = 1.9$. Notice that 1.2 and 1.9 are values representing variances and not standard deviations. The χ^2 formula requires the variance; there is no need to square the variances again.

$$\chi^2 = \frac{(n - 1)s^2}{\sigma^2} = \frac{(51 - 1)1.9}{1.2} = \frac{(51)1.9}{1.2} = \frac{95}{1.2} = 79.167$$

A LEARNING AID

Classical Testing for Chi-Square

Consider the variance of exam scores in statistics courses as 81. A random sample of 31 students produces a variance of 64. Test, using the classical approach, the hypothesis that the variance of the sample is significantly smaller than the variance of the population. Let $\alpha = .10$.

Step 1 State the hypotheses. A hypothesis statement is contained in the statement that the sample variance is significantly smaller than the population variance. The parameter in question is the population variance, σ^2. The direction of the challenge is smaller, which means less than. A less than sign ($<$) can go only in the alternative hypothesis. If the alternative is less than, then the null hypothesis is greater than or equal to. The hypotheses are written:

$$H_0:\ \ \sigma^2 \geq 81 \quad \text{and} \quad H_1:\ \ \sigma^2 < 81$$

Step 2 Identify the test criteria. The test criteria begins with identifying the level of significance, alpha. Alpha is noted as .10. The test statistic is chi-square. Chi-square tests for one variance or standard deviation. If a null hypothesis includes σ^2 or σ, the test statistic is chi-square. The critical region is to the left, because the alternative hypothesis contains a less than sign. The critical value is determined by the degrees of freedom and alpha. The degrees of freedom are 30 ($n - 1$). Although alpha is .10, a left-tailed region requires alpha to be subtracted from 1. The alpha for the left tail at .1 is $1 - .10$, or .90. Reading from Table A.5 trace *down* to 30 df and *across* to the alpha value of .90. The critical value is 20.599.

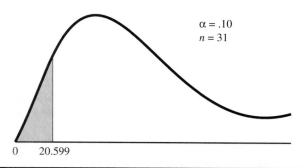

Step 3 Calculate the test statistic. The calculation requires $\sigma^2 = 81$, $s = 64$, and $n = 31$.

$$\chi^2 = \frac{(n-1)s^2}{\sigma^2} = \frac{(31-1)64}{81}$$
$$= \frac{(30)64}{81} = \frac{1920}{81} = 23.704$$

Step 4 Place the calculated value on the distribution. Note that the calculated value, 23.704, falls slightly to the right of the critical value, 20.599.

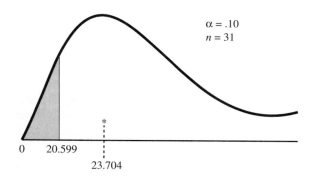

Step 5 Make a decision. The calculated value does not fall in the critical region. The decision is to fail to reject H_0.

Step 6 Interpret the results. A decision that fails to reject the null hypothesis suggests that this sample does not provide sufficient evidence to challenge the null successfully. Applying the decision directly to the experiment, the interpretation is as follows: There is insufficient evidence, at the .10 level of significance, to reject the null hypothesis. The variance of scores of the sampled students is not significantly smaller.

Place the calculated value, 79.167, on the distribution curve. Its placement is determined by comparing 79.167 to the critical value already placed on the curve.

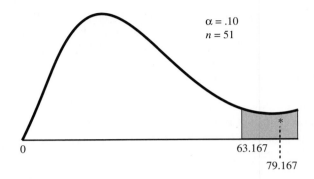

$\alpha = .10$
$n = 51$

0

63.167

79.167

The next step is to make a decision. If the calculated value falls in the critical region, as it does here, the decision is to reject the null hypothesis.

Reject H_0

The final step is to interpret the decision. Rejecting the null hypothesis suggests that there is sufficient proof based on this sample at this level of significance that the null hypothesis is incorrect. There is sufficient evidence at the .10 level of significance to reject the null hypothesis that the variance in body temperature is no more than 1.2°.

Chi-Square Testing Using *P*-Values

The *P*-value approach to hypothesis testing takes the classical approach one step further by transforming the calculated value into a probability and comparing the probability to an alpha level. *P*-values, whether for χ^2, z, t, or other test statistics, are probabilities presenting the level of significance at which the test statistic becomes significant provided the null hypothesis is true. Because *P*-values and alphas are probabilities, one compared to the other leads to decisions about the null hypothesis.

Computerized statistical programs typically report calculated χ^2 values with an associated *P*-value. The calculated value may be used to conduct a classical hypothesis test, whereas the *P*-value may be used to conduct a *P*-value hypothesis test. When a *P*-value is offered by a computerized program or by another source, a comparison of the *P*-value with the alpha level is necessary. If the *P*-value is less than or equal to α, then the null hypothesis is rejected. The null hypothesis fails to be rejected if the *P*-value is greater than α.

A complete hypothesis test using the *P*-value approach for χ^2 is like the *P*-value approach for t. The six steps identified for t in Chapter 11 are repeated here for χ^2.

Steps in Hypothesis Testing Using the *P*-Value Approach

1. State H_0 and H_1.
2. Identify the test criteria.
    a. Level of significance
    b. Test statistic
3. Calculate the test statistic.
4. Calculate the *P*-value.
    a. One-tailed test
    b. Two-tailed test
5. Make a decision.
    a. Fail to reject H_0.
    b. Reject H_0.
6. Interpret the results.

The first step in *P*-value testing is to identify the null and alternative hypotheses. Step 2 is to determine two aspects of the test criteria, the level of significance and the test statistic. The level of significance is usually given as α in the problem or must be determined by considering the acceptance of a type I error—that is, rejecting a true hypothesis. The test statistic must be determined by reviewing the parameter in the hypotheses. The parameters used in testing so far are the population mean (μ), the population variance (σ^2), and the population standard deviation (σ). When the mean is tested, the test statistic is z or t. When the population variance or the population standard deviation is tested, the test statistic is χ^2. Step 3 is to calculate the test statistic. The calculation for χ^2 is:

$$\chi^2 = \frac{(n - 1)s^2}{\sigma^2}$$

Step 4 involves finding the probability associated with the calculated test statistic. The transformation of χ^2 is exactly like t. The alpha levels reported in Table A.5 are used as estimates of *P*-values. The *P*-value for χ^2 is determined by noting the calculated value from step 3 with the degrees of freedom from step 2. Using Table A.5, move *down* to the appropriate degrees of freedom. Read *across* all the values of that row, finding the value closest to the calculated value. The value in the table closest to the calculated value serves as a guide to the probability used as the *P*-value. The *P*-value is the alpha level associated with the column in which the value closest to the calculated value is found. For example, if the value calculated in step 3 equals 26.27 for a sample of 19 with 18 (19 − 1 = 18) degrees of freedom, then the *P*-value is .10. The *P*-value .10 is found by moving *down* to 18 degrees of freedom, *across* to the value 25.989, which is closest to the calculated value 26.27, and *up* to the alpha value .10 associated with the column in which 25.989 is found.

Degrees of Freedom	Alpha			
	.10		.05	.025
1	. . .	. . .	. . .	. . .
2	. . .	. . .	. . .	. . .
. . .	. . .	. . .	. . .	. . .
18	. . .	25.989	. . .	. . .

$$P\text{-value}_{(26.27, df18)} = .10$$

Because only a few alpha levels are reported in Table A.5, χ^2 P-value estimates tend to fall between two reported alphas. If the calculated value falls between two critical values, then use both alpha values to denote the range of values within which the P-value lies. For example, if a calculated χ^2 value in step 3 equals 31.023 for a sample of 23, which has 22 degrees of freedom, the χ^2 P-value ranges from .05 to .10. Both values become the P-values and are compared to the original alpha in making a decision about the hypothesis. The P-value for a χ^2 calculated value of 31.023 is found by moving *down* the χ^2 table to 22 degrees of freedom, *over* to the closest value, and *up* to the alpha levels. The values closest to 31.023 at 22 df are 33.924 and 30.813. Tracing up the columns, 33.924 is associated with an alpha of .05, and 30.813 is associated with .10. The P-value falls between .05 and .10.

Degrees of Freedom	.01	Alpha	.05	.025
1	. . .		. . .	. . .
2	. . .		. . .	. . .
. . .	. . .		. . .	. . .
22	30.813	←——————→	33.924	. . .

$$P\text{-value}_{(31.023, df22)} = (.05 < P < .10)$$

Remember that a two-tailed test requires the P-value to be multiplied by 2 before comparing it to alpha. It is important to be aware of the left-tailed alpha values reported in Table A.5. Remember that left-tailed alphas such as .90 and .95 are related to alphas of .10 and .05, respectively. Left-tailed alphas are found by subtracting the given alpha from 1.0. Reversing this process, subtracting left-tailed alpha from 1.0 results in the original right-tailed alpha. Therefore, if a one-tailed alpha representing the P-value is found to be .995, then the P-value is $1.0 - .995$, or .005. If a two-tailed alpha representing the P-value is .995, then the P-value is $2(1.0 - .995)$, or $2(.005) = .01$.

The next step in P-value testing requires comparing the P-value to alpha and making a decision about the hypothesis. The rule for the decision using P-values remains constant for all test statistics, whether χ^2, z, or t. If the P-value is less than or equal to alpha, then the null hypothesis is rejected. If the P-value is greater than alpha, then the null hypothesis fails to be rejected.

$P \leq \alpha$:   Reject H_0.

$P > \alpha$:   Fail to reject H_0.

The final step is interpreting the decision. It is important to remember that rejecting the null hypothesis does not suggest that the sample information is true or that the new parameter is represented by the sample statistic. Likewise, failing to reject the null hypothesis suggests only that the sample does not provide sufficient evidence to challenge the null hypothesis.

EXAMPLE 12.8

Experiment   Test the null hypothesis $\sigma = 5$ using the *P*-value approach. Use a sample of 25 with a sample standard deviation 3. Let $\alpha = .10$.

Answer   Reject the null hypothesis. There is sufficient evidence at the .10 level of significance to reject the null hypothesis that the standard deviation equals 5.

Solution   There are six steps in hypothesis testing using the *P*-value approach: State the hypothesis; identify the test criteria; calculate the test statistic; calculate the *P*-value; make a decision; and interpret the results. The experiment states the null hypothesis as $\sigma = 5$. The alternative hypothesis must challenge the null hypothesis by containing the contrasting mathematical symbol. If the null hypothesis is equal to, then the alternative hypothesis is not equal to. The parameter is sigma, σ, representing the population standard deviation. State the hypotheses:

$$H_0: \quad \sigma = 5 \qquad H_1: \quad \sigma \neq 5$$

The test criteria for *P*-value testing require identification of the test statistic and level of confidence. The test statistic for standard deviation or variance is chi-square. The level of significance is given as .10.

The third step in using the *P*-value approach is to calculate the test statistic. The calculation for χ^2 requires the following information derived from the experiment: $\sigma = 5$, $s = 3$, and $n = 25$. Notice the formula actually requires the population variance and sample variance. The experiment reports standard deviations. Standard deviations become variances by squaring them. Calculate the χ^2 value.

$$\chi^2 = \frac{(n-1)s^2}{\sigma^2} = \frac{(25-1)3^2}{5^2} = \frac{(24)9}{25} = \frac{216}{25} = 8.64$$

Transform the calculated χ^2 value into a probability using Table A.5. The *P*-value for the χ^2 statistic is determined by moving *down* the degrees of freedom column, *across* to the value closest to the calculated value, and *up* to the alpha associated with that column. The degrees of freedom are $25 - 1$, or 24. The calculated value is 8.64. Trace *down* to df 24. Reading *across* this row only, notice the closest value to 8.64 is 9.886. Trace *up* the column where 9.886 is located and find the alpha, .995. The alpha .995 is for a left-tailed test. χ^2 left-tailed critical values are found by subtracting alpha from 1.0. Reversing this process, the value for the left-tailed test is subtracted from 1 to give the desired alpha value. Therefore, $1.0 - .995$ yields an alpha of .005. The value .005 is the

P-value associated with the calculated value 8.64 at 24 degrees of freedom if the test were a one-tailed test. Because the test is two-tailed, the alpha associated with 8.64 must be multiplied by 2.

Degrees of Freedom	Alpha .995
1	$\uparrow$ . . .
2	. . .
. . .	. . .
24	$\longrightarrow$ 9.886

$$1.0 - .995 = .005 \qquad .005(2) = .01$$

$$\text{\textit{P}-value}_{(8.644, \text{df}24)} = .01$$

Compare the *P*-value to the original alpha given in the experiment. If *P* $\leq \alpha$, then reject the null hypothesis. If *P* > α, then fail to reject the null hypothesis. *P* at .01 is less than α at .10; therefore, reject the null hypothesis.

$$P_{(.01)} \leq \alpha_{(.10)} \qquad \text{Reject } H_0$$

The final step in *P*-value testing is interpreting the results. Rejecting the null hypothesis suggests that there is sufficient evidence provided by this sample

A LEARNING AID

Chi-Square Testing Using *P*-Values

The standard deviation of life expectancy at birth for the world is 5.32 y. A sample of 31 countries produces a standard deviation of 6.31. Does the sample provide sufficient evidence that the standard deviation of life expectancy is greater than 5.32 y ($\alpha = .05$)?

Step 1 Identify the null and alternative hypotheses. The hypothesis statement is contained in the last sentence, where a challenge is asserted that the standard deviation (σ) is greater than 5.32 y. Because the null hypothesis must always contain an equal sign, the greater than (>) symbol must be placed in the alternative hypothesis. The null hypothesis will include the equal sign as well as the less than sign; therefore, the hypotheses are

$$H_0: \quad \sigma \leq 5.32 \qquad H_1: \quad \sigma > 5.32$$

Step 2 Identify the level of significance and the test statistic. The level of significance is reported as

alpha = .05. Chi-square must be the test statistic since the standard deviation is in question. The *z* and *t* distributions are reserved for testing means, whereas χ^2 tests for a variance or standard deviation.

Step 3 Calculate the test statistic. Chi-square requires the following information derived from the problem: $n = 31$, $s = 6.31$, and $\sigma = 5.32$. Notice the values for *s* and σ are standard deviations and must be squared in the calculation. Calculate χ^2:

$$\chi^2 = \frac{(n-1)s^2}{\sigma^2} = \frac{(31-1)6.31^2}{5.32^2} = \frac{(30)39.816}{28.302} =$$

$$\frac{1194.483}{28.302} = 42.204$$

Step 4 Transform the calculated value into a probability using Table A.5. The *P*-value is the alpha associated with the nearest critical value that has the same degrees of freedom as the calculated value of 25 at the .10 level of significance that the standard deviation is not equal to 5.

EXAMPLE 12.9

Experiment   A computer software program reports a calculated χ^2 value 27.204 with a *P*-value .10. What decision can be made for a one-tailed hypothesis test at an $\alpha = .05$?

Answer   Fail to reject H_0.

Solution   Computer software programs often report *P*-values representing the level of significance at which the test statistic becomes significant. When a *P*-value is given, proceed directly to step 5 in hypothesis testing. The determination of the calculated value and its transformation into a probability are already represented in the *P*-value. Simply compare the *P*-value to alpha and make a decision. If the *P*-value is less than or equal to alpha, then reject the null hypothesis. If *P* is greater than alpha, then fail to reject the null hypothesis. In this experiment, *P* at .10 is greater than alpha at .05. Fail to reject the null hypothesis.

$$P\text{-value}_{(.10)} > \alpha_{(.05)} \qquad \text{Fail to reject } H_0$$

(42.204). The degrees of freedom for χ^2 are $n - 1$, or 30. Trace along the row for 30 df and find the value nearest to 42.204. The value 42.204 falls between two values, 40.256 and 43.773. The alphas associated with both critical values are reported as the *P*-value. In other words, the *P*-value for 42.204 at 30 df is greater than .05 but less than .10.

$$\chi^2_{(42.204,30\text{df})} = (.05 < P < .10)$$

Degrees of Freedom	Alpha		
	.10	$\longleftrightarrow$	.05
1	. . .		. . .
2	. . .		. . .
. . .	. . .		. . .
30	40.256	$\longleftrightarrow$	43.773

Step 5   Compare the *P*-value to the original alpha and make a decision. If the *P*-value is greater than alpha, then fail to reject the null hypothesis. If the *P*-

value is less than or equal to alpha, then reject the null hypothesis. The *P*-value for the calculated value 42.204 is between .05 and .10, whereas the alpha is .05. Although it appears the *P*-value is equal to alpha since both contain the value .05, the *P*-value is actually understood to be greater than .05 but less than .10. Therefore, the *P*-value is greater than .05, and because alpha is .05, the *P*-value is greater than alpha. The decision is to fail to reject the null hypothesis.

$$(.10 > P > .05) > \alpha_{(.05)} \qquad \text{Fail to reject } H_0$$

Step 6   Interpret the results. The decision to fail to reject the null hypothesis suggests that the sample does not successfully challenge the null. The sample of 31 countries does not provide sufficient evidence at the .05 level of significance to reject the null hypothesis that the standard deviation of life expectancy at birth for the world is less than or equal to 5.32 y.

SECTION 4

Confidence Interval for Chi-Square

A confidence interval for estimating a population variance or standard deviation is calculated using the chi-square test statistic. Recall that a population parameter can be estimated from sample data using a confidence interval. The confidence interval for χ^2 establishes a range of values around a sample variance or standard deviation. Recall the definition of a confidence interval.

> **Confidence interval** Estimating a population parameter from sample statistics given a specified level of confidence.

A confidence interval establishes a range of values around the sample information where the population parameter will fall given a particular degree of confidence. The sample statistic used as the point of departure to determine the range of values for the interval is known as the point estimate. The point estimate for calculated confidence intervals using chi-square is the sample variance or sample standard deviation.

The degree of confidence, or level of confidence, establishes the probability that the population parameter will fall inside the range of values set by the point estimate. Recall that Chapter 10 presents the concept of the level of confidence as the opposite of alpha. Alpha is the probability of committing an error, and the level of confidence is the probability of being correct. The level of confidence is usually given as a percentage. If a researcher wishes to be 90% certain that the population parameter falls within a range around the point estimate, the level of confidence is .90 and alpha is .10. Alpha and the level of confidence must have a sum of 1.0.

Confidence intervals for χ^2 are found the same way as confidence intervals for t. Chi-square requires transforming the level of confidence directly into a χ^2 critical value by using the degrees of freedom and alpha divided by 2. *Remember that all confidence intervals are two-tailed, requiring that alpha be divided by 2.* Chi-square critical values are dependent on the sample size, which determines degrees of freedom, or $n - 1$. Identify the degrees of freedom and the alpha level, $\alpha/2$. Use Table A.5. Go *down* to the appropriate degrees of freedom and *across* to the value under the correct alpha level. The critical value found in the intersection is noted as $\chi^2_{(df, \alpha/2)}$. Retain this value for the calculation of the confidence interval.

EXAMPLE 12.10

Experiment Find the critical value associated with a 95% confidence interval for χ^2 where $n = 41$.

Answer $\chi^2_{(40, .025)} = 59.342$

Solution Critical values for χ^2 are found in Table A.5. Alpha and degrees of freedom are required for χ^2 critical values. If a 95% (.95) confidence level is required, alpha is 5%, or .05. All confidence intervals are two-tailed. Divide alpha by 2 so that half of the probability of an error is on both sides of the point estimate. Alpha divided by two is .05/2, or .025. The degrees of freedom are n

− 1, or 41 − 1 = 40. Using Table A.5, go *down* the df 40 and *across* to the $\alpha/2$ value, .025. The value 59.342 is found in the intersection and is the critical value to be placed in the calculation of the confidence interval.

The calculation of the confidence interval for a population variance or population standard deviation is chi-square.

The Chi-Square Confidence Interval Formula for Estimating a Population Variance

$$\frac{(n-1)s^2}{\chi^2_{(df,\alpha/2)}} < \sigma^2 < \frac{(n-1)s^2}{\chi^2_{(df,1-\alpha/2)}}$$

where

E is the estimate of the population variance.

n is sample size.

s^2 is the sample variance, known as the point estimate.

$\chi^2_{(df,\alpha/2)}$ is the critical right-tailed value found in Table A.5.

$\chi^2_{(df,1-\alpha/2)}$ is the critical left-tailed value found in Table A.5.

A special condition exists for calculating a confidence interval for estimating a standard deviation. The preceding formula will result in estimating a variance. Recall from earlier chapters that the square root of the variance is the standard deviation. When a standard deviation is estimated, take the square root of the variance formula just presented.

$$\sigma = \sqrt{\sigma^2}$$

As with other procedures, there are several steps that help organize the calculation and interpretation of the confidence interval.

Steps in Calculating a Confidence Interval for a Population Parameter

1. Identify the level of confidence.
2. Identify the test statistic (z, t, χ^2, or F).
3. Determine the critical value with $\alpha/2$.
4. Calculate the interval.
5. State the interval.

Step 1 identifies the problem as a confidence interval and the level of confidence. Key words to keep in mind are *interval, confidence,* and *estimate.* Also, the level of confidence is usually given within the statement, such as "estimate with 90% confidence" or "calculate a 90% interval." Questions asking for a confidence interval for the variance or standard deviation would not make such statements.

Step 2 is to identify the test statistic. Thus far, z, t, and χ^2 have been described. Use z for normally distributed means with large samples and where the standard deviation of the population is known. Use t for normally distributed means with small samples ($n \leq 30$) or when the population standard deviation is unknown. Use χ^2 for one population variance or standard deviation.

The third step is to determine the critical value. The χ^2 statistic requires the degrees of freedom and an alpha level. The degrees of freedom are equal to $n - 1$. Alpha is determined by subtracting the level of confidence from 1. If a 90% level of confidence is desired, then alpha is $1 - .9$, or $.10$. *All alphas must be divided by 2 when calculating a confidence interval.* Use Table A.5. For the right-tailed critical value, go *down* to the degrees of freedom and *across* to the alpha column. The value in the intersections is the critical value. The left-tailed critical value requires subtracting the divided alpha from 1.0. Left-tailed χ^2 values are reported in separate columns in Table A.5. The values are found the same way as right-tailed values except by using the left-tailed alphas. Subtract the divided alpha from 1, go *down* to the degrees of freedom and *across* to the alpha column. Retain these values for the calculation in step 4.

The fourth step is to calculate the confidence interval. The calculation must be performed twice to establish the lower limit of the range and the upper limit of the range. The formulas are essentially the same; in one formula the numerator is divided by a right-tailed critical value and in the other, the numerator is divided by a left-tailed critical value. The calculation for the χ^2 confidence interval is

$$\frac{(n - 1)s^2}{\chi^2_{(df, \alpha/2)}} < \sigma^2 < \frac{(n - 1)s^2}{\chi^2_{(df, 1 - \alpha/2)}}$$

If the confidence interval relates to the variance, then go on to step 5. If the confidence interval is for a standard deviation, be sure to take the square root of the values calculated in this step before going to step 5.

Step 5 is to restate the calculated values in the appropriate format for reporting confidence intervals. The notation for an interval places the parameter inside the lower and upper limit of the values calculated in step 4. The parameter of σ^2 is the population variance, whereas σ is the population standard deviation.

$$\text{lower limit} < \sigma^2 < \text{upper limit}$$

$$\text{lower limit} < \sigma < \text{upper limit}$$

EXAMPLE 12.11

Experiment Find the 90% confidence interval for the variance in the heights of female students using a sample of 51 with a variance of 25.

Answer 90% confidence interval: $18.52 < \sigma^2 < 35.96$

Solution Begin by identifying the experiment as a confidence interval. The statement asks for a confidence interval. The level of confidence is given at 90%. A 90% level of confidence means that the population parameter should fall in the range of values 90% of the time with a 10% error, 5% on both sides of the point estimator.

Use the χ^2 statistic for the problem, because it asks for an estimate of population variance. Two critical values must be determined for a chi-square confidence interval. Both critical values require the degrees of freedom and alpha. The degrees of freedom, $n - 1$, are 50. Alpha must be determined by subtracting the level of confidence from 1: $1 - .9 = .10$. Remember that all confidence intervals require $\alpha/2$, so divide alpha by 2. Alpha divided by 2 is .10/2, or .05. The right-tailed critical value is found in Table A.5. Go *down* to 50 degrees of freedom and *across* to an alpha ($\alpha/2$) of .05. The value 67.505 is found in the intersection. Retain this value for the calculation of the lower limit of the confidence interval.

$$\chi^2_{(50,.05)} = 67.505$$

The left-tailed critical value is found by subtracting the divided alpha from 1.0. Chi-square is not symmetric, as are z and t. Left-tailed χ^2 values are reported as alpha levels reflecting the area of the curve to the right of the critical value. Therefore, the left-tailed critical value for a divided alpha of .05 is .95 ($1.0 - .05 = .95$). Move *down* to 50 degrees of freedom and *across* to the column of values under an alpha of .95. The critical value 34.764 is found in the intersection.

$$\chi^2_{(50,.95)} = 34.764$$

To calculate the interval, the following information is necessary: $s^2 = 25$, $n = 51$, $\chi^2_{(df,\alpha/2)} = 67.505$, and $\chi^2_{(df,1-\alpha/2)} = 34.764$.

$$\frac{(n - 1)s^2}{\chi^2_{(df,\alpha/2)}} < \sigma^2 < \frac{(n - 1)s^2}{\chi^2_{(df,1-\alpha/2)}}$$

$$\frac{(51 - 1)25}{67.505} < \sigma^2 < \frac{(51 - 1)25}{34.764}$$

$$\frac{(50)25}{67.505} < \sigma^2 < \frac{(50)25}{34.764}$$

$$\frac{1250}{67.505} < \sigma^2 < \frac{1250}{34.764}$$

$$18.52 < \sigma^2 < 35.96$$

The lower limit of the interval is 18.52 and the upper limit is 35.96. This suggests that with 90% confidence, the variance of heights for female students is between 18.52 and 35.96.

$$18.52 < \sigma^2 < 35.96$$

A LEARNING AID

Confidence Intervals for Chi-Square

Calculate the 95% confidence interval for the variance in IQ tests from a sample of 41 randomly selected students producing a variance of 223.96.

Step 1   Identify the level of confidence. The level of confidence is the probability the parameter will be contained in the interval. The experiment requires a 95% level of confidence suggesting that the parameter should fall in the range of values 95% of the time with a 5% error. To write 95% as a probability, drop the percent sign and move the decimal two places to the left (.95).

Step 2   Identify the test statistic. Use chi-square when estimating one population variance or standard deviation. Notice the experiment does not estimate a mean, which would require z or t.

Step 3   Determine the critical value with $\alpha/2$. Because chi-square is not symmetric, two critical values must be determined for the left and right tails. Critical values for χ^2 require degrees of freedom and alpha. Degrees of freedom are $n - 1$: $41 - 1 = 40$. Divide alpha by 2 for all confidence intervals. Alpha is $1 -$ the level of confidence: $1 - .95 = .05$. Divide .05 by 2 and adjust as needed for the left and right critical values. The right tail is .05/2, or .025. The left tail is adjusted by subtracting the divided alpha from 1.0: $1 - .05/2 = .975$. Find the right-tailed critical value by tracing *down* Table A.5 to 40 degrees of freedom and *over* to $\alpha = .025$. The critical value for the right tail is 59.342. The left-tailed value is also found in Table A.5 by tracing *down* to 50 degrees of freedom

and *over* to $\alpha = .975$. The left-tailed critical value is 24.433. Retain these values for the calculation.

$$\chi^2_{(40,.025)} = 59.242 \qquad \chi^2_{(40,.975)} = 24.433$$

Step 4   Calculate the interval. The following information is necessary for estimating a variance with chi-square: $n = 41$, $s^2 = 223.96$, $\chi^2_{(40,.025)} = 59.242$, and $\chi^2_{(40,.975)} = 24.433$.

$$\frac{(n-1)s^2}{\chi^2_{(40,.025)}} < \sigma^2 < \frac{(n-1)s^2}{\chi^2_{(40,.975)}}$$

$$\frac{(41-1)233.96}{59.342} < \sigma^2 < \frac{(41-1)233.96}{24.433}$$

$$\frac{(40)233.96}{59.342} < \sigma^2 < \frac{(40)233.96}{24.433}$$

$$\frac{8958.4}{59.342} < \sigma^2 < \frac{8958.4}{24.433}$$

$$150.96 \qquad < \sigma^2 < 366.65$$

Step 5   State the interval. The lower limit of the interval is 150.96 and the upper limit is 366.65. This suggests that with 95% confidence, the variance in IQ tests is between 150.96 and 366.65. The interval notation is

$$150.96 < \sigma^2 < 366.65$$

CHAPTER 12 IN REVIEW

12.1   Find the χ^2 critical values:

   a. $\chi^2_{(20,.025)}$
   b. $\chi^2_{(2,.05)}$
   c. $\chi^2_{(18,.10)}$
   d. $\chi^2_{(16,.95)}$
   e. $\chi^2_{(30,.90)}$
   f. $\chi^2_{(80,.995)}$

12.2   Find the χ^2 critical values:

   a.

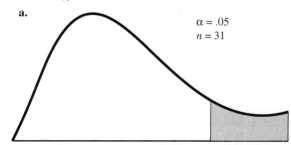

$\alpha = .05$
$n = 31$

b.

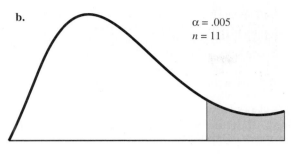

$\alpha = .005$
$n = 11$

c.

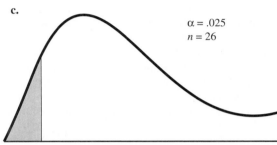

$\alpha = .025$
$n = 26$

d.

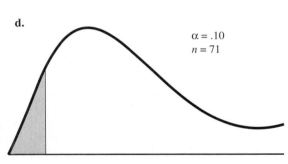

$\alpha = .10$
$n = 71$

e.

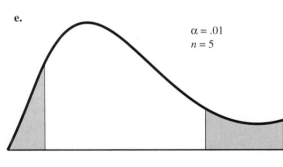

$\alpha = .01$
$n = 5$

f.

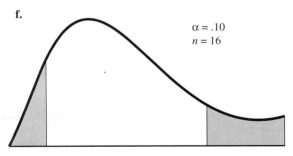

$\alpha = .10$
$n = 16$

12.3   Find the critical value(s) for the following hypotheses.

a. $H_0: \sigma^2 = 20$, $H_1: \sigma^2 \neq 20$, $n = 20$, $\alpha = .10$

b. $H_0: \sigma \leq 5$, $H_1: \sigma > 5$, $n = 6$, $\alpha = .05$

c. $H_0: \sigma^2 = 0$, $H_1: \sigma^2 \neq 0$, $n = 30$, $\alpha = .01$

d. $H_0: \sigma \geq 0$, $H_1: \sigma < 0$, $n = 4$, $\alpha = .01$

e. $H_0: \sigma \geq 3$, $H_1: \sigma < 3$, $n = 91$, $\alpha = .005$

12.4   In the appropriate format, state the null and alternative hypotheses.

a. The variance in age of patients is no more than 7.62 y.

b. The standard deviation in the price of cement is 75¢.

c. The standard deviation in the per capita GNP is $5263.

d. The variance in temperature is no less than 60°.

e. The variance in the weight of babies is different than 7.2 lb.

12.5   In the appropriate format, state the null and alternative hypotheses.

a. The variance in weight of students is not less than 150 lb.

b. The variance in the cost of medicines is greater than 2.23.

c. The standard deviation of exam scores is greater than 10.2.

d. The standard deviation of heights of students is 5 ft 8 in.

e. The variance in caffeine in soft drinks is less than 2.0 mg.

12.6   The standard deviation of a machine pouring soda into a bottle is .4 oz. A sample of 50 bottles produces a standard deviation of .32. At the .05 level of significance, test the claim that the standard deviation equals .4.

12.7   The ages of 12 randomly selected graduate students are as follows. At the .025 level of significance, test the claim that the standard deviation of ages for graduate students is less than 5.33 y.

24.2	33.7	31.9	34.3	31.6	32.7
33.1	25.2	21.6	32.9	23.0	42.4

12.8   One large law school has found that applicants taking the entrance exam earn scores with a variance of 529. A counselor claims that the current group of students produces a larger variance of scores. Test the claim, using the P-value approach, that the variance is larger than 529 if a random sample of 61 students produces a variance of 564. Use a .10 level of significance.

12.9   Test the null hypothesis $\sigma = 15$ where $n = 24$, $s^2 = 10$, and $\alpha = .01$. Use both the classical and P-value approach.

12.10   Find the 90% confidence interval for the variance in the costs of textbooks using a sample of 101 books with a variance of 5.25.

12.11   Find the 95% confidence interval for the standard deviation of the prices on the stock market using a sample of 31 stocks producing a standard deviation of 3.25.

12.12   Given here are total fertility rates of 12 countries. Test the claim that this sample comes from a population with a standard deviation equal to .457. Use $\alpha = .10$.

$$3.03 \quad 3.37 \quad 3.13 \quad 2.33 \quad 4.33 \quad 3.28$$
$$3.72 \quad 4.79 \quad 2.72 \quad 3.13 \quad 3.77 \quad 4.92$$

12.13 At $\alpha = .025$, test the claim that $\sigma^2 > 282$ if a random sample of 30 yields $s^2 = 294$.

12.14 At $\alpha = .025$, test the claim that a population has a standard deviation less than 34.3. A random sample of 51 items yields a standard deviation of 22.1.

12.15 A potato chip company bought a new dispensing machine. The manufacturer of the machine claims it dispenses on average 6 oz, with a standard deviation of 1.0. The chip company feels the standard deviation is much larger than the company claims. A sample of 20 bags was taken reporting a mean of 5.8 and a standard deviation of 1.2. Does the evidence support the manufacturer's claim at the .10 level of significance?

12.16 In the appropriate format, state the null and alternative hypotheses.

    a. The variance in effectiveness of the leading nasal spray is .5 hours.

    b. The standard deviation of the pulse rate of aerobic dancers is lower than 4 beats per minute.

    c. A diet cola has a variance of 35 mg of sodium.

    d. The variance in time it takes the Hometown police to arrive at the scene of a crime is 3 min.

12.17 A random sample of the costs of 20 used cars in the suburb produces a standard deviation of $300. Do the data show that the standard deviation of used cars in the suburb is significantly less than $340, which is the standard deviation of all cars in the city? Use $\alpha = .05$.

12.18 The average number of years it will take the population of a country to double is 41, with a standard deviation of 4.26. Test the claim that the standard deviation is greater than 4.26 using a sample of 20 countries whose variance is 22.35. Let $\alpha = .05$.

12.19 The variance in education spending for a nation is $2.978 million per year. A researcher believes this value is too low and tests the claim using the last 10 y of spending, which produces a variance of $4.142 million. Is there sufficient evidence to suggest the researcher may be correct ($\alpha = .025$)?

12.20 The election commission claims that the variance in voter turnout across the states in a national election is 958,441. Does a sample of 28 states with a variance of 914,950 support the claim? Use a .10 level of significance.

12.21 Estimate the variance of strength of a new metal for airplane manufacturing using a sample of 30 with a variance of 5.381 ($\alpha = .10$).

12.22 Find the 95% confidence interval for the variance in completing a baccalaureate degree with a sample of 101 students with a variance of 7.88 years.

12.23 True or false?

    a. A confidence interval for chi-square establishes a range of values around the sample mean.

    b. All confidence intervals are one-tailed to the right.

    c. The standard deviation is the square root of the variance.

    d. If the P-value is .05 and alpha is .10, the decision is to reject the null hypothesis.

12.24 True or false?

    a. The chi-square test statistic is applied to testing means.

    b. The chi-square zero value is located in the middle of the distribution.

    c. A critical chi-square value of 20.345 must be located in the right tail.

    d. If a calculated value is 25.62 and a critical chi-square value is 32.45, then the decision is to fail to reject the null hypothesis.

12.25 Identify the correct decision concerning the following χ^2 P-values for a one-tailed test to the right.

    a. $P = .05$, $\alpha = .05$ **c.** $P = .025$, $\alpha = .01$

    b. $.025 < P < .05$, $\alpha = .10$ **d.** $P < .01$, $\alpha = .01$

Testing and Estimating Two Populations 13

Situations often exist in which hypothesis testing or estimation is necessary using two samples and/or two populations, as when comparing exam scores of one statistics course to a second statistics course. Previous chapters focused on inferential testing and estimating for means and standard deviations of one population. Adjusting the formulas to include two samples or two populations is easily achieved. Conceptually the process remains the same; most formulas are adjusted by adding a second sample statistic and/or a second parameter. Where means are tested for large samples and population standard deviations are known, the central limit theorem is applied using the normal z distribution. Where means are tested for small samples or where the population standard deviations are not known, the t distribution must be applied. When variances or standard deviations are tested, a skewed distribution similar to chi-square must be applied.

Before the various hypothesis tests are discussed, the terms independent and dependent must be reviewed. Independence is a concern in regression, correlation, probabilities, and sampling. Sampling independence occurs when data are taken from two populations or from independent sources of one population. Independence occurs when the outcomes of one event do not affect the outcomes of another event. For example, a coin landing heads up on one toss does not affect whether the same coin lands heads up the second, third, or fourth tosses. The outcomes from tossing a coin two or more times are independent. However, drawing a coin from one's pocket without replacing it before drawing a second coin makes the second outcome dependent on the first. Any time the sample space is altered, the events are dependent.

Sampling independence or dependence concerns the effect one sample has on another. If two independent samples are drawn, one sample will not affect the other. Random sampling is the best indicator of independent sampling. Random sampling ensures that each element of the population has an equal chance of being selected.

Random sampling is especially important when two samples are selected from the same population.

Dependent sampling usually contains the same elements twice. A very common sampling technique in most social, health, and behavioral sciences is pretest/posttest sampling. For example, a group of individuals is selected and observed, a test or experiment is performed, and a second observation is conducted. The second test results are affected by the observations obtained by the first test. Testing the same individuals twice results in dependent sampling.

Two Independent Means: z

When two large independent samples are drawn from one or two populations where the population standard deviations are known, the central limit theorem is applied in testing and estimating the difference between the means. The central limit theorem (described in Chapter 10) asserts that if random samples are taken from a population, then the sampling distribution approaches the normal probability distribution. A normal distribution is represented by the bell-shaped z distribution. Therefore, testing or estimating two sampling distributions can be achieved using the normal z distribution.

Several conditions are necessary before applying the normal z distribution for two means. First, the samples must be independent; that is, the outcomes of one sample do not affect the outcomes of the second. Next, both population standard deviations must be known. Sample standard deviations cannot be substituted for population standard deviations. Finally, both samples must be large; that is, the sample size of each must be greater than 30.

Criteria for Using z for Two Means

1. Samples are independent.
2. σ_1 and σ_2 are known.
3. n_1 and n_2 are greater than 30.

Hypothesis testing using the classical approach for two large population means follows the same six steps as other types of testing. The hypotheses must be written, the test criteria identified, the calculated value obtained, the calculated value compared to the critical value, a decision made, and an interpretation given.

Steps in Hypothesis Testing Using the Classical Approach

1. State H_0 and H_1.
2. Identify the test criteria.
   a. Level of significance, α
   b. Test statistic (z, t, χ^2, F)
   c. Critical region
      (1) One-tailed test
      (2) Two-tailed test
   d. Critical value

3. Calculate the test statistic.
4. Place the calculated value on distribution curve.
5. Make a decision.
    a. Fail to reject H_0.
    b. Reject H_0.
6. Interpret the results.

The hypotheses are adjusted to represent the comparison of the two population means. Thus far, hypotheses contain one parameter, mathematical symbol, and value. Testing two population means requires two parameters, μ_1 and μ_2. Subscripts are added to denote the first and second means, respectively. Which population to denote by 1 and which to denote by 2 is determined in the hypotheses and not necessarily the first population information provided in the experiment. The three mathematical symbols used in the null hypothesis are $\leq$, $=$, and $\geq$, whereas the three symbols for the alternative hypothesis are $>$, $\neq$, and $<$. Hypotheses for two populations contain a value representing the expected difference between the parameters. Where no difference is expected, include the value 0 in the hypotheses. Therefore, the notation for testing two population means follows the format: parameter one, minus parameter two, mathematical symbol, and value. Some examples are as follows:

$$\text{If } H_0 \text{ is } \mu_1 - \mu_2 \geq 2, \text{ then } H_1 \text{ is } \mu_1 - \mu_2 < 2.$$

$$\text{If } H_0 \text{ is } \mu_1 - \mu_2 = 0, \text{ then } H_1 \text{ is } \mu_1 - \mu_2 \neq 0.$$

$$\text{If } H_0 \text{ is } \mu_1 - \mu_2 \leq 5, \text{ then } H_1 \text{ is } \mu_1 - \mu_2 > 5.$$

EXAMPLE 13.1

Experiment   State the null and alternative hypotheses: There is no more than a 10-lb difference between the mean weight of women and the mean weight of men.

Answer H_0: $\mu_1 - \mu_2 \leq 10$, H_1: $\mu_1 - \mu_2 > 10$

Solution   Begin by identifying the parameters. The Greek symbol μ represents a population mean. The experiment questions the difference between the mean weights of two groups, men and women. Therefore, $\mu_1 - \mu_2$ represents the difference between the means. The words no more than are represented by the math symbol $\leq$, which can only be placed in the null hypothesis. If $\leq$ is in the null hypothesis, then $>$ must be placed in the alternative hypothesis. The expected difference is more than 10 lb. The value 10 is placed in the hypotheses.

The test criteria include identifying the level of significance, test statistic, critical region, and critical value. These steps are achieved exactly as they were in Chapter 10. The level of significance, represented by alpha, is usually established in the experiment. The test statistic z is applied to two population means where the standard deviations are known and samples are large. The critical region is guided by the mathematical symbol of the alternative hypothesis. The critical region is to the left when the alternative hypothesis is $<$, to the right when the symbol is $>$, and two-tailed when the symbol is $\neq$. The critical value for z is determined by placing the alpha in the critical region (first dividing it by 2 if a two-tailed test) and subtracting it from .5000. The subtracted probability is matched to the z critical values in Table A.3 of Appendix A. Notice that z is the only test statistic where probabilities are reported in the body of the table, with critical values on the rim. All other test statistics involve degrees of freedom along the outside of the tables, with critical values in the bodies. Remember that z represents a normal bell-shaped curve whose mean, mode, and median are in the center. Critical values, not probabilities, below the mean, 0, are negative. Probabilities are never negative.

EXAMPLE 13.2

Experiment   Find the critical z value for H_1: $\mu_1 - \mu_2 > 10$; $\alpha = .05$.

Answer   1.645

Solution   The critical value cannot be determined until the critical region is set. The critical region is guided by the alternative hypothesis, which requires only values greater than 10. The test is a one-tailed z test to the right, because the symbol $>$ is in the alternative hypothesis. The normal curve is drawn. Alpha is placed in the critical region in the right tail. Because alpha is .05, the area of the noncritical region is found by subtracting .05 from .5000, the probability of half a normal curve. The probability of the noncritical region is .5000 $-$ .05, or .4500. Using Table A.3, find the probability closest to .4500. The value .4500 is exactly between the reported values .4495 and .4505. Reading *across* and *up* to the z critical values in the margins, .4500 falls between 1.64 and 1.65. The critical value is the z value halfway between 1.64 and 1.65, or 1.645.

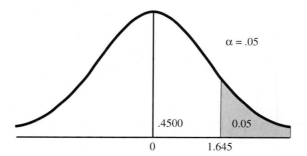

EXAMPLE 13.3

Experiment   Find the critical z value for H_1: $\mu_1 - \mu_2 \neq 4$; $\alpha = .05$.

Answer   1.96 and -1.96

Solution   The critical value cannot be determined until the critical region is set. The critical region is guided by the alternative hypothesis, which requires values not equal to 4. The test is a two-tailed z test, because the symbol $\neq$ is in the alternative hypothesis. The normal curve is drawn. Divide alpha by 2 before placing it in the critical regions of the right and left tails: $.05/2 = .025$. The area of the noncritical region is found by subtracting .025 from .5000, the probability of half a normal curve. The probability of the noncritical region is $.5000 - .025$, or .4750. Using Table A.3, find the probability .4750. Reading *across* and *up* to the z critical values in the margins, .4750 is associated with the z value 1.96. Because the normal curve is symmetric, 1.96 for the right tail is -1.96 for the left tail.

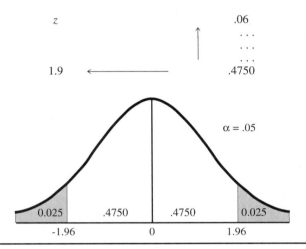

Once the hypotheses and test criteria are determined, the test statistic can be calculated. The test involves calculating the sample information offered as the challenge to the null hypothesis. The calculation for z when the difference between two population means is calculated is similar to the z formula presented in Chapter 10, but with added symbols representing the second sample and population information.

One population: $z = \dfrac{\bar{x} - \mu}{\sigma/\sqrt{n}}$

Two population: $z = \dfrac{(\bar{x}_1 - \bar{x}_2) - (\mu_1 - \mu_2)}{\sqrt{(\sigma_1^2/n_1) + (\sigma_2^2/n_2)}}$

Formula for Calculating z for Two Population Means

$$z = \dfrac{(\bar{x}_1 - \bar{x}_2) - (\mu_1 - \mu_2)}{\sqrt{(\sigma_1^2/n_1) + (\sigma_2^2/n_2)}}$$

The formula tests the difference between the sample and population means. The value placed in parentheses $(\mu_1 - \mu_2)$ is the expected difference stated in the hypotheses. That is, if the hypothesis states the difference is greater than 10, then the value 10 is placed in parentheses. If no difference is expected, then the value is 0.

EXAMPLE 13.4

Experiment Calculate the z test statistic using the following information: $\bar{x}_1 = 20$, $\bar{x}_2 = 19$, $\sigma_1^2 = 4.5$, $\sigma_2^2 = 5.6$, $n_1 = 40$, and $n_2 = 50$.

Answer 2.11

Solution The experiment requires the calculation of the test statistic z. Use the two-population z formula, because two sample means, two sample sizes, and two population standard deviations are given. Notice the calculation requires the retention of the square root sign over the whole denominator until it contains one value.

$$z = \frac{(\bar{x}_1 - \bar{x}_2) - (\mu_1 - \mu_2)}{\sqrt{(\sigma_1^2/n_1) + (\sigma_2^2/n_2)}} = \frac{(20 - 19) - (0)}{\sqrt{(4.5/40) + (5.5/50)}}$$

$$= \frac{(1) - (0)}{\sqrt{(.1125) + (.112)}}$$

$$= \frac{1}{\sqrt{(.2245)}}$$

$$= \frac{1}{.4738}$$

$$= 2.11$$

The fourth step of hypothesis testing is placing the calculated value on the curve to determine its placement relative to the critical value. Remember that negative z critical and calculated values are to the left of the mean 0, located in the middle of the curve.

The final steps of hypothesis testing are the decision and interpretation. There are only two decisions that can be made. The decision is either to reject the null hypothesis or to fail to reject the null hypothesis. If the calculated value is in the critical region, then the decision must be to reject the null hypothesis. If the calculated value does not fall in the critical region, then the decision is to fail to reject the null hypothesis. The interpretation of the decision requires applying the original language contained in the experiment.

EXAMPLE 13.5

Experiment Farmer A claims that the difference in the mean weights of her turkeys and Farmer B's turkeys is no more than 2 pounds. A random sample of 50 of Farmer A's turkeys produces a mean of 11.2 lb, whereas a random sample of 50 of Farmer B's turkeys produces a mean of 8.75 lb. If the population standard deviations are 1.3 and 2.6, respectively, do the samples support Farmer A's claim at the .01 level of significance?

Answer Yes, the samples do support Farmer A's claim.

Solution   Step 1 is to state the hypotheses. The claim that the mean weight of one farmer's turkeys is no more than 2 lb greater than the mean weight of her neighbor's turkeys leads to hypotheses concerning two populations. The parameter for means is μ. The difference between two means is written $\mu_1 - \mu_2$. The mathematical symbol representing no more than is $\leq$, less than or equal to. The symbol $\leq$ can be placed only in the null hypothesis. The symbol in the alternative hypothesis must, therefore, be $>$. The value for both hypotheses is the expected difference, which is no more than 2 lb. The hypotheses are

$$H_0: \quad \mu_1 - \mu_2 \leq 2 \qquad H_1: \quad \mu_1 - \mu_2 > 2$$

Step 2 is the identification of the test criteria. The level of significance, alpha, is .01. The test statistic is z. The normal z distribution is applied, because two populations are tested, both samples are large and randomly selected assuring independence, and both standard deviations of the populations are known. The critical region is placed in the right tail, as determined by the $>$ in the alternative hypothesis. The critical value requires subtracting alpha, .01, from .5000, the probability of half the curve, and finding the z score associated with the remaining probability. Because $.5000 - .01$ equals .4900, the critical z value in Table A.3 associated with the probability .4900 is 2.33.

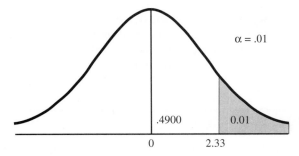

$$\alpha = .01$$

.4900   0.01

0   2.33

The third stage is the calculation of the test statistic. All the necessary information is given in the problem. Remember that the value for the difference of the population means is the 2 contained in the hypotheses. Also notice that the formula requires the population variances, but the experiment gives standard deviations. The standard deviations must be squared for the calculation. $\bar{x}_1 = 11.2$, $\bar{x}_2 = 8.75$, $n_1 = 50$, $n_2 = 50$, $\sigma_1 = 1.3$, and $\sigma_2 = 2.6$.

$$z = \frac{(\bar{x}_1 - \bar{x}_2) - (\mu_1 - \mu_2)}{\sqrt{(\sigma_1^2/n_1) + (\sigma_2^2/n_2)}} = \frac{(11.2 - 8.75) - (2)}{\sqrt{(1.3^2/50) + (2.6^2/50)}}$$

$$= \frac{(2.45) - (2)}{\sqrt{(1.69/50) + (6.75/50)}}$$

$$= \frac{.45}{\sqrt{(.0338) + (.135)}}$$

$$= \frac{.45}{\sqrt{(.1688)}}$$

$$= \frac{.45}{.4121}$$

$$= 1.09$$

The fourth stage is to place the calculated value 1.09 on the distribution curve. It is placed to the left of the critical value 2.33, in the noncritical region.

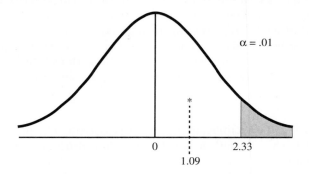

Step 5 is to make a decision based on the placement of the calculated value on the curve. Since the calculated value is not in the critical region, the decision is to fail to reject the null hypothesis.

$$\text{Fail to reject } H_0$$

The final step is to interpret the decision incorporating the language of the experiment. Failing to reject the null hypothesis suggests that the samples support Farmer A's claim that the difference in the mean weights of her turkeys and Farmer B's turkeys is no more than 2 lb.

EXAMPLE 13.6

Experiment Does the quality of Work Life Program help productivity as measured by the average number of defects per finished product? One hundred units were randomly selected after the program's implementation, producing a mean of 1.3 defects. One hundred units were randomly selected before the program's implementation, producing a mean of 2.5 defects. Assume the population standard deviation after the program is 1.1 and that before the program is 1.9; $\alpha = .05$.

Answer Reject the null hypothesis; there is sufficient evidence at the .05 level to suggest that the program has substantially helped productivity.

Solution Identify the hypotheses. For the program to be viewed as a success, the number of defects per unit must decrease after its implementation. Therefore, the alternative hypothesis is that mean number of defects is less ($<$) than mean number of defects before. The null hypothesis must use the contrasting symbol, greater than or equal to ($\geq$). Because no value is stated, the value placed in the hypotheses is 0.

$$H_0: \quad \mu_1 - \mu_2 \geq 0 \qquad H_1: \quad \mu_1 - \mu_2 < 0$$

Step 2 is to identify the test criteria. The test statistic is z for two populations with large sample sizes and both population standard deviations known. The alpha level is .05. The critical region is to the left. The critical value is determined by subtracting .05 from .5000 and identifying the z value in Table A.3 associated with the probability .4500. The critical value is -1.645 (the negative sign is added to z values located to the left of 0).

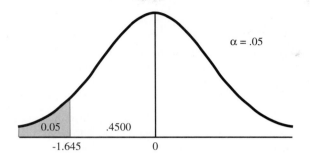

The third stage is the calculation of the test statistic. All the necessary information is given in the problem. Notice that the formula requires the population variances, but the experiment gives standard deviations. The standard deviations must be squared for the calculation: $\bar{x}_1 = 1.3, \bar{x}_2 = 2.5, n_1 = 100, n_2 = 100, \sigma_1 = 1.1$, and $\sigma_2 = 1.9$.

$$z = \frac{(\bar{x}_1 - \bar{x}_2) - (\mu_1 - \mu_2)}{\sqrt{(\sigma_1^2/n_1) + (\sigma_2^2/n_2)}} = \frac{(1.3 - 2.5) - (0)}{\sqrt{(1.1^2/100) + (1.9^2/100)}}$$

$$= \frac{(-1.2) - (0)}{\sqrt{(1.21/100) + (3.61/100)}}$$

$$= \frac{-1.2}{\sqrt{(.0121) + (.0361)}}$$

$$= \frac{-1.2}{\sqrt{(.0482)}}$$

$$= \frac{-1.2}{.2195}$$

$$= -5.47$$

The fourth stage is to place the calculated value, -5.47, on the distribution curve. It is placed to the left of the critical value -1.645, in the critical region.

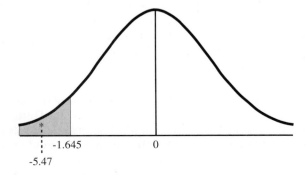

Step 5 is to make a decision based on the placement of the calculated value on the curve. Because the calculated value is in the critical region, the decision is to reject the null hypothesis.

$$\text{Reject } H_0$$

The final step is to interpret the decision incorporating the language of the experiment. Rejecting the null hypothesis suggests productivity decreased, as measured by the number of defects per unit.

The P-value approach for two-population z testing is the same as for one-population z testing. The P-value approach goes one step further than the classical approach by transforming the calculated value into a probability that can be compared to alpha for a decision. The first three steps of the P-value approach are similar to the classical approach. Only two aspects of the test criteria are necessary: the level of significance and the identification of the test statistic. The hypotheses statements and the calculation of the test statistic are the same. Once the calculated test statistic is determined, it is transformed into a probability using Table A.3. The P-value associated with the probability is determined and then compared to alpha. If the P-value is less than or equal to alpha, then the decision is to reject the null hypothesis. If the P-value is greater than alpha, then the decision is to fail to reject the null hypothesis. The final step is the interpretation of the decision to the experiment.

> **Steps in Hypothesis Testing Using the P-Value Approach**
>
> 1. State H_0 and H_1.
> 2. Identify the test criteria.
>   a. Level of significance
>   b. Test statistic
> 3. Calculate the test statistic.
> 4. Calculate the P-value.
>   a. One-tailed test
>   b. Two-tailed test
> 5. Make a decision.
>   a. Fail to reject H_0.
>   b. Reject H_0.
> 6. Interpret results.

Step 4 is the step that needs special attention when using the z statistic. Unlike t and χ^2, z does not contain degrees of freedom. Begin by noting the calculated z value. Find the corresponding probability associated with the calculated z value reported in Table A.3. Subtract this probability from .5000, the probability of half of the normal curve. The remaining probability represents the area of the curve and is known as the P-value if the test is one-tailed. Two-tailed tests require the probability of the tail to be multiplied by 2 to represent the full P-value probability. For example, if a calculated value 1.78 has an associated probability from Table A.3 of

.4625, then .4625 is subtracted from .5000 for a probability of a tail of .0375. See Figure 13.1. If the test is one-tailed, then the P-value is .0375. However, if the test is two-tailed, .0375 must be multiplied by 2 for a combined P-value of .0375(2) = .075. Remember that left-tailed z calculated values are negative, but the probability is never negative.

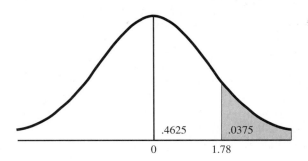

FIGURE 13.1

The other steps in P-value testing remain the same. State the hypotheses, identify the test criteria, calculate the test statistic, calculate the P-value, make a decision, and interpret the results.

EXAMPLE 13.7

Experiment   The registrar of State University claims the mean age of evening students is no more than 5 y greater than the mean age of day students. A random sample of 32 day students produces a mean of 26, whereas a random sample of 40 evening students produces a mean of 33. The population standard deviation of day students is 4 and the standard deviation of evening students is 3. Test using the P-value approach at the .05 level of significance.

Answer   Reject the null hypothesis; there is sufficient evidence at the .05 level of significance to suggest that the mean age of evening students is more than 5 y greater than the mean age of day students.

Solution   Step 1 is to state the hypotheses. The statement of the registrar is that the mean age of evening students is no more than 5 y greater than the mean age of day students. This statement is the null hypothesis, because the symbol representing no more than (less than or equal to) can be placed only in the null hypothesis. If the null contains the symbol $\leq$, then the alternative hypothesis must contain the symbol $>$. The difference between two means requires the parameters $\mu_1 - \mu_2$. The hypothesized difference is 5 y.

$$H_0: \quad \mu_1 - \mu_2 \leq 5 \qquad H_1: \quad \mu_1 - \mu_2 > 5$$

Step 2 is to identify the test criteria. The level of significance is .05, and the test statistic is the two-population z distribution. The z distribution is applied to two random samples, where both sample sizes are larger than 30 and both population standard deviations are known.

Step 3 is to calculate the test statistic. The information for evening students is population 1, and the information for day students is population 2. This order is required by the hypotheses statements, which assume the mean age of evening students is larger than that of day students. Standard deviations are given, but the formula requires variances. Thus, the standard deviations must be squared. The value 5 must be placed in the formula for the expected difference of the population means. The information is $\bar{x}_1 = 33$, $\bar{x}_2 = 26$, $n_1 = 40$, $n_2 = 32$, $\sigma_1 = 3$, and $\sigma_2 = 4$.

$$z = \frac{(\bar{x}_1 - \bar{x}_2) - (\mu_1 - \mu_2)}{\sqrt{(\sigma_1^2/n_1) + (\sigma_2^2/n_2)}} = \frac{(33 - 26) - (5)}{\sqrt{(3^2/40) + (4^2/32)}}$$

$$= \frac{(7) - (5)}{\sqrt{(9/40) + (16/32)}}$$

$$= \frac{2}{\sqrt{(.225) + (.5)}}$$

$$= \frac{2}{\sqrt{.725}}$$

$$= \frac{2}{.8515}$$

$$= 2.35$$

The *P*-value is found by finding the probability associated with the calculated test statistic, 2.35. Table A.3 gives a probability .4906 for $z = 2.35$. The probability .4906 must be subtracted from .5000 to give the probability of the curve from $z = 2.35$ out to the end of the tail. The value is $.5000 - .4906 = .0094$. This is the *P*-value, because this is a one-tailed test.

P-value = .0094

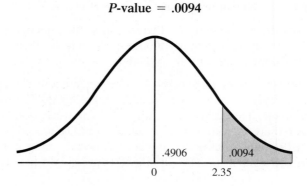

The *P*-value must be compared to alpha to make a decision about the null hypothesis. Compare the *P*-value, .0094, to alpha, .05. Because $P < \alpha$, reject the null hypothesis.

$$P_{(.0094)} \leq \alpha_{(.05)} \qquad \text{Reject } H_0$$

Rejecting the null hypothesis suggests there is sufficient proof at the .05 level of significance that the mean age of evening students is more than 5 y greater than the mean age of day students.

The confidence interval for two-population z estimation is similar to that for one-population estimation. The only difference is in the formula, which must now represent two sample means. Confidence intervals estimate parameters. When estimating the difference of two population means, the estimation is based on the difference of two sample means. The confidence interval establishes a range around the difference of the sample means in which the difference of the population means should fall.

The level of confidence establishes the width of the interval and thus the probability that the parameter will be contained in the interval. The level of confidence is usually reported as a percentage; to rewrite a percentage as a probability requires dropping the percent sign and moving the decimal two places to the left. If a level of confidence is 95%, then the probability is .95. Alpha is the opposite of the level of confidence. If the level of confidence is .95, then alpha is .05. The level of confidence and alpha have a sum of 1. Because the interval establishes a range of values around the sample statistic, the probability of an error is divided by 2, with half the error in each tail of the curve. In other words, all confidence intervals require dividing alpha by 2.

The critical value for z requires alpha and Table A.3. Alpha is divided by 2 and then subtracted from .5000. If alpha is .05, alpha divided by 2 is .025. Subtracting .025 from .5000 results in .4750. Using Table A.3, the probability of .4750 is associated with a critical z value of 1.96. The critical value is noted as $z_{(\alpha/2)}$ and is retained for the calculation of the interval.

The formula for estimating two large, independent means results from algebraic manipulation of the test statistic formula. To apply this formula for estimating means, both samples must be large, the samples must be independent, and the standard deviations of the populations must be known; all three conditions must be met before using the formula.

> ### The Formula for a Confidence Interval for the Difference of Two Population Means Where the Samples Are Independent, Samples Are Size >30, σ_1 and σ_2 Are Known
>
> $$\begin{cases} (\bar{x}_1 - \bar{x}_2) + z_{(\alpha/2)} \sqrt{\dfrac{\sigma_1^2}{n_1} + \dfrac{\sigma_2^2}{n_2}} \\ (\bar{x}_1 - \bar{x}_2) - z_{(\alpha/2)} \sqrt{\sigma_1^2/n_1 + \sigma_2^2/n_2} \end{cases}$$

The first formula establishes the upper limit of the interval, and the second formula establishes the lower limit. The value representing $z_{(\alpha/2)}$ is the critical value identified in an earlier step. Be sure to notice whether the information given in an experiment is a standard deviation or a variance. The formula requires the variance. Standard deviations are squared to give variances. The notation of the interval derived from the calculation is written in terms of the difference of the population means.

$$\text{lower limit} < (\mu_1 - \mu_2) < \text{upper limit}$$

Steps in Calculating a Confidence Interval for a Population Parameter

1. Identify the level of confidence.
2. Identify the test statistic (z, t, χ^2, or F).
3. Determine the critical value with $\alpha/2$.
4. Calculate the interval.
5. State the interval.

A LEARNING AID

Two Independent Means: z

Test whether the average cost of repairs at Maria's Garage is greater than the average cost of repairs at Dino's Garage. A random selection of 50 repairs at Maria's garage produces a mean of $100.15. A random selection of 60 repairs at Dino's Garage produces a mean of $90.55. Assume the standard deviation of all repairs at Maria's is $25.33 and at Dino's is $18.79. Use the classical approach with alpha of .05.

Step 1   State the hypotheses. The claim is that the average cost of repairs at Maria's is greater than the average cost of repairs at Dino's. The test is for two populations, because it is asking about average costs at two garages. The test is for means, because two means are being tested, the mean cost of repairs at the two garages. Randomization ensures independent samples. The greater than symbol is used in the claim, which makes the claim an alternative hypothesis. If the alternative hypothesis is greater than ($>$), then the null hypothesis must be less than or equal to ($\leq$). The value placed in the hypothesis is 0, unless otherwise stated in the claim. The hypotheses for two population means are written:

$$H_0: \quad \mu_1 - \mu_2 \leq 0 \qquad H_1: \quad \mu_1 - \mu_2 > 0$$

Step 2   Identify the test criteria. Alpha is given as .05. Use the test statistic z for two population means that are independent with large samples (both n_1 and n_2 are greater than 30) and where both population standard deviations are known. The critical region is placed in the right tail, as determined by the $>$ symbol in the alternative hypothesis. The critical value requires subtracting alpha .05 from .5000, the probability of half of the curve, and finding the z score associated with the remaining probability. Because .5000 $-$ .05 equals .4500, the critical z value in Table A.3 in the appendix associated with the probability .4500 is 1.645.

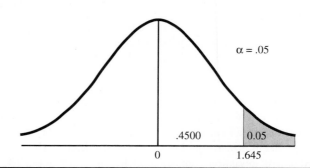

EXAMPLE 13.8

Experiment   Estimate with 90% certainty the difference between the mean grocery bill at Food Mart and the mean grocery bill at Savon Market. A random sample of 40 bills from Food Mart produces a mean of $69.50; the population standard deviation is $16.91. A random sample of 40 bills from Savon Market produces a mean of $61.25 and a population standard deviation of $19.35.

Answer $\$1.566 < (\mu_1 - \mu_2) < \$14.934$

Solution   The problem requires a 90% confidence interval for the difference of two population means. The level of confidence and alpha must have a sum of 1. If the confidence level is .90, then alpha must be $1 - .90$, or .10. The test statistic is z for two population means. Both samples are large (>30), both samples are randomly selected (resulting in independence), and both population

---

Step 3   Calculate the test statistic. The test statistic is z for two independent large samples. Because the hypothesis statement tests whether the cost of repairs at Maria's garage is greater than Dino's, Maria's Garage is population 1 and Dino's is population 2. The information given is $\bar{x}_1 = 100.15$, $\bar{x}_2 = 90.55$, $n_1 = 50$, $n_2 = 60$, $\sigma_1 = 25.33$, and $\sigma_2 = 18.79$.

$$z = \frac{(\bar{x}_1 - \bar{x}_2) - (\mu_1 - \mu_2)}{\sqrt{(\sigma_1^2/n_1) + (\sigma_2^2/n_2)}}$$

$$= \frac{(100.15 - 90.55) - (0)}{\sqrt{(25.33^2/50) + (18.79^2/60)}}$$

$$= \frac{9.6 - 0}{\sqrt{(641.60/50 + 353.064/60)}}$$

$$= \frac{9.6}{\sqrt{(12.832 + 5.884)}}$$

$$= \frac{9.6}{\sqrt{(18.716)}}$$

$$= \frac{9.6}{4.326}$$

$$= 2.22$$

Step 4   Place the calculated value on the curve. The calculated value is 2.22; place it to the right of the critical value 1.645.

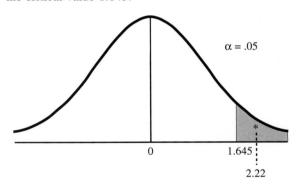

Step 5   Make a decision. Because the calculated value is in the critical region, the decision must be to reject the null hypothesis.

Reject H_0

Step 6   Interpret the results. Rejecting the null hypothesis suggests that there is sufficient evidence at the .05 level of significance that the average cost of repairs for Maria's Garage is greater than the average cost at Dino's Garage.

standard deviations are reported. All three conditions are required before the z test statistic can be used. The critical value is determined by alpha and Table A.3. Alpha must always be divided by 2 when estimating parameters. Divide .10 by 2. The divided alpha is .05. Subtract the divided alpha, .05, from .5000 and find the associated critical z value reported in Table A.3. The subtraction gives $.5000 - .05 = .4500$. The critical value associated with the probability .4500 is 1.645, because .4500 falls exactly between the probabilities associated with 1.64 and 1.65. Retain 1.645 for the calculation as $z_{(\alpha/2)}$.

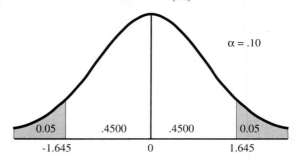

The next step is to calculate the interval. The calculation of the estimation of the test statistic z requires the following information: $\bar{x}_1 = 69.50$, $\bar{x}_2 = 61.25$, $n_1 = 40$, $n_2 = 40$, $\sigma_1^2 = 16.91$, $\sigma_2^2 = 19.35$, and $z_{(\alpha/2)} = 1.645$.

Because the only difference between the calculation of the upper limit and lower limit is the addition and subtraction, respectively, of the right part of the formula, the calculation can be performed once, with the appropriate addition or subtraction at the end.

$$= (\bar{x}_1 - \bar{x}_2) \pm z_{(\alpha/2)} \sqrt{\frac{\sigma_1^2}{n_1} + \frac{\sigma_2^2}{n_2}}$$

$$= (69.50 - 61.25) \pm 1.645 \sqrt{\frac{16.91^2}{40} + \frac{19.35^2}{40}}$$

$$= 8.25 \pm 1.645 \sqrt{\frac{285.948}{40} + \frac{374.423}{40}}$$

$$= 8.25 \pm 1.645\sqrt{7.149 + 9.361}$$

$$= 8.25 \pm 1.645\sqrt{16.51}$$

$$= 8.25 \pm 1.645(4.063)$$

$$= 8.25 \pm 6.684$$

$$\text{Lower limit} = 8.25 - 6.684 = 1.566$$

$$\text{Upper limit} = 8.25 + 6.684 = 14.934$$

The confidence interval has a lower limit of 1.566 and an upper limit of 14.934. Therefore, with 90% confidence, the difference between the mean grocery bills from Food Mart and Savon Market is between \$1.566 and \$14.934.

$$\$1.566 < (\mu_1 - \mu_2) < \$14.934$$

Two Independent Means: *t*

The *z* normal distribution represents the probability distribution of means for large independent samples where the population standard deviation is known. It is rare that the population standard deviation is known, given the population mean is being tested. Also it is common that the sample size is small. Recall from Chapter 11 that the *Student t* distribution is a probability distribution similar to *z*, but it represents small samples where the population standard deviation is not known. The *t* distribution is also applied to two population mean testing where the samples are small or the population standard deviations are not known.

The *t* distribution is symmetric and approximately normal, with the mean, mode, and median denoted by 0 and located in the middle of the curve. All *t* values below the mean are negative. Each probability distribution represented by *t* is dependent on the degrees of freedom and the level of significance. See Figure 13.2.

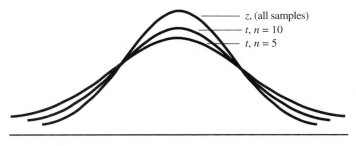

FIGURE 13.2

Hypothesis testing for two independent population means with small sample sizes or with unknown population standard deviations follows the same six steps as do the other test statistics. State the hypotheses, identify the test criteria, calculate the test statistic, place the calculated value on the distribution curve, make a decision, and interpret the results.

Steps in Hypothesis Testing Using the Classical Approach

1. State H_0 and H_1.

2. Identify the test criteria.

   a. Level of significance, α

   b. Test statistic (z, t, χ^2, F)

   c. Critical region

      (1) One-tailed test

      (2) Two-tailed test

   d. Critical value

3. Calculate the test statistic.

4. Place the calculated value on the distribution curve.

5. Make a decision.

   a. Fail to reject H_0.

   b. Reject H_0.

6. Interpret the results.

The hypotheses statements for t are written exactly as they are for z. The parameters are μ_1 and μ_2, the mathematical symbol is determined by the claim, and a value represents the expected difference between the population means. If no difference is expected, then the value is 0. For example, the hypothesis for "no difference" is written:

$$H_0: \quad \mu_1 - \mu_2 = 0 \qquad H_1: \quad \mu_1 - \mu_2 \neq 0$$

The critical value for t requires the level of significance and the degrees of freedom. The degrees of freedom for t when testing for two population means are found by adding the sample sizes and subtracting 2 (df $= n_1 + n_2 - 2$). The number of degrees of freedom for two populations differs from $n - 1$, for one population; both sample sizes must be considered for the degrees of freedom. Alpha is usually reported in an experiment. Remember that alpha is divided by 2 for two-tailed tests. All critical values below the mean are negative. Table A.4 reports the critical values for the t distribution.

> **Degrees of Freedom for Two-Population t Tests When the Variances Are Assumed Equal**
>
> $$df = n_1 + n_2 - 2$$

EXAMPLE 13.9

Experiment Find the critical t values for the following information.

a. $H_0: \quad \mu_1 - \mu_2 = 0, \qquad H_1: \quad \mu_1 - \mu_2 \neq 0, n_1 = 30, n_2 = 25, \alpha = .05$
b. $H_0: \quad \mu_1 - \mu_2 \leq 0, \qquad H_1: \quad \mu_1 - \mu_2 > 0, n_1 = 7, n_2 = 8, \alpha = .01$
c. $H_0: \quad \mu_1 - \mu_2 \geq 0, \qquad H_1: \quad \mu_1 - \mu_2 < 0, n_1 = 12, n_2 = 15, \alpha = .10$

Answer

a. **1.96 and −1.96**
b. **2.650**
c. **−1.316**

Solution Critical values for t require alpha and degrees of freedom. The degrees of freedom for the two-population t are $n_1 + n_2 - 2$. The existence of two populations is evident in that the hypotheses contain two parameters, μ_1 and μ_2.

a. This experiment is a two-tailed test. The mathematical symbol $=$ in the alternative denotes a two-tailed test. Divide alpha by two: $.05/2 = .025$. The degrees of freedom are $n_1 + n_2 - 2$, or $30 + 25 - 2$, which is 53. Use Table A.4. Trace *down* to 53 degrees of freedom and *across* to alpha $= .025$. The degrees of freedom reported at the bottom of the df column represent all degrees of freedom larger than 29. The value found in this row under the alpha of .025

is 1.96. Because this is a two-tailed test and t is symmetric, the value 1.96 is the right-tailed value; -1.96 is the left-tailed value. The notations are

$$t_{(53,.025)} = 1.96 \quad \text{and} \quad -t_{(53,.025)} = -1.96$$

b. The second experiment is one-tailed to the right, as determined by the symbol $>$ in the alternative hypothesis. Alpha is not divided for one-tailed tests. Alpha is .01. Degrees of freedom are $n_1 + n_2 - 2$, or $7 + 8 - 2$, or 13. Trace *down* Table A.4 to 13 degrees of freedom and *across* to alpha $= .01$. The critical value is 2.65:

$$t_{(13,.01)} = 2.65$$

c. The third experiment is one-tailed to the left, as determined by the symbol $<$ in the alternative hypothesis. Alpha is .10. The degrees of freedom are $12 + 15 - 2$, or 25. Trace *down* Table A.4 to df 25 and *across* to alpha $= .10$. The critical value is -1.316. Do not forget the negative sign, because the critical value falls below the mean in the left tail of the distribution curve:

$$t_{(25,.10)} = -1.316$$

The calculation of the t test statistic for two populations is different than the formula for one-population t and one- or two-population z. Recall the adjustment of the calculation for the one-population z test statistic for the t calculation. The population standard deviation in the z formula is replaced by the sample standard deviation in the t test.

$$z = \frac{\bar{x} - \mu}{\sigma/\sqrt{n}} \qquad t = \frac{\bar{x} - \mu}{s/\sqrt{n}}$$

The adjustment for two populations cannot be accomplished this easily. Recall that the denominator in z is referred to as the standard error. Because the standard error involves an error, the error is slightly increased in t with the substitution of s for σ. If the same substitution is done for the two-population z calculation containing two standard errors, then the error will greatly increase. Several statistical approaches are available to avoid the increased error. Some test the equality of the variances (contained in the standard error) before applying one of two calculations for t. Others simply accept the substitution of the population variances with the sample variances when samples are large; another accepts substitution when samples are small. One uniform rule is used in this text. Any time either sample is small or either population standard deviation or variance is unknown, the following t test statistic is applied:

$$t = \frac{(\bar{x}_1 - \bar{x}_2) - (\mu_1 - \mu_2)}{\sqrt{\dfrac{(n_1 - 1)s_1^2 + (n_2 - 1)s_2^2}{n_1 + n_2 - 2}} \sqrt{\dfrac{1}{n_1} + \dfrac{1}{n_2}}}$$

Formula Calculating t for Two Independent Population Means

$$t = \frac{(\bar{x}_1 - \bar{x}_2) - (\mu_1 - \mu_2)}{\sqrt{\dfrac{(n_1 - 1)s_1^2 + (n_2 - 1)s_2^2}{n_1 + n_2 - 2}}\sqrt{\dfrac{1}{n_1} + \dfrac{1}{n_2}}}$$

The formula appears complicated. The complexity results from the estimation of the unknown population variances. The first part of the denominator is referred to as the estimate of the pooled variances. The notation for the estimate of the pooled variances is s_p.

This calculated value is placed on the distribution curve and compared to the critical value. If the calculated value is in the critical region, then the decision is to reject the null hypothesis. If the calculated value is not in the critical region, then the decision is to fail to reject the null hypothesis.

EXAMPLE 13.10

Experiment   A study was designed to compare the attitudes of two groups of nursing students toward computers. Group 1 had previously taken a statistical methods course that involved significant computer interaction. Group 2 had taken a statistical methods course that did not use computers. Using an index of anxiety, random samples were drawn, producing the following measures.

$$\text{Group 1:} \quad n = 12 \quad \bar{x} = 60.3 \quad s = 5.62$$
$$\text{Group 2:} \quad n = 14 \quad \bar{x} = 67.2 \quad s = 4.39$$

Do the data show that the mean score for those with computer experience was significantly less than the mean score for those without computer experience? Use $\alpha = .05$.

Answer   Yes, there is sufficient evidence to suggest that the mean score for those with computer experience was significantly less than the mean score for those without computer experience.

Solution   To state the hypotheses, determine if this is one population or two. Two groups are sampled and the difference between the means is tested. The samples are independent; randomization ensures independent sampling. The experiment questions whether the nursing students with computer experience have, on the average, less anxiety than those without computer experience. The parameters are μ_1 and μ_2. The words less than denote the alternative hypothesis, because the symbol $<$ can be placed only in the alternative hypothesis. The null hypothesis must then be $\geq$. Place the value 0 in the hypothesis as the expected difference, because no other difference is stated. The 0 implies that any difference less than 0 is sufficient to reject the null hypothesis. The hypotheses are

$$H_0: \quad \mu_1 - \mu_2 \geq 0 \qquad H_1: \quad \mu_1 - \mu_2 < 0$$

The test criteria include the level of significance, test statistic, critical region, and critical value. The level of significance is reported as .05. The test statistic is t. Use t when *either* sample is small ($n \leq 30$) or when *either* population standard deviation is unknown. Both samples of nursing students are small and neither report a population standard deviation, only the sample standard deviations. The critical region is to the left, as determined by the $<$ symbol in the alternative hypothesis. The critical value is determined by alpha and the degrees of freedom. Alpha is .05. The degrees of freedom are $n_1 + n_2 - 2$, or $12 + 14 - 2 = 24$. Use Table A.4. Trace *down* to df 24 and *across* to alpha .05. The critical value is -1.711. The negative sign denotes its location below the mean.

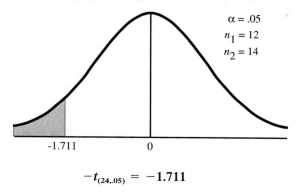

$\alpha = .05$
$n_1 = 12$
$n_2 = 14$

-1.711   0

$$-t_{(24,.05)} = -1.711$$

The calculation of the test statistic t for two populations is the formula containing the pooled-variance denominator.

$$t = \frac{(\bar{x}_1 - \bar{x}_2) - (\mu_1 - \mu_2)}{\sqrt{\dfrac{(n_1 - 1)s_1^2 + (n_2 - 1)s_2^2}{n_1 + n_2 - 2}} \sqrt{\dfrac{1}{n_1} + \dfrac{1}{n_2}}}$$

$$= \frac{(60.3 - 67.2) - (0)}{\sqrt{\dfrac{(12 - 1)5.62^2 + (14 - 1)4.39^2}{12 + 14 - 2}} \sqrt{\dfrac{1}{12} + \dfrac{1}{14}}}$$

$$= \frac{(-6.9) - (0)}{\sqrt{\dfrac{(11)31.584 + (13)19.272}{24}} \sqrt{.083 + .071}}$$

$$= \frac{-6.9}{\sqrt{\dfrac{(347.428) + (250.537)}{24}} \sqrt{.154}}$$

$$= \frac{-6.9}{\sqrt{\dfrac{597.965}{24}} \sqrt{.154}}$$

$$= \frac{-6.9}{\sqrt{24.915} \sqrt{.154}}$$

$$= \frac{-6.9}{(4.99)(.393)}$$

$$= \frac{-6.9}{1.961}$$

$$= -3.519$$

Place the calculated value, -3.519, on the distribution curve. The calculated value, -3.519, falls to the left of the critical value, -1.711.

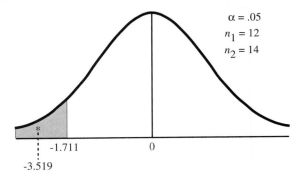

The decision is to reject the null hypothesis. The interpretation is that the samples do provide sufficient evidence at the .05 level of significance that the mean score for those with computer experience was significantly less than the mean score for those without computer experience.

The P-value approach for testing with t for two population means is exactly the same as it is for the one-population t. The P-value approaches extend the classical approach by transforming the calculated value into a probability that is compared to alpha for a decision. P-value testing requires several steps similar to the classical approach. The hypotheses are stated, the test criteria are identified, and the test statistic is calculated. The P-value approach for t requires a probability to be determined from the calculated t value by using Table A.4. The P-value is compared to alpha. If the P-value is less than or equal to alpha, then decision is to reject the null hypothesis. If the P-value is greater than alpha, then decision is to fail to reject the null hypothesis.

Steps in Hypothesis Testing Using the P-Value Approach

1. State H_0 and H_1.
2. Identify the test criteria.
   a. Level of significance
   b. Test statistic
3. Calculate the test statistic.
4. Calculate the P-value.
   a. One-tailed test
   b. Two-tailed test
5. Make a decision.
   a. Fail to reject H_0.
   b. Reject H_0.
6. Interpret the results.

The fourth step in P-value testing differs from the classical approach. The probability of the calculated value must be found and adjusted if it represents a two-tailed test. Using Table A.4, the P-value is the alpha associated with the critical value with the same degrees of freedom nearest to the calculated value determined in step

3. That is, to find the probability for *t*, note the calculated value from step 3 with the degrees of freedom from step 2. Using Table A.4, move *down* to the appropriate degrees of freedom. Read *across* all the values of that row, finding the value nearest to the calculated value. The *P*-value is the alpha level associated with the column where the value nearest to the calculated value is found. If the calculated value falls between two critical values, then use both alpha values to denote the range of values in which the *P*-value lies. If the test is two-tailed, then the alpha value identified by this method must be multiplied by 2 before noting it as a *P*-value.

The final stages of *P*-value testing require decision and interpretation. The decision is made by comparing the *P*-value to the alpha reported in the experiment. If *P* is less than or equal to alpha, then the decision is to reject the null hypothesis. If the *P*-value is greater than alpha, then the decision is to fail to reject the null hypothesis.

P-value $\leq$ alpha   Reject H_0
P-value $>$ alpha   Fail to reject H_0

EXAMPLE 13.11

Experiment It is argued that the risk of complications in pregnancy is greater for women over age 35 than for women 34 y old and younger. A random sample of 10 women age 35 and older produces an average of 5.2 complications, with a standard deviation of 1.2. A random sample of 20 women age 34 and younger produces an average of 4.1, with a standard deviation of .95. Use the *P*-value approach. Do the samples provide sufficient evidence to support the assumption that the risk of complications in pregnancy increases with the age of the mother? Use $\alpha = .05$.

Answer Yes, there is sufficient evidence to suggest that the mean number of complications for women age 35 and older is greater than those age 34 and younger.

Solution To state the hypotheses, determine if this is one population or two. Two groups are sampled and the difference between the means is tested. Randomization ensures independent sampling. The experiment questions whether complications are greater for those women over 35 than for those younger. The parameters are μ_1 and μ_2. The words greater than indicate the alternative hypothesis, because the symbol $>$ can be placed only in the alternative hypothesis. The null hypothesis must then be $\leq$. Place the value 0 in the hypothesis as the expected difference, because no other difference is stated. The 0 implies that any difference less than 0 is sufficient to reject the null hypothesis. The hypotheses are

$$H_0: \quad \mu_1 - \mu_2 \leq 0 \qquad H_1: \quad \mu_1 - \mu_2 > 0$$

The test criteria include alpha, test statistic, critical region, and critical value. Alpha is reported as .05. The test statistic is *t*. Use *t* when *either* sample is small ($n \leq 30$) or when *either* population standard deviation is unknown. Both samples are small and population standard deviations are not given in either case, only the sample standard deviations. The critical region is to the right, as determined by the $>$ symbol in the alternative hypothesis. The critical value is determined by alpha and the degrees of freedom. Alpha is .05. The degrees of freedom are $n_1 + n_2 - 2$, or $10 + 20 - 2 = 28$. Use Table A.4. Move *down* to 28 df and *across* to alpha $= .05$. The critical value is 1.701.

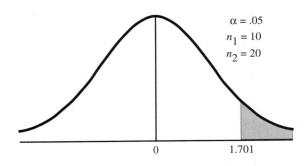

$$\alpha = .05$$
$$n_1 = 10$$
$$n_2 = 20$$

$$t_{(28,.05)} = 1.701$$

The calculation of the test statistic t for two populations is the formula containing the pooled-variance denominator. Arrange the data for the calculation: $\bar{x}_1 = 5.2$, $\bar{x}_2 = 4.1$, $n_1 = 10$, $n_2 = 20$, $s_1 = 1.2$, and $s_2 = .95$.

$$t = \frac{(\bar{x}_1 - \bar{x}_2) - (\mu_1 - \mu_2)}{\sqrt{\dfrac{(n_1 - 1)s_1^2 + (n_2 - 1)s_2^2}{n_1 + n_2 - 2}}\sqrt{\dfrac{1}{n_1} + \dfrac{1}{n_2}}}$$

$$= \frac{(5.2 - 4.1) - (0)}{\sqrt{\dfrac{(10 - 1)(1.2)^2 + (20 - 1)(.95)^2}{10 + 20 - 2}}\sqrt{\dfrac{1}{10} + \dfrac{1}{20}}}$$

$$= \frac{(1.1) - (0)}{\sqrt{\dfrac{(9)(1.44) + (19)(.9025)}{28}}\sqrt{.1 + .05}}$$

$$= \frac{1.1}{\sqrt{\dfrac{12.96 + 17.1475}{28}}\sqrt{.15}}$$

$$= \frac{1.1}{\sqrt{\dfrac{30.1075}{28}}\sqrt{.154}}$$

$$= \frac{1.1}{\sqrt{1.10753}\sqrt{.15}}$$

$$= \frac{1.1}{(1.037)(.387)}$$

$$= \frac{1.1}{.4016}$$

$$= 2.739$$

Determine the probability value associated with this calculated value using Table A.4. The *P*-value for the *t* statistic is determined by moving *down* to the degrees of freedom ($n_1 + n_2 - 2$), *across* to the values nearest the calculated value (2.739), and *up* to the alpha associated with that column. Trace *down* to df 28. Reading *across* this row only, notice the nearest value to 2.739 is 2.763. Move *up* the column where 2.763 is located and find alpha = .005. Alpha = .005 is the *P*-value associated with the calculated value 2.739 at 28 degrees of freedom.

$$P\text{-value}_{(2.739, \text{df}28)} = .005$$

Compare the *P*-value to the original alpha given in the experiment. If *P* $\leq \alpha$, then reject the null hypothesis. If *P* $> \alpha$, then fail to reject the null hypothesis. *P* at .005 is less than α at .05; therefore, reject the null hypothesis.

$$P_{(.005)} \leq \alpha_{(.05)} \qquad \text{Reject } H_0$$

The interpretation is that the samples do provide sufficient evidence at the .05 level of significance that the mean number of complications for women over age 35 is greater than the mean number of complications for women 34 and younger.

The confidence interval for two-population *t* estimation is similar to that for one-population estimation. The confidence interval establishes a range of values around the sample information in which the population parameter will fall. With two population means, the confidence interval establishes a range around the difference of the sample means in which the difference of the population means will fall.

To estimate the difference between two population means with the *t* statistic, the samples must be independent, with either sample size less than or equal to 30 or either population standard deviation unknown. Any of these conditions is sufficient for estimating with *t*.

> **The Formula for a Confidence Interval for the Difference of Two Population Means Where the Samples Are Independent, Sample Size $\leq$ 30, or σ_1 and σ_2 Are Unknown**
>
> $$(\bar{x}_1 - \bar{x}_2) \pm t_{(\text{df}, \alpha/2)} \sqrt{\frac{(n-1)s_1^2 + (n-1)s_2^2}{n_1 + n_2 - 2}} \sqrt{\frac{1}{n} + \frac{1}{n}}$$
>
> where df = $n_1 + n_2 - 2$.

This formula estimates the difference between the population means based on the difference of the sample means. The $\pm$ symbol indicates the data to the right of the symbol should be added to $x_1 - x_2$ to determine the upper limit of the confidence interval and subtracted to find the lower limit of the interval. Because the data to the right of the symbol remains constant, the addition and subtraction occurs at the end of the calculation.

The critical value represented by $t_{(\alpha/2)}$ must be determined before beginning any calculation. The critical value is determined by identifying the degrees of freedom and alpha. The degrees of freedom are $n_1 + n_2 - 2$. Alpha is always divided by two when estimating parameters. Use Table A.4. Move *down* to the appropriate degrees of freedom and *across* to the divided alpha level. Retain the critical value for the calculation of the interval.

Steps in Calculating a Confidence Interval for a Population Parameter

1. Identify the level of confidence.
2. Identify the test statistic (z, t, χ^2, or F).
3. Determine the critical value with $\alpha/2$.
4. Calculate the interval.
5. State the interval.

A LEARNING AID

Two Independent Means: *t*

A random sample of 20 used cars in the suburbs produces a mean of $1200 with a standard deviation of $300. A random sample of 25 used cars in the city produces a mean of $800 with a standard deviation of $340. Do the data show that the mean of used cars in the suburbs is significantly greater than the mean in the city? Use $\alpha = .05$.

Step 1 State the hypotheses. Begin by determining if there is one population or two. Two groups are sampled and the difference between the means is tested. Randomization ensures independent sampling. The experiment questions whether the cost of cars in the suburbs is greater than the cost of cars in the city. The parameters are μ_1 and μ_2. The words greater than indicate the alternative hypothesis, because the symbol $>$ can be placed only in the alternative hypothesis. The null hypothesis must then be $\leq$. Place the value 0 in the hypothesis as the expected difference, because no other difference is stated. The 0 implies that any difference greater than 0 is sufficient to reject the null hypothesis. The hypotheses are

$$H_0: \quad \mu_1 - \mu_2 \leq 0 \qquad H_1: \quad \mu_1 - \mu_2 > 0$$

Step 2 Identify the test criteria. The test criteria include the level of significance, test statistic, critical region, and critical value. The level of significance is reported as .05. The test statistic is t. Use t when *either*

sample is small ($n \leq 30$) or when *either* population standard deviation is unknown. Both samples of cars are small and a population standard deviation is not given in either case. The critical region is to the right, as determined by the $>$ symbol in the alternative hypothesis. The critical value is determined by alpha and the degrees of freedom. The degrees of freedom are $n_1 + n_2 - 2$, or $20 + 25 - 2 = 43$. Use Table A.4. Move *down* to df 43 and *across* to alpha $= .05$. The critical value is 1.645.

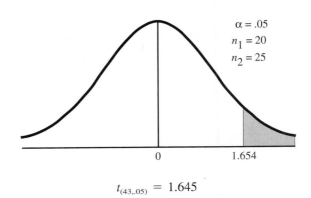

$$t_{(43,.05)} = 1.645$$

Step 3 Calculate the test statistic t. The calculation of t for two populations is the formula containing the pooled-variance denominator. The necessary

EXAMPLE 13.12

Experiment   Find the 90% confidence interval for the difference between the mean age of members in the U.S. Senate and U.S. House of Representatives. Twenty members from both institutions are randomly selected, producing means of 45 and 39, respectively, and variances of 19.2 and 28.26, respectively.

Answer $3.468 < \mu_1 - \mu_2 < 8.532$

Solution   Begin by identifying the experiment as a confidence interval. The experiment asks for a 90% confidence interval. A 90% level of confidence means that the difference of the population parameters should fall in the range of values 90% of the time. Stated another way, the probability of estimating correctly is .9.

---

information is $\bar{x}_1 = 1200$, $\bar{x}_2 = 800$, $s_1 = 300$, $s_2 = 340$, $n_1 = 20$, and $n_2 = 25$.

$$t = \frac{(\bar{x}_1 - \bar{x}_2) - (\mu_1 - \mu_2)}{\sqrt{\dfrac{(n_1 - 1)s_1^2 + (n_2 - 1)s_2^2}{n_1 + n_2 - 2}}\sqrt{\dfrac{1}{n_1} + \dfrac{1}{n_2}}}$$

$$= \frac{(1200 - 800) - (0)}{\sqrt{\dfrac{(20 - 1)(300)^2 + (25 - 1)(340)^2}{20 + 25 - 2}}\sqrt{\dfrac{1}{20} + \dfrac{1}{25}}}$$

$$= \frac{400 - 0}{\sqrt{\dfrac{(19)(90{,}000) + (24)(115{,}600)}{43}}\sqrt{.05 + .04}}$$

$$= \frac{400}{\sqrt{\dfrac{(1{,}710{,}000) + (2{,}774{,}400)}{43}}\sqrt{.09}}$$

$$= \frac{400}{\sqrt{\dfrac{4{,}484{,}400}{43}}\sqrt{.09}}$$

$$= \frac{400}{\sqrt{104{,}288.37}\sqrt{.09}}$$

$$= \frac{400}{(322.937)(.3)}$$

$$= \frac{400}{96.881}$$

$$= 4.129$$

Step 4   Place the calculated value 4.133 on the distribution curve. The calculated value, 4.133, falls to the left of the critical value, 1.645.

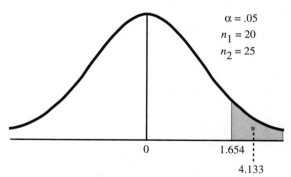

$\alpha = .05$
$n_1 = 20$
$n_2 = 25$

0   1.654
            4.133

Step 5   Make a decision. The decision is to reject the null hypothesis, because the calculated value falls in the critical region.

Step 6   Interpret the results. The interpretation is that the samples do provide sufficient evidence at the .05 level of significance that the mean cost of used cars in the suburbs is greater than the mean cost of used cars in the city.

Use the t statistic for the experiment, because the sample sizes are both small, the samples are independent, and the population standard deviations are unknown.

The critical value for t requires the degrees of freedom and alpha. The degrees of freedom are $n_1 + n_2 - 2$, which is $20 + 20 - 2$, or 38. Alpha must be determined by subtracting the level of confidence from 1, or $1 - .9 = .10$. Divide alpha by 2 before going into the t table. Remember, all confidence intervals require $\alpha/2$. Alpha divided by 2 is $.10/2$, or $.05$. Using Table A.4, move *down* to 38 df and *across* to alpha ($\alpha/2$) $.05$. All degrees of freedom greater than 29 are read from the bottom row of numbers. The value 1.645 is the critical value. Retain this value for the calculation of the interval.

To calculate the interval, the following information is necessary: $\bar{x}_1 = 45$, $\bar{x}_2 = 39$, $s_1^2 = 19.2$, $s_2^2 = 28.26$, $n_1 = 20$, $n_2 = 20$, and $t_{(\alpha/2)} = 1.645$.

$$E_{(\mu_1 - \mu_2)} = (\bar{x}_1 - \bar{x}_2) \pm t_{(df, \alpha/2)} \sqrt{\frac{(n-1)s_1^2 + (n-1)s_2^2}{n_1 + n_2 - 2}} \sqrt{\frac{1}{n} + \frac{1}{n}}$$

$$= (45 - 39) \pm 1.645 \sqrt{\frac{(20-1)(19.2) + (20-1)(28.26)}{20 + 20 - 2}} \sqrt{\frac{1}{20} + \frac{1}{20}}$$

$$= 6 \pm 1.645 \sqrt{\frac{(19)(19.2) + (19)(28.26)}{38}} \sqrt{.05 + .05}$$

$$= 6 \pm 1.645 \sqrt{\frac{364.8 + 536.94}{38}} \sqrt{.10}$$

$$= 6 \pm 1.645 \sqrt{\frac{(901.74)}{38}} \sqrt{.10}$$

$$= 6 \pm 1.645 \sqrt{23.73} \sqrt{.10}$$

$$= 6 \pm 1.645(4.87)(.316)$$

$$= 6 \pm 2.532$$

$$\text{Lower limit} = 6 - 2.532 = 3.468$$
$$\text{Upper limit} = 6 + 2.532 = 8.532$$

The confidence interval has a lower limit of 3.468 and an upper limit of 8.532. Therefore, with 90% confidence, the difference between the average ages of U.S. Senators and Representatives is between 3.468 and 8.532 y.

$$3.468 < \mu_1 - \mu_2 < 8.532$$

Two Dependent Means: t

The t distribution is also applied in testing and estimating two dependent samples. Recall that dependent sampling occurs when the same data are sampled twice. Many of the social and behavioral sciences conduct experiments where the same individuals are tested twice. Many tests are referred to as *pretests* and *posttests;* others are called *before* and *after* tests. All the stages of hypothesis testing and estimation remain the same for the t test for dependent sampling as for the t test for independent sampling. The only major adjustment occurs in the adjusted formula for the calculated t value.

The hypotheses are written slightly differently than they are written for independent sampling. Because the difference between the first sample mean and the second sample mean is in question, the notation for the difference in dependent means is written μ_d. An example of hypotheses with no expected difference is written

$$H_0: \quad \mu_d = 0 \qquad H_1: \quad \mu_d \neq 0$$

If a difference is expected, then a value will replace the 0 in the hypotheses. Remember that the symbols $\leq$, $=$, and $\geq$ are placed in the null hypothesis and $>$, $\neq$, and $<$ are placed in the alternative hypothesis.

The critical region and calculated value are determined by reading Table A.4. The degrees of freedom for dependent testing with t are $n - 1$, where n represents the number of paired observations. For example, if 10 people are tested twice, although there are a total of 20 responses, the sample size is 10 and df $=$ $10 - 1 = 9$.

Degrees of Freedom for t Dependent Means

$$\text{df} = n - 1$$

where n is the number of paired observations.

The formula for the calculated t value requires the calculation of the sample mean difference and the sample standard deviation difference. The formula for the mean difference is the sum of the differences divided by the number of paired observations. Subtract each value of x of the first test from its corresponding x value in the second test. The summation occurs after each difference is determined. The sample statistic is d.

Formula for Calculating the Mean Difference for Dependent Samples

$$\bar{d} = \frac{\Sigma d}{n}$$

where

d is the difference between members of each ordered pair: $d = (x_2 - x_1)$.

n is the number of ordered pairs.

The calculation of the standard deviation difference for dependent samples is similar to the standard deviation presented in earlier chapters, but d replaces x in the calculation.

Formula for Calculating the Standard Deviation for Dependent Samples

$$s_d = \sqrt{\frac{\Sigma d^2 - \frac{(\Sigma d)^2}{n}}{n - 1}}$$

The calculated t value requires subtracting the expected mean difference from the sample mean difference and dividing by the standard error. The calculation of the sample mean difference and the standard deviation, which is a component of the standard error, must be completed before using the t formula.

Formula for t Dependent Means

$$t = \frac{\bar{d} - \mu_d}{s_d/\sqrt{n}}$$

where

$\bar{d}$ is the sample mean difference.

$\mu_{\bar{d}}$ is the expected population mean difference.

$s_{\bar{d}}$ is the sample standard deviation difference.

n is the number of ordered pairs.

EXAMPLE 13.13

Experiment   To test the effect of a computer training session, employees at the university were asked to test their knowledge of computer skills before and after the training session. Six employees scored as shown here. Can it be concluded that a significant difference in their computer skills is due to the training session? Let $\alpha = .05$.

Before	After
61	75
43	71
71	93
66	82
59	69
60	80

Answer   Yes, it can be concluded that the difference in computer skills is due to the training session.

Solution   To state the hypotheses, determine if this is one population or two. One group is sampled twice, resulting in testing the difference in the responses from the first test to the second. The samples are not independent, because the same people are sampled twice. A before-and-after test that is not randomized usually implies dependent sampling. The parameter for two dependent means is μ_d. The symbol for an expected difference is $\neq$, which must be placed in the alternative hypothesis. The null hypothesis must contain the contrasting symbol, $=$. The value 0 is placed in the hypothesis as the expected difference.

$$H_0: \quad \mu_d = 0 \qquad H_1: \quad \mu_d \neq 0$$

The test criteria include the level of significance, test statistic, critical region, and critical value. The level of significance is reported as alpha $= .05$.

The test statistic for two dependent means is t. The critical region is in both tails, as determined by the $\neq$ symbol in the alternative hypothesis. The critical t value for dependent means requires the degrees of freedom and the alpha. The degrees of freedom for dependent sampling is $n - 1$, where n is the number of ordered pairs. Six people are sampled; $n - 1$ is $6 - 1$, or 5. Alpha is divided by 2 for a two-tailed test: .05/2 is .025. Use Table A.4. Move *down* to 5 df and *across* to alpha = .025. The critical value for the right tail is 2.571. The left-tailed value is determined by adding a negative sign to the right-tailed value. The left-tailed critical value is -2.571.

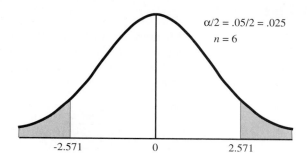

$\alpha/2 = .05/2 = .025$

$n = 6$

-2.571   0   2.571

The calculation of the test statistic t for two dependent means requires the mean difference and the standard deviation difference. The formulas for the mean and standard deviation follow. Notice the data are restated and arranged to illustrate the calculations.

Before	After	$(x_2 - x_1)$ d	d^2
61	75	14	196
43	71	28	784
71	93	22	484
66	82	16	256
59	69	10	100
60	80	20	400
		$\Sigma d = 110$	$\Sigma d^2 = 2220$

$$\bar{d} = \frac{\Sigma d}{n} = \frac{110}{6} = 18.33$$

$$s_d = \sqrt{\frac{\Sigma d^2 - (\Sigma d)^2/n}{n - 1}} = \sqrt{\frac{2220 - 110^2/6}{6 - 1}}$$

$$= \sqrt{\frac{2220 - 2016.67}{5}} = \sqrt{\frac{203.33}{5}} = \sqrt{40.666} = 6.377$$

With the sample mean difference of 22 and the sample standard deviation difference of 20.88, the t test statistic can be calculated.

$$t = \frac{\bar{d} - \mu_d}{s_d/\sqrt{n}} = \frac{18.33 - 0}{6.377/\sqrt{6}} = \frac{18.33}{6.377/2.449} = \frac{18.33}{2.604} = 7.04$$

Place the calculated value, 7.04, on the curve. The value 7.04 falls to the right of 2.571, in the critical region. The decision is to reject the null hypothesis.

$$\text{Reject } H_0$$

There is sufficient evidence, at the .05 level of significance, to suggest that the training course affected the computer skills of the employees at the university.

EXAMPLE 13.14

Experiment   A political scientist interested in the relationship between redistricting and incumbency advantage in city council elections collects the following data for six districts. Test the null hypothesis that redistricting makes no difference in the incumbents' vote margins. Let $\alpha = .05$.

Average Margin of Victory	
Before	**After**
56	53
60	57
52	50
57	59
62	60
54	52

Answer   Fail to reject the null hypothesis. There is not sufficient evidence to reject the null hypothesis that redistricting makes no difference in the incumbents' vote margins.

Solution   One group is sampled twice resulting in testing the difference in the responses from the first test to the second. The samples are not independent, because the same people are sampled twice. A before-and-after test that is not randomized usually implies dependent sampling. The parameter for two dependent means is μ_d. The symbol for an expected difference is $\neq$, which must be placed in the alternative hypothesis. The null hypothesis must contain the contrasting symbol, $=$. The value 0 is placed in the hypothesis as the expected difference.

$$H_0: \quad \mu_d = 0 \qquad H_1: \mu_d \neq 0$$

The test criteria include the level of significance, test statistic, critical region, and critical value. The level of significance is reported as alpha $= .05$. The test statistic for two dependent means is t. The critical region is in both tails, as determined by the $\neq$ symbol in the alternative hypothesis. The critical t value for dependent means requires the degrees of freedom and the alpha. The degrees of freedom for dependent sampling are $n - 1$, where n is the number of ordered pairs. Six people are sampled, so $n - 1$ is $6 - 1$, or 5. Alpha is divided by 2 for a two-tailed test: .05/2 is .025. Use Table A.4. Move *down* to 5 df and *across* to alpha $= .025$. The critical value for the right tail is 2.571. The left-tail value is determined by adding a negative sign to the right-tail value. The left-tail critical value is -2.571.

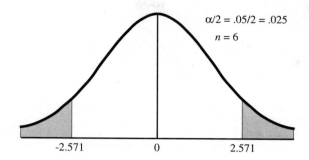

$\alpha/2 = .05/2 = .025$

$n = 6$

-2.571   0   2.571

The calculation of the test statistic t for two dependent means requires the mean difference and the standard deviation difference. The formulas for the mean and standard deviation follow. The data are restated and arranged to illustrate the calculations.

Before	After	$(x_2 - x_1)$ d	d^2
56	53	3	9
60	57	3	9
52	50	2	4
57	59	-2	4
62	60	2	0
54	52	2	4
		$\Sigma d = 10$	$\Sigma d^2 = 30$

$$\bar{d} = \frac{\Sigma d}{n} = \frac{10}{6} = 1.67$$

$$s_d = \sqrt{\frac{\Sigma d^2 - (\Sigma d)^2/n}{n - 1}} = \sqrt{\frac{30 - 10^2/6}{6 - 1}} = \sqrt{\frac{30 - 16.67}{5}}$$

$$= \sqrt{\frac{13.33}{5}} = \sqrt{2.667} = 1.63$$

With the sample mean difference of 1.67 and the sample standard deviation difference 1.63, the t test statistic can be calculated.

$$t = \frac{\bar{d} - \mu_d}{s_d/\sqrt{n}} = \frac{1.67 - 0}{1.63/\sqrt{6}} = \frac{1.67}{1.63/2.449} = \frac{1.67}{.665} = 2.510$$

Place the calculated value, 2.510, on the curve. The value 2.510 falls to the left of 2.571, in the noncritical region. The decision is to fail to reject the null hypothesis.

Fail to reject H_0

There is sufficient evidence, at the .05 level of significance, to suggest that the training course affected the computer skills of the employees at the university.

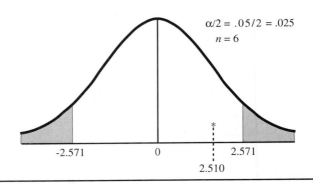

$\alpha/2 = .05/2 = .025$
$n = 6$

-2.571   0   2.571

2.510

A LEARNING AID

Two Dependent Means: t

A major retail chain store believes that sales have decreased since the most recent recession. To test the claim, five stores were surveyed over a period of time before and after the recession, producing the following data ($\alpha = .01$):

Average Sales (in thousands of dollars)

Before	After
102	100
203	195
156	158
157	159
260	257

Step 1 There are two populations, because each store was surveyed twice. The experiment is to test if there is a decrease in sales from the first test to the second. The samples are not independent, because the same stores are sampled twice. A before-and-after test that is not randomized usually implies dependent sampling. The parameter for two dependent means is μ_d. The symbol for the expected decrease in sales is $<$, which must be placed in the alternative hypothesis. The null hypothesis must contain the contrasting symbol, $\geq$. The value 0 is placed in the hypothesis as the expected difference.

$$H_0: \quad \mu_d \geq 0 \qquad H_1: \quad \mu_d < 0$$

Step 2 Identify the test criteria. The test criteria include the level of significance, test statistic, critical region, and critical value. The level of significance is reported as alpha = .05. The test statistic for two dependent means is t. The critical region is to the left, as determined by the $<$ symbol in the alternative hypothesis. The critical t value for dependent means requires the degrees of freedom and the alpha. The degrees of freedom for dependent sampling are $n - 1$, where n is the number of ordered pairs. Five stores are sampled, so $n - 1 = 5 - 1$, or 4. Use Table A.4. Move *down* to 4 df and *across* to alpha = .01. The critical value is -3.747. Left-tailed values include a negative sign.

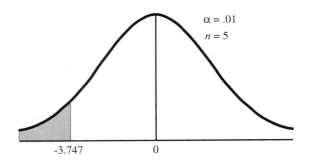

$\alpha = .01$
$n = 5$

-3.747   0

Step 3 The calculation of the test statistic t for two dependent means requires the mean difference and the standard deviation difference. The formulas for the

P-value testing for t dependent means is exactly the same as for t independent means. The calculated value is transformed into a probability representing the alpha value of the critical value nearest the calculated value. The decision concerning the null hypothesis is made by comparing the P-value to the alpha reported in the experiment.

EXAMPLE 13.15

Experiment   Find the P-value for a one-tailed calculated t value of 1.722 for a dependent sample with the sample size 19.

Answer $P_{(1.722, 18)} = .05$

Solution   The P-value for two-population t is determined by identifying the alpha associated with the nearest critical value at the same degrees of freedom

---

mean and standard deviation follow. The data are restated and arranged to illustrate the calculations. The *before* data are subtracted from the *after*.

Before	After	$(x_2 - x_1)$ d	d^2
102	100	−2	4
203	195	−8	64
156	158	2	4
157	159	2	4
260	257	−3	9
		$\Sigma d = -9$	$\Sigma d^2 = 85$

$$\bar{d} = \frac{\Sigma d}{n} = \frac{-9}{5} = -1.80$$

$$s_d = \sqrt{\frac{\Sigma d^2 - (\Sigma d)^2/n}{n-1}} = \sqrt{\frac{85 - (-9)^2/5}{5-1}}$$

$$= \sqrt{\frac{85 - 16.2}{4}} = \sqrt{\frac{68.8}{4}}$$

$$= \sqrt{17.20} = 4.15$$

With the sample mean difference of -1.80 and the sample standard deviation difference of 4.15, the t test statistic can be calculated.

$$t = \frac{\bar{d} - \mu_d}{s_d/\sqrt{n}} = \frac{-1.8 - 0}{4.15/\sqrt{5}} = \frac{-1.8}{4.15/2.24}$$

$$= \frac{-1.8}{1.85} = -.972$$

Step 4   Place the calculated value, $-.972$, on the curve. The value $-.972$ falls to the right of -3.747, in the noncritical region.

Step 5   Make a decision. Because the value is in the noncritical region, the decision is to fail to reject the null hypothesis.

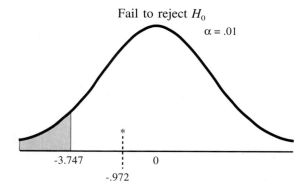

Fail to reject H_0

$\alpha = .01$

-3.747   -.972   0

Step 6   Interpret the results. There is not sufficient evidence, at the .01 level of significance, to suggest that retail sales declined significantly after the recession.

as the calculated value. Use Table A.4. Trace *down* to 18 degrees of freedom (19 − 1 = 18), *across* to the critical value 1.734, which is nearest the calculated value of 1.722, and *up* to the alpha level for that column. The alpha associated with 18 df and the critical value 1.734 is .05. The *P*-value for 1.722 is .05.

Confidence intervals for *t* dependent means estimate the population mean difference based on the sample mean difference. The formula is similar to the one-population *t* formula.

Confidence Interval for *t* Dependent Means

$$\overline{d} \pm t_{(df, \alpha/2)} \frac{s_d}{\sqrt{n}}$$

where df = $n - 1$.

The confidence interval for *t* dependent means is used infrequently in most of the social sciences, because rarely can a researcher predict the occurrence of a social or political event.

Two Variances: *F* Distribution

The previous sections of this chapter show how to test and estimate population means from independent populations that are normally distributed. The formulas in this section test and estimate variances of two independent populations that are normally distributed. Recall that chi-square tests and estimates a variance from one population, whereas the *F* distribution tests and estimates the equality of the variances from two populations. Many similarities exist between χ^2 and *F*. Both distributions represent variances, are skewed to the right, and contain only nonnegative values. The skewness reflects the nonnormal distribution of the variances, although the population means are normally distributed. Variances are dependent on sample size, resulting in several distribution curves based on degrees of freedom. See Figure 13.3.

0

FIGURE 13.3

> ***F* distribution** A distribution representing the equality of variances from two populations.
>
> **1.** *F* is nonsymmetric, skewed to the right.
> **2.** *F* is nonnegative, greater than or equal to 0.
> **3.** The two populations are normally distributed.
> **4.** The two populations are independent of each other.

As with the two-population *t* distribution, the *F* distribution can be approached in several ways. The *F* distribution can be very complicated, with the skewed distribution determining which variances represent the first population and which represent the second. Many researchers prefer to treat the distribution differently when the test is one-tailed as opposed to two-tailed. A uniform rule is applied in this text; it essentially allows all tests to concentrate on the right tail of the curve.

The six steps of the classical hypothesis test are the same for *F* as for the other test statistics: State the hypotheses, identify the test criteria, calculate the test statistic, place the calculated value on the curve, make a decision, and interpret the results. The hypotheses for *F* are stated slightly differently than they are for other test statistics. All other hypotheses contain the parameter(s), a mathematical symbol, and a value. *F* tests for the equality of the variances; therefore, a value representing a difference is not usually in question. Hypotheses for *F* contain the parameters σ_1^2 and σ_2^2 and a mathematical symbol. For example, an experiment may question whether the variance of rainfall in Wayne County is less than the variance in rainfall in Oakland County. That hypothesis statement must be the alternative hypothesis, because it includes the less than symbol. The null hypothesis uses the symbol for greater than or equal to. The parameters are the variances. The statements are written as

$$H_0: \quad \sigma_1^2 \geq \sigma_2^2 \qquad H_1: \quad \sigma_1^2 < \sigma_2^2$$

Remember that $\leq$, $=$, and $\geq$ are the only three mathematical symbols acceptable in the null hypothesis, whereas $>$, $\neq$, and $<$ are the three mathematical symbols acceptable in the alternative hypothesis.

The critical value for *F* requires the degrees of freedom for the sample with the larger variance, the degrees of freedom for the sample with the smaller variance, and alpha. Degrees of freedom are determined by $n - 1$. The notation for the *F* critical value always places the degrees of freedom for the sample with the larger variance first, with the degrees of freedom for the sample with the smaller variance second. Table A.6 gives critical values for the *F* distribution. Notice that Table A.6 is composed of several tables, each reflecting a different alpha and each identifying one number of degrees of freedom as the numerator and the second as the denominator. The uniform rule is that the numerator is always the sample with the larger variance, and the denominator is always the sample with the smaller variance. The separate tables for each alpha are required because all alphas and all degrees of freedom cannot be contained in a one-page table. The notation is

$$F_{(\mathrm{df}_n, \mathrm{df}_d, \alpha)}$$

The subscripts n and d represent the numerator and denominator. *It is important to remember that the numerator represents the sample containing the larger variance, and the denominator represents the sample containing the smaller variance.*

Degrees of Freedom for F

$$df_n: \quad n - 1$$
$$df_d: \quad n - 1$$

where

df_n is the degrees of freedom for the larger variance.
df_d is the degrees of freedom for the smaller variance.

If the test is two-tailed, then alpha must be divided by 2. Because the larger variance information serves as the guide for the numerator, the calculated value and the critical value will fall toward the right tail of the distribution. Alpha is divided by 2 and the critical value for the right tail is determined by the procedure described earlier. Only the right-tail critical value is determined with the degrees of freedom for the sample with the larger variance, the degrees of freedom for the sample with the smaller variance, and alpha divided by 2. The left tail is noted as a critical region but does not need to be identified with a critical value.

EXAMPLE 13.16

Experiment   Find the critical F value for the following information:

  a. Two-tailed: $\sigma_1^2 = 24$, $\sigma_2^2 = 33$, $n_1 = 10$, $n_2 = 21$, $\alpha = .05$
  b. One-tailed: $\sigma_1^2 = 14$, $\sigma_2^2 = 13$, $n_1 = 25$, $n_2 = 26$, $\alpha = .05$

Answer

  a. 3.6669
  b. 1.9643

Solution   a. A two-tailed F critical value requires identifying the degrees of freedom for the sample with the larger variance, the degrees of freedom for the sample with the smaller variance, and alpha divided by 2. The second variance, $\sigma^2 = 33$, is larger. The degrees of freedom for this sample are used as the df numerator and are equal to $n - 1 = 21 - 1$, or 20. The first variance, 24, is smaller than 33, and its degrees of freedom form the df denominator. The degrees of freedom for the denominator equal $10 - 1$, or 9. Alpha divided by 2 is .05/2, or .025. Begin by identifying the correct F table. The critical values for alpha .025 are reported in Table A.6b. Read *across* to the df numerator 20 (found on the second page of the table) and *down* to the df denominator 9. The value 3.6669 in the intersection is the critical value for the right tail. The left tail is shaded as a critical region but is not assigned a critical value.

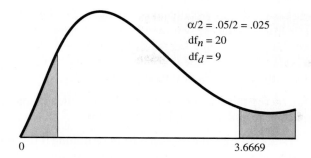

$\alpha/2 = .05/2 = .025$
$df_n = 20$
$df_d = 9$

0   3.6669

b. A one-tailed F critical value can be placed on the right tail if the degrees of freedom are adjusted to represent the numerator with the larger variance. The variance 14 is larger than 13. Therefore, the degrees of freedom for the numerator represent the sample size 25; that is, the degrees of freedom for the numerator are $25 - 1$, or 24. The degrees of freedom for the denominator are $26 - 1$, or 25. The test is one-tailed, which means alpha is not divided by 2. Alpha is .05. Use Table A.6c, which gives values for alpha $= .05$. Read *across* to 24 degrees of freedom for the numerator and *down* to 25 degrees of freedom for the denominator. The value 1.9643 is the critical value.

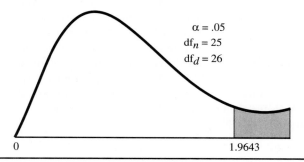

$\alpha = .05$
$df_n = 25$
$df_d = 26$

0   1.9643

The calculated F value is perhaps the simplest calculation of all the test statistics. It is the ratio of the two sample variances. The rule for F is to place the larger sample variance in the numerator and the smaller in the denominator; thus, the ratio is always greater than 1.0.

Calculation of the Test Statistic F

$$F = \frac{s_1^2}{s_2^2}$$

EXAMPLE 13.17

Experiment   The variability in potency for drugs is very important. A pharmacist wants to test whether the variability in a generic drug is different than the variability in the commercially named drug. A random sample of 21 tablets of the generic drug produces a variance of .02 mg, whereas a random sample of 31 tablets of the commercially named drug produces a variance of .04. Do the samples provide sufficient evidence to conclude that there is a significant variability between the two kinds of tablets? Use $\alpha = .05$.

Answer   No, there is no evidence that there is a significant amount of variability between the generic and commercially named drug.

Solution   To state the hypotheses, begin by determining if this is one population or two. Two sets of data are provided, with a test for the difference between the variances. The samples are independent, because both samples are randomly selected. The words no difference indicate the null hypothesis, because the $=$ symbol can be placed only in the null hypothesis. The alternative hypothesis is then $\neq$. The parameters are σ_1^2 and σ_2^2.

$$H_0: \quad \sigma_1^2 = \sigma_2^2 \qquad H_1: \quad \sigma_1^2 \neq \sigma_2^2$$

The test criteria begin with identifying alpha. Alpha is reported as .05. The test statistic is F, representing two population variances. The test is two-tailed, requiring the critical region to be placed in both tails and alpha to be divided by 2. However, by placing the sample with the larger variance in the numerator and its degrees of freedom first in the notation, only the right-tailed critical F value must be determined. The variance .04 is larger than .02. Therefore, the commercially named data are treated as the first variance and are placed in the numerator. The sample size for the commercially named drug is 31, with degrees of freedom $= 31 - 1 = 30$. The degrees of freedom for the denominator are $21 - 1$, or 20. Alpha must be divided by 2 for the two-tailed test: $.05/2 = .025$. Use Table A.6b for alpha $= .025$. Read *across* to 30 df and *down* to 20 df. The critical value is 2.3486.

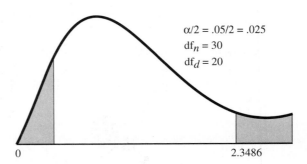

$$\alpha/2 = .05/2 = .025$$
$$df_n = 30$$
$$df_d = 20$$

$$F_{(30,20,.05/2)} = 2.3486$$

Calculate the test statistic. The F calculation involves the ratio of the sample variances, placing the larger variance in the numerator and the smaller variance in the denominator.

$$F = \frac{s_1^2}{s_2^2} = \frac{.04}{.02} = 2.00$$

Place the calculated value on the distribution curve: 2.00 falls to the left of the critical value, 2.3486. The decision is to fail to reject the null hypothesis.

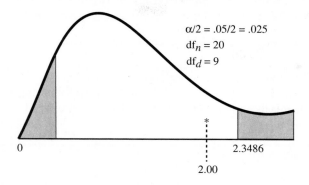

$\alpha/2 = .05/2 = .025$

$df_n = 20$

$df_d = 9$

2.3486

2.00

0

Failing to reject the null hypothesis is interpreted to mean that the sample does not provide sufficient evidence at the .05 level of significance to reject the null hypothesis that there is no difference in the variability of the generic drug and the commercially named drug.

The P-value approach for F is similar to χ^2 and t in that the P-value is the alpha associated with the critical value nearest the calculated value. Once the calculated value is obtained, refer to all three parts of Table A.6. All three parts must be consulted, because different alphas are not reported on the same table. Move *across* to the degrees of freedom associated with the numerator and *down* to the degrees of freedom associated with the denominator. Note the value in this position for each table, each representing a different alpha. Because there are three tables, there should be three critical values noted, each with its appropriate alpha. Choose the alpha with the critical value nearest to the calculated value. The alpha becomes the P-value for a one-tailed test. For a two-tailed test, the alpha is multiplied by 2 before noting it as the P-value. If the calculated value falls to either side of the alpha, then note the direction of the P-value as being in the same direction. If the value falls between two alpha levels, then note the P-value as being between both alphas. That is, if a calculated value is 1.4567, then one critical value is 1.9876 at an alpha of .025, and another critical value is 1.2432 at an alpha of .05. The P-value is between .025 and .05 (greater than .025 but less than .05).

EXAMPLE 13.18

Experiment   Find the P-value for a calculated value of 3.1031 with 24 df in the numerator and 9 df in the denominator.

Answer $F_{(3.1031 \text{ at } 24 \ df_n \text{ and } 9 \ df_d)} = (.025 < P < .05)$

Solution   Using Table A.6a, A.6b, and A.6c, find the critical value for each alpha with numerator 24 df and denominator 9 df. For alpha = .01 (Table A.6a), the critical value found by tracing *across* to 24 degrees of freedom for the numerator and *down* to 9 degrees of freedom for the denominator is 4.7290. For alpha df is 3.6142. At alpha = .05 (Table A.6c), the critical value is 2.9005 for numerator 24 df and denominator 9 df. Compare the calculated value 3.1031 to the three critical values. The value 3.1031 falls between 3.6142 for alpha = .025 and 2.9005 for alpha = .05. Therefore, the P-value is greater than .025 but less than .05.

The other steps for the P-value approach remain the same. The hypotheses are stated, the test criteria are identified, the test statistic is calculated, the P-value is calculated, the decision is made, and the decision is interpreted.

EXAMPLE 13.19

Experiment   Using the P-value approach, test the claim that the variance in the time it takes the local police force to arrive at the scene of a traffic accident is greater than the variance in the time it takes the local fire department. A random sample of 10 calls to the police department produced a variance of 2.5 min, whereas a random sample of 10 calls to the fire department produced a variance of 1.54 min; $\alpha = .01$.

Answer   There is not sufficient evidence to suggest that the variance in time it takes the local police force to arrive at the scene of a traffic accident is greater than the variance in the time it takes the local fire department.

Solution   To state the hypotheses, begin by determining if this is one population or two. Two sets of data are provided with a test for the difference between the variances. The samples are independent, because both samples are randomly selected. The words greater than indicate the alternative hypothesis, because the symbol $>$ can be placed only in the alternative hypothesis. The null hypothesis is then $\leq$. The parameters are σ_1^2 and σ_2^2. The hypotheses are

$$H_0: \quad \sigma_1^2 \leq \sigma_2^2 \qquad H_1: \quad \sigma_1^2 > \sigma_2^2$$

The test criteria begin with identifying alpha. Alpha is reported as .05. The test statistic is F, representing two population variances. The test is one-tailed, as determined by the $>$ symbol in the alternative hypothesis.

Calculate the test statistic. The F calculation involves the ratio of the sample variances, placing the larger variance as the numerator and the smaller as the denominator.

$$F = \frac{s_1^2}{s_2^2} = \frac{2.50}{1.54} = 1.6234$$

Transform the calculated value into a P-value by noting all the alphas for the critical values with the same degrees of freedom from Table A.6a, A.6b, and A.6c. The degrees of freedom associated with the numerator, the police department, are $10 - 1$, or 9. The degrees of freedom for the denominator, the fire department, are also $10 - 1$, or 9. Begin with Table A.6a for alpha .01. The critical value at alpha = .01 and degrees of freedom 9 and 9 is 5.3511. For alpha = .025 (Table A.6b) with df 9 and 9, the critical value is 4.0260. For alpha = .05 (Table A.6c) with df 9 and 9, the critical value is 3.1789. The calculated value

A LEARNING AID

F Distribution

A potato chip company is purchasing a new dispensing machine. Two machines dispense, on the average, the same number of ounces. The variance of a random sample of 20 bags for the brand X machine is 1.22 oz and the variance of a random sample of 13 bags for the brand Y machine is 1.96 oz. Do the samples provide sufficient evidence that there is significant difference in the variability of the machines? Let $\alpha = .1$.

Step 1   State the hypotheses. Begin by determining if there is one population or two. Two machines are providing two sets of data. The samples are independent, because both are randomly selected. Variances are being tested. The parameters are σ^2 and σ^2. The mathematical symbol referred to by the experiment as a difference is $\neq$. The $\neq$ must be placed in the alternative hypothesis. The null hypothesis then uses $=$.

$$H_0: \quad \sigma_1^2 = \sigma_2^2 \qquad H_1: \quad \sigma_1^2 \neq \sigma_2^2$$

Step 2   Identify the test criteria. Alpha is reported as .1. The test statistic for two variances is F. The test is two-tailed, as determined by the $=$ in the alternative hypothesis. By placing the sample with the larger variance as the numerator and its degrees of freedom first in the notation, only the right-tailed critical F value must be determined. The variance 1.96 is larger than 1.22. Therefore, brand Y is treated as the first variance and is placed in the numerator. The degrees of freedom for brand Y are $n - 1 = 13 - 1$, or 12. The degrees of freedom for the denominator, brand X, are $n - 1 = 20 - 1$, or 19. Alpha must be divided by 2 for the two-tailed test: .1 divided by 2 is .05. Use Table A.6c for alpha = .05. Move *across* to 12 degrees of freedom for the numerator and *down* to 19 degrees of freedom for the denominator. The critical value is 2.3080.

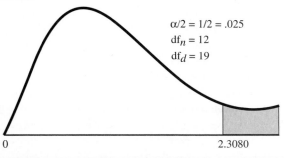

Step 3   Calculate the test statistic. The F calculation is the ratio of the sample variances, placing the larger variance in the numerator and the smaller variance in the denominator.

$$F = \frac{s_1^2}{s_2^2} = \frac{1.96}{1.22} = 1.6066$$

Step 4   Place the calculated value on the distribution curve. Place the value 1.6066 to the left of 2.3080.

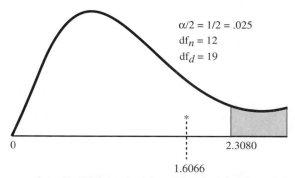

Step 5   Make a decision. The decision is to fail to reject the null hypothesis, because the calculated value does not fall in the critical region.

Fail to reject H_0

Step 6   Interpret the results. Failing to reject the null hypothesis is interpreted with the original information provided in the experiment. There is not sufficient evidence at the .1 level of significance to conclude the variances of the machines differ.

1.6234 is nearest, but greatly below, 3.1789 for alpha = .05. Because an alpha greater than .05 is not reported in the table, the P-value should be reported as being greater than .05.

$$F_{(1.6234 \text{ at } 9 \text{ df}_n \text{ and } 9 \text{ df}_d)} = .05 < P$$

Compare the P-value to the original alpha. If P is less than or equal to alpha, then reject the null hypothesis. If P is greater than alpha, then fail to reject the null hypothesis. Because P is greater than alpha = 1.01, the decision is to fail to reject the null hypothesis.

$$P\text{-value}_{(.05<P)} > \alpha_{(.01)} \qquad \text{Fail to reject } H_0$$

The interpretation is that there is not sufficient evidence to suggest the variance in time it takes the local police force to arrive at the scene of a traffic accident is greater than the variance in the time it takes the local fire department.

The confidence interval for estimating the equality of variances is rarely used in statistics. Because of the difficulty of the skewed distribution for two population variances, the F confidence interval is difficult to calculate without the left-tail critical values. Although the discussion here is limited, the formula involves the algebraic manipulation of the test statistic.

> **Confidence Interval for Estimating the Equality of Two Variances Using F**
>
> $$\frac{s_1^2}{s_2^2} \frac{1}{F_{(\text{df}_n,\text{df}_d,1-\alpha/2)}} < \frac{\sigma_1^2}{\sigma_2^2} < \frac{s_1^2}{s_2^2} \frac{1}{F_{(\text{df}_n,\text{df}_d,\alpha/2)}}$$
>
> where
>
> s_1^2 is the larger variance and s_2^2 is the smaller variance.
> $$F_{(\text{df}_n,\text{df}_d,1-\alpha/2)} = 1/F(\text{df}_d, \text{df}_n, \alpha/2)$$

CHAPTER 13 IN REVIEW

13.1 Find the following critical values for two-tailed z tests.

    a. $\alpha = .025$ **c.** $\alpha = .10$

    b. $\alpha = .05$ **d.** $\alpha = .01$

13.2 In the appropriate format, state the null and alternative hypotheses:

    a. Test the claim that two ambulance services have the same mean response time.

    b. The mean of brand Y is lower than brand X.

    c. The variance of fatalities in time period 1 is equal to the variance of fatalities in time period 2.

    d. The mean time of two flights to St. Louis is equal.

13.3 Find the critical values for the following one-tailed F tests.

    a. $n_n = 10$, $n_d = 10$, $\alpha = .05$

    b. $n_n = 10$, $n_d = 7$, $\alpha = .05$

    c. $n_n = 10$, $n_d = 25$, $\alpha = .02$

    d. $n_n = 25$, $n_d = 10$, $\alpha = .02$

    e. $n_n = 7$, $n_d = 10$, $\alpha = .01$

    f. $n_n = 5$, $n_d = 5$, $\alpha = .05$

13.4 Find the critical values for the following two-tailed t tests.

    a. $n_1 = 20$, $n_2 = 15$, $\alpha = .05$

b. $n_1 = 10, n_2 = 12, \alpha = .10$

c. $n_1 = 5, n_2 = 8, \alpha = .01$

d. $n_1 = 8, n_2 = 8, \alpha = .01$

13.5 When 10 randomly selected adult males are given a test on reaction times, their scores produce a variance of 2.04. When 21 other randomly selected adult males are given a training session before taking the same test, their scores produce a variance of 3.44. At the .05 significance level, test the claim that the population of nontrained males will have a variance larger than the population of the trained males.

13.6 An experiment is devised to study the variability of grading procedures among college professors. Two different professors are asked to grade the same set of 25 exams, and their grades have variances of 24.4 and 39.7, respectively. At the .05 significance level, test the claim that the first professor's grading exhibits greater variance.

13.7 As part of the National Health Care Survey, data are collected on the weights of men. For 100 men aged 25 to 34, the mean is 176 lb and the standard deviation is 35 lb. For 150 men aged 65 to 74, the mean is 164 with a standard deviation of 27.0. Test the claim that the mean weight difference is no greater than 8.4 lb. Use $\alpha = .05$.

13.8 The telephone company collects sample data on the lengths, in minutes, of telephone calls made to foreign countries. A random sample of 40 calls to Greece produces a mean of 12.65 min. A random sample of 40 calls to Italy produces a mean of 11.24 min. The standard deviation of all calls to these countries is 7.23 and 8.99, respectively. At the .02 level of significance, test the claim that there is no difference between the mean times of all long-distance calls made to the two countries.

13.9 Find the 90% confidence interval for the mean difference of the pulse rate between aerobic dancers and tennis players. A random sample of 50 aerobic dancers produces a mean pulse rate of 63, with a population standard deviation of 3.25. A random sample of 50 tennis players produces a mean pulse rate of 69, with a population standard deviation of 2.33.

13.10 Suppose a random sample of 10 people was conducted on the day the U.S. invasion of Kuwait occurred to measure the public's support of the invasion. Respondents rated their support from a low of 1 to a high of 10. After President Bush addressed the United States on national television, the respondents were asked again to rate their support. At the .10 level of significance, can we say that there was no major change in opinion due to Bush's speech? The responses were as follows:

Poll 1	Poll 2
5	5
3	7
7	8
9	9
7	8
6	8
10	10
2	4
4	3
7	9

13.11 Workers in a region where a caste system is thought to exist among workers were surveyed to determine job satisfaction. Group A believes the caste system does exist. Group B believes the caste system does not exist. Test at the .1 level that the mean of Group A equals the mean of Group B. Assume the samples are independent.

$$n_a = 175 \qquad n_b = 277$$
$$\bar{x}_a = 5.42 \qquad \bar{x}_b = 5.19$$
$$\sigma_a = 1.24 \qquad \sigma_b = 1.17$$

13.12 True or false?

a. The test statistic for two population variances is χ^2.

b. If the outcomes of one sample affect the outcomes of another sample, then the samples are independent.

c. If a z P-value is .004 and alpha is .005, then the decision is to fail to reject the null hypothesis.

d. Confidence intervals are always two-tailed.

13.13 True or false?

a. The F distribution test is usually concerned with the right tail of the distribution curve.

b. Critical values for t may be negative.

c. Critical values for F may be negative.

d. Critical values for z may be negative.

13.14 An achievement test given to 6- and 7-y-old girls produced the following results. At the .05 level, perform a P-value test on the equality of the means.

	Sample Size	Mean	Standard Deviation
6-y-olds	12	37.5	10.02
7-y-olds	16	44	13.2

13.15 Using the information in Problem 13.14, test the equality of the variances at the .05 level.

14

Additional Inferential Statistics

The previous chapters on inferential statistics discussed testing and estimating parameters for one or two populations that are normally distributed, typically interval- or ratio-level data. This chapter discusses testing and estimating parameters for nominal-level data and for means from three or more populations. Essentially, this chapter combines procedures presented in several previous chapters that focused on graphs with hypothesis testing presented in later chapters. Multinomial experiments extend binomial experiments and test the expected outcomes with observed outcomes. Contingency tables, which have been presented several times, are also tested for a difference between the expected outcomes and observed outcomes. Finally, analysis of variance (ANOVA) tests differences among three or more means.

SECTION 1

Multinomial Experiments

Chapter 7 introduced the binomial probability distribution, in which a discrete random variable has only two possible outcomes, known as success and failure. The probability of success and failure remained constant throughout the experiment. Multinomial experiments are exactly like binomial experiments, except that multinomial experiments may have three or more outcomes. Remember the binomial experiment referred to in Chapter 7 in which people are asked to identify their religion. If a researcher is concerned with the respondents who are Catholic, a binomial experiment collapses all religions other than Catholic into a category labeled failure, with success reserved for those reporting Catholic. A multinomial experiment does not collapse the categories into two. If five religions are reported, then five categories are created. As with binomial experiments multinomial experiments have a fixed number of trials, the trials must be independent, an outcome can qualify for only one category, and the probabilities remain constant across all trials.

Conditions for a Multinomial Experiment

1. There is a fixed number of trials, n.
2. The trials are independent.
3. There are more than two possible outcomes.
4. The probability for each outcome remains constant on all trials.
5. The probability of all outcomes must have a sum of 1.0.

A multinomial experiment allows a researcher to test the difference between the observed outcomes of an experiment and the theoretical outcomes. Remember that any observed outcome does not necessarily match a theoretical outcome. The question then is to determine if the differences between the proportions in the observed outcomes and the expected theoretical outcomes are statistically significant. The test statistic for multinomials is chi-square. Chi-square tests the variance in the difference between the observed frequencies and the expected frequencies. Recall from Chapter 13 that the chi-square distribution is a nonnegative right-skewed distribution (Figure 14.1). Its critical values are reported in Table A.5.

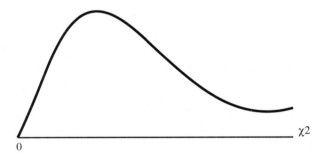

χ^2

0

FIGURE 14.1

A special rule must be emphasized: Because the calculated chi-square value will be very small if no difference is measured, any significant difference will have a large chi-square value. Therefore, *all multinomial experiments are tested as right-tailed χ^2 tests.*

The first step in hypothesis testing for multinomials is to state the hypotheses. The hypotheses for multinomials can be written with symbols or with verbal descriptions. The null hypothesis is often written with symbols stating the probability of each outcome and its value. The probability, p, for each outcome must remain constant, but each outcome is not necessarily equal to the other outcomes. The alternative hypothesis is almost always stated verbally, challenging that at least one of the probabilities in the null hypothesis is not equal to the value claimed. For example, if the null hypothesis claims that, of a random sample of students' religions, the probability of answering Protestant is .60, Catholic, .35, Jewish, .03, and other, .02, then the alternative hypothesis challenges that at least one of these proportions is not equal to the value claimed.

H_0: $p_1 = .60, p_2 = .35, p_3 = .03$, and $p_4 = .02$

H_1: At least one of the proportions is not equal to the value claimed

The test criteria include the identification of the level of significance, test statistic, critical region, and critical value. The level of significance is usually reported in the experiment or must be determined by considering the probability of a type I error. The test statistic for multinomials is chi-square. *The critical region is always one-tailed to the right. Never divide alpha by 2 when testing a multinomial experiment.* The critical value is determined by the degrees of freedom and alpha. The degrees of freedom for the multinomial chi-square test is $k - 1$, where k is the number of possible outcomes (not the number of trials). For example, if 100 people surveyed indicated five different religions, k is 5, not 100.

Degrees of Freedom for a Multinomial

$$k - 1$$

where k equals the number of possible outcomes or categories.

The third step in hypothesis testing is to calculate the test statistic. The test statistic is chi-square; however, its calculation is different than the chi-square calculation in Chapter 12. A multinomial tests the difference between the observed proportions for each outcome and the expected proportions for each outcome based on a theoretical distribution. Therefore, the expected outcomes are subtracted from the observed outcomes, squared, divided by the expected probability, and summed.

Formula for Chi-Square Multinomial Calculated Value

$$\chi^2 = \sum \frac{(O - E)^2}{E}$$

where

O is the observed frequency of an outcome.

E is the expected frequency, equal to np.

Σ is the summation, which occurs at the end of the calculations.

Note the summation sign in the test statistic calculation. The summation occurs at the end of the calculations. The expected frequency for each outcome is subtracted from its observed frequency, squared, and divided by the expected frequency. This process is performed for each category. When the formula is applied to each category, the values are then summed. Arrange the data with columns for O, E, $(O - E)$, $(O - E)^2$, and $(O - E)^2/E$. Sum the last column for the χ^2 calculated value. If E is given as a proportion, E must be calculated for each category by multiplying the total number of responses in the survey by the probability of the category.

Expected Frequency for a Multinomial

$$E = np$$

where

E is the expected frequency for a category.

n is the total number of responses in the survey.

p is the probability for that category.

The fourth step in hypothesis testing is placing the calculated value on the distribution curve. The calculated value is placed on the curve relative to the critical value.

The fifth step is to make a decision. If the calculated value falls in the critical region, then the decision is to reject the null hypothesis. If the calculated value does not fall in the critical region, then the decision is to fail to reject the null hypothesis.

The final step in hypothesis testing is to interpret the results. In multinomial testing rejecting the null hypothesis implies that at least one of the proportions in the null hypothesis is different than the value claimed—that is, a significant difference is found between the observed frequencies and the expected frequencies.

EXAMPLE 14.1

Experiment   The registrar claims that 60% of the students in the university are Protestant, 35% are Catholic, 3% are Jewish, and 2% are other religions. To test this claim, two hundred students are surveyed, producing the following results: 106 Protestants, 80 Catholics, 10 Jewish, and 4 other. Test the registrar's claim at the .01 level of significance.

Answer   Fail to reject the null hypothesis. There is not sufficient proof at the .01 level of significance to reject the null hypothesis that the proportions of religion among the students is different than that claimed by the registrar.

Solution   This is a multinomial experiment, because four categories are represented in 200 independent trials, where the probabilities of the outcomes have a sum of 1.0. (the percentages are probabilities. As percentages they must have a sum of 100%.) Begin by stating the hypotheses. The null hypothesis for a multinomial states that the proportions are equal to the claimed values. The percentages are written as probabilities by dropping the percent sign and moving the decimal point two places to the left.

H_0: $p_1 = .60$, $p_2 = .35$, $p_3 = .03$, and $p_4 = .02$

H_1:   At least one of the proportions is not equal to the value claimed

The level of significance is .01. The test statistic is chi-square. The critical region for multinomial testing is always one-tailed to the right. The critical value is determined by the degrees of freedom $k - 1$ and alpha. The k is equal to the number of categories. There are four categories of religion reported in the hypotheses; therefore, $k - 1$ is $4 - 1$, or 3. Read *down* Table A.5 to 3 degrees of freedom and *across* to alpha $= .01$. The critical value is 11.345.

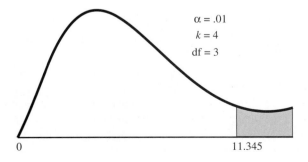

$\alpha = .01$
$k = 4$
$df = 3$

0   11.345

Calculate the test statistic. Chi-square is calculated differently for a multinomial than it is when testing a single variance. Arrange the data in columns for O, E, $(O - E)$, $(O - E)^2$, and $(O - E)^2/E$. The sample data are the observed data, O. E is determined by multiplying n and p for each category, where n is 200. As a check on the mathematics, the sum of O must equal n, the sum of E must also equal n, and the sum of $(O - E)$ must equal O. The summation of the $(O - E)^2/E$ column is the calculated χ^2 value.

Category	O	$(np) = E$	$(O - E)$	$(O - E)^2$	$(O - E)^2/E$
Protestant	106	$[200(.60)] = 120$	-14	$14^2 = 196$	$196/120 = 1.633$
Catholic	80	$[200(.35)] = 70$	10	$10^2 = 100$	$100/70 = 1.429$
Jewish	10	$[200(.03)] = 6$	4	$4^2 = 16$	$16/6 = 2.667$
Other	4	$[200(.02)] = 4$	0	$0^2 = 0$	$0/4 = 0.000$
	200	200	0		5.729

The calculated value is 5.729. This value must be placed on the distribution curve relative to the critical value.

A LEARNING AID

Multinomial Experiment

A local department store claims that 28% of their sales is in women's clothes, 24% is in cosmetics, 18% is in jewelry, 15% is in men's clothes, and 15% is in other departments. A random sample of 400 sales produces the following results: 138 sales in women's clothes, 107 sales in cosmetics, 65 sales in jewelry, 51 sales in men's clothes, and 39 sales in other departments. Test the department's claim at alpha = .05.

Step 1 This is a multinomial experiment, because five categories are represented in 400 independent (random) trials, where the probabilities of the outcomes have a sum of 1.0. (The percentages are probabilities. As percentages, they must have a sum of 100%).

State the hypotheses. The null hypothesis for a multinomial experiment reports that the proportions are equal to the claimed values. The percentages are written as probabilities by dropping the percent sign and moving the decimal left two places. State each category with the probability claimed by the store.

H_0: $p_1 = .28$, $p_2 = .24$, $p_3 = .18$, $p_4 = .15$, and $p_5 = .15$

H_1: At least one of the proportions is not equal to the value claimed

Step 2 Identify the test criteria. The level of significance is .05. The test statistic for a multinomial is chi-square. The critical region for multinomial testing is always one-tailed to the right. The critical value is determined by the degrees of freedom $k - 1$ and alpha. k is equal to the number of categories. There are five departments reported in the hypotheses; therefore, $k - 1$ is $5 - 1$, or 4. Read *down* Table A.5 in the appendix to 4 degrees of freedom and *across* to alpha = .05. The critical value is 9.488.

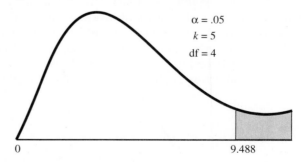

$\alpha = .05$
$k = 5$
$df = 4$

Step 3 Calculate the test statistic. Chi-square is calculated for the difference between the observed frequencies and the expected frequencies. Arrange the data in columns for O, E, $(O - E)$, $(O - E)^2$, and $(O - E)^2/E$. The sample data are the observed data, O.

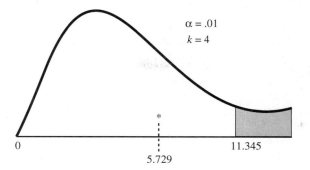

Because the calculated value, 5.729, does not fall in the critical region, the decision is to fail to reject the null hypothesis. The interpretation of the decision in the experiment is that there is not sufficient proof at the .01 level of significance to reject the null hypothesis that the proportions of religion among the students is different than that claimed by the registrar.

E is determined by multiplying n and p for each category, where n is 400. As a check on the mathematics, the sum of O must equal n, the sum of E must also equal n, and the sum of $(O - E)$ must equal 0. The summation of the $(O - E)^2/E$ column is the calculated χ^2 value.

Category	O	$np = E$	$(O - E)$
Women's	138	$[400(.28)] = 112$	26
Cosmetics	107	$[400(.24)] = 96$	11
Jewelry	65	$[400(.18)] = 72$	−7
Men's	51	$[400(.15)] = 60$	−9
Other	39	$[400(.15)] = 60$	−21
	400	400	0

Category	$(O - E)^2$	$(O - E)^2/E$
Women's	$26^2 = 676$	$676/112 = 6.036$
Cosmetics	$11^2 = 121$	$121/96 = 1.260$
Jewelry	$-7^2 = 49$	$49/72 = 0.681$
Men's	$-9^2 = 81$	$81/60 = 1.350$
Other	$-21^2 = 441$	$441/60 = 7.350$
		16.677

Step 4   Place the calculated value on the distribution curve. The calculated value is the sum of the last column, 16.677. This value must be placed on the distribution curve relative to the critical value.

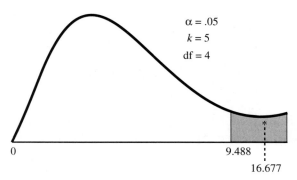

Step 5   Make a decision. Because the calculated value, 16.677, falls in the critical region, the decision is to reject the null hypothesis.

Reject the null hypothesis

Step 6   Interpret the results. The interpretation of the decision with regard to the experiment is that there is sufficient evidence at the .05 level of significance to reject the null hypothesis that at least one of the proportions in sales in the department store is different than that claimed by the store.

Testing Contingency Tables

Chapter 4 describes the contingency table as a two-way display of two nominal-level variables. Chapter 7 also describes the transformation of a contingency table into a theoretical probability distribution. Both of these processes are combined in this chapter to determine if the variables are independent or dependent. The table, also referred to as a crosstab, represents the relationships of two variables and their events. The relationship of the variables in a contingency table is determined by comparing a sample's observed frequencies with the expected frequencies based on a theoretical distribution.

The variables in a contingency table are assumed independent until a challenge proves the variables are dependent. Independence is implied when there is no difference between the observed frequencies and the expected frequencies. If a difference exists, then the variables are said to be dependent. The chi-square test statistic measures the degree of variance in the observed and expected frequencies. As with the multinomial experiment, *all tests for contingency tables are one-tailed to the right.*

The first step in hypothesis testing for contingency tables is to state the hypotheses. The null hypothesis is completely narrative, stating that the two variables are independent. The alternative hypothesis, also narratively stated, claims that the two variables are dependent.

The test criteria are the same as with the multinomial experiment. The level of significance is reported in the experiment or determined by considering the seriousness of a type I error. The test statistic for a contingency table is chi-square. *The critical region is always one-tailed to the right,* and the critical value is determined by the degrees of freedom and alpha, as reported in Table A.5. The degrees of freedom for a contingency table differ from other test statistics. The degrees of freedom equal the number of rows minus one multiplied by the number of columns minus one. The table is reviewed to determine the number of rows and columns.

> **Degrees of Freedom for a Contingency Table**
>
> $$df = (r - 1)(c - 1)$$
>
> where
>
> r equals the number of rows in the table.
> c equals the number of columns in the table.

The degrees of freedom for a table where five values for a variable are presented in the rows and three values for a second variable are presented in the columns are $(5 - 1)(3 - 1)$, or 8.

The third step in hypothesis testing is to calculate the test statistic. The chi-square calculation for a contingency table is identical to the calculation for the multinomial experiment. However, the calculation of the expected values differs. In a multinomial experiment, $E = np$, but the contingency table requires the expected values to be calculated by multiplying the row total by the column total and then dividing by the total number of responses in the sample. This calculation must occur for each cell in the contingency table.

Expected Frequency for Each Cell in a Contingency Table

$$E = \frac{(\text{row total})(\text{column total})}{\text{total sample size}} = \frac{(R)(C)}{N}$$

where

R equals the row total for a cell.

C equals the column total for a cell.

N equals the total sample size.

The expected frequency for a cell whose row total is 200, column total is 300, and with a total sample size of 600 is 100 {$(E = [200(300)]/600 = 100$}. The expected frequency for each cell must be calculated. Either the expected frequency is placed in parentheses inside each cell of the table or the data are arranged in columns comparing the observed frequencies to the expected frequencies. If a table has eight cells, the data are given with eight columns, one representing each of the cells.

Chi-square is then calculated in the same way as for a multinomial experiment. The data are arranged in the following columns: O, E, $(O - E)$, $(O - E)^2$, and $(O - E)^2/E$.

Chi-Square Formula for a Contingency Table

$$\chi^2 = \sum \frac{(O - E)^2}{E}$$

where

O is the observed frequency of an outcome.

E is the expected frequency $[(R)(C)]/N$.

Σ is the summation, which occurs at the end of the calculation.

Note that the summation in the calculation occurs at the end. Each expected frequency is subtracted from its observed frequency, squared, and divided by the expected frequency. This process is performed for each category.

The fourth step in hypothesis testing is to place the calculated value on the distribution curve relative to the critical value.

The fifth step is to make a decision. If the calculated value falls in the critical region, then the decision is to reject the null hypothesis. If the calculated value does not fall in the critical region, then the decision is to fail to reject the null hypothesis.

The final step is to interpret the results. Rejecting a null hypothesis for a contingency table implies that the two variables are dependent—that a significant difference is found between the observed values and the expected values. Failing to reject the null hypothesis implies that the variables are independent; that is, no difference is found between the observed and expected values.

EXAMPLE 14.2

Experiment   For a sample of 810 voters, determine if gender and party identification are independent at alpha $= .05$.

Answer Reject the null hypothesis. The variables gender and party identification appear to be dependent, with a significant difference between the observed and expected values. It appears that women tend to be Democrats and males tend to be Republicans.

Gender	Party Identification			Total
	Democrat	Independent	Republican	
Female	205	102	93	400
Male	112	114	184	410
Total	317	216	277	810

Solution The contingency table shows the intersection of two variables, sex and party identification. The table also represents observed frequencies as obtained for a sample of 810 voters. Begin by stating the hypotheses. The null hypothesis states that the variables are independent—that there is no difference between the observed and expected frequencies. The alternative hypothesis states that there is a difference between the observed and expected frequencies.

H_0: Gender and party identification are independent

H_1: Gender and party identification are dependent

The test criteria include alpha, the test statistic, critical region, and critical value. Alpha is reported as .05. The test statistic for contingency tables is chi-square. The critical region is always to the right for chi-square testing of contingency tables and multinomial cases. The critical value is determined by the degrees of freedom and alpha. The degrees of freedom for a contingency table are $(r - 1)(c - 1)$, where r is the number of rows and c is the number of columns. The variable sex is reported with two rows and the variable party identification is reported with three columns. The degrees of freedom are $(2 - 1)(3 - 1) = 2$. Use Table A.5. Trace *down* to 2 degrees of freedom and *across* to alpha = .05. The critical value is 5.991. Place the critical value on the distribution curve.

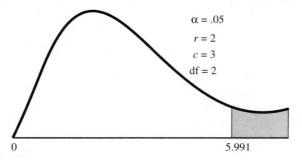

$\alpha = .05$
$r = 2$
$c = 3$
df $= 2$

0   5.991

Calculate the expected frequencies for each cell by multiplying the row total by the column total and then dividing by the sample size. For example, for the upper left cell, a female Democrat, the expected frequency is [400(317)]/810, or 156.54. For female Independents, the expected value is [400(216)]/810, or 106.67. The expected value for female Republicans is [400(277)]/810, or 136.79. Complete this process for the males, replacing the row totals with 410.

Gender	Party Identification			Total
	Democrat	Independent	Republican	
Female	205 (156.54)	102 (106.67)	93 (136.79)	400
Male	112 (160.46)	114 (109.33)	184 (140.21)	410
Total	317	216	277	810

Calculate the χ^2 statistic. Arrange the data in columns for O, E, $(O - E)$, $(O - E)^2$, and $(O - E)^2/E$. Each cell must be labeled. There are six cells in the contingency table. Remember that the columns for O and E must each sum to the sample size, 810. Also, the column $(O - E)$ must sum to zero. The sum of the last column is the calculated χ^2 value.

Cell	O	E	$(O - E)$	$(O - E)^2$	$(O - E)^2/E$
Female Democrat	205	156.54	48.46	2348.37	15.002
Female Independent	102	106.67	− 4.67	21.81	0.204
Female Republican	93	136.79	−43.79	1917.56	14.018
Male Democrat	112	160.46	−48.46	2348.37	14.635
Male Independent	114	109.33	4.67	21.81	0.199
Male Republican	184	140.21	43.79	1917.56	13.676
	810	810.00	00.00		57.734

Place the calculated value, 57.734, on the distribution curve. The value 57.734 falls to the right of the critical value in the critical region.

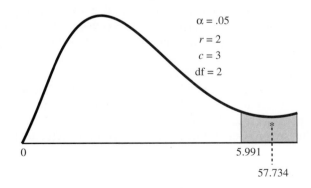

$\alpha = .05$
$r = 2$
$c = 3$
$df = 2$

5.991

57.734

The decision must be to reject the null hypothesis that the variables are independent. Based on this sample, the interpretation is that there is sufficient evidence at the .05 level of significance that gender and party identification are dependent.

Reject the null hypothesis

In most computerized statistical programs, contingency tables are known as crosstabulations, or crosstabs. Chi-square statistics are usually available for a cross-tabulation. Because chi-square is always one-tailed to the right for a contingency table, if a reported calculated chi-square value exceeds the critical value, then the decision is to reject the null hypothesis.

EXAMPLE 14.3

Experiment The following crosstab is given with the corresponding statistics. Are the variables independent?

Crosstab: Gender and Age of Students

Gender	Under 25	Age 25–34	35–44	Over 44	Total
Female	2,900	3,254	1,120	438	7,712
Male	2,460	3,196	1,088	544	7,288
Total	5,360	6,450	2,208	982	15,000

Chi-square = 36.6

Critical value = 7.8

Degrees of freedom = 3

Significance level = .05

Answer No, the variables are not independent.

Solution A contingency table (crosstab) can be tested to determine if two variables are independent by comparing the observed and expected frequencies. The null hypothesis for a contingency table always is that the variables are independent. The alternative hypothesis is that they are dependent. The contingency table is reported with the calculated value. Compare the calculated value to the critical value. At the .05 level of significance and at 3 degrees of freedom, the calculated value, 36.6, exceeds the critical value, 7.8. The decision is to reject the null hypothesis that the variables are independent. There is sufficient evidence at the .05 level of significance that age and the gender of students are dependent.

EXAMPLE 14.4

Experiment The following is a contingency table representing the amount of political information Southerners receive from church and their level of support for liberal political causes. Are the variables independent at the .01 level of significance?

		Church Information		
		Low	High	Total
Support for	High	70	30	100
Liberalism	Low	30	70	100
	Total	100	100	200

Answer   No, reject the null hypothesis that the variables are independent.

Solution   The contingency table represents the overlapping of two variables, information and liberalism. Begin by stating the hypotheses. The null hypothesis states that the variables are independent—that there is no difference between the observed and expected frequencies. The alternative hypothesis states that there is a difference between the observed and expected frequencies.

H_0:   Information and liberalism are independent

H_1:   Information and liberalism are dependent

The test criteria include alpha, the test statistic, critical region, and critical value. Alpha is reported as .01. The test statistic for contingency tables is chi-square. The critical region is always to the right for chi-square testing of contingency tables and multinomial cases. The critical value is determined by the degrees of freedom and alpha. The degrees of freedom for a contingency table are $(r - 1)(c - 1)$, where r is the number of rows and c is the number of columns. The variable liberalism is reported with two rows and the variable information is reported with two columns. The degrees of freedom are $(2 - 1)(2 - 1) = 1$. Use Table A.5. Move *down* to 1 degree of freedom and *across* to alpha = .01. The critical value is 6.635. Place the critical value on the distribution curve.

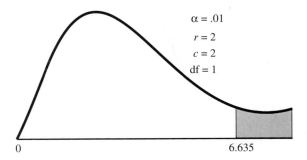

$\alpha = .01$
$r = 2$
$c = 2$
$df = 1$

0   6.635

Calculate the expected frequencies for each cell by multiplying the row total by the column total and then dividing by the sample size. For example, for the upper left cell, a person with low information and high support for liberalism, the expected frequency is [100(100)]/200, or 50. Place the expected frequency in parentheses below each observed value. Complete this process for the other three cells.

		Low	High	Total
		Church Information		
		Low	High	Total
Support for	High	70 (50)	30 (50)	100
Liberalism	Low	30 (50)	70 (50)	100
	Total	100	100	200

Calculate the χ^2 statistic. Arrange the data in columns headed O, E, $(O - E)$, $(O - E)^2$, and $(O - E)^2/E$. Each cell must be labeled. There are six cells in the contingency table. Remember that the columns for O and E must each have

A LEARNING AID

Testing Contingency Tables

For a sample of 400 registered voters, determine if voters' preference for an increase in sales tax is independent of their preference for an income tax to pay for a new education program (alpha = .05).

		Sales Tax		Total
		Yes	No	Total
Income Tax	Yes	108	92	200
	No	66	134	200
	Total	174	226	400

Step 1   Identify the table as a contingency table. Two nominal variables are overlapped with the joint observed frequencies reported in the cells. Begin by stating the hypotheses. The null hypothesis states that the variables are independent. The alternative hypothesis states that the variables are dependent. No symbols or values are used in the statements for contingency tables.

H_0: Preferences for sales taxes or income taxes are independent

H_1: Preferences for sales taxes or income taxes are dependent

Step 2   Identify the test criteria. Alpha is reported as .05. The test statistic for a contingency table is chi-square. The critical region for a contingency table always is one-tailed to the right. The degrees of freedom are equal to $(r - 1)(c - 1)$, where r is the number of rows and c is the number of columns. Since the table is two by two, df = $(2 - 1)(2 - 1) = 1$. Move *down* Table A.5 to 1 df, and move *across* to alpha = .05. The critical value is 3.841.

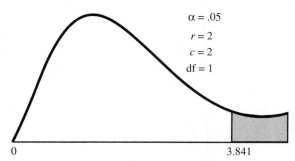

$\alpha = .05$
$r = 2$
$c = 2$
df = 1

Step 3   Calculate the expected frequencies for each cell by multiplying the row total by the column total and then dividing by the sample size. For example, for the upper left cell, yes and yes, the expected frequency is [200(174)]/400, or 87. For no and no, the expected value is [200(226)]/400, or 113. Complete a sum equal to the sample size, 810. Also, the column $(O - E)$ must have a sum of zero. The sum of the last column is the calculated χ^2 value.

Cell	O	E	$(O - E)$	$(O - E)^2$	$(O - E)^2 E$
High/Low	70	50	20	400	8
High/High	30	50	−20	400	8
Low/Low	30	50	−20	400	8
Low/High	70	50	20	400	8
	200	200	00		32

Place the calculated value, 32, on the distribution curve. The value 32 falls to the right of the critical value in the critical region.

---

this process for the other two cells. Place the expected values in parentheses in each cell.

	Sales Tax		
	Yes	**No**	**Total**
Income Tax Yes	108 (87)	92 (113)	200
No	66 (87)	134 (113)	200
Total	174	226	400

Calculate the χ^2 statistic. Arrange the data in columns for O, E, $(O - E)$, $(O - E)^2$, and $(O - E)^2/E$. Each cell must be represented. The sum of the last column is the calculated χ^2 value.

Cell	O	E	$(O - E)$	$(O - E)^2$	$(O - E)^2/E$
Yes/yes	108	87	21	441	5.069
Yes/no	92	113	−21	441	3.903
No/yes	66	87	−21	441	5.069
No/no	134	113	21	441	3.903
	400	400	0		17.944

Step 4   Place the calculated value on the distribution curve. The calculated value is 17.944. Place 17.944 to the right of the critical value, 3.841.

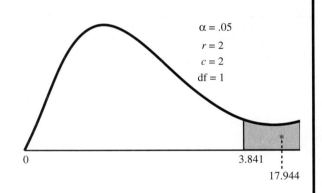

$\alpha = .05$
$r = 2$
$c = 2$
df $= 1$

0   3.841
                  17.944

Step 5   Make a decision. The calculated value 33.501 falls in the critical region. Therefore, reject the null hypothesis.

Reject H_0

Step 6   Interpret the results. Rejecting the null hypothesis in a contingency table suggests that the variables are dependent; that is, the difference between the observed and expected values is significant. There is sufficient evidence at the .05 level of significance to show that there is a relationship between voters' preferences between sales taxes and income taxes.

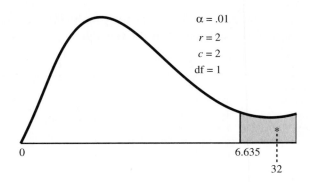

$\alpha = .01$
$r = 2$
$c = 2$
$df = 1$

0   6.635

32

The decision must be to reject the null hypothesis that the variables are independent. Based on this sample, the interpretation is that there is sufficient evidence at the .01 level of significance that the amount of information a Southerner receives is independent of support for liberal causes.

Reject the null hypothesis

Analysis of Variance

Although the most common statistical measures test the difference between two samples, testing with three or more samples is also necessary. Situations often occur in which there are several methods, several products, or several types of items that are compared. For example, an instructor may want to compare student performance based on academic major. The z and t test statistics compare only two majors at a time. If six majors exist, then 15 separate tests, working with two majors at a time, would need to be performed. Separate testing is inefficient, and the chance of errors is substantially increased.

A method of testing three or more means focuses on analyzing the variance within and across the samples. This method is known as the *analysis of variance,* or ANOVA. There are several types of analysis of variance, of which two are discussed in this chapter: a one-way ANOVA and a two-way ANOVA. The simplest type of analysis is the one-way ANOVA, in which observations are classified into groups on the basis of a single characteristic, such as, a one-way analysis comparing student performance based on majors. The two-way analysis of variance is more complicated. Observations are classified into groups on the basis of two characteristics. For example, a two-way analysis compares student performance based on majors and year in school.

Although means are being tested, analysis of variance compares the variation between the samples to the variation within the sample. If the variance between the samples is larger than the variation within the samples, then it is concluded that the means of each sample are not the same. For example, if the normal curves in Figure 14.2 represent three samples, then the analysis of variance can be conceptualized as measuring the difference between the means of each sample (represented by the peaks in the curve) and the difference within each sample (represented by the width of each curve).

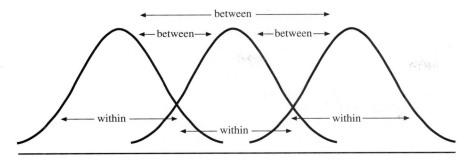

FIGURE 14.2

There are several conditions necessary for applying the analysis of variance. The first condition is that at least three population means are tested. All populations are considered normally distributed. Populations that are not normally distributed should be tested using other methods (such as the Kruskal-Wallis test). The standard deviations of the population must be equal and the samples must be independent.

The F distribution is used in testing three or more means with ANOVA. Recall from Chapter 13 that the F distribution is not symmetric, but is skewed to the right (Figure 14.3). It has values of 0 or more, and degrees of freedom associated with the numerator and the denominator. Critical values for F are reported in Table A.6a, A.6b, and A.6c. Each table represents a different alpha level.

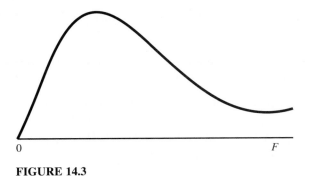

FIGURE 14.3

The six steps in hypothesis testing are followed when testing with the analysis of variance. State the hypotheses, identify the test criteria, calculate the test statistic, place the calculated value on the curve, make a decision, and interpret the results.

The null hypothesis is written with the parameters and an equal sign. The null hypothesis states that the means of all the populations are equal. The alternative hypothesis is written narratively stating that the means are not all equal. For example, for three population means the hypotheses are written as

$$H_0: \quad \mu_1 = \mu_2 = \mu_3$$

$$H_1: \quad \text{The means are not equal}$$

The test criteria include the level of significance, test statistic, critical region, and critical value. The level of significance is typically given as alpha. If alpha is not given, then it must be set by considering the seriousness of a type I error. The test statistic for three or more normally distributed means is the F test, as determined by the analysis of variance. As with multinomials and contingency tables, *the critical region for ANOVA testing is always one-tailed to the right.* The critical value is determined by identifying the degrees of freedom for the numerator, degrees of freedom for the denominator, and alpha. The degrees of freedom for the numerator is associated with the difference between the samples and is equal to $k - 1$, where k is the number of samples, or categories. The degrees of freedom for the denominator is associated with the difference within the samples and is equal to $N - k$, where N is the total number of outcomes in all samples combined and k is the number of samples. As a check on the degrees of freedom, the numerator df and denominator df should have a sum of $n - 1$, as calculated for most other test statistics.

Degrees of Freedom for ANOVA

$$\mathrm{df}_n = k - 1$$

$$\mathrm{df}_d = N - k$$

where

k equals the number of samples (which must be at least 3).

N is the total number of outcomes in all samples combined.

df_n is associated with the difference between samples.

df_d is associated with the difference within samples.

EXAMPLE 14.5

Experiment If three different methods are used to teach statistics, determine the degrees of freedom associated with a survey of 20 students in method I, 25 students in method II, and 20 students in method III.

Answer $\mathrm{df}_n = 2$, $\mathrm{df}_d = 62$

Solution The degrees of freedom associated with the difference between the samples are determined by $k - 1$, where k is the number of samples. There are three samples, so $k - 1 = 3 - 1 = 2$. The degrees of freedom associated with the difference within the samples is determined by $N - k$, where N is the total number of outcomes and k is the number of samples. The total number of outcomes is found by adding the number of students in each sample: $20 + 25 + 20 = 65$. There are three samples, so the degrees of freedom for the denominator are $65 - 3 = 62$.

The critical value is determined by noting the degrees of freedom for the numerator, the degrees of freedom for the denominator, and alpha. Begin by identifying the correct alpha in Table A.6a, A.6b, and A.6c. After identifying alpha, move *across* the table to the appropriate degrees of freedom for the numerator and *down* to the appropriate degrees of freedom for the denominator. The value in the intersection is the critical F value.

The calculation of the test statistic is lengthy. The variation within the samples is measured, the variation across the samples is measured, the total variation is measured, and then a ratio of the mean square estimates results in a calculated F value. Each of these calculations is performed separately. After the initial calculations, the full process can be summarized in a table that organizes the calculations.

Begin by calculating the sum of squares for the total variation that exists. Recall that the sum of squares is the numerator of the variance formula presented in earlier chapters and is denoted by 55. Use the subscript t to denote the sum of squares for the total. The calculation is the same as in earlier chapters. Notice that N replaces n, as a reminder in ANOVA that N is the total number of observations for all samples combined. The lowercase n is reserved for identifying the number of observations in any one sample.

Sum of Squares for the Total Variation

$$SS_t = \Sigma x^2 - \frac{(\Sigma x)^2}{N}$$

The total variance is now partitioned into two parts, one measuring the difference between the samples and the other measuring the difference within the samples. It is also common to refer to the difference between the samples as the *sum of squares between, sum of squares factor,* or *sum of squares treatment.* Each of the terms refers to the fact that the test is measuring whether a difference exists between the populations. The difference within the samples is associated with error and is therefore commonly referred to as the *sum of squares within* or *sum of squares error.*

The calculation for the sum of squares between is done by squaring each sample's total and dividing by the sample's size. Then these values are added after being determined for each sample. From this summation is subtracted the square of the sum of x divided by N. The data are usually arranged in columns, where each column represents a sample. The C in the formula represents the sum of the values in a column. Each column total is squared and divided by its n; then it is added to the values obtained for the other samples. The lowercase n is the number of values in a sample, and the uppercase N is the total number of values in all samples combined.

Sum of Squares between (Factor, Treatment)

$$SS_b = \Sigma \left(\frac{C^2}{n} \right) - \frac{(\Sigma x)^2}{N}$$

where

   C^2 is the square of the column total.

   n is the number of values in a sample.

   $(\Sigma x)^2$ is the sum of all values, squared.

   N is the total number of values in all samples combined.

The sum of squares within (error) is the remaining unexplained variance after the sum of squares between is subtracted from the total sum of squares. The sum of squares error can be calculated by formula or by subtracting the sum of squares between from the sum of squares total. If the full formula is used, the sum of the two partitions should be the total.

Sum of Squares Within (Error)

$$SS_w = SS_t - SS_b \quad \text{or} \quad SS_w = \sum x^2 - \sum \left(\frac{C^2}{n} \right)$$

where

C^2 is the square of the column total.

n is the number of values in a sample.

$\sum x^2$ is the square of all values, summed.

N is the total number of values in all samples combined.

Arranging the calculations for the sum of squares in a table will guide the final calculations. Each sum of squares is divided by its degrees of freedom. The result of the division is referred to as the mean square, which estimates the variance. The ratio of the mean square between and within results in the calculated F statistic. The table should contain a column for the source of variance, the sum of squares (55), degrees of freedom (df), mean square (MS), and F. Three rows should exist representing the source of variance: between (factor), within (error), and total.

Source of Variation	SS	df	MS	F
Between (factor)	$SS_b = \sum \left(\frac{C^2}{n} \right) - \frac{(\sum x)^2}{N}$	$k - 1$	$\dfrac{SS_b}{df_b}$	$\dfrac{MS_b}{MS_N}$
Within (error)	$SS_w = \sum x^2 - \sum \left(\frac{C^2}{n} \right)$	$N - k$	$\dfrac{SS_w}{df_w}$	
Total	$SS_t = \sum x^2 - \frac{(\sum x)^2}{N}$	$N - 1$		

The F test statistic is the ratio of the mean squares for between and mean squares for within. The calculated F statistic is placed on the distribution curve relative to the critical value. If the calculated value falls in the critical region, then the decision is to reject the null hypothesis. If the calculated value does not fall in the critical region, then the decision is to fail to reject the null hypothesis.

Failing to reject the null hypothesis implies that there is no difference in the means. A calculated F value near 1.0 suggests that there is no significant difference between the sample means. If the calculated F value is large, then a significant difference exists between the sample means, and the null hypothesis is rejected. Rejecting the null hypothesis implies only that at least one mean is not equal to the others. It does not specify which mean is not equal. There are a variety of tests called multiple comparison procedures (for example, the Tukey β test) that can be used to specify the inequality.

EXAMPLE 14.6

Experiment University students are randomly assigned to one of three different courses in statistics: a self-study course, a lecture course, or a computer-assisted course. An exam is given to determine if there is a significant difference in knowledge of statistics among the students taking the different courses. Is there a significant difference in the outcomes from the teaching methods at the .01 level?

Self-Study	Lecture	Computer-Assisted
60	90	83
72	75	76
64	88	55
62	75	79
52	72	66
58	82	76
	63	89
	71	73

Answer No, there is no significant difference in the teaching methods.

Solution Identify the data as an ANOVA by identifying the necessary conditions. There are three samples of students. The samples are randomly selected, which ensures independent sampling. The standard deviations can be calculated.

State the hypotheses. The null hypothesis for ANOVA is that there is no difference between the population means. The alternative hypothesis is that at least one mean is statistically unequal to the others.

$$H_0: \quad \mu_1 = \mu_2 = \mu_3 \qquad H_1: \quad \text{The means are not equal}$$

Identify the test criteria. The alpha is reported as .01. The test statistic for ANOVA is F. *The critical region for ANOVA is always one-tailed to the right.* The critical value is determined by degrees of freedom for the numerator, degrees of freedom for the denominator, and alpha. The degrees of freedom for the numerator are $k - 1$, where k is the number of samples. Therefore, numerator df $= 3 - 1$, or 2. The degrees of freedom for the denominator are $N - k$, where N is the total number of outcomes for all samples combined. Twenty-two students are tested; therefore, the degrees of freedom for the denominator are $N - k = 22 - 3 = 19$.

$$\text{df}_n = k - 1 = 3 - 1 = 2$$
$$\text{df}_d = N - k = 22 - 3 = 19$$

Use Table A.6a, which is for critical F values at alpha .01. Read *across* the table to numerator df-2 and *down* to the denominator df $= 19$. The critical value in the intersection is 5.9259. Place the value on the distribution curve.

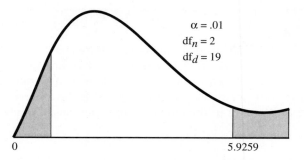

$$\alpha = .01$$
$$df_n = 2$$
$$df_d = 19$$

0   5.9259

To calculate the test statistic, arrange the data in the columns. Calculate x^2 for each value reported and sum all columns.

Self-Study	x^2	Lecture	x^2	Computer-Assisted	x^2
60	3,600	90	8,100	83	6,889
72	5,184	75	5,625	76	5,776
64	4,096	88	7,744	55	3,025
62	3,844	75	5,625	79	6,241
52	2,704	72	5,184	66	4,356
58	3,364	82	6,724	76	5,776
		63	3,969	89	7,921
		71	5,041	73	5,329
$C_1 = 368$	22,792	$C_2 = 616$	48,012	$C_3 = 597$	45,313
$n_1 = 6$		$n_2 = 8$		$n_3 = 8$	

$$\Sigma x^2 = 22,792 + 48,012 + 45,313 = 116,117$$
$$(\Sigma x) = 368 + 616 + 597 = 1581$$
$$N = n_1 + n_2 + n_3 = 6 + 8 + 8 = 22$$

Calculate the sum of squares total. Then calculate the sum of squares between. Subtract the between value from the total, resulting in the sum of squares within.

$$SS_t = \Sigma x^2 - \frac{(\Sigma x)^2}{N} = 116,117 - \frac{1581^2}{22} = 116,117 - \frac{2,499,561}{22}$$

$$= 116,117 - 113,616.4$$

$$= 2500.6$$

$$SS_b = \Sigma \left(\frac{C^2}{n} \right) - \frac{(\Sigma x)^2}{N} = \left(\frac{368^2}{6} + \frac{616^2}{8} + \frac{597^2}{8} \right) - \frac{1581^2}{22}$$

$$= \left(\frac{135,424}{6} + \frac{379,456}{8} + \frac{356,409}{8} \right) - \frac{2,499,561}{22}$$

$$= [22,570.667 + 47,432 + 44,551.125] - 113,616.4$$

$$= 114,553.79 - 113,616.4$$

$$= 939.39$$

$$SS_w = SS_t - SS_b = 2500.6 - 937.39 = 1563.21$$

Place these values in a table to clarify the calculations.

Source of Variation	SS	df	MS	F
Between (factor)	937.39	$k - 1$ 2	SS_b/df_b 468.695	
Within (error)	1563.21	$N - k$ 19	SS_w/df_w 82.274	$\dfrac{MS_b}{MS_w} = 5.697$
Total	2500.60	21		

Place the calculated value 5.697 on the distribution curve.

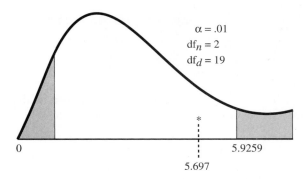

$$\alpha = .01$$
$$df_n = 2$$
$$df_d = 19$$

0   5.9259

5.697

Fail to reject the null hypothesis, because the calculated value does not fall in the critical region. Failing to reject the null implies that there is no significant difference in the methods of teaching statistics courses.

The one-way analysis of variance determines whether differences in sample means exist with the data classified according to one characteristic. Often data are classified by several characteristics, known as factors. For example, the success of students in class may be determined by the method of teaching. But it may be important to factor in grade-point average, year in school, or other characteristics that may affect student performance. When data are classified by two factors, a two-way ANOVA determines whether differences in sample means exist due to one or the other characteristic or both.

Several hypotheses are tested when conducting a two-way analysis of variance. Hypotheses must measure the effect of each factor and their interaction. Three separate null hypotheses are tested: (1) test to determine if there is no interaction between the two factors, (2) test to determine if there are effects from one of the factors, and (3) test to determine if there are effects from the second factor.

Each hypothesis is tested separately. The null hypothesis for the interaction is very important. If it is rejected, then there is no need to test the factors separately. That is, if there is interaction between the two factors, the factors do not need to be tested separately.

The calculations for the various sums of squares for the two-way analysis of variance are very involved and are best left for a computer software program. The mean square, the degrees of freedom, and identification of the F test statistic are described here.

The mean square for interaction is determined by dividing the sum of squares for interaction by the degrees of freedom for the interaction. The degrees of freedom for the interaction are $c - 1$, where c is the number of columns.

Mean Square for the Interaction of Two Factors

$$MS_{interaction} = \frac{SS_{interaction}}{df_{interaction}}$$

The mean square for within (also referred to as error or residual) is determined by dividing the sum of squares for within by the degrees of freedom for within.

Mean Square for Within (Error)

$$MS_{within} = \frac{SS_{within}}{df_{within}}$$

The test statistic F for the interaction is determined by the ratio of the mean square for the interaction and the mean square for within.

F Test Statistic for the Interaction of Two Factors

$$F_{interaction} = \frac{MS_{interaction}}{MS_{within}}$$

The effect of the factor presented in the rows of the data is tested if the interaction testing fails to reject the null hypothesis. The mean square for the row factor is determined by dividing the sum of squares for the row factor by its degrees of freedom. The test statistic F for the row factor is determined by the ratio of the mean square for the row and the mean square for within. Rejecting the null hypothesis for the row factor implies that the row factor affects the equality of the means.

F Test Statistic for the Row Factor

$$F_{row} = \frac{MS_{row}}{MS_{within}}$$

The effect due to the factor presented in the columns must also be tested if the interaction testing fails to reject the null hypothesis. The mean square for the column factor is determined by dividing the sum of squares for the column by its degrees of freedom. The test statistic F for the column is determined by the ratio of the mean square for the column and the mean square for within. Rejecting the null hypothesis for the column factor implies that the column factor affects the equality of the means.

F Test Statistic for the Column Factor

$$F_{column} = \frac{MS_{column}}{MS_{within}}$$

EXAMPLE 14.7

Experiment The following two-way ANOVA table represents grade-point average based on year in school and major. Analyze the effect of the year in school and major on grade-point average. Let $\alpha = .01$.

Source of Variation	SS	df	MS	F
Year in school (row, factor 1)	3.108	3	1.036	2.584
Major (column, factor 2)	2.549	6	.425	1.060
Interaction (year and major)	2.277	18	.127	.317
Within (error)	9.213	23	.401	
Total	17.147	50		

Answer There appears to be no effect on the grade-point average based on the year in school, major, or these variables' interaction.

Solution Begin by testing the effect of the interaction. The null hypothesis is that there is no interaction between the two factors. The alternative hypothesis suggests that there is an interaction between the two factors. Draw a distribution curve and note the critical value. The critical value has numerator degrees of freedom associated with the interaction, reported as 18, and denominator degrees of freedom associated with within, reported as 23. Using Table A.6a for alpha $= .01$, read *over* to 20 df (nearest estimate for 18 df) and *down* to 23 df. The value 2.7805 is in the intersection and is the critical value. Place the calculated F value, 0.317, on the curve relative to the critical value, 2.7805.

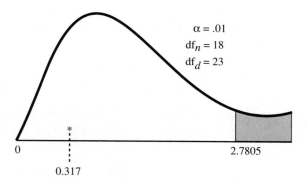

$$\alpha = .01$$
$$df_n = 18$$
$$df_d = 23$$

The calculated value, .317, is not in the critical region; therefore, the decision is to fail to reject the null hypothesis. There appears to be no interaction between the two factors.

Test the first factor, year in school. The null hypothesis is that there are no effects from the row factor—that is, year in school has no effect on the student's grade point average. The critical value has numerator degrees of freedom equal to 3 denominator degrees of freedom of 23. Read *across* Table A.6a to 3 df and *down* to 23 df; 4.7649 is the critical value. Place the critical and calculated values on a distribution curve.

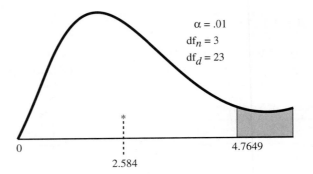

ANOVA

The following data give the number of children born to women in various parts of the country according to a random survey of women from the North, South, East and West. Determine if there are significant differences in the mean based on region for $\alpha = .05$.

North	South	East	West
3	2	4	5
3	5	4	1
0	1	2	3
1	6	0	4
2	5	2	1
2		1	2
2			2

Step 1 Identify the data as an ANOVA by identifying the necessary conditions. There are four samples of women. The samples are randomly selected, which ensures independent sampling.

State the hypotheses. The null hypothesis for ANOVA is that there is no difference between the population means. The alternative hypothesis is that at least one mean is statistically not equal to the others.

$$H_0: \quad \mu_1 = \mu_2 = \mu_3 = \mu_4$$

$$H_1: \quad \text{The means are not equal}$$

Step 2 Identify the test criteria. The alpha is reported as .05. The test statistic for ANOVA is F. *The critical region for ANOVA is always one-tailed to the right.* The critical value is determined by degrees of freedom for the numerator, degrees of freedom for the denominator, and alpha. The degrees of freedom for

the numerator are $k - 1$, where k is the number of samples; therefore numerator df $= 4 - 1$, or 3. The degrees of freedom for the denominator are $N - k$, where N is the total number of outcomes for all samples combined. Twenty-five women are surveyed; therefore the degrees of freedom for the denominator are equal $N - k = 25 - 4$, or 21. Read *across* Table A.6c to 3 df and *down* to 21 df. The critical value is 3.0725.

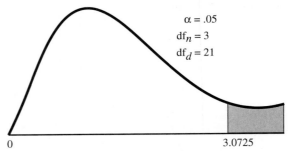

Step 3 Calculate the test statistic. Arrange the data in the columns. Calculate x^2 for each value reported and sum all columns.

North	x^2	South	x^2	East	x^2	West	x^2
3	9	2	4	4	16	5	25
3	9	5	25	4	16	1	1
0	0	1	1	2	4	3	9
1	1	6	36	0	0	4	16
2	4	5	25	2	4	1	1
2	4			1	1	2	4
2	4					2	4
$C_1 = 13$	31	$C_2 = 19$	91	$C_3 = 13$	41	$C_4 = 18$	60
$n_1 = 7$		$n_2 = 5$		$n_3 = 6$		$n_4 = 7$	

The decision is to fail to reject the null hypothesis, because the calculated value, 2.584, does not fall in the critical region. Year in school does not appear to have an effect on a student's grade-point average.

Finally, test the effect of the second variable, major. The null hypothesis states that there is no effect from the column factor—that is, a student's major does not affect the student's grade-point average. Identify the critical value. The numerator degrees of freedom, from the major, are 6 and the denominator, error, is 23. Read *across* Table A.6a to 6 df and *down* to 23 df. The critical value is 3.7102. Place the calculated and critical values on the distribution curve.

$\Sigma x^2 = 31 + 91 + 41 + 60 = 223$

$(\Sigma x) = 13 + 19 + 13 + 18 = 63$

$N = n_1 + n_2 + n_3 + n_4 = 7 + 5 + 6 + 7 = 25$

Calculate the sum of squares for the total. Then calculate the sum of squares for the between. Finally, subtract the between value from the total value, resulting in the sum of squares for within.

$$SS_t = \Sigma x^2 - \frac{(\Sigma x)^2}{N} = 223 - \frac{63^2}{25} = 223 - \frac{3969}{25}$$

$$= 223 - 158.76 = 64.24$$

$$SS_b = \Sigma \left(\frac{C^2}{n} \right) - \frac{(\Sigma x)^2}{N}$$

$$= \left(\frac{13^2}{7} + \frac{19^2}{5} + \frac{13^2}{6} + \frac{18^2}{7} \right) - \frac{63^2}{25}$$

$$= \left(\frac{169}{7} + \frac{361}{5} + \frac{169}{6} + \frac{324}{7} \right) - \frac{3969}{25}$$

$$= (24.14 + 72.2 + 28.17 + 46.29) - 158.76$$

$$= 170.8 - 158.76$$

$$= 12.04$$

$$SS_w = SS_t - SS_b = 64.24 - 12.04 = 52.2$$

Place these values in the table in order to organize the calculations.

Source of Variation	SS	df	MS	F
Between (factor)	12.04	$k - 1$ 3	SS_B/df_B 4.013	$\dfrac{MS_B}{MS_w} =$ 1.6142
Within (error)	52.2	$N - k$ 21	SS_w/df_w 2.486	
Total	64.24	24		

Step 4 Place the calculated value, 1.6142, on the distribution curve.

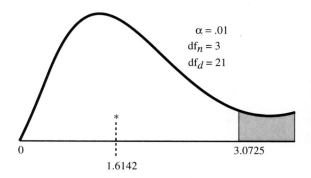

$\alpha = .01$
$df_n = 3$
$df_d = 21$

0   1.6142   3.0725

Step 5 Make a decision. Fail to reject the null hypothesis, because the calculated value does not fall in the critical region.

Step 6 Interpret the results. Failing to reject the null hypothesis implies that there is no significant difference in the number of children born to women based on the region of the country.

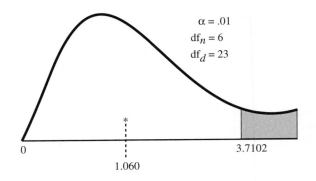

$\alpha = .01$
$\text{df}_n = 6$
$\text{df}_d = 23$

0   1.060   3.7102

The decision again is to fail to reject the null hypothesis. There appears to be no effect of the column factor. The student's major does not appear to affect the student's grade-point average.

CHAPTER 14 IN REVIEW

14.1 Find the critical value for the following one-tailed data.

a. $\chi^2_{(15,.025)}$ **c.** $\chi^2_{(12,.05)}$

b. $\chi^2_{(26,.05)}$ **d.** $\chi^2_{(6,.005)}$

14.2 Find the critical value for the following one-tailed data.

a. $F_{(5,6,.025)}$ **d.** $F_{(2,6,.05)}$

b. $F_{(4,2,.05)}$ **e.** $F_{(4,3,.01)}$

c. $F_{(4,2,.01)}$ **f.** $F_{(5,3,.05)}$

14.3 Find the following critical chi-square values for a multinomial test.

a. $k = 5$, $\alpha = .05$ **c.** $k = 4$, $\alpha = .05$

b. $k = 8$, $\alpha = .025$ **d.** $k = 6$, $\alpha = .10$

14.4 Find the following critical chi-square values for a contingency table.

a. $r = 3$, $c = 4$,   **c.** $r = 7$, $c = 5$,
$\alpha = .05$ $\alpha = .025$

b. $r = 2$, $c = 3$, $\alpha = .10$ **d.** $r = 4$, $c = 4$, $\alpha = .01$

14.5 Determine, at the .05 level of significance, if there is a relationship between the occupational background of members of state legislatures and their party identification.

| | **Party Membership** | | |
	Democrat	**Republican**	**Total**
Law	224	122	346
Business/banking	136	176	312
Agriculture	100	100	200
Public service	159	135	294
Education	124	114	238
Other	60	50	110
Total	803	697	1500

14.6 The following data are prices (in thousands of dollars) of houses in three suburban communities. Is there a significant difference between the average price across the suburbs? Let $\alpha = .01$.

Chesterfield	Ladue	Bloomfield
116	132	108
117	144	196
138	161	126
100	131	111
135	109	128
134	200	
122	165	

14.7 A polling organization claims that 54% of the U.S. public feel that television news is the most believable source of news, 22% say that newspapers are the most believable source, 6% think radio is the most believable source, and 7% say that magazines are most believable. A student challenges this claim and conducts a survey of 800 voters who respond with the following answers ($\alpha = .05$):

Television	480
Newspapers	240
Radio	64
Magazines	16

14.8 Market tests for preferences of toothpaste produced the following results for a random sample of 200 consumers:

Brand	A	B	C	D
Preference	64	24	57	55

At the .10 level, does there appear to be a preference in toothpaste?

14.9   A researcher wants to compare the amount of weight loss from a popular liquid diet to weight loss from an exercise program. Five hundred people were randomly assigned one of the programs, and the amount of weight loss after 6 mo was noted. Test to determine if there is a relationship between the amount of weight loss and program ($\alpha = .10$).

	Liquid Diet	Exercise	Total
More than 10 lb	17	115	132
5–9 lb	103	94	197
0–4 lb	128	43	171
Total	248	252	500

14.10   Five different brands of aspirin are compared based on the amount of time it took for the aspirin to become effective. Is there sufficient evidence to support that the average length of time (in minutes) for effectiveness is the same? Let $\alpha = .01$.

Brand of Aspirin

A	B	C	D	E
19	8	10	8	15
12	15	9	9	10
16	11	12	10	14
15	10	9	13	13
16	14	11	12	15

14.11   The number of bankruptcies filed in one federal court for a month by type of business is reported here. Is there evidence that the number of bankruptcies differs based on the type of business? Let $\alpha = .05$.

Retail	Restaurants	Construction	Manufacturing
23	42	48	36

14.12   The following data are scores on a standardized exam for admission to graduate school based on the type of student preparation. Test for the equality of the mean scores for each type of preparation. Let $\alpha = .01$.

Method

Self-Study	Prep. Course	No Preparation
116	132	108
117	137	109
138	131	131
100	125	130
125	111	110
134	140	
122		

14.13   True or false?
   a. ANOVA tests three or more means.
   b. The test statistic for ANOVA is χ^2.
   c. ANOVA compares the variation between the sample to the variation within the sample.
   d. ANOVA testing is always two-tailed.

14.14   True or false?
   a. The contingency table is a two-way display of two nominal level variables.
   b. The null hypothesis for a contingency table assumes the variables are dependent.
   c. Two variables are said to be independent if no difference exists between the observed and expected frequencies.
   d. Testing contingency tables is always two-tailed.

14.15   True or false?
   a. The probabilities of all the outcomes in a multinomial experiment must have a sum of 0.
   b. All multinomial experiments are two-tailed.
   c. The expected frequencies for each category in a multinomial experiment is determined by multiplying the total number of responses by the probability for the category.
   d. The test statistic for testing multinomial cases is F.

15

Case Study

The case study presented in this chapter serves as an overview of many of the techniques that are presented in this text.* A common question asked by students of statistics is, How do all the techniques relate? This chapter attempts to answer that question by presenting a case study as it develops from the early stages of descriptive statistics to some of the later stages of inferential statistics.

Statistical analysis begins by identifying the purpose of the study and the source and nature of the data. The case study focuses on the factors pertaining to fertility. Identifying these factors allows a nation to develop public policy to encourage or discourage social behavior. A case study is employed using the country of Cyprus. Cyprus is a sovereign state in the Mediterranean Sea between the countries of Greece and Turkey. Cyprus is selected for the study because it presents an interesting situation as a nation that is sometimes considered developed and sometimes considered a developing country. Its economic and social indicators are characteristic of a transitional society. It has regressed as a developed country due to military and economic turmoil in the 1970s. Cyprus is also selected because of the availability of data from a household survey conducted from 1974 to 1976. A total of 34,413 persons were sampled and interviewed out of a total population of 600,000. Surveys did not include households in the northern part of the country, which has been held by Turkish forces since 1974.

The second major area to address in a statistical analysis is the operational definitions of the variables. The dependent variable is the one that is being explained, and the independent variables are the variables that explain the dependent variable. The study attempts to explain fertility by illustrating what factors lead couples to have few or many children. Fertility is the dependent variable and is measured as

*Victoria L. (Armstrong) Mantzopolous, *Differential Fertility in Cyprus: A Micro-Analysis* (Detroit: Wayne State University, 1987).

346

the number of children born to all women who have ever been married. As the study develops, it becomes apparent that a major factor in explaining fertility is the number and timing of a loss of a child through death. Therefore, a second dependent variable is identified and defined as the number of children ever born after the occurrence of the first infant or child death.

The factors that explain fertility are referred to as the independent variables. Twelve independent variables are included in the study and are categorized into four groups: (1) demographic variables, (2) economic indicators, (3) social-economic indicators, and (4) controlling variables. Each category and each variable are specifically defined so that another researcher is able to repeat the measurements.

The demographic variables are age at which the woman married, whether a woman experienced the death of a child, and the birth order of a child who died. Economic indicators include the employment activity of a woman, the employment activity of her husband, and residency. Social-economic indicators include the employment status of a woman, the employment status of her husband, the education of a woman, and the education of her husband. The controlling variables are the current age of a woman and the duration of marriage.

Once the data are collected, they must be coded and entered into a computer. Coding assigns numerical values to responses of variables that have no inherent values. For example, sex of a respondent has two responses, male and female. The responses do not have inherent numerical value. Numerical values must be assigned, such as coding a response for a female as a 1 and a response for a male as a 2. The values are arbitrarily assigned but are necessary for the mathematical calculations. Entering the data in a computer is necessary if the data are numerous. The most popular software packages are Statistical Package for the Social Sciences (SPSS), Minitab, and Statdisk. A command file for the data is written that identifies the necessary statistical procedures.

One of the first statistical procedures that should be completed is a frequency distribution. A frequency distribution not only provides valuable information, but it also allows a researcher to check the coding and reliability of the data. For example if sex is coded 1 for a female and 2 for a male and a value of 3 appears in the frequency distribution, an error in the coding occurred. A frequency distribution also illustrates the number of people for each response of a variable. The percentages of each response are also presented in a frequency distribution. Table 15.1 gives the frequency distribution for the number of households in the four areas of the country.

TABLE 15.1   Frequency Distribution of Households

Residency	Count	Percent	Cumulative Percent
Nicosia	4,110	41.29	41.29
Limassol	3,114	30.53	71.82
Larnaca	2,010	19.71	91.53
Paphos	966	9.47	100.00
Total	10,200	100.00	

The column for the count reflects the number of households who report residency in each of the regions. The total, 10,200, is the total number of households surveyed in the study. The percent column reflects the relative proportion of each response. For example, 41.29% of the households surveyed report residency in the region of Nicosia. The number 41.29 is obtained by dividing the number of house-holds in the category (4110) by the total number of households in the survey (10,200). The cumulative percent reflects the cumulative relative proportions. A cumulative count adds all the responses preceding each response. For example, 71.82% of the households report residency in either Nicosia or Limassol, and 91.52% report residency in either Nicosia, Limassol, or Larnaca.

Frequency distributions should be obtained for each variable. They are an important tool for checking the data for errors and for understanding the nature of the data. For example, a frequency distribution on the number of years a woman is married produced values such as 90 y and even 100 y. Although a value of 90 may be possible, the two or three women who reported being married for 100 y probably did not understand the question. The error is supported by a frequency distribution on the current age of women. No woman reported being older than 85. If no one is older than 85, it would not be possible for a few to be married for 90 or 100 y.

Frequency distributions can also be obtained with additional descriptive infor-mation, such as means and standard deviations, that offer further insight into the data. Frequencies of two variables may be overlapped to produce a crosstabulation table. The table can also reveal errors in the data by highlighted intersections of two variables that should or should not exist. A crosstab overlays two variables and can determine if an association exists between the variables. Crosstabulations also should be one of the first procedures performed on the data. Crosstabulations reflect if two variables are independent or dependent.

Table 15.2 overlays the educational level of a wife with that of her husband. The upper left cell reflects 96 respondents where both the wife and husband have no formal schooling. The adjacent cell reflects 117 respondents where the wife has a primary education and the husband has no formal schooling. Careful analysis of the table and with measurements such as chi-square show that there is a relationship between the husband's and wife's educational attainment. A pattern exists in which the husband's education increases as the wife's education increases; however, the husband's education increases at a faster rate. Notice that the husbands tend to have the same or slightly higher levels of education as their wives. For example, 3282 husbands and wives have the same primary education. However, 710 husbands with a primary education have wives with no schooling, but only 117 wives with a primary education have husbands with no schooling.

Crosstabulation tables provide insight into the relationship and association of two variables. Although crosstabs may include statistics measuring the strength and

TABLE 15.2 Crosstabulation of Education of Wife with Education of Husband

Education of Husband	Education of Wife				
	No School	Primary	Secondary	University	Total
No School	96	117	6	0	219
Primary	710	3282	209	11	4212
Secondary	34	756	698	78	1566
University	3	81	294	200	578
Total	843	4236	1207	289	6575

significance of the relationships, correlation analysis, regression analysis, and hypothesis testing are typically performed.

A correlation matrix should be obtained to illustrate further the relationships between the variables. Correlations measure the strengths and directions of linear relationships between two variables. The matrix produced by most software packages reports a correlation coefficient, the number of responses included in each calculation, and the level of significance, which describes whether the relationship is statistically significant or the outcome of sampling error. Other matrices exclude the latter two measurements and report only the correlation coefficient, with asterisks next to the coefficients that are significant. Table 15.3 is a partial correlation matrix for selected variables. A partial matrix, as presented here, describes only selected variables. The ellipses on the matrix represent correlations of the same two variables that are presented somewhere else in the table. For example, age and the education of the wife has the same correlation coefficient ($-.455$) as does education of the wife and age. In order not to clutter the matrix, only one of the relationships is reported, with the other noted by an ellipsis.

TABLE 15.3   Correlation Matrix for Selected Variables

	Fertility	Age	Educ. of Wife	Educ. of Husband	Work Status of Wife	Work Status of Husband
Age	.317*	1.000	. . . .	. . . .	. . . .	. . . .
Education of Wife	−.328*	−.455*	1.000	. . . .	. . . .	. . . .
Education of Husband	−.293*	−.331*	.622*	1.000	. . . .	. . . .
Work Status of Wife	.050	.249*	−.132	−.018	1.000	. . . .
Work Status of Husband	.137	.588*	−.299*	−.183	.255*	1.000
Child Death	.568*	.344*	−.266*	−.194	.090	.248*

*Significant at the .01 level.

The appearance of the matrix reflects the correlation coefficients for two variables. The first cell in the second row contains the coefficient .317 for fertility and age. The value .317 implies that a positive relationship exists between fertility and age. A positive relationship means that the values of the two variables increase or decrease together; therefore, as the current age of a woman increases, so too does the level of fertility. In other words, older women tend to have more children than younger women. A negative coefficient implies that the variables move in opposite directions. For example, the value −.328 for fertility and the educational level of a woman means that as a woman's educational level increases, she tends to have fewer children. Given the large sample size of more than 8000 women, any coefficient greater than .196 is considered significant. A coefficient greater than .196 suggests that there is a clear pattern of movement of the two variables. None of the coefficients for the work status of the husband is above .196. Although a pattern may exist between the relationship between the work status of the husband and the other variables, the relationship is not considered significant.

Although many other procedures were performed on the data, such as the t test and ANOVA, performing a multiple regression analysis was the objective. A regression analysis measures the predictive value of the independent variables to the dependent variables. A multiple regression analysis implies that there are three or more independent variables that may predict a dependent variable. The computer software packages produce a variety of statistics with a multiple regression procedure. Typically, standardized beta coefficients report a significance level based on a test known as an F test. The researcher introduces all the independent variables and specifies the level of statistical significance. The procedure then controls relationships between the independent variables and reports only those variables that are statistically significant. Statistics known as multiple R and R square report the amount of variance in the dependent variable explained by the independent variables. Table 15.4 is a partial list of a multiple regression report.

TABLE 15.4   Multiple Regression Report for the Number of Children Ever Born

Variable	B	Beta	Std. Error	F
Child Mortality	1.2796	.4200	.0505	641.389
Age at Marriage	−.1263	−.2919	.0040	962.278
Education: Husband	−.2863	−.0839	.0415	47.484
Current Age	.3903	.2251	.0023	276.638
Employment: Husband	−1.5688	−.3090	.1237	160.686
Urban/Rural Residency	.2612	.0548	.504	26.852

Multiple R .6862
R square   .4708

The matrix reports a variety of statistics that help determine if the relationship of the independent variables is significant to the dependent variable. The direction of the beta value, whether positive or negative, determines the relationship of that independent variable to the dependent variable. For example, the beta value for age at marriage is −.2919, which implies that as the age at which a woman marries increases, the number of children she is likely to bear decreases. The R square of .4708 implies that 47.08% of the variance in the number of children ever born to all ever married women is explained by these few variables.

A regression analysis is often repeated for the dependent variables as well as for some of the independent variables. Some independent variables pass through other independent variables before affecting the dependent variable. That is, there are some variables that directly and/or indirectly affect the dependent variable. Repeating regressions by substituting some of the independent variables as dependent variables creates a maze of paths that more completely explain the dependent variables. The paths are overlaid and referred to as a path analysis. Although this is an advanced statistical procedure, it is important to understand how many of the procedures contained in this text will relate to each other. The following figure illustrates the final path analysis for the dependent variable, the number of children ever born. The values on the path are beta coefficients. Notice that child mortality serves not only as an independent variable directly related to the number of children born, but also as a variable through which other independent variables pass, indirectly explaining the number of children. Some variables, such as the education of the wife, have paths directly to the number of children born and indirectly through child mortality and the age at marriage. See Figure 15.1.

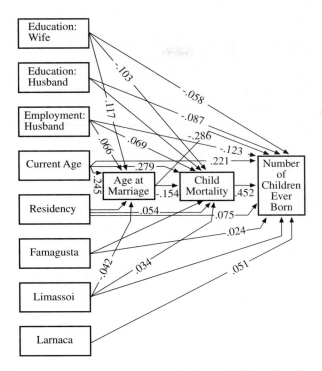

FIGURE 15.1   Path Analysis for the Number of Children Ever Born

The conclusions drawn from this case study are that child mortality is a significant factor in explaining fertility. When a woman loses a child, she is likely to replace the child with more than one additional child. Also, the younger the woman is when she marries, the more children she is likely to have. Other variables that are directly related to fertility are the education of the wife, the education of the husband, the employment status of the husband, the current age of the woman, rural residency, and residency in selected regions of the country. Interestingly, most of these variables also explain age at marriage and child mortality.

The case study is presented to allow an understanding of how the statistical procedures throughout this text relate. Not all the procedures contained in the text were discussed here because not all relate to the case study.

Appendix A
Tables

TABLE A.1   Critical Values for *r*

Critical Values of the Pearson Correlation Coefficient *r*

n	$\alpha = .05$	$\alpha = .01$
4	.950	.999
5	.878	.959
6	.811	.917
7	.754	.875
8	.707	.834
9	.666	.798
10	.632	.765
11	.602	.735
12	.576	.708
13	.553	.684
14	.532	.661
15	.514	.641
16	.497	.623
17	.482	.606
18	.468	.590
19	.456	.575
20	.444	.561
25	.396	.505
30	.361	.463
35	.335	.430
40	.312	.402
45	.294	.378
50	.279	.361
60	.254	.330
70	.236	.305
80	.220	.286
90	.207	.269
100	.196	.256

To test H_0: $\rho = 0$ against H_1: $\rho \neq 0$, reject H_0 if the absolute value of *r* is greater than the critical value in the table.

Source: Biometrika Tables for Statisticians, third ed., vol. 1, T13, 1966. Reproduced with permission of the Biometrika Trustees.

TABLE A.2   Binomial Probabilities

n	x	.01	.05	.10	.20	.30	.40	ρ .50	.60	.70	.80	.90	.95	.99	x
2	0	980	902	810	640	490	360	250	160	090	040	010	002	0+	0
	1	020	095	180	320	420	480	500	480	420	320	180	095	020	1
	2	0+	002	010	040	090	160	250	360	490	640	810	902	980	2
3	0	970	857	729	512	343	216	125	064	027	008	001	0+	0+	0
	1	029	135	243	384	441	432	375	288	189	096	027	007	0+	1
	2	0+	007	027	096	189	288	375	432	441	384	243	135	029	2
	3	0+	0+	001	008	027	064	125	216	343	512	729	857	970	3
4	0	961	815	656	410	240	130	062	026	008	002	0+	0+	0+	0
	1	039	171	292	410	412	346	250	154	076	026	004	0+	0+	1
	2	001	014	049	154	265	346	375	346	265	154	049	014	001	2
	3	0+	0+	004	026	076	154	250	346	412	410	292	171	039	3
	4	0+	0+	0+	002	008	026	062	130	240	410	656	815	961	4
5	0	951	774	590	323	168	078	031	010	002	0+	0+	0+	0+	0
	1	048	204	328	410	360	259	156	077	028	006	0+	0+	0+	1
	2	001	021	073	205	309	346	312	230	132	051	008	001	0+	2
	3	0+	001	008	051	132	230	312	346	309	205	073	021	001	3
	4	0+	0+	0+	006	028	077	156	259	360	410	328	204	048	4
	5	0+	0+	0+	0+	002	010	031	078	168	328	590	774	951	5
6	0	941	735	531	262	118	047	016	004	001	0+	0+	0+	0+	0
	1	057	232	354	393	303	187	094	037	010	002	0+	0+	0+	1
	2	001	031	098	246	324	311	234	138	060	015	001	0+	0+	2
	3	0+	002	015	082	185	276	312	276	185	082	015	002	0+	3
	4	0+	0+	001	015	060	138	234	311	324	246	098	031	001	4
	5	0+	0+	0+	002	010	037	094	187	303	393	354	232	057	5
	6	0+	0+	0+	0+	001	004	016	047	118	262	531	735	941	6
7	0	932	698	478	210	082	028	008	002	0+	0+	0+	0+	0+	0
	1	066	257	372	367	247	131	055	017	004	0+	0+	0+	0+	1
	2	002	041	124	275	318	261	164	077	025	004	0+	0+	0+	2
	3	0+	004	023	115	227	290	273	194	097	029	003	0+	0+	3
	4	0+	0+	003	029	097	194	273	290	227	115	023	004	0+	4
	5	0+	0+	0+	004	025	077	164	261	318	275	124	041	002	5
	6	0+	0+	0+	0+	004	017	055	131	247	367	372	257	066	6
	7	0+	0+	0+	0+	0+	002	008	028	082	210	478	698	932	7
8	0	923	663	430	168	058	017	004	001	0+	0+	0+	0+	0+	0
	1	075	279	383	336	198	090	031	008	001	0+	0+	0+	0+	1
	2	008	051	149	294	296	209	109	041	010	001	0+	0+	0+	2
	3	0+	005	033	147	254	279	219	124	047	009	0+	0+	0+	3
	4	0+	0+	005	046	136	232	273	232	136	046	005	0+	0+	4
	5	0+	0+	0+	009	047	124	219	279	254	147	033	005	0+	5
	6	0+	0+	0+	001	010	041	109	209	296	294	149	051	003	6
	7	0+	0+	0+	0+	001	008	031	090	198	336	383	279	075	7
	8	0+	0+	0+	0+	0+	001	004	017	058	168	430	663	923	8
9	0	914	630	387	134	040	010	002	0+	0+	0+	0+	0+	0+	0
	1	083	299	387	302	156	060	018	004	0+	0+	0+	0+	0+	1
	2	003	063	172	302	267	161	070	021	004	0+	0+	0+	0+	2
	3	0+	008	045	176	267	251	164	074	021	003	0+	0+	0+	3
	4	0+	001	007	066	172	251	246	167	074	017	001	0+	0+	4
	5	0+	0+	001	017	074	167	246	251	172	066	007	001	0+	5
	6	0+	0+	0+	003	021	074	164	251	267	176	045	008	0+	6

TABLE A.2 continued

n	x	.01	.05	.10	.20	.30	.40	ρ .50	.60	.70	.80	.90	.95	.99	x
	7	0+	0+	0+	0+	004	021	070	161	267	302	172	063	003	7
	8	0+	0+	0+	0+	0+	004	018	160	156	302	387	299	083	8
	9	0+	0+	0+	0+	0+	0+	002	010	040	134	387	630	914	9
10	0	904	599	349	107	028	006	001	0+	0+	0+	0+	0+	0+	0
	1	091	315	387	268	121	040	010	002	0+	0+	0+	0+	0+	1
	2	004	075	194	302	233	121	044	011	001	0+	0+	0+	0+	2
	3	0+	010	057	201	267	215	117	042	009	001	0+	0+	0+	3
	4	0+	001	011	088	200	251	205	111	037	006	0+	0+	0+	4
	5	0+	0+	001	026	103	201	246	201	103	026	001	0+	0+	5
	6	0+	0+	0+	006	037	111	205	251	200	088	011	001	0+	6
	7	0+	0+	0+	001	009	042	117	215	267	201	057	010	0+	7
	8	0+	0+	0+	0+	001	011	044	121	233	302	194	075	004	8
	9	0+	0+	0+	0+	0+	002	010	040	121	268	387	315	091	9
	10	0+	0+	0+	0+	0+	0+	001	006	028	107	349	599	904	10
11	0	895	569	314	086	020	004	0+	0+	0+	0+	0+	0+	0+	0
	1	099	329	384	236	093	027	005	001	0+	0+	0+	0+	0+	1
	2	005	087	213	295	200	089	027	005	001	0+	0+	0+	0+	2
	3	0+	014	071	221	257	177	081	023	004	0+	0+	0+	0+	3
	4	0+	001	016	111	220	236	161	070	017	002	0+	0+	0+	4
	5	0+	0+	002	039	132	221	226	147	057	010	0+	0+	0+	5
	6	0+	0+	0+	010	057	147	226	221	132	039	002	0+	0+	6
	7	0+	0+	0+	002	017	070	161	236	220	111	016	001	0+	7
	8	0+	0+	0+	0+	004	023	081	177	257	221	071	014	0+	8
	9	0+	0+	0+	0+	001	005	027	089	200	295	213	087	005	9
	10	0+	0+	0+	0+	0+	001	005	027	093	236	384	329	099	10
	11	0+	0+	0+	0+	0+	0+	0+	004	020	086	314	569	895	11
12	0	886	540	282	069	014	002	0+	0+	0+	0+	0+	0+	0+	0
	1	107	341	377	206	071	017	003	0+	0+	0+	0+	0+	0+	1
	2	006	099	230	283	168	064	016	002	0+	0+	0+	0+	0+	2
	3	0+	017	085	236	240	142	054	012	001	0+	0+	0+	0+	3
	4	0+	002	021	133	231	213	121	042	008	001	0+	0+	0+	4
	5	0+	0+	004	053	158	227	193	101	029	003	0+	0+	0+	5
	6	0+	0+	0+	016	079	177	226	177	079	016	0+	0+	0+	6
	7	0+	0+	0+	003	029	101	193	227	158	053	004	0+	0+	7
	8	0+	0+	0+	001	008	042	121	213	231	133	021	002	0+	8
	9	0+	0+	0+	0+	001	012	054	142	240	236	085	017	0+	9
	10	0+	0+	0+	0+	0+	002	016	064	168	283	230	099	006	10
	11	0+	0+	0+	0+	0+	0+	003	017	071	206	377	341	107	11
	12	0+	0+	0+	0+	0+	0+	0+	002	014	069	282	540	886	12

TABLE A.2   **continued**

n	x	.01	.05	.10	.20	.30	.40	ρ .50	.60	.70	.80	.90	.95	.99	x
13	0	878	513	254	055	010	001	0+	0+	0+	0+	0+	0+	0+	0
	1	115	351	367	179	054	011	002	0+	0+	0+	0+	0+	0+	1
	2	007	111	245	268	139	045	010	001	0+	0+	0+	0+	0+	2
	3	0+	021	100	246	218	111	035	006	001	0+	0+	0+	0+	3
	4	0+	003	028	154	234	184	087	024	003	0+	0+	0+	0+	4
	5	0+	0+	006	069	180	221	157	066	014	001	0+	0+	0+	5
	6	0+	0+	001	023	103	197	209	131	044	006	0+	0+	0+	6
	7	0+	0+	0+	006	044	131	209	197	103	023	001	0+	0+	7
	8	0+	0+	0+	001	014	066	157	221	180	069	006	0+	0+	8
	9	0+	0+	0+	0+	003	024	087	184	234	154	028	003	0+	9
	10	0+	0+	0+	0+	001	006	035	111	218	246	100	021	0+	10
	11	0+	0+	0+	0+	0+	001	010	045	139	268	245	111	007	11
	12	0+	0+	0+	0+	0+	0+	002	011	054	179	367	351	115	12
	13	0+	0+	0+	0+	0+	0+	0+	001	010	055	254	513	878	13
14	0	869	488	229	044	007	001	0+	0+	0+	0+	0+	0+	0+	0
	1	123	359	356	154	041	007	001	0+	0+	0+	0+	0+	0+	1
	2	008	123	257	250	113	032	006	001	0+	0+	0+	0+	0+	2
	3	0+	026	114	250	194	085	022	003	0+	0+	0+	0+	0+	3
	4	0+	004	035	172	229	155	061	014	001	0+	0+	0+	0+	4
	5	0+	0+	008	086	196	207	122	041	007	0+	0+	0+	0+	5
	6	0+	0+	001	032	126	207	183	092	023	002	0+	0+	0+	6
	7	0+	0+	0+	009	062	157	209	157	062	009	0+	0+	0+	7
	8	0+	0+	0+	002	023	092	183	207	126	032	001	0+	0+	8
	9	0+	0+	0+	0+	007	041	122	207	196	086	008	0+	0+	9
	10	0+	0+	0+	0+	001	014	061	155	229	172	035	004	0+	10
	11	0+	0+	0+	0+	0+	003	022	085	194	250	114	026	0+	11
	12	0+	0+	0+	0+	0+	001	006	032	113	250	257	123	008	12
	13	0+	0+	0+	0+	0+	0+	001	007	041	154	356	359	123	13
	14	0+	0+	0+	0+	0+	0+	0+	001	007	044	229	488	869	14
15	0	860	463	206	035	005	0+	0+	0+	0+	0+	0+	0+	0+	0
	1	130	366	343	132	031	005	0+	0+	0+	0+	0+	0+	0+	1
	2	009	135	267	231	092	022	003	0+	0+	0+	0+	0+	0+	2
	3	0+	031	129	250	170	063	014	002	0+	0+	0+	0+	0+	3
	4	0+	005	043	188	219	127	042	007	001	0+	0+	0+	0+	4
	5	0+	001	010	103	206	186	092	024	003	0+	0+	0+	0+	5
	6	0+	0+	002	043	147	207	153	061	012	001	0+	0+	0+	6
	7	0+	0+	0+	014	081	177	196	118	035	003	0+	0+	0+	7
	8	0+	0+	0+	003	035	118	196	177	081	014	0+	0+	0+	8
	9	0+	0+	0+	001	012	061	153	207	147	043	002	0+	0+	9
	10	0+	0+	0+	0+	003	024	092	186	206	103	010	001	0+	10
	11	0+	0+	0+	0+	001	007	042	127	219	188	043	005	0+	11
	12	0+	0+	0+	0+	0+	002	014	063	170	250	129	031	0+	12
	13	0+	0+	0+	0+	0+	0+	003	022	092	231	267	135	009	13
	14	0+	0+	0+	0+	0+	0+	0+	005	031	132	343	366	130	14
	15	0+	0+	0+	0+	0+	0+	0+	0+	005	035	206	463	860	15

(0+ represents a positive probability less than .0005)

Source: Frederick Mosteller, Robert E. K. Rourke, and George B. Thomas, Jr., *Probability with Statistical Applications,* Second Edition. © 1970 by Addison-Wesley Publishing Company, Inc. Reprinted by permission of the publisher.

TABLE A.2   continued
Binomial Coefficients

n	$\binom{n}{0}$	$\binom{n}{1}$	$\binom{n}{2}$	$\binom{n}{3}$	$\binom{n}{4}$	$\binom{n}{5}$	$\binom{n}{6}$	$\binom{n}{7}$	$\binom{n}{8}$	$\binom{n}{9}$	$\binom{n}{10}$
0	1										
1	1	1									
2	1	2	1								
3	1	3	3	1							
4	1	4	6	4	1						
5	1	5	10	10	5	1					
6	1	6	15	20	15	6	1				
7	1	7	21	35	35	21	7	1			
8	1	8	28	56	70	56	28	8	1		
9	1	9	36	84	126	126	84	36	9	1	
10	1	10	45	120	210	252	210	120	45	10	1
11	1	11	55	165	330	462	462	330	165	55	11
12	1	12	66	220	495	792	924	792	495	220	66
13	1	13	78	286	715	1287	1716	1716	1287	715	286
14	1	14	91	364	1001	2002	3003	3432	3003	2002	1001
15	1	15	105	455	1365	3003	5005	6435	6435	5005	3003
16	1	16	120	560	1820	4368	8008	11440	12870	11440	8008
17	1	17	136	680	2380	6188	12376	19448	24310	24310	19448
18	1	18	153	816	3060	8568	18564	31824	43758	48620	43758
19	1	19	171	969	3876	11628	27132	50388	75582	92378	92378
20	1	20	190	1140	4845	15504	38760	77520	125970	167960	184756

Source: John E. Freund and Gary A. Simon, *Statistics, A First Course,* fifth ed. © 1991, p. 553. Reprinted by permission of Prentice-Hall, Inc., Englewood Cliffs, N.J.

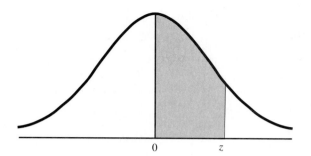

0   z

TABLE A.3   Normal Probability Distribution

z	.00	.01	.02	.03	.04	.05	.06	.07	.08	.09
.0	.0000	.0040	.0080	.0120	.0160	.0199	.0239	.0279	.0319	.0359
.1	.0398	.0438	.0478	.0517	.0557	.0596	.0636	.0675	.0714	.0753
.2	.0793	.0832	.0871	.0910	.0948	.0987	.1026	.1064	.1103	.1141
.3	.1179	.1217	.1255	.1293	.1331	.1368	.1406	.1443	.1480	.1517
.4	.1554	.1591	.1628	.1664	.1700	.1736	.1772	.1808	.1844	.1879
.5	.1915	.1950	.1985	.2019	.2054	.2088	.2123	.2157	.2190	.2224
.6	.2257	.2291	.2324	.2357	.2389	.2422	.2454	.2486	.2517	.2549
.7	.2580	.2611	.2642	.2673	.2704	.2734	.2764	.2794	.2823	.2852
.8	.2881	.2910	.2939	.2967	.2995	.3023	.3051	.3078	.3106	.3133
.9	.3159	.3186	.3212	.3238	.3264	.3289	.3315	.3340	.3365	.3389
1.0	.3413	.3438	.3461	.3485	.3508	.3531	.3554	.3577	.3599	.3621
1.1	.3643	.3665	.3686	.3708	.3729	.3749	.3370	.3790	.3810	.3830
1.2	.3849	.3869	.3888	.3907	.3925	.3944	.3962	.3980	.3997	.4015
1.3	.4032	.4049	.4066	.4082	.4099	.4115	.4131	.4147	.4162	.4177
1.4	.4192	.4207	.4222	.4326	.4251	.4265	.4279	.4292	.4306	.4319
1.5	.4332	.4345	.4357	.4370	.4382	.4394	.4406	.4418	.4429	.4441
1.6	.4452	.4463	.4474	.4484	.4495	.4505	.4515	.4525	.4535	.4545
1.7	.4554	.4564	.4573	.4582	.4591	.4599	.4608	.4616	.4625	.4633
1.8	.4641	.4649	.4656	.4664	.4671	.4678	.4686	.4693	.4699	.4706
1.9	.4713	.4719	.4726	.4732	.4738	.4744	.4750	.4756	.4761	.4767
2.0	.4772	.4778	.4783	.4788	.4793	.4798	.4803	.4808	.4812	.4817
2.1	.4821	.4826	.4830	.4834	.4838	.4842	.4846	.4850	.4854	.4857
2.2	.4861	.4864	.4868	.4871	.4875	.4878	.4881	.4884	.4887	.4890
2.3	.4893	.4896	.4898	.4901	.4904	.4906	.4909	.4911	.4913	.4916
2.4	.4918	.4920	.4922	.4925	.4927	.4929	.4931	.4932	.4934	.4936
2.5	.4938	.4940	.4941	.4943	.4945	.4946	.4948	.4949	.4951	.4952
2.6	.4953	.4955	.4956	.4957	.4959	.4960	.4961	.4962	.4963	.4964
2.7	.4965	.4966	.4967	.4968	.4969	.4970	.4971	.4972	.4973	.4974
2.8	.4974	.4975	.4976	.4977	.4977	.4978	.4979	.4979	.4980	.4981
2.9	.4981	.4982	.4982	.4983	.4984	.4984	.4985	.4985	.4986	.4986
3.0	.4987	.4987	.4987	.4988	.4988	.4989	.4989	.4989	.4990	.4990

Notes: 1. For values of z above 3.09, use .4999 for the area.
    2. Use these common values that result from interpolation:

z score	Area
1.645	.4500
1.96	.4750
2.575	.4950

Source: Frederick Mosteller and Robert E. K. Rourke, *Sturdy Statistics* Table A-1 (Reading, Mass.: Addison-Wesley, 1973). Reprinted with permission of the author.

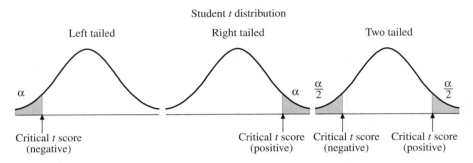

Student *t* distribution

TABLE A.4   *t* Distribution

Degrees of Freedom	α					
	.005	**.01**	**.025**	**.05**	**.10**	**.25**
1	63.657	31.821	12.706	6.314	3.078	1.000
2	9.925	6.965	4.303	2.920	1.886	.816
3	5.841	4.541	3.182	2.353	1.638	.765
4	4.604	3.747	2.776	2.132	1.533	.741
5	4.032	3.365	2.571	2.015	1.476	.727
6	3.707	3.143	2.447	1.943	1.440	.718
7	3.500	2.998	2.365	1.895	1.415	.711
8	3.355	2.896	2.306	1.860	1.397	.706
9	3.250	2.821	2.262	1.833	1.383	.703
10	3.169	2.764	2.228	1.812	1.372	.700
11	3.106	2.718	2.201	1.796	1.363	.697
12	3.054	2.681	2.179	1.782	1.356	.696
13	3.012	2.650	2.160	1.771	1.350	.694
14	2.977	2.625	2.145	1.761	1.345	.692
15	2.947	2.602	2.132	1.753	1.341	.691
16	2.921	2.584	2.120	1.746	1.337	.690
17	2.898	2.567	2.110	1.740	1.333	.689
18	2.878	2.552	2.101	1.734	1.330	.688
19	2.861	2.540	2.093	1.729	1.328	.688
20	2.845	2.528	2.086	1.725	1.325	.687
21	2.831	2.518	2.080	1.721	1.323	.686
22	2.819	2.508	2.074	1.717	1.321	.686
23	2.807	2.500	2.069	1.714	1.320	.685
24	2.797	2.492	2.064	1.711	1.318	.685
25	2.787	2.485	2.060	1.708	1.316	.684
26	2.779	2.479	2.056	1.706	1.315	.684
27	2.771	2.473	2.052	1.703	1.314	.684
28	2.763	2.467	2.048	1.701	1.313	.683
29	2.756	2.462	2.045	1.699	1.311	.683
Large (*z*)	2.575	2.327	1.960	1.645	1.282	.675

Source: Biometrika Tables for Statisticians, third ed., T12, 1966. Reproduced with permission of the Biometrika Trustees.

TABLE A.5   Chi-Square Distribution

Area to the Right of the Critical Value

Degrees of Freedom	0.995	0.99	0.975	0.95	0.90	0.10	0.05	0.025	0.01	0.005
1	—	—	.001	.004	.016	2.706	3.841	5.024	6.635	7.879
2	.010	.020	.051	.103	.211	4.605	5.991	7.378	9.210	10.597
3	.072	.115	.216	.352	.584	6.251	7.815	9.348	11.345	12.838
4	.207	.297	.484	.711	1.064	7.779	9.488	11.143	13.277	14.860
5	.412	.554	.831	1.145	1.610	9.236	11.071	12.833	15.086	16.750
6	.676	.872	1.237	1.635	2.204	10.645	12.592	14.449	16.812	18.548
7	.989	1.239	1.690	2.167	2.833	12.017	14.067	16.013	18.475	20.278
8	1.344	1.646	2.180	2.733	3.490	13.362	15.507	17.535	20.090	21.955
9	1.735	2.088	2.700	3.325	4.168	14.684	16.919	19.023	21.666	23.589
10	2.156	2.558	3.247	3.940	4.865	15.987	18.307	20.483	23.209	25.188
11	2.603	3.053	3.816	4.575	5.578	17.275	19.675	21.920	24.725	26.757
12	3.074	3.571	4.404	5.226	6.304	18.549	21.026	23.337	26.217	28.299
13	3.565	4.107	5.009	5.892	7.042	19.812	22.362	24.736	27.688	29.819
14	4.075	4.660	5.629	6.571	7.790	21.064	23.685	26.119	29.141	31.319
15	4.601	5.229	6.262	7.261	8.547	22.307	24.996	27.488	30.578	32.801
16	5.142	5.812	6.908	7.962	9.312	23.542	26.296	28.845	32.000	34.267
17	5.697	6.408	7.564	8.672	10.085	24.769	27.587	30.191	33.409	35.718
18	6.265	7.015	8.231	9.390	10.865	25.989	28.869	31.526	34.805	37.156
19	6.844	7.633	8.907	10.117	11.651	27.204	30.144	32.852	36.191	38.582
20	7.434	8.260	9.591	10.851	12.443	28.412	31.410	34.170	37.566	39.997
21	8.034	8.897	10.283	11.591	13.240	29.615	32.671	35.479	38.932	41.401
22	8.643	9.542	10.982	12.338	14.042	30.813	33.924	36.781	40.289	42.796
23	9.260	10.196	11.689	13.091	14.848	32.007	35.172	38.076	41.638	44.181
24	9.886	10.856	12.401	13.848	15.659	33.196	36.415	39.364	42.980	45.559
25	10.520	11.524	13.120	14.611	16.473	34.382	37.652	40.646	44.314	46.928
26	11.160	12.198	13.844	15.379	17.292	35.563	38.885	41.923	45.642	48.290
27	11.808	12.879	14.573	16.151	18.114	36.741	40.113	43.194	46.963	49.645
28	12.461	13.565	15.308	16.928	18.939	37.916	41.337	44.461	48.278	50.993
29	13.121	14.257	16.047	17.708	19.768	39.087	42.557	45.772	49.588	52.336
30	13.787	14.954	16.791	18.493	20.599	40.256	43.773	46.979	50.892	53.672
40	20.707	22.164	24.433	26.509	29.051	51.805	55.758	59.342	63.691	66.766
50	27.991	29.707	32.357	34.764	37.689	63.167	67.505	71.420	76.154	79.490
60	35.534	37.485	40.482	43.188	46.459	74.397	79.082	83.298	88.379	91.952
70	43.275	45.442	48.758	51.739	55.329	85.527	90.531	95.023	100.425	104.215
80	51.172	53.540	57.153	60.391	64.278	96.578	101.829	106.629	112.329	116.321
90	59.196	61.754	65.647	69.126	73.291	107.565	113.145	118.136	124.116	128.299
100	67.328	70.065	74.222	77.929	82.358	118.498	124.342	129.561	135.807	140.169

Source: Donald B. Owen, *Handbook of Statistical Tables.* © 1962 by Addison-Wesley Publishing Company, Inc. Reprinted with permission of the publisher.

TABLE A.6a   *F* **Distribution** $\alpha = .01$

<table>
<tr><th colspan="11">Numerator Degrees of Freedom</th></tr>
<tr><th rowspan="2"></th><th>df_1</th><th colspan="9"></th></tr>
<tr><th>df_2</th><th>1</th><th>2</th><th>3</th><th>4</th><th>5</th><th>6</th><th>7</th><th>8</th><th>9</th></tr>
<tr><td rowspan="30" style="writing-mode: vertical-rl">Denominator degrees of freedom</td><td>1</td><td>4052.2</td><td>4999.5</td><td>5403.4</td><td>5624.6</td><td>5763.6</td><td>5859.0</td><td>5928.4</td><td>5981.1</td><td>6022.5</td></tr>
<tr><td>2</td><td>98.503</td><td>99.000</td><td>99.166</td><td>99.249</td><td>99.299</td><td>99.333</td><td>99.356</td><td>99.374</td><td>99.388</td></tr>
<tr><td>3</td><td>34.116</td><td>30.817</td><td>29.457</td><td>28.710</td><td>28.237</td><td>27.911</td><td>27.672</td><td>27.489</td><td>27.345</td></tr>
<tr><td>4</td><td>21.198</td><td>18.000</td><td>16.694</td><td>15.977</td><td>15.522</td><td>15.207</td><td>14.976</td><td>14.799</td><td>14.659</td></tr>
<tr><td>5</td><td>16.258</td><td>13.274</td><td>12.060</td><td>11.392</td><td>10.967</td><td>10.672</td><td>10.456</td><td>10.289</td><td>10.158</td></tr>
<tr><td>6</td><td>13.745</td><td>10.925</td><td>9.7795</td><td>9.1483</td><td>8.7459</td><td>8.4661</td><td>8.2600</td><td>8.1017</td><td>7.9761</td></tr>
<tr><td>7</td><td>12.246</td><td>9.5466</td><td>8.4513</td><td>7.8466</td><td>7.4604</td><td>7.1914</td><td>6.9928</td><td>6.8400</td><td>6.7188</td></tr>
<tr><td>8</td><td>11.259</td><td>8.6491</td><td>7.5910</td><td>7.0061</td><td>6.6318</td><td>6.3707</td><td>6.1776</td><td>6.0289</td><td>5.9106</td></tr>
<tr><td>9</td><td>10.561</td><td>8.0215</td><td>6.9919</td><td>6.4221</td><td>6.0569</td><td>5.8018</td><td>5.6129</td><td>5.4671</td><td>5.3511</td></tr>
<tr><td>10</td><td>10.044</td><td>7.5594</td><td>6.5523</td><td>5.9943</td><td>5.6363</td><td>5.3858</td><td>5.2001</td><td>5.0567</td><td>4.9424</td></tr>
<tr><td>11</td><td>9.6460</td><td>7.2057</td><td>6.2167</td><td>5.6683</td><td>5.3160</td><td>5.0692</td><td>4.8861</td><td>4.7445</td><td>4.6315</td></tr>
<tr><td>12</td><td>9.3302</td><td>6.9266</td><td>5.9525</td><td>5.4120</td><td>5.0643</td><td>4.8206</td><td>4.6395</td><td>4.4994</td><td>4.3875</td></tr>
<tr><td>13</td><td>9.0738</td><td>6.7010</td><td>5.7394</td><td>5.2053</td><td>4.8616</td><td>4.6204</td><td>4.4410</td><td>4.3021</td><td>4.1911</td></tr>
<tr><td>14</td><td>8.8616</td><td>6.5149</td><td>5.5639</td><td>5.0354</td><td>4.6950</td><td>4.4558</td><td>4.2779</td><td>4.1399</td><td>4.0297</td></tr>
<tr><td>15</td><td>8.6831</td><td>6.3589</td><td>5.4170</td><td>4.8932</td><td>4.5556</td><td>4.3183</td><td>4.1415</td><td>4.0045</td><td>3.8948</td></tr>
<tr><td>16</td><td>8.5310</td><td>6.2262</td><td>5.2922</td><td>4.7726</td><td>4.4374</td><td>4.2016</td><td>4.0259</td><td>3.8896</td><td>3.7804</td></tr>
<tr><td>17</td><td>8.3997</td><td>6.1121</td><td>5.1850</td><td>4.6690</td><td>4.3359</td><td>4.1015</td><td>3.9267</td><td>3.7910</td><td>3.6822</td></tr>
<tr><td>18</td><td>8.2854</td><td>6.0129</td><td>5.0919</td><td>4.5790</td><td>4.2479</td><td>4.0146</td><td>3.8406</td><td>3.7054</td><td>3.5971</td></tr>
<tr><td>19</td><td>8.1849</td><td>5.9259</td><td>5.0103</td><td>4.5003</td><td>4.1708</td><td>3.9386</td><td>3.7653</td><td>3.6305</td><td>3.5225</td></tr>
<tr><td>20</td><td>8.0960</td><td>5.8489</td><td>4.9382</td><td>4.4307</td><td>4.1027</td><td>3.8714</td><td>3.6987</td><td>3.5644</td><td>3.4567</td></tr>
<tr><td>21</td><td>8.0166</td><td>5.7804</td><td>4.8740</td><td>4.3688</td><td>4.0421</td><td>3.8117</td><td>3.6396</td><td>3.5056</td><td>3.3981</td></tr>
<tr><td>22</td><td>7.9454</td><td>5.7190</td><td>4.8166</td><td>4.3134</td><td>3.9880</td><td>3.7583</td><td>3.5867</td><td>3.4530</td><td>3.3458</td></tr>
<tr><td>23</td><td>7.8811</td><td>5.6637</td><td>4.7649</td><td>4.2636</td><td>3.9392</td><td>3.7102</td><td>3.5390</td><td>3.4057</td><td>3.2986</td></tr>
<tr><td>24</td><td>7.8229</td><td>5.6136</td><td>4.7181</td><td>4.2184</td><td>3.8951</td><td>3.6667</td><td>3.4959</td><td>3.3629</td><td>3.2560</td></tr>
<tr><td>25</td><td>7.7698</td><td>5.5680</td><td>4.6755</td><td>4.1774</td><td>3.8550</td><td>3.6272</td><td>3.4568</td><td>3.3239</td><td>3.2172</td></tr>
<tr><td>26</td><td>7.7213</td><td>5.5263</td><td>4.6366</td><td>4.1400</td><td>3.8183</td><td>3.5911</td><td>3.4210</td><td>3.2884</td><td>3.1818</td></tr>
<tr><td>27</td><td>7.6767</td><td>5.4881</td><td>4.6009</td><td>4.1056</td><td>3.7848</td><td>3.5580</td><td>3.3882</td><td>3.2558</td><td>3.1494</td></tr>
<tr><td>28</td><td>7.6356</td><td>5.4529</td><td>4.5681</td><td>4.0740</td><td>3.7539</td><td>3.5276</td><td>3.3581</td><td>3.2259</td><td>3.1195</td></tr>
<tr><td>29</td><td>7.5977</td><td>5.4204</td><td>4.5378</td><td>4.0449</td><td>3.7254</td><td>3.4995</td><td>3.3303</td><td>3.1982</td><td>3.0920</td></tr>
<tr><td>30</td><td>7.5625</td><td>5.3903</td><td>4.5097</td><td>4.0179</td><td>3.6990</td><td>3.4735</td><td>3.3045</td><td>3.1726</td><td>3.0665</td></tr>
<tr><td>40</td><td>7.3141</td><td>5.1785</td><td>4.3126</td><td>3.8283</td><td>3.5138</td><td>3.2910</td><td>3.1238</td><td>2.9930</td><td>2.8876</td></tr>
<tr><td>60</td><td>7.0711</td><td>4.9774</td><td>4.1259</td><td>3.6490</td><td>3.3389</td><td>3.1187</td><td>2.9530</td><td>2.8233</td><td>2.7185</td></tr>
<tr><td>120</td><td>6.8509</td><td>4.7865</td><td>3.9491</td><td>3.4795</td><td>3.1735</td><td>2.9559</td><td>2.7918</td><td>2.6629</td><td>2.5586</td></tr>
<tr><td>∞</td><td>6.6349</td><td>4.6052</td><td>3.7816</td><td>3.3192</td><td>3.0173</td><td>2.8020</td><td>2.6393</td><td>2.5113</td><td>2.4073</td></tr>
</table>

Source: Biometrika Tables for Statisticians, third ed., vol. 1, T18, 1966. Reproduced with permission of the Biometrika Trustees.

	Numerator Degrees of Freedom									
df_1 df_2	**10**	**12**	**15**	**20**	**24**	**30**	**40**	**60**	**120**	**∞**
1	6055.8	6106.3	6157.3	6208.7	6234.6	6260.6	6286.8	6313.0	6339.4	6365.9
2	99.399	99.416	99.433	99.449	99.458	99.466	99.474	99.482	99.491	99.499
3	27.229	27.052	26.872	26.690	26.598	26.505	26.411	26.316	26.221	26.125
4	14.546	14.374	14.198	14.020	13.929	13.838	13.745	13.652	13.558	13.463
5	10.051	9.8883	9.7222	9.5526	9.4665	9.3793	9.2912	9.2020	9.1118	9.0204
6	7.8741	7.7183	7.5590	7.3958	7.3127	7.2285	7.1432	7.0567	6.9690	6.8800
7	6.6201	6.4691	6.3143	6.1554	6.0743	5.9920	5.9084	5.8236	5.7373	5.6495
8	5.8143	5.6667	5.5151	5.3591	5.2793	5.1981	5.1156	5.0316	4.9461	4.8588
9	5.2565	5.1114	4.9621	4.8080	4.7290	4.6486	4.5666	4.4831	4.3978	4.3105
10	4.8491	4.7059	4.5581	4.4054	4.3269	4.2469	4.1653	4.0819	3.9965	3.9090
11	4.5393	4.3974	4.2509	4.0990	4.0209	3.9411	3.8596	3.7761	3.6904	3.6024
12	4.2961	4.1553	4.0096	3.8584	3.7805	3.7008	3.6192	3.5355	3.4494	3.3608
13	4.1003	4.9603	3.8154	3.6646	3.5868	3.5070	3.4253	3.3413	3.2548	3.6154
14	3.9394	3.8001	3.6557	3.5052	3.4274	3.3476	3.2656	3.1813	3.0942	3.0040
15	3.8049	3.6662	3.5222	3.3719	3.2940	3.2141	3.1319	3.0471	2.9595	2.8684
16	3.6909	3.5527	3.4089	3.2587	3.1808	3.1007	3.0182	2.9330	2.8447	2.7528
17	3.5931	3.4552	3.3117	3.1615	3.0835	3.0032	2.9205	2.8348	2.7459	2.6530
18	3.5082	3.3706	3.2273	3.0771	2.9990	2.9185	2.8354	2.7493	2.6597	2.5660
19	3.4338	3.2965	3.1533	3.0031	2.9249	2.8442	2.7608	2.6742	2.5839	2.4893
20	3.3682	3.2311	3.0880	2.9377	2.8594	2.7785	2.6947	2.6077	2.5168	2.4212
21	3.3098	3.1730	3.0300	2.8796	2.8010	2.7200	2.6359	2.5484	2.4568	2.3603
22	3.2576	3.1209	2.9779	2.8274	2.7488	2.6675	2.5831	2.4951	2.4029	2.3055
23	3.2106	3.0740	2.9311	2.7805	2.7017	2.6202	2.5355	2.4471	2.3542	2.2558
24	3.1681	3.0316	2.8887	2.7380	2.6591	2.5773	2.4923	2.4035	2.3100	2.2107
25	3.1294	2.9931	2.8502	2.6993	2.6203	2.5383	2.4530	2.3637	2.2696	2.1694
26	3.0941	2.9578	2.8150	2.6640	2.5848	2.5026	2.4170	2.3273	2.2325	2.1315
27	3.0618	2.9256	2.7827	2.6316	2.5522	2.4699	2.3840	2.2938	2.1985	2.0965
28	3.0320	2.8959	2.7530	2.6017	2.5223	2.4397	2.3535	2.2629	2.1670	2.0642
29	3.0045	2.8685	2.7256	2.5742	2.4946	2.4118	2.3253	2.2344	2.1379	2.0342
30	2.9791	2.8431	2.7002	2.5487	2.4689	2.3860	2.2992	2.2079	2.1108	2.0062
40	2.8005	2.6648	2.5216	2.3689	2.2880	2.2034	2.1142	2.0194	1.9172	1.8047
60	2.6318	2.4961	2.3523	2.1978	2.1154	2.0285	1.9360	1.8363	1.7263	1.6006
120	2.4721	2.3363	2.1915	2.0346	1.9500	1.8600	1.7628	1.6557	1.5330	1.3805
∞	2.3209	2.1847	2.0385	1.8783	1.7908	1.6964	1.5923	1.4730	1.3246	1.0000

Denominator degrees of freedom

TABLE A.6b *F* Distribution α = .025

					Numerator Degrees of Freedom				
df₂ \ df₁	**1**	**2**	**3**	**4**	**5**	**6**	**7**	**8**	**9**
1	647.79	799.50	864.16	899.58	921.85	937.118	948.22	956.55	963.28
2	38.506	39.000	39.165	39.248	39.298	39.331	39.335	39.373	39.387
3	17.443	16.044	15.439	15.101	14.885	14.735	14.624	14.540	14.473
4	12.218	10.649	9.9792	9.6045	9.3645	9.1973	9.0741	8.9796	8.9047
5	10.007	8.4336	7.7636	7.3879	7.1464	6.9777	6.8531	6.7572	6.6811
6	8.8131	7.2599	6.5988	6.2272	5.9876	5.8198	5.6955	5.5996	5.5234
7	8.0727	6.5415	5.8898	5.5226	5.2852	5.1186	4.9949	4.8993	4.8232
8	7.5709	6.0595	5.4160	5.0526	4.8173	4.6517	4.5286	4.4333	4.3572
9	7.2093	5.7147	5.0781	4.7181	4.4844	4.3197	4.1970	4.1020	4.0260
10	6.9367	5.4564	4.8256	4.4683	4.2361	4.0721	3.9498	3.8549	3.7790
11	6.7241	5.2559	4.6300	4.2751	4.0440	3.8807	3.7586	3.6638	3.5879
12	6.5538	5.0959	4.4742	4.1212	3.8911	3.7283	3.6065	3.5118	3.4358
13	6.4143	4.9653	4.3472	3.9959	3.7667	3.6043	3.4827	3.3880	3.3120
14	6.2979	4.8567	4.2417	3.8919	3.6634	3.5014	3.3799	3.2853	3.2093
15	6.1995	4.7650	4.1528	3.8043	3.5764	3.4147	3.2934	3.1987	3.1227
16	6.1151	4.6867	4.0768	3.7294	3.5021	3.3406	3.2194	3.1248	3.0488
17	6.0420	4.6189	4.0112	3.6648	3.4379	3.2767	3.1556	3.0610	2.9849
18	5.9781	4.5597	3.9539	3.6083	3.3820	3.2209	3.0999	3.0053	2.9291
19	5.9216	4.5075	3.9034	3.5587	3.3327	3.1718	3.0509	2.9563	2.8801
20	5.8715	4.4613	3.8587	3.5147	3.2891	3.1283	3.0074	2.9128	2.8365
21	5.8266	4.4199	3.8188	3.4754	3.2501	3.0895	2.9686	2.8740	2.7977
22	5.7863	4.3828	3.7829	3.4401	3.2151	3.0546	2.9338	2.8392	2.7628
23	5.7498	4.3492	3.7505	3.4083	3.1835	3.0232	2.9023	2.8077	2.7313
24	5.7166	4.3187	3.7211	3.3794	3.1548	2.9946	2.8738	2.7791	2.7027
25	5.6864	4.2909	3.6943	3.3530	3.1287	2.9685	2.8478	2.7531	2.6766
26	5.6586	4.2655	3.6697	3.3289	3.1048	2.9447	2.8240	2.7293	2.6528
27	5.6331	4.2421	3.6472	3.3067	3.0828	2.9228	2.8021	2.7074	2.6309
28	5.6096	4.2205	3.6264	3.2863	3.0626	2.9027	2.7820	2.6872	2.6106
29	5.5878	4.2006	3.6072	3.2674	3.0438	2.8840	2.7633	2.6686	2.5919
30	5.5675	4.1821	3.5894	3.2499	3.0265	2.8667	2.7460	2.6513	2.5746
40	5.4239	4.0510	3.4633	3.1261	2.9037	2.7444	2.6238	2.5289	2.4519
60	5.2856	3.9253	3.3425	3.0077	2.7863	2.6274	2.5068	2.4117	2.3344
120	5.1523	3.8046	3.2269	2.8943	2.6740	2.5154	2.3948	2.2994	2.2217
∞	5.0239	3.6889	3.1161	2.7858	2.5665	2.4082	2.2875	2.1918	2.1136

Denominator degrees of freedom

	Numerator Degrees of Freedom									
df_2 \ df_1	**10**	**12**	**15**	**20**	**24**	**30**	**40**	**60**	**120**	**∞**
1	968.63	976.71	984.87	993.10	997.25	1001.4	1005.6	1009.8	1014.0	1018.3
2	39.398	39.415	39.431	39.448	39.456	39.465	39.473	39.481	39.490	39.498
3	14.419	14.337	14.253	14.167	14.124	14.081	14.037	13.992	13.947	13.902
4	8.8439	8.7512	8.6565	8.5599	8.5109	8.4613	8.4111	8.3604	8.3092	8.2573
5	6.6192	6.5245	6.4277	6.3286	6.2780	6.2269	6.1750	6.1225	6.0693	6.0153
6	5.4613	5.3662	5.2687	5.1684	5.1172	5.0652	5.0125	4.9589	4.9044	4.8491
7	4.7611	4.6658	4.5678	4.4667	4.4150	4.3624	4.3089	4.2544	4.1989	4.1423
8	4.2951	4.1997	4.1012	3.9995	3.9472	3.8940	3.8398	3.7844	3.7279	3.6702
9	3.9639	3.8682	3.7694	3.6669	3.6142	3.5604	3.5055	3.4493	3.3918	3.3329
10	3.7168	3.6209	3.5217	3.4185	3.3654	3.3110	3.2554	3.1984	3.1399	3.0798
11	3.5257	3.4296	3.3299	3.2261	3.1725	3.1176	3.0613	3.0035	2.9441	2.8828
12	3.3736	3.2773	3.1772	3.0728	3.0187	2.9633	2.9063	2.8478	2.7874	2.7249
13	3.2497	3.1532	3.0527	2.9477	2.8932	2.8372	2.7797	2.7204	2.6590	2.5955
14	3.1469	3.0502	2.9493	2.8437	2.7888	2.7324	2.6742	2.6142	2.5519	2.4872
15	3.0602	2.9633	2.8621	2.7599	2.7066	2.6437	2.5850	2.5242	2.4611	2.3953
16	2.9862	2.8890	2.7875	2.6808	2.6252	2.5678	2.5085	2.4471	2.3831	2.3163
17	2.9222	2.8249	2.7230	2.6158	2.5598	2.5020	2.4422	2.3801	2.3153	2.2474
18	2.8664	2.7689	2.6667	2.5590	2.5027	2.4445	2.3842	2.3214	2.2558	2.1869
19	2.8172	2.7196	2.6171	2.5089	2.4523	2.3937	2.3329	2.2696	2.2032	2.1333
20	2.7737	2.6758	2.5731	2.4645	2.4076	2.3486	2.2873	2.2234	2.1562	2.0853
21	2.7348	3.6368	2.5338	3.4247	2.3675	2.3082	2.2465	2.1819	2.1141	2.0422
22	2.6998	2.6017	2.4984	2.3890	2.3315	2.2718	2.2097	2.1446	2.0760	2.0032
23	2.6682	2.5699	2.4665	2.3567	2.2989	2.2389	2.1763	2.1107	2.0415	1.9677
24	2.6396	2.5411	2.4374	2.3273	2.2693	2.2090	2.1460	2.0799	2.0099	1.9353
25	2.6135	2.5149	2.4110	2.3005	2.2422	2.1816	2.1183	2.0516	1.9811	1.9055
26	2.5896	2.4908	2.3867	2.2759	2.2174	2.1565	2.0928	2.0257	1.9545	1.8781
27	2.5676	2.4688	2.3644	2.2533	2.1946	2.1334	2.0693	2.0018	1.9299	1.8527
28	2.5473	2.4484	2.3438	2.2324	2.1735	2.1121	2.0477	1.9797	1.9072	1.8291
29	2.5286	2.4295	2.3248	2.2131	2.1540	2.0923	2.0276	1.9591	1.8861	1.8072
30	2.5112	2.4120	2.3072	2.1952	2.1359	2.0739	2.0089	1.9400	1.8664	1.7867
40	2.3882	2.2882	2.1819	2.0677	2.0069	1.9429	1.8752	1.8028	1.7242	1.6371
60	2.2702	2.1692	2.0613	1.9445	1.8817	1.8152	1.7440	1.6668	1.5810	1.4821
120	2.1570	2.0548	1.9450	1.8249	1.7597	1.6899	1.6141	1.5299	1.4327	1.3104
∞	2.0483	1.9447	1.8326	1.7085	1.6402	1.5660	1.4835	1.3883	1.2684	1.0000

Denominator degrees of freedom

TABLE A.6c   *F* **Distribution** $\alpha = .05$

	df$_1$	1	2	3	4	5	6	7	8	9
	df$_2$									
	1	161.45	199.50	215.71	224.58	230.16	233.99	236.77	238.88	240.54
	2	18.513	19.000	19.164	19.247	19.296	19.330	19.353	19.371	19.385
	3	10.128	9.5521	9.2766	9.1172	9.0135	8.9406	8.8867	8.8452	8.8123
	4	7.7086	9.9443	6.5914	6.3882	6.2561	6.1631	6.0942	6.0410	6.9988
	5	6.6079	5.7861	5.4095	5.1922	5.0503	4.9503	4.8759	4.8183	4.7725
	6	5.9874	5.1433	4.7571	4.5337	4.3874	4.2839	4.2067	4.1468	4.0990
	7	5.5914	4.7374	4.3468	4.1203	3.9715	3.8660	3.7870	3.7257	3.6767
	8	5.3177	4.4590	4.0662	3.8379	3.6875	3.5806	3.5005	3.4381	3.3881
	9	5.1174	4.2565	3.8625	3.6331	3.4817	3.3738	3.2927	3.2296	3.1789
	10	4.9646	4.1028	3.7083	3.4780	3.3258	3.2172	3.1355	3.0717	3.0204
	11	4.8443	3.9823	3.5874	3.3567	3.2039	3.0946	3.0123	2.9480	2.8962
	12	4.7472	3.8853	3.4903	3.2592	3.1059	2.9961	2.9134	2.8486	2.7964
	13	4.6672	3.8056	3.4105	3.1791	3.0254	2.9153	2.8321	2.7669	2.7144
	14	4.6001	3.7389	3.3439	3.1122	2.9582	2.8477	2.7642	2.6987	2.6458
	15	4.5431	3.6823	3.2874	3.0556	2.9013	2.7905	2.7066	2.6408	2.5876
	16	4.4940	3.6337	3.2389	3.0069	2.8524	2.7413	2.6572	2.5911	2.5377
	17	4.4513	3.5915	3.1968	2.9647	2.8100	2.6987	2.6143	2.5480	2.4943
	18	4.4139	3.5546	3.1599	2.9277	2.7729	2.6613	2.5767	2.5102	2.4563
	19	4.3807	3.5219	3.1274	2.8951	2.7401	2.6283	2.5435	2.4768	2.4227
	20	4.3512	3.4928	3.0984	2.8661	2.7109	2.5990	2.5140	2.4471	2.3928
	21	4.3248	3.4668	3.0725	2.8401	2.6848	2.5727	2.4876	2.4205	2.3660
	22	4.3009	3.4434	3.0491	2.8167	2.6613	2.5491	2.4638	2.3965	2.3419
	23	4.2793	3.4221	3.0280	2.7955	2.6400	2.5277	2.4422	2.3748	2.3201
	24	4.2597	3.4028	3.0088	2.7763	2.6207	2.5082	2.4226	2.3551	2.3002
	25	4.2417	3.3852	2.9912	2.7587	2.6030	2.4904	2.4047	2.3371	2.2821
	26	4.2252	3.3690	2.9752	2.7426	2.5868	2.4741	2.3883	2.3205	2.2655
	27	4.2100	3.3541	2.9604	2.7278	2.5719	2.4591	2.3732	2.3053	2.2501
	28	4.1960	3.3404	2.9467	2.7141	2.5581	2.4453	2.3593	2.2913	2.2360
	29	4.1830	3.3277	2.9340	2.7014	2.5454	2.4324	2.3463	2.2783	2.2229
	30	4.1709	3.3158	2.9223	2.6896	2.5336	2.4205	2.3343	2.2662	2.2107
	40	4.0847	3.2317	2.8387	2.6060	2.4495	2.3359	2.2490	2.1802	2.1240
	60	4.0012	3.1504	2.7581	2.5252	2.3683	2.2541	2.1665	2.0970	2.0401
	120	3.9201	3.0718	2.6802	2.4472	2.2899	2.1750	2.0868	2.0164	1.9588
	∞	3.8415	2.9957	2.6049	2.3719	2.2141	2.0986	2.0096	1.9384	1.8799

Numerator Degrees of Freedom

Denominator degrees of freedom

	df₁				**Numerator Degrees of Freedom**						
df₂		**10**	**12**	**15**	**20**	**24**	**30**	**40**	**60**	**120**	**∞**
	1	241.88	243.91	245.95	248.01	249.05	250.10	251.14	252.20	253.25	254.31
	2	19.396	19.413	19.429	19.446	19.454	19.462	19.471	19.479	19.487	19.496
	3	8.7855	8.7446	8.7029	8.6602	8.6385	8.6166	8.5944	8.5720	8.5494	8.5264
	4	5.9644	5.9117	5.8578	5.8025	5.7744	5.7459	5.7170	5.6877	5.6581	5.6281
	5	4.7351	4.6777	4.6188	4.5581	4.5272	4.4957	4.4638	4.4314	4.3985	4.3650
	6	4.0600	3.9999	3.9381	3.8742	3.8415	3.8082	3.7743	3.7398	3.7047	3.6689
	7	3.6365	3.5747	3.5107	3.4445	3.4105	3.3758	3.3404	3.3043	3.2674	3.2298
	8	3.3472	3.2839	3.2184	3.1503	3.1152	3.0794	3.0428	3.0053	2.9669	2.9276
	9	3.1373	3.0729	3.0061	2.9365	2.9005	2.8637	2.8259	2.7872	2.7475	2.7067
	10	2.9782	2.9130	2.8450	2.7740	2.7372	2.6996	2.6609	2.6211	2.5801	2.5379
	11	2.8536	2.7876	2.7186	2.6464	2.6090	2.5705	2.5309	2.4901	2.4480	2.4045
	12	2.7534	2.6866	2.6169	2.5436	2.5055	2.4663	2.4259	2.3842	2.3410	2.2962
	13	2.6710	2.6037	2.5331	2.4589	2.4202	2.3803	2.3392	2.2966	2.2524	2.2064
	14	2.6022	2.5342	2.4630	2.3879	2.3487	2.3082	2.2664	2.2229	2.1778	2.1307
	15	2.5437	2.4753	2.4034	2.3275	2.2878	2.2468	2.2043	2.1601	2.1141	2.0658
	16	2.4935	2.4247	2.3522	2.2756	2.2354	2.1938	2.1507	2.1058	2.0589	2.0096
	17	2.4499	2.3807	2.3077	2.2304	2.1898	2.1477	2.1040	2.0584	2.0107	1.9604
	18	2.4117	2.3421	2.2686	2.1906	2.1497	2.1071	2.0629	2.0166	1.9681	1.9168
	19	2.3779	2.3080	2.2341	2.1555	2.1141	2.0712	2.0264	1.9795	1.9302	1.8780
	20	2.3479	2.2776	2.2033	2.1242	2.0825	2.0391	1.9938	1.9464	1.8963	1.8432
	21	2.3210	2.2504	2.1757	2.0960	2.0540	2.0102	1.9645	1.9165	1.8657	1.8117
	22	2.2967	2.2258	2.1508	2.0707	2.0283	1.9842	1.9380	1.8894	1.8380	1.7831
	23	2.2747	2.2036	2.1282	2.0476	2.0050	1.9605	1.9139	1.8648	1.8128	1.7570
	24	2.2547	2.1834	2.1077	2.0267	1.9838	1.9390	1.8920	1.8424	1.7896	1.7330
	25	2.2365	2.1649	2.0889	2.0075	1.9643	1.9192	1.8718	1.8217	1.7684	1.7110
	26	2.2197	2.1479	2.0716	1.9898	1.9464	1.9010	1.8533	1.8027	1.7488	1.6906
	27	2.2043	2.1323	2.0558	1.9736	1.9299	1.8842	1.8361	1.7851	1.7306	1.6717
	28	2.1900	2.1179	2.0411	1.9586	1.9147	1.8687	1.8203	1.7689	1.7138	1.6541
	29	2.1768	2.1045	2.0275	1.9446	1.9005	1.8543	1.8055	1.7537	1.6981	1.6376
	30	2.1646	2.0921	2.0148	1.9317	1.8874	1.8409	1.7918	1.7396	1.6835	1.6223
	40	2.0772	2.0035	1.9245	1.8389	1.7929	1.7444	1.6928	1.6373	1.5766	1.5089
	60	1.9926	1.9174	1.8364	1.7480	1.7001	1.6491	1.5943	1.5343	1.4673	1.3893
	120	1.9105	1.8337	1.7505	1.6587	1.6084	1.5543	1.4952	1.4290	1.3519	1.2539
	∞	1.8307	1.7522	1.6664	1.5705	1.5173	1.4591	1.3940	1.3180	1.2214	1.0000

Denominator degrees of freedom

TABLE A.7   Random Digits

997	828	347	853	635	454	793	759	522	001	119	632	671	062	248	391	317	515
726	606	098	005	339	335	212	666	821	415	754	418	622	531	704	884	929	938
832	144	540	450	459	589	490	676	682	393	552	474	284	593	132	372	598	949
861	734	164	032	199	071	154	704	835	588	651	225	968	371	616	097	373	432
530	841	450	203	068	071	126	485	092	312	939	274	482	045	152	256	624	950
067	679	461	169	303	361	205	549	914	099	627	747	575	081	169	761	615	228
884	889	983	374	000	974	589	872	302	704	394	595	552	954	314	292	175	467
370	049	952	462	151	591	795	263	075	485	151	129	902	082	825	416	228	201
326	435	295	510	958	190	682	311	954	995	149	074	467	042	351	135	741	729
924	122	665	912	769	906	494	031	152	191	213	441	482	157	868	878	699	755
087	135	052	217	041	927	412	292	042	205	203	805	569	049	070	933	300	455
473	037	788	957	595	720	717	920	371	925	879	954	041	465	521	629	028	682
482	228	523	370	229	798	857	834	671	015	974	913	722	002	917	043	395	552
947	047	372	219	391	201	685	858	518	191	619	412	905	673	126	196	561	595
748	545	252	247	196	191	136	724	916	967	312	718	517	313	618	314	485	212
712	299	238	432	058	700	011	129	927	842	634	495	671	221	117	246	746	627
727	707	816	200	583	212	051	701	111	383	850	075	279	954	458	909	824	444
990	005	049	217	379	190	209	290	041	314	132	302	107	632	785	458	367	912
932	231	413	140	092	910	792	612	179	139	130	721	242	257	859	021	839	987
432	234	198	808	629	941	421	202	024	468	861	816	594	519	725	332	699	925
637	427	814	224	502	779	007	293	198	147	992	461	633	338	353	196	782	956
565	012	337	273	372	610	137	478	169	187	413	309	335	574	609	780	484	598
558	151	890	911	872	829	496	211	598	529	952	367	786	298	290	018	697	993
105	612	354	438	321	818	976	027	195	144	798	288	210	022	787	638	062	809
916	423	524	533	582	696	387	373	481	909	899	752	754	608	332	594	598	301
291	413	491	915	299	923	129	928	783	807	482	013	034	202	139	780	387	926
743	529	063	318	383	847	476	136	924	998	967	673	778	514	942	289	987	436
389	873	083	920	387	198	734	878	478	308	657	651	704	756	876	517	494	574
509	817	409	196	988	758	617	461	546	509	617	408	746	583	498	754	645	766
774	562	327	849	282	101	874	865	537	478	670	987	873	821	212	308	729	746
074	563	488	598	782	932	876	530	859	656	709	844	546	745	684	371	918	968
650	949	786	184	572	641	876	571	014	701	264	564	746	815	176	426	842	874
319	912	314	310	010	439	020	290	158	922	946	919	549	456	440	019	837	843
018	347	837	465	465	895	656	861	487	587	785	376	665	695	753	431	819	239
104	293	629	043	120	150	151	032	510	511	766	264	919	401	017	401	470	917
409	874	785	076	456	677	634	565	476	187	553	854	289	432	979	389	697	929
086	348	997	592	784	078	757	239	363	043	925	321	356	789	485	084	356	764
585	671	745	086	435	238	585	686	140	597	672	277	765	922	345	133	966	377
544	329	500	740	536	409	504	832	232	165	295	896	761	164	549	989	320	208
186	816	889	093	193	225	285	576	296	269	062	686	652	263	276	928	525	588
599	872	448	935	841	122	094	747	399	374	399	265	460	408	009	302	218	602
992	986	234	337	273	654	332	196	732	011	575	653	302	320	098	074	349	364
947	467	382	456	654	187	390	184	473	298	398	756	209	498	567	093	865	485
335	389	245	665	559	123	875	349	956	225	316	958	846	993	828	847	928	748
395	549	498	986	582	467	763	189	928	373	847	874	917	476	545	434	563	243
873	976	549	034	324	168	787	908	234	440	856	642	315	921	870	974	331	843
476	535	410	587	450	987	485	750	914	545	258	356	194	565	443	023	487	076

TABLE A.8 Hypothesis Testing Formulas

Population Parameter	H_0	H_1	Conditions	Formula	Degrees of Freedom
One population Mean, μ	$\mu = 0$ $\mu \leq 0$ $\mu \geq 0$	$\mu \neq 0$ $\mu > 0$ $\mu < 0$	Normal distribution Large sample, $n > 30$ σ known	$z = \dfrac{\bar{x} - \mu}{\sigma/\sqrt{n}}$	None
One population mean, μ	$\mu = 0$ $\mu \leq 0$ $\mu \geq 0$	$\mu \neq 0$ $\mu > 0$ $\mu < 0$	Normal distribution Small sample, $n \leq 30$ σ unknown	$t = \dfrac{\bar{x} - \mu}{s/\sqrt{n}}$	$n - 1$
Two population means, μ	$\mu_1 - \mu_2 = 0$ $\mu_1 - \mu_2 \leq 0$ $\mu_1 - \mu_2 \geq 0$	$\mu_1 - \mu_2 \neq 0$ $\mu_1 - \mu_2 > 0$ $\mu_1 - \mu_2 < 0$	Normal distribution Large samples, $n > 30$ Independent σ_1 and σ_2 known	$z = \dfrac{(\bar{x}_1 - \bar{x}_2) - (\mu_1 - \mu_2)}{\sqrt{\sigma_1^2/n_1 + \sigma_2^2/n_2}}$	None
Two population means, μ	$\mu_1 - \mu_2 = 0$ $\mu_1 - \mu_2 \leq 0$ $\mu_1 - \mu_2 \geq 0$	$\mu_1 - \mu_2 \neq 0$ $\mu_1 - \mu_2 > 0$ $\mu_1 - \mu_2 < 0$	Normal distribution Small samples, $n \leq 30$ Independent σ_1 and σ_2 unknown Assumed $\sigma_1 = \sigma_2$	$t = \dfrac{(\bar{x}_1 - \bar{x}_2) - (\mu_1 - \mu_2)}{\sqrt{\dfrac{(n_1 - 1)s_1^2 + (n_2 - 1)s_2^2}{n_1 + n_2 - 2}}\sqrt{\dfrac{1}{n_1} + \dfrac{1}{n_2}}}$	$n_1 + n_2 - 2$
Two population means, μ_d	$\mu_d = 0$ $\mu_d \leq 0$ $\mu_d \geq 0$	$\mu_d \neq 0$ $\mu_d > 0$ $\mu_d < 0$	Dependent samples Paired observations	$t = \dfrac{\bar{d} - \mu_d}{s_d/\sqrt{n}}$	$n - 1$
One population variance or standard deviation, σ^2 or σ	$\sigma^2 = 0$ $\sigma^2 \leq 0$ $\sigma^2 \geq 0$	$\sigma^2 \neq 0$ $\sigma^2 > 0$ $\sigma^2 < 0$	Variance or standard deviation	$\chi^2 = \dfrac{(n - 1)s^2}{\sigma^2}$	$n - 1$
Two population variances or standard deviations	$\sigma_1^2 = \sigma_2^2$ $\sigma_1^2 \leq \sigma_2^2$ $\sigma_1^2 \geq \sigma_2^2$	$\sigma_1^2 \neq \sigma_2^2$ $\sigma_1^2 > \sigma_2^2$ $\sigma_1^2 < \sigma_2^2$	Variance or standard deviation, σ^2 or σ	$F = \dfrac{s_1^2}{s_2^2}$	$\mathrm{df}_n = n_n - 1$ $\mathrm{df}_d = n_d - 1$

Appendix B
Dictionary
and Formulas

Addition theorem for two events: Adding the elements in A to those in B and subtracting the overlap so the elements are counted only once. The addition theorem for two events is $P(A \cup B) = P(A) + P(B) - P(A \cap B)$.

Alternative hypothesis: A statement that the value of the population parameter is different from that specified by the null hypothesis. It carries the burden of proof. It is denoted by H_1 or H_a.

Analysis of variance (ANOVA): A method of testing three or more means that focuses on analyzing the variance within and across the samples.

Source	Sum of the Squares (SS)	Degrees of Freedom	Mean Square	F
Between	$SSb = \Sigma \left(\dfrac{c^2}{n} \right) - \dfrac{(\Sigma x)^2}{n}$	$k - 1$	SS/df	$\dfrac{MS_B}{MS_w}$
Within	$SSw = \Sigma x^2 - \Sigma \left(\dfrac{c^2}{n} \right)$	$N - k$	SS/df	
Error	$SSt = \Sigma x^2 - (\Sigma x)^2/n$	$N - 1$		

Bar chart: A graph that displays discrete and continuous data for any level of measurement.

Binomial probability distribution: A distribution of a discrete random variable that has only two possible outcomes. The chance of one thing happening is often asked. By dividing the outcomes in only two categories, a binomial distribution usually results. For example a two-group classification of Catholic or non-Catholic represents a binomial random variable.

$$P(x) = \binom{n}{x} p^x q^{n-x}$$

Bivariate analysis: A technique for describing the relationship between two variables.

Branches: Each ordered pair of a sample space illustrated in a tree diagram represents a branch of the tree. Each branch can be numbered.

Cells: The outcomes of a variable are overlapped with the outcomes of another variable. The overlaps are referred to as cells.

Central limit theorem: Applied to sampling distributions approaching the normal distribution, where the mean of the sample means equals the population mean, and the standard deviation of the sample means is the standard error.

Chi-square distribution, χ^2: A distribution representing variances of one population. Chi is a Greek letter written as χ and pronounced as ki in kite. The square represents the square of the variance, is skewed to the right, and contains only nonnegative values: $\chi^2 = \dfrac{(n-1)s^2}{\sigma^2}$.

Cluster sampling: A technique that limits sampling to a few subsets of the population considered to be representative of the population.

Complementary sets: The complementary set of set A is the set of all elements in the universal set that are not in set A. The complementary set of A is denoted by A' or $\overline{A}$.

Conditional probability: The probability of the second event is dependent on the conditions of the first event: $P(A|B) = P(A \cap B)/P(B)$.

Confidence interval: A technique for estimating a population parameter from sample statistics given a specified level of confidence.

Contingency table: Also known as a crosstabulation, or crosstab; a table that represents the relationships of two variables and their events. The outcomes of a variable are overlapped with the outcomes of another variable. The overlaps are referred to as cells.

Continuous random variable: A variable that describes a measurement. It can take on an infinite number of values. When describing intervals, there is an infinite number of possible values that a continuous random variable can take on in the interval. It often describes a measurement between two designated points.

Critical value: The first value of the critical region, which will be used to compare with the calculated test statistic.

Cumulative frequency distribution: A count of the frequencies or relative proportions of a value to all preceding counts.

Data: The value of a variable associated with one element of the population or sample or the set of values of a variable for each of the elements of the population or sample.

Degrees of freedom: The number of values in a sample that are independent of others. This number determines which distribution represents a particular population. Most test statistics require $n - 1$ degrees of freedom: df = $n - 1$.

Dependent variable y: The variable that is explained or predicted by the independent variable or variables.

Discrete probability function: Any mathematical formula that allows the calculation of the probability for each x cited. It represents a probability distribution.

Discrete random variable: A variable that assumes a numerical value for each outcome or element of the sample space, represented by a capital letter such as X, Y, or Z.

Empty set: A set with no elements. An empty set is represented by $\emptyset$.

Event: Any set or subset of outcomes in a sample space. Each outcome is known as an element of the event.

Experiment: A planned activity that generates a set of data.

Experimental probabilities: Also known as empirical or observational; the observed proportion of times an event occurs in a series of similar experiments, denoted by P'.

F test distribution: A test or estimate for the equality of the variances from two populations. F, like chi-square, represents variances, is skewed to the right, and contains only nonnegative values: $F = s_1^2/s_2^2$.

Fail to reject the null hypothesis: The decision that must be made if the calculated value of a test statistic falls in the non-critical region.

Frequency distribution: A distribution providing a simple count of data in terms of the number or percentage for each value of a variable.

Grouped frequency distribution: A frequency distribution where values are collapsed into groups or classes.

Histogram: A special type of bar chart displaying continuous data at the interval or ordinal levels.

Hypothesis testing (classical approach): The process of testing and deciding whether to reject hypotheses. This process follows six steps. First, state the hypotheses. Second, establish test criteria. Third, calculate the test statistic. Fourth, place calculated value on distribution curve. Fifth, make a decision. Sixth, interpret results.

Hypothesis testing (P-value): Also called prob-value, the smallest level of significance for the sample test statistic at which it becomes significant, provided the null hypothesis is true. P is considered significant when it is less than or equal to the type I error. (The five steps are very much like those of the classical approach.)

Independent variable x: The variable that predicts change in the dependent variable y.

Inferential statistics: A discipline in which population information is predicted from a sample. Decisions about various hypotheses may lead to accepting or discarding policies, behavior, and even theories.

Intersection: For two sets A and B, the set of elements that are in both A and B. It is the area where two sets overlap. The intersection of A and B is denoted by $A \cap B$.

Interval-level measurements: Measurements whose values are ordered and have measurable differences, such as temperature.

Joint probability: The probability that two events happen at the same time: $P(A \cap B) = P(A)P(B|A)$.

Law of large numbers: A law stating that as the number of times an experiment is repeated, the observed probability will approach the theoretical probability.

Level of confidence: The probability that a parameter is contained in the confidence interval established around a sample statistic. It is also known as a confidence coefficient and is $1 - \alpha$.

Level of significance: The probability of committing a type I error (the probability of rejecting the H_0 when it is actually true). The level of significance is represented by the Greek letter α (alpha) and is usually set as .025, .05, .01, or .10.

Mean: A measure of central tendency that describes the average response when the data are summed and divided by the total number of elements or observations. The symbol for the mean of a sample is $\bar{x}$; for a population, the symbol is μ. Both are calculated as $\Sigma x/n$.

Mean-square interaction: Determined by dividing the sum of square interaction by the degrees of freedom for the interaction.

Mean square for the within (error): Also referred to as error or residual; determined by dividing the sum of squares for within by the degrees of freedom for within.

Mean for a frequency distribution: Whether data are grouped or ungrouped, $\Sigma xf/\Sigma f$.

Measure of central tendency: A locator of the center of a set of data. A measure of central tendency is a single number that describes the general order or magnitude of a set of data. The more common measure of central tendency is the mean, often known as the average.

Measures of dispersion: The degree to which observations vary from the average. The variations can be calculated with a measure of dispersion. The larger the measure of dispersion, the more variability exists. If no variation exists, the measure of dispersion is 0.

Measures of position: Comparing data within one population or between different populations. The standard score, or z score, is a measure of position that allows data from the same or different populations to be compared. Proportions and quartile descriptions are also measures of position within one population.

Median, x: The middle value of a set of data when the data are arranged in order. Half the data values are above and half are below the median. The position at which the median is located in a set of data is calculated by $(n + 1)/2$.

Mode: The most commonly occurring observed value in a set of data.

Multinomial experiment: Similar to a binomial experiment, with the exception that multinomial experiments may have three or more outcomes. An example is the five (or more) categories of response for the variable religious preference. The *chi-square statistic* is a common measure of a multinomial experiment.

Multiplication theorem for two dependent events: Requires the multiplication of the probability of event A with the conditional probability of event B: $P(A \cap B) = P(A)P(B|A)$.

Multivariate analysis: A technique for describing the relationship between three or more variables. An example of multivariate analysis is describing the age, sex, and religious affiliation of students.

Mutually exclusive: When two events cannot happen together.

Nominal-level measurements: Also known as attribute or categorical measurements; variables whose values describe attributes that do not imply magnitude or value, such as marital status.

Nominal probability distribution: A probability distribution describing continuous random variables. The distribution is plotted as a bell-shaped curve that is symmetric, with the mean, mode, and median in the center. It is also known as the *normal curve.*

Null hypotheses: A statement that there is no difference between the hypothesized value of the population parameter and a sample statistic. It carries the benefit of the doubt. It is denoted by H_0.

One-tailed test: When a critical region falls to only one side of a probability distribution. This occurs when the H_1 involves less than ($<$) or greater than ($>$).

Ordered pairs: A pair of numbers in which a value for a variable X is given with its corresponding value for variable Y.

Ordinal-level measurement: Measurements whose values can be ranked or ordered from lowest to highest, such as military rankings, alphabetizing a seating chart, arranging people according to weight or height, or positioning military leaders according to rank.

Parameter: A numerical characteristic of an entire population. Parameters are usually represented by Greek letters such as μ or σ.

Pearson's product moment correlation coefficient: A measure of the strength and direction of the relationship between two interval or ratio variables. The notation is r. The value r ranges from -1 to 1.

$$r = \frac{n\Sigma xy - \Sigma x \Sigma y}{\sqrt{n\Sigma x^2 - (\Sigma x)^2}\ \sqrt{n\Sigma y^2 - (\Sigma y)^2}}$$

Percentile: A measure of position that divides data into 100 equal parts. Each percentile is written as P with a subscript indicating the value of the percentile, such as P_{30}.

Pie chart: Also known as a circle graph; a circular diagram displaying nominal-level discrete variables and representing relative proportions.

Point estimate: The sample statistic used to estimate the population parameter. When estimating the parameter mean (μ), the point estimate is the sample statistic ($\bar{x}$).

Population: A universal set of all individuals, objects, or measurements whose properties are being analyzed.

Probabilities: Educated guesses about what might happen or what has happened, based on information that has been obtained or observed.

Quartiles: A measure of position that divides data into four equal parts. The first quarter is denoted by Q_1, the second, or midquartile, by Q_2, and the third by Q_3.

Random sample: A sample in which every element of the population has an equal probability of being included in the sample.

Range: A measure of dispersion that identifies the difference between the lowest and highest value. Range = $H - L$.

Ratio-level measurements: Measurements whose values can be ordered, have measurable differences, and have a zero starting point that implies an absence of the measurement, such as age.

Reject the null hypothesis: A decision that must be made if the calculated value of a test statistic falls in the critical region.

Repeated sampling: When several samples are obtained from the same population.

Replacement: During an experiment, when an element is withdrawn and then replaced in the original sample space. Each event with replacement is independent. Events without replacement are dependent.

Regression line: Also known as the line of best fit; a straight line predicting values of y from values of x. The bivariate regression line is $\hat{y} = b + mx$.

Relative frequency: The proportion of the frequency of a value to the total number of occurrences: $f/\Sigma f$.

Sample: A subset of the population.

Sample space: The set of all possible outcomes of an experiment. The format for the sample space is $S = \{(\ ), (\ ), (\ ), \ldots\}$.

Sampling distribution of the mean: The probability distribution of the values of the sample mean from all possible samples of the same size.

Sampling error: An error attributed to the chance that the elements chosen for the sample are not representative of the population.

Sampling mean: When random samples of size n are drawn from a population, the expected value of the mean of the sample means is the population mean. $\mu_{\bar{x}} = \mu$

Slope (m): A value that describes how a regression line ascends or descends through the data. The slope describes the unit increase or decrease in y for every unit increase in x.

$$m = \frac{n(\Sigma xy) - \Sigma x \Sigma y}{n(\Sigma x^2) - (\Sigma x)^2}$$

Spearman's rank correlation coefficient: A measure of the strength and direction of the relationship between two ordinal variables. The notation is r_s. The value r_s ranges from -1 to 1.

$$r_s = 1 - \frac{6\Sigma d^2}{n(n^2 - 1)}$$

Special addition rule: Used when sets or events are mutually exclusive. Events that are mutually exclusive cannot happen together. The rule for addition of two mutually exclusive events is $P(A \cup B) = P(A) + P(B)$

Standard deviation: The square root of the average squared deviations from the mean. The standard deviation is the square-root of the variance. The symbol for the standard deviation of a sample is s, and the symbol for a population standard deviation is σ.

$$\sigma = \sqrt{\frac{\Sigma(x - \bar{x})^2}{n - 1}} \ \text{or} \ \sqrt{\frac{\Sigma x^2 - \frac{(\Sigma x)^2}{n}}{n - 1}}$$

Standard score, z score: A measure of position based on the number of standard deviations that a given value is from the mean. It is calculated as $z = (x - \bar{x})/n$.

Statistic: A numerical characteristic of a sample. Statistics are usually represented by English letters such as $\bar{x}$ or s.

Stratified random sample: A simple random sample taken from each subset or strata of the population.

Subjective probabilities: Educated guesses based on personal judgment.

Systematic error: An error in the process of selecting elements in the sample, it is not corrected by increasing sample size.

Systematic sample: Accomplished by choosing every kth element after having begun by choosing the first element randomly.

***t* distribution:** A probability distribution that depicts sampling means. It has several characteristics similar to the normal z distribution. The t distribution is symmetric, its mean is 0, and its variance is greater than 1, but it decreases toward 1 as n increases.

$$t = \frac{\bar{x} - \mu}{s/\sqrt{n}}$$

Test criteria: Criteria allowing a researcher to determine the level of significance, or the type I error. They also determine the exact test to be performed that will challenge the null hypothesis and the values of a test that may result in its rejection.

Test statistic: The random variable used to calculate and compare the sample statistic to the hypothesized population parameter. The test statistics used in this book are z, $t\chi^2$, and F.

Theoretical probabilities: Probabilities determined when all sample points are equally likely to occur. A theoretical probability is denoted by P.

Tree diagram: A way of illustrating sample space using branches to represent each possible outcome or ordered pair.

Two-tailed test: When a critical region is divided with half of its area on both ends of the probability distribution. This situation occurs when H_1 indicates a parameter is not equal to a hypothesized value.

Union: For two sets A and B, the set of all elements that are in A or B or in both. Union is denoted by $A \cup B$.

Univariate analysis: A technique for describing a single variable.

Universal set: Also known as population; the set of all elements that occur in an overall frame of reference. All other sets occurring within its boundaries are subsets of the universal set.

Value: One of the categories or responses of a variable.

Variable: A characteristic about objects, events, or individuals that has or can be assigned a numerical value.

Variance: The average squared deviations of values from their mean. The symbol for a variance for a sample is s^2, and the symbol for a population variance is σ^2. The formulas for either are

$$\frac{\Sigma(x - \bar{x})^2}{n - 1} \quad \text{or} \quad \frac{\Sigma x - (\Sigma x)^2 n}{n - 1}$$

Venn diagrams: A pictorial illustration of sets or subsets of a sample space. A rectangle usually represents the sample space. Subsets are also known as events and are usually represented by capital letters.

***y*-intercept, *b*:** As a component of the regression line, a description of the predicted y value when x is zero.

$$b = \frac{(\Sigma y)(\Sigma x^2) - \Sigma x \Sigma y}{n(\Sigma x^2) - (\Sigma x)^2}$$

Answers to Selected Questions

Chapter 2 in Review

2.1

x	f
19	3
20	2
21	5
25	6
27	3
28	1
30	4
31	2
32	2
34	2

2.3

Response	f	Rel. Freq.	Cum. Freq.	Cum. Rel. Freq.
Pop	18	.257	18	.257
Classical	12	.171	30	.428
Country	17	.243	47	.671
Rock	10	.143	57	.814
Oldies	13	.186	70	1.000

2.5

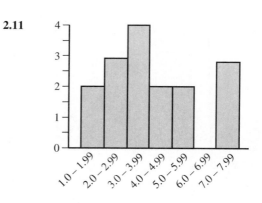

2.7

2.9

x	f
20–22	5
23–25	4
26–28	6
29–31	7
32–34	1
35–37	2
Total	25

2.11

2.13

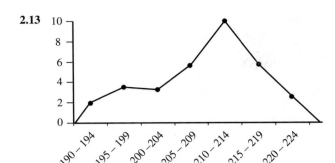

2.15

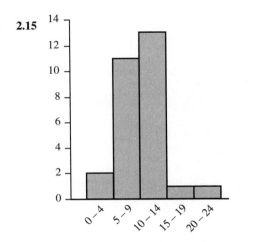

Chapter 3 in Review

3.1 $\bar{x} = 27.67$, $i = 8$, $\tilde{x} = 28$, mode $= 28$

3.3 $\bar{x} = 20.47$, $s^2 = 94.74$, $s = 9.73$, mark $= 12$, median $=$ 5th class, mode $= 17$

3.5 **a.** $i = 2$, $Q_1 = 24.5$

   b. $i = 6$, $Q_3 = 28.3$

   c. $i = 5$, $P_{60} = 28.2$

   d. $i = 2$, $P_{20} = 24.5$

3.7 $\bar{x} = 21.78$, $s = 5.95$

3.9 $\bar{x} = 209.10$, $s = 7.83$

3.11 $\bar{x} = 24.44$, $\tilde{x} = 21.8$, mode $= 20.8$, range $= 17.7$, $s^2 = 26.33$, $s = 5.12$, $Q_1 = 20.8$, $Q_2 = 21.8$, $P_{40} = 20.8$, $P_{79} = 28.3$

3.13 $\bar{x} = 41.65$, $s^2 = 224.32$, $s = 14.98$

3.15 lead, $z = 1.27$, $z = 1.00$

Chapter 4 in Review

4.1 $r = 1.00$, yes, yes, $\hat{y} = 0 + .12x$, $\hat{y} = 24$

4.3 $r = .58$, $\hat{y} = 17.4 + .65x$, $\hat{y} = \$21,300$

4.5 $r = .84$, strong positive relationship, $\hat{y} = -.16 + .55x$, $\hat{y} = 3.69$, $\hat{y} = 2.59$

4.7 $r = .45$

4.9 $\hat{y} = 18.27$

4.13 False, false, false, false

4.15 .98

4.19 18.164

Chapter 5 in Review

5.1 $S = \{(1), (2), (3), (4), (5), (6)\}$

5.3 $S = \{(\text{heads}), (\text{tails})\}$

5.5 $S = \{(\text{BBB}), (\text{GGG})\}$

5.7 $S = \{(\text{start}), (\text{no start})\}$

5.9

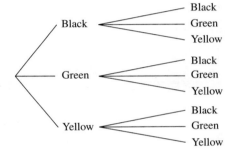

   c. $S = \{(\text{BB}), (\text{BG}), (\text{BY}), (\text{GB}), (\text{GG}), (\text{GY}), (\text{YB}), (\text{YG}), (\text{YY})\}$

5.11 True

5.13 False, false, true

5.15 No

5.17 Universal set

5.19 False

Chapter 6 in Review

6.1 $P(A) = .44$, no

6.3 $P(A \cap B) = .64$

6.5 $P(A \cap B) = 0$, or ϕ

6.7 $P(A \cup B) = .5$, no

6.9 $P(A|B) = .74$

6.11 $P(A) = .60$

6.13 $P(A) = 1.0$

6.15 $P(q) = .5$, $P(q \cap q) = .2$, $P(d') = .2$, $P(q \cap d) \cup P(d \cap q) = .6$, $P(d \cap d) = .2$

6.17 $P(\text{Rep.}) = .4$, $P(\text{Dem.} \cap \text{yes}) = .5$, $P(\text{no}) = .22$ $P(R')$ $= .6$, $P(\text{no}|\text{Dem.}) = .17$

6.19 $P(A \cup B) = .7$, $P(A|B) = .2$, $P(B') = .5$, $P(A') = .7$

Chapter 7 in Review

7.1 Yes, no, no, yes

7.3 $\mu = 4.67$, $\sigma^2 = 1.52$, $\sigma = 1.23$

7.5 $P(x = 3) = .246$

7.7 $\mu = 15$, $\sigma = 1.94$

7.9 $P(x = 4) = .063$, $P(x = 0) = .063$, $P(x > 2) = .313$

7.11 $P(x \geq 6) = .012$, $P(x \geq 6) = .109$, $\mu = 3.776$, $\sigma = 1.41$

7.13 $\mu = 17$, $\sigma = 1.6$

7.15 $P(x \geq 3) = .189$

7.17 $\mu = 11.2$

7.19 $P(x \geq 2) = .434$

Chapter 8 in Review

8.1 $P(.4738)$, $P(.4922)$, $P(.1879)$, $P(.1879)$, $P(.2881)$, $P(.4750)$

8.3 $P(.0250)$, $P(.1685)$, $P(.0013)$, $P(.9750)$, $P(.6879)$, $P(.3121)$

8.5 $P(.0000)$

8.7 $P(.6826)$, $P(.9544)$, $P(.9974)$

8.9 2.05, $.02$, 3.09, 1.64

8.11 2.33, 1.96, -1.65, -2.58

8.13 $z = -.5$, $P = .3085$, $z = -.5$, $z = 1.5$, $P = .6247$, $z = .5$, $P = .3085$

8.15 $z = -1$, $z = .5$, $P = .5328$, $z = 0$, $P = .5000$, $z = -1$, $P = .1587$

8.17 $\mu = 3.2$, $\sigma = 1.39$, $z = .94$, $P = .1736$

8.19 $\mu = 2.4$, $\sigma = 1.3$, $z = .08$, $P = .5319$

8.21 $\mu = 120$, $\sigma = 7.75$

8.23 $x = 2459.48$

8.25 $P(x \leq 2) = .0618$

Chapter 9 in Review

9.1 Yes

9.3 $P = .3944$, $P = .3944$, $P = .2486$, $P = .4999$

9.5 $P = .2344$, $P = .0673$, $P = .4772$, $P = .0752$

9.7 $z = 1.20$, $P = .8489$

9.9 Systematic sampling

9.11 $\mu_{\bar{x}} = 35$, $\sigma_{\bar{x}} = 1.2$, $z = -1.67$, $P = .0475$

9.13 Every element has an equal chance of being selected; there are no biases introduced as part of the selection process.

9.15 $z = 16$, $P = .4364$, $z = .88$, $P = .1894$; the first asks for the probability of one employee, the second asks for that of a sample.

9.17 $\mu_{\bar{x}} = 12.5$, $\sigma_{\bar{x}} = .73$, $z = 0$, $P = .5000$, $P = .5000$, $z = .68$, $P = .7517$, $z = .68$, $P = .2483$

9.19 $\mu_{\bar{x}} = 8.9$, $\sigma_{\bar{x}} = .32$, $z = 1.58$, $P = .0571$

Chapter 10 in Review

10.1 2.33, 1.96, -1.96, -1.645

10.3 **a.** H_0: $\mu = 27$, H_1: $\mu \neq 27$
 b. H_0: $\mu \geq 30$, H_1: $\mu < 30$
 c. H_0: $\mu \leq 75,000$, H_1: $\mu > 75,000$
 d. H_0: $\mu = 7.2$, H_1: $\mu \neq 7.2$
 e. H_0: $\mu = 13,560$, H_1: $\mu \neq 13,560$

10.5 **a.** One-tailed right
 b. Two-tailed
 c. One-tailed right
 d. One-tailed left
 e. Two-tailed
 f. One-tailed left

10.7 $z = 2.36$; reject null

10.9 $P = .1446$, fail to reject null

10.11 Type I error: the bag really opens but was not approved.
 Type II error: the bag does not open but was approved.
 Type II error is more serious.

10.13 **a.** Fail to reject null
 b. Fail to reject null
 c. Reject null
 d. Fail to reject null
 e. Reject null
 f. Fail to reject null

10.15 $z = -2.81$; reject null

10.17 $(1738 < \mu < 1774)$

10.19 False, true, false, false

Chapter 11 in Review

11.1 2.462, 2.228, −2.179, −1.753

11.3 **a.** H_0: $\mu \geq 7$, H_1: $\mu < 7$
  b. H_0: $\mu \geq 30$, H_1: $\mu < 30$
  c. H_0: $\mu \leq 1.25$, H_1: $\mu > 1.25$
  d. H_0: $\mu = 7.2$, H_1: $\mu \neq 7.2$
  e. H_0: $\mu = 32$, H_1: $\mu \neq 32$

11.5 **a.** H_0: $\mu \geq 150$, H_1: $\mu < 150$
  b. H_0: $\mu = 9.5$, H_1: $\mu \neq 9.5$
  c. H_0: $\mu \leq 30{,}000$, H_1: $\mu > 30{,}000$
  d. H_0: $\mu = 5$ ft 8 in., H_1: $\mu \neq 5$ ft 8 in.
  e. H_0: $\mu \leq 110$, H_1: $\mu > 110$

11.7 $t = 2.598$; reject null

11.9 $t = 3.444$; reject null

11.11 $t = 4.174$; reject null

11.13 $t = -2.8$; reject null

11.15 $t = .764$; reject null; $P = .25$; reject null

11.17 **a.** Fail to reject null
  b. Fail to reject null
  c. Reject null
  d. Reject null
  e. Fail to reject null

11.19 $E = (84.710 < \mu < 97.681)$

Chapter 12 in Review

12.1 34.170, 5.991, 25.989, 7.962, 20.599, 51.172

12.3 30.144 and 10.177, 11.071, 52.336 and 13.121, .115, 59.196

12.5 **a.** H_0: $\sigma^2 \geq 150$, H_1: $\sigma^2 < 150$
  b. H_0: $\sigma^2 \leq 2.23$ H_1: $\sigma^2 > 2.23$
  c. H_0: $\sigma \leq 10.2$, H_1: $\sigma > 10.2$
  d. H_0: $\sigma = 5$ ft 8 in., H_1: $\sigma \neq 5$ ft 8 in.
  e. H_0: $\sigma^2 \geq 2.0$, H_1: $\sigma^2 < 2.0$

12.7 $\chi^2 = 13.73$; fail to reject null

12.9 $\chi^2 = 1.022$, $P(<.01)$; reject H_0

12.11 $E = (2.597 < \sigma < 4.344)$

12.13 $\chi^2 = 30.234$; fail to reject null

12.15 $\chi^2 = 20.757$; reject null

12.17 $\chi^2 = 14.792$; fail to reject null

12.19 $\chi^2 = 12.518$; fail to reject null

12.21 $E = (3.667 < \sigma^2 < 8.812)$

Chapter 13 in Review

13.1 ±2.24, ±1.96, ±1.645, ±2.575

13.3 3.1789, 4.0990, 2.7027, 3.6142, 5.8018, 6.3882

13.5 $F = 1.686$; fail to reject null

13.7 $t = 1.220$; fail to reject null

13.9 $E = (5.069 < (\mu_2 - \mu_1) < 6.931)$

Chapter 14 in Review

14.1 27.488, 38.885, 21.026, 18.548

14.3 9.488, 16.013, 7.815, 9.236

14.5 $\chi^2 = 31.151$; reject null

14.7 $\chi^2 = 60.254$; reject null

14.9 $\chi^2 = 115.386$; reject null

14.11 $\chi^2 = 9.255$; reject null

Index

NOTES

NOTES

NOTES

NOTES